Synthesizing Research on Language Learning and Teaching

Language Learning and Language Teaching

The *LL&LT* monograph series publishes monographs as well as edited volumes on applied and methodological issues in the field of language pedagogy. The focus of the series is on subjects such as classroom discourse and interaction; language diversity in educational settings; bilingual education; language testing and language assessment; teaching methods and teaching performance; learning trajectories in second language acquisition; and written language learning in educational settings.

Series editors

Nina Spada
Ontario Institute for Studies in Education, University of Toronto

Jan H. Hulstijn
Department of Second Language Acquisition, University of Amsterdam

Volume 13

Synthesizing Research on Language Learning and Teaching
Edited by John M. Norris and Lourdes Ortega

Synthesizing Research on Language Learning and Teaching

Edited by

John M. Norris
Lourdes Ortega

University of Hawai'i at Mānoa

John Benjamins Publishing Company
Amsterdam / Philadelphia

™ The paper used in this publication meets the minimum requirements
of American National Standard for Information Sciences – Permanence
of Paper for Printed Library Materials, ANSI z39.48-1984.

Library of Congress Cataloging-in-Publication Data

Synthesizing Research on Language Learning and Teaching / edited by John M.
    Norris and Lourdes Ortega.
        p.   cm. (Language Learning and Language Teaching, ISSN 1569–9471
; v. 13)
        Includes bibliographical references and indexes.
        1. Second language acquisition--Research--History. 2. Language and
    languages--Study and teaching--Research--History. I. Norris, John
    Michael. II. Ortega, Lourdes. III. Series.

    P118.2.S96 2006
    418.0072--dc22   2006042702
    ISBN 90 272 1965 6 (Hb; alk. paper)
    ISBN 90 272 1966 4 (Pb; alk. paper)

John Benjamins Publishing Co. · P.O. Box 36224 · 1020 ME Amsterdam · The Netherlands
John Benjamins North America · P.O. Box 27519 · Philadelphia PA 19118-0519 · USA

In memory of Charlie Sato

Table of contents

Contributors

J. William Asher, Purdue University
Craig Chaudron, University of Hawai'i at Mānoa
Thomas H. Dinsmore, University of Cincinnati–Clermont College
Nick C. Ellis, University of Michigan
Gina Iberri-Shea, Northern Arizona University
Eun Hee Jeon, Northern Arizona University
Tadayoshi Kaya, Northern Arizona University
Casey M. Keck, Northern Arizona University
John M. Norris, University of Hawai'i at Mānoa
Lourdes Ortega, University of Hawai'i at Mānoa
Jane Russell, University of Toronto
Nina Spada, University of Toronto
John R. Stevens, Utah State University
Alan M. Taylor, Brigham Young University–Idaho
Kip Téllez, University of California Santa Cruz
Margaret Thomas, Boston College
Nicole Tracy-Ventura, Northern Arizona University
Safary Wa-Mbaleka, Northern Arizona University
Hersh C. Waxman, University of Houston

E-mail addresses

J. William Asher	asher@purdue.edu
Craig Chaudron	chaudron@hawaii.edu
Thomas H. Dinsmore	Thomas.Dinsmore@uc.edu
Nick C. Ellis	ncellis@umich.edu
Gina Iberri-Shea	Gina.Iberri-Shea@nau.edu
Eun Hee Jeon	EunHee.Jeon@nau.edu
Tadayoshi Kaya	Tadayoshi.Kaya@nau.edu
Casey M. Keck	Casey.Keck@nau.edu
John M. Norris	jnorris@hawaii.edu
Lourdes Ortega	lortega@hawaii.edu
Jane Russell	janeyjane00@yahoo.com
Nina Spada	nspada@oise.utoronto.ca
John R. Stevens	jrstevens@stat.purdue.edu
Alan M. Taylor	tayloral@byui.edu
Kip Téllez	ktellez@cats.ucsc.edu
Margaret Thomas	thomasm@bc.edu
Nicole Tracy-Ventura	Nicole.Tracy@nau.edu
Safary Wa-Mbaleka	Safary.Wa-Mbaleka@nau.edu
Hersh C. Waxman	hwaxman@uh.edu

Preface

Research synthesis pursues systematic (i.e., exhaustive, trustworthy, and replicable) understandings of the state of knowledge that has accumulated about a given problem across primary research studies. Its foremost purpose is to integrate available research evidence, such that both patterns and inconsistencies (in both findings and methods) may be identified with precision. Research synthesis emerged from a methodological movement in the 1970s, in response to dissatisfaction with several major weaknesses inherent in traditional approaches to reviewing. By the late 1970s it had crystallized into a formal methodological approach, and since the 1990s its application to synthesizing primary research in a variety of fields has become widespread.

In applied linguistics, research synthesis is still relatively novel, despite early voices arguing its potential for our field (e.g., Chaudron 1988; Hammadou 1993). In recent years, however, interest has gained momentum, with a few second language (L2) research topics being submitted to meta-analysis (Goldschneider & DeKeyser 2001; Masgoret & Gardner 2003; Norris & Ortega 2000; Ross 1998), and with the exploration of other synthetic methodologies (Ortega 2003; Thomas 1994). These developments are no doubt partly motivated by the exponential growth of research on language learning and language teaching (LL&LT) during the same time period. Even within a limited focus on "the field of language pedagogy" – the main concern of this *LL & LT* series – the existing literature base consists of a daunting and rapidly expanding amount of published work (never mind unpublished). For example, already by the mid-1980s, Chaudron (1988) was able to identify 70-plus studies that had investigated L2 teaching and learning in the classroom context, and by the late 1990s, we identified in excess of 250 studies that focused specifically on the topic "effectiveness of L2 instruction" (Norris & Ortega 2000).

To be sure, such an expanded substantive and methodological research landscape exerts pressing needs for researchers to take stock of the extant knowledge in LL&LT. Research synthesis can help those interested in LL&LT and applied linguistics "make sense" of this daunting body of research to degrees of precision and insight that the traditional literature review approach can not. It can help identify patterns in and relationships among accumulated findings and uncover gaps and methodological weaknesses. It also has the potential to generate original theoretical knowledge not found in any single primary study, by resolving the extent to which theoretical tenets and constructs actually hold as increasing empirical light is shed upon them. However, systematic research synthesis is not easy, and it depends as much on the quality and availability of good primary research as it does on the capabilities of secondary researchers. In order for synthesis to fulfill its potential in LL&LT, it will probably require something of a sea change in how all of us go about our interactions with L2 research. Our basic premise here is that anyone involved in LL&LT research, whether we participate from the perspective of knowledge generation or knowledge utilization, will need to begin thinking and acting synthetically, if the field is to make truly worthwhile contributions to human understanding of language learning and teaching phenomena.

The ten contributions assembled in this volume constitute the first collection of substantial work on research synthesis within applied linguistics and, more specifically, focusing on LL&LT topics. With it, we hope to illustrate the many ins and outs of research synthesis and to provide guidance and models for its complex application, its diverse epistemological choices, and its demanding methodologies. The book is intended for a wide readership in applied linguistics. It can be of value to *graduate students* embarking on a course paper or proposing a dissertation topic, who want to know what the research to date has already shown and what added value their own primary research studies might contribute; to *methodologists* who want to know how L2 research questions have been addressed, in order to suggest improvements in how they should be addressed; and to *senior academics and theoreticians* who want to take stock of entire domains of inquiry in order to identify trends in our thinking, to propose nuanced research questions most in need of our attention, and to evaluate the theories that provide structure and meaning to LL&LT as a field of inquiry. We also hope the book will appeal to *teachers, curriculum developers,* and *policy makers* who want to become better and more independent judges of what research has indicated to be the best practices in high-quality L2 education.

This volume would not have been possible without the collective efforts of many individuals. We thank the external reviewers for providing expert and insightful commentaries on the chapters: Carol Chapelle, Alister Cumming, Robert DeKeyser, William Grabe, Gabriele Kasper, Mary McGroarty, Teresa Pica, and Margaret Thomas. Our gratitude also goes to the *LL & LT* series editors, Jan Hulstijn and Nina Spada (and previously, Birgit Harley), and to Kees Vaes at John Benjamins, for their enthusiasm and support. Finally, our special thanks go to the contributors, who represent a courageous first generation of second language research synthesists. Their rare combination of substantive and methodological expertise enabled the realization of this volume, and their efforts indicate a watershed point in the maturation of LL&LT research.

We dedicate this book to the memory of Charlene "Charlie" Sato, friend and mentor at the University of Hawai'i. Charlie's work, at the interface between second language acquisition and language use in context, was exemplary. In tackling the most difficult – and most worthwhile – problems, she drew on diverse theoretical underpinnings, demanded rigorous methods of inquiry, and, most importantly, advocated the generation of knowledge that could actually be utilized for the social good. Her ethic is very much what we strive for, and what we hope to encourage here as well.

John M. Norris and *Lourdes Ortega*
Cádiz, December 2005

References

Chaudron, C. (1988). *Second language classrooms: Research on teaching and learning.* Cambridge, UK: Cambridge University Press.

Hammadou, J. (1993). Inquiry in language teacher education. In G. Guntermann (Ed.), *Developing language teachers for a changing world* (pp. 76–103). Lincolnwood, IL: National Textbook Company.

Goldschneider, J., & DeKeyser, R. M. (2001). Explaining the "natural order of L2 morpheme acquisition" in English: A meta-analysis of multiple determinants. *Language Learning, 51,* 1–50.

Masgoret, A.-M., & Gardner, R. C. (2003). Attitudes, motivation, and second language learning: A meta-analysis of studies conducted by Gardner and associates. *Language Learning, 53,* 123–163.

Norris, J. M., & Ortega, L. (2000). Effectiveness of L2 instruction: A research synthesis and quantitative meta-analysis. *Language Learning, 50,* 417–528.

Ortega, L. (2003). Syntactic complexity measures and their relationship to L2 proficiency: A research synthesis of college-level L2 writing. *Applied Linguistics, 24,* 492–518.

Ross, S. (1998). Self-assessment in second language testing: A meta-analysis and analysis of experiential factors. *Language Testing, 15,* 1–20.

Thomas, M. (1994). Assessment of L2 proficiency in second language acquisition research. *Language Learning, 44,* 307–336.

SECTION I

Introduction

CHAPTER 1

The value and practice of research synthesis for language learning and teaching

John M. Norris and Lourdes Ortega
University of Hawai'i at Mānoa

In this chapter, we introduce readers to the value of research synthesis, both as a systematic approach to conducting useful secondary reviews and as an ethical approach to understanding, informing, and utilizing second language research of all kinds. We also outline key components in the practice of research synthesis, focusing in particular on the conduct of quantitative meta-analysis. The chapter is organized as follows. We first situate research synthesis in relation to work on language learning and teaching, and we outline the defining features of a synthetic approach. We then consider challenges in applying research synthesis for distinct purposes and in domains characterized by distinct epistemologies. Next, in order to illustrate how synthesis proceeds, we articulate its stages within the focused methodology of quantitative meta-analysis. Extending well beyond this specific practice, we then propose the notion of synthesis as a research ethic, and we suggest implications for practice among distinct participants in the research community. We close the chapter by forecasting a few key challenges and contributions that we think will define the immediate future of research synthesis in the field of language learning and teaching.

Introduction

Research on language learning and language teaching is simple. Regardless of ontological-epistemological persuasion, theoretical outlook, or research purpose, the questions that interest all of us are quite straightforward: How do people learn languages other than their first? What factors (linguistic, cognitive, social, educational, affective, material) may moderate or enhance their learning of another language? Via what externally arranged processes (especially language teaching) can language learning be initiated, accelerated, and ultimately made more successful? What do the outcomes of language learning look like, for individuals and for society?

At the same time, research on language learning and language teaching is complex and vast. The existing literature base consists of a daunting and rapidly expanding amount of published work (see Hinkel 2005), never mind unpublished. Also on the rise is the array of methodologies being brought to bear on questions about language learning and teaching (LL&LT henceforth), including among others: (a) experimental and quasi-experimental research; (b) case studies; (c) surveys; (d) micro-analyses; and (e) ethnographies (Brown & Rodgers 2002). Within each of these traditions, in turn, a wealth of knowledge has begun to accumulate, as researchers have addressed the fundamental problems that define the field. Given this substantial and multi-methodological foundation of work on LL&LT, researchers, educators, and others have rightly begun to ask "How do we make sense of it all?" and "What are the answers to the 'simple' questions of the field?"

Research synthesis – that is, the systematic secondary review of accumulated primary research studies – has tremendous potential value for helping those interested in LL&LT "make sense" of research. Rigorous syntheses enable the research community to compare and combine findings across individual studies, to authoritatively answer particular research questions, and to identify gaps in research methodologies. In addition, we believe that research synthesis is much more than the sum of its parts, that it has more to offer than just improved secondary reviews of accumulated research, as valuable as these are in their own right. More to the point, and more challenging, we propose in this chapter that a *synthetic research ethic* should be adopted as a guide for all empirical work within our field. We believe that such a research ethic, calling for all of us involved in research to think and act synthetically rather than idiosyncratically, would enable resolution of weaknesses that characterize contemporary practices in LL&LT. To be sure, this is a call for change in how we go about all aspects of research, from primary to secondary, and from the perspective of knowledge generation as well as knowledge utilization. However, fundamentally, we do not believe that research on LL&LT will achieve much more than it already has, unless we all embrace this synthetic ethic. To borrow from Wittgenstein (1969/1972), "If experience is the ground of our certainty, then naturally it is past experience. And it isn't merely my experience, but other people's, that I get knowledge from." (pp. 35–36, our translation). In the current chapter, we begin down this challenging path by offering a rationale and methodology for helping the LL&LT research community to think and act synthetically.

What is research synthesis?

It is customary in the social sciences to engage in secondary research, that is, to review the available literature at important watershed points in the progress of a research domain. Broadly speaking, we review in order to get a sense of what is already known about a particular question or problem, to understand how it has been addressed methodologically, and to figure out where we need to go next with our research. In some fields, long-lived refereed journals are devoted exclusively to the publication of secondary reviews. Perhaps the most well-known examples come from psychology and education: *Psychological Bulletin* and *Review of Educational Research*, established in 1881 and 1930 respectively. In applied linguistics, as well, two journals that have provided persistent venues for secondary research are *Language Teaching* (since 1968) and *Annual Review of Applied Linguistics* (since 1980). They are unique in our field not only because they exclusively publish reviews of research, but also because submissions are not accepted; instead contributions are commissioned from authorities in each research area. In addition, *Language Learning*, a journal which typically publishes primary research, established in 1994 a special Review Article section devoted to "publishing review articles that synthesize and rigorously assess data, findings, and key concepts from a significant range of previous research on a single topic" (*Language Learning*, 44(1), Editor's statement, p. 3). Other applied linguistics journals also publish reviews of the literature on selected topics on a regular basis.

Research synthesis, then, falls within a broad and lengthy tradition of research review. However, reviewing can take many forms, some of which have predominated in LL&LT while others have remained relatively untapped. The most traditional form is the narrative review, with its goal to scope out and 'tell a story' about the empirical territory in order to identify a gap in which to situate new primary research, as is customary in the literature review sections of dissertations and empirical articles. Another form of review is the 'authoritative tour,' in which subject-matter authorities seek to distill an original argument about what the evidence really means in a body of literature. Seminal examples in applied linguistics are two reviews of age effects in second language acquisition by Krashen et al. (1979) and Long (1990), as well as the oft-cited review of recasts in second language learning by Nicholas et al. (2001). Occupying other places along the reviewing continuum are the comprehensive bibliographical review (many of the articles published in the *Annual Review of Applied Linguistics* and *Language Teaching*), the vote-counting review (e.g., Long 1983), the historiographical review (e.g., Henning 1986; Lazaraton

2000), the integrative review (e.g., Chaudron 1988; Reichelt 2001; Spada 1997), and the critical review (e.g., Marinova-Todd et al. 2000; Truscott 1996, 1999). Each of these forms of review has a distinct purpose, and each adopts specific ways of surveying, critiquing, and presenting the collective wisdom that has accumulated within a particular domain (on types of secondary research review, see Cooper 1988; Light & Pillemer 1984; see also Chaudron, Chapter 10, this volume).

Where does research synthesis fit within this array and how is it distinguished from other types of review? Synthesis comprises one end of the reviewing continuum, in that it pursues a systematic (i.e., exhaustive, trustworthy, and replicable) understanding of the state of accumulated knowledge; its foremost purpose is to integrate available research, such that both patterns and inconsistencies (in both findings and methods) may be identified with accuracy (Cooper & Hedges 1994b). The research synthetic approach to reviewing emerged from a methodological movement in the 1970s, in response to dissatisfaction with several major weaknesses inherent in traditional approaches (see Jackson 1980; Light & Smith 1971). The essential weaknesses include, foremost, a tendency to select the studies under consideration unsystematically and idiosyncratically, resulting in incomplete, biased, or simply unwarranted claims about the state of knowledge. In addition, traditional reviewers tend to distill generalizations, and to argue their positions, on the basis of theoretical predilections rather than inspection of the actual evidence that may be compiled systematically across studies, including evidence regarding the extent to which study methodologies themselves may be influencing study results. In response, research synthesis adopts three defining features:

1. *Research synthesis always includes an explicit articulation of how the relevant literature was searched and how primary studies were selected for review.*
   Just as sampling and careful description of study participants is a key consideration when planning primary research of any kind, the identification, selection, and characterization of studies is a main concern when planning a research synthesis.
2. *Research synthesis focuses on the actual variables, characteristics, and data reported in primary studies, rather than on the study-specific conclusions offered by primary researchers.*
   Because the conclusions of primary researchers may be influenced by a variety of factors, synthesists generally look to the data themselves as a source for their own interpretations, to whatever extent primary study reports enable them to do so.

3. *Research synthesis compiles findings and seeks generalizations by examining categories of data and methodology that cut across studies, in order to create as systematic a depiction as possible about what we know, what we do not know, and why.*
   The systematic integration of existing evidence calls for synthesists to work with super-ordinate categories, according to which primary studies can be coded, compared, contrasted, and compiled into a clear picture of what research to date has to say.

Given these three defining features, research synthesists obviously tackle reviewing as an empirical task in its own right, subscribing to a "review-as-research" perspective (Cooper & Hedges 1994b:6). By the same token, syntheses constitute an empirical genre of their own, in that they generate new findings that transcend the findings and interpretations proposed within any one individual study.

Despite sharing the basic tenets above, research syntheses can take many forms, depending on the research questions posed, the purposes pursued, the maturity of the target domain, and the nature of the data contained in the primary studies to be synthesized. For example, syntheses can be integrative (looking for patterns and clear moderating factors in the data) or critical (of methods and interpretations), and they can even include a large narrative component (e.g., where clarification of constructs is called for). Likewise, as we will discuss in the next section, not only quantitative but also qualitative bodies of literature can be synthesized systematically, and there are diverse choices available for those LL&LT researchers interested in broaching the task within distinct research traditions.

Initial options and choices in research synthesis

Systematic research synthesis crystallized into a methodological approach to reviewing by the late 1970s, and its application to problems in a variety of fields gained momentum during the 1980s and 1990s. It is noteworthy that early discussions on why and how to go about synthesis were concerned almost exclusively with the review of quantitative and experimental bodies of research, related no doubt to the locus and focus of the research being synthesized (i.e., primarily in well-established sub-disciplines of experimental psychology, medicine, sociology, and education). Among the available options, quantitative meta-analysis has become the best described and most frequently practiced form of research synthesis, to the extent that, in certain quarters, it has been ensconced as the preferred scientific means for generating answers to research problems (e.g., Cooper & Hedges 1994a). However, in recent years, along with the diversification of epistemologies, models, and methods in the social sciences and education, an expansion of purposes for research review was inevitable; as a result, there has been a concomitant exploration and diversification of approaches to research synthesis.

At the outset of any synthetic review of primary studies, the synthesist is faced with several choices and options, which in turn determine the methodologies adopted for the review. These initial considerations we summarize in the form of several guiding questions:

1.   What is the *epistemological and methodological nature* of the domain of research to be synthesized? Do studies utilize 'quantitative' (e.g., experimental, quasi-experimental, correlational, survey, numeric description), 'qualitative' (e.g., interpretive ethnographic, conversation analytic), or 'mixed-methods' (e.g., program evaluative) designs and data?

2.   What is the *maturity* of the targeted domain? Have numerous primary studies been conducted, including purposeful replication of specific variables? Do primary researchers discuss their studies in terms of exploration and description, or are they more interested in testing, confirming, or resolving? Have researchers come to some agreement on terms, definitions, and methodological features, or is there considerable apparent discord?

3.   What is the *purpose* for synthesizing research within the domain, and who is going to use the findings? Will the synthesis seek to establish a definitive answer to a much studied research question, to test a hypothesis, or to identify the 'best practices' among a series of intervention or program types? Will it explore what research to date seems to be indicating about the effect of certain variables or contextual factors on teaching and learning? Will it assess the quality of methods that have been deployed (and those that have not) in response to a particular research problem? Will it seek to clarify the theoretical frameworks or the construct definitions at stake?

Of course, these questions overlap to some extent, as will their answers. However, through their careful consideration, synthesists can arrive at a sound basis for choosing an approach that is best suited for responding to the needs of the domain. Pondering over these initial questions should also help synthesists and others avoid the risks incurred when certain forms of research synthesis are misapplied or misinterpreted. In the following, we highlight a few of the distinct purposes for synthesis and we address major related concerns.

By the numbers: Synthesizing quantitative research

The central purpose of systematic research synthesis, as it was originally conceived, was to make cumulative (quantifiable) sense of primary studies that are themselves quantitative. Lipsey and Wilson (2001) capture well this original spirit of research synthesis as:

> [...] a form of survey research in which research reports, rather than people, are surveyed. A coding form (survey protocol) is developed, a sample or population of research reports is gathered, and each research study is "interviewed" by a coder who reads it carefully and codes the appropriate information about its characteristics [...]. (pp. 1–2)

Syntheses that focus on quantitative primary studies often take the specific form of a meta-analysis, but they need not do so. Put differently, all meta-analyses are research syntheses (and perhaps for this reason the two terms frequently are used as if they were synonymous, as in the title of Cooper & Hedges 1994a), but not all syntheses are meta-analyses. Generally speaking, meta-analyses are conducted (a) on 'quantitative' domains of inquiry in which (b) considerable replication of specific independent, dependent, and moderating variables has occurred, and (c) for the specific purposes of clarifying the actual relationship among main study variables, as well as the potential moderating effects of contextual and other variables on this relationship. In the case of meta-analysis, therefore, data from original study findings are summarized into effect sizes (to be explained later), and these in turn are "analyzed using special adaptations of conventional statistical techniques to investigate and describe the pattern of findings in the selected set of studies" (Lipsey & Wilson 2001:2).

By now, several meta-analyses have emerged in response to particular areas of LL&LT research. In chronological order, these include: Ross (1998) on the validity of self-report measures of proficiency, Norris and Ortega (2000) on the effectiveness of L2 instruction, Goldschneider and DeKeyser (2001) on explanations for the accuracy orders uncovered in morpheme studies, and Masgoret and Gardner (2003) on the relationship between motivation and language learning achievement. The present volume adds five new LL&LT meta-analyses to this list: Dinsmore (Chapter 2) on the magnitude of differences between native and non-native speakers' grammatical intuitions, Keck et al. (Chapter 3) on the acquisitional benefits of native-speaker to non-native speaker interaction, Russell and Spada (Chapter 4) on the effectiveness of providing negative feedback in speaking and writing, Jeon and Kaya (Chapter 5) on the effectiveness of instruction on L2 pragmatics, and Taylor et al. (Chapter 6) on the benefits of reading strategy training.

When the focus is on quantitative primary studies, a positivist orientation to synthesizing is common. Thus, proponents use metaphors like "summing up" (Light & Pillemer 1984) and "taking stock" (Hunt 1997), and they advocate "orderly knowledge building" (Cooper 1998:1). They emphasize systematicity, replicability, and reduced bias as major strengths of the approach. They depict scholarship as a process of the cumulative generation of knowledge that gradually approximates an unbiased truth, adopting a modernist grand narrative of progression towards ever more accurate and better knowledge. In this sense, meta-analyses frequently seek "final answers" about a contentious problem.

In some areas of research, we stand to gain immensely when we can distill "final answers" through the aggregation of findings across many studies. The precursor of contemporary meta-analysis, Karl Pearson, showed this potential in 1904 when he was able to conclude that inoculation against typhoid fever really worked, simply by averaging the correlations between inoculation and mortality rates across five individual studies, each of which was too small to provide a single-study answer to this important question (Hunt 1997:8). Similarly, at the origin of classic Glassian meta-analysis, Gene Glass and his colleague Mary Lee Smith sought a method that would allow them to bring the quantitative findings reported across 375 studies onto a common scale, in order to silence persistent attacks against psychotherapy that Hans Eysenck and other British psychologists had been publishing for almost 20 years. Glass laid the foundations for a new methodology of what he coined "meta-analysis" (an analysis of analyses) in his presidential address for the American Educational Research Association (Glass 1976), and the first official meta-analysis was published the next year (Smith & Glass 1977). Via the painstaking calculation and aggregation of 833 effect sizes, Glass and Smith showed that groups receiving psychotherapy were on average two-thirds of a standard deviation better by the end of the treatment than control groups, thus conclusively demonstrating that psychotherapy was an effective treatment for neurosis.

Despite the potential benefits evident in such examples of meta-analysis at work, certain dangers need to be considered, as Ellis (Chapter 9, this volume) rightly warns. For one, there are without doubt occasions when quantitative domains of research are best left un-meta-analyzed, for example, when only a few studies have been conducted on the same topic. Furthermore, even when enough primary studies have accumulated, the certainty and authority that is implied by a convincing meta-analytic finding has the potential to do considerable harm. Premature closure of a research domain may ensue when primary researchers or pundits incorrectly assume that there is nothing more to be learned following a 'conclusive' meta-analysis. Also problematic is the tendency of subsequent users of meta-analyses (other researchers, theoreticians, policy-makers, etc.) to focus on only a portion of the meta-analysis in arguing their cases. For example, they may consider: (a) the main effects in absence of moderating effects; or (b) the central tendency of an effect in absence of the variability associated with it; or (c) the role played by one variable, such as measurement type, in absence of the host of other variables investigated. In doing so, such *a-synthetic* commentaries actually obscure the intent of the original synthesis to sort out what is and what is not yet known, never mind why. As we will discuss at the end of the chapter, other dangers are also incurred when synthesists are seduced by meta-analytic technocracy.

In part because of such risks, other applications of quantitative research synthesis have evolved beyond traditional meta-analysis, as secondary reviewers have sought to understand, clarify, and improve upon work in fields like psychology, education, policy analysis, medicine, and so on. Where meta-analysis of the traditional sort is not warranted – or where purposes beyond the pursuit of "final answers" are addressed – the principles of research synthesis offer additional options. In quantitative research on LL&LT, some examples of synthesis in response to distinct purposes are in evidence. Thus, Ortega (2003) synthesized existing measures of syntactic complexity used in second language writing research, in order to clarify their inter-relationships as well as their relationship with L2 development. In the present collection, Thomas (Chapter 8) offers another example, through her historiographical synthesis that compares how practices of proficiency measurement have been used in L2 research during two different periods over an intervening twelve years.

It is also possible to combine meta-analytic purposes with others into a single synthesis. In Norris and Ortega (2000), for example, we pursued two distinct purposes, including not only a meta-analysis of existing quantitative research findings, but also a critical synthesis of research practices, in order to assess what kinds of research had been conducted (and features in need of attention) within the L2 instructional effectiveness domain. In another example of non-traditional approaches to meta-analysis, Glass himself has grown cautious against technocratic applications of meta-analysis (Glass 1999) and has employed the methodology in diverse ways. Recently, he and his colleagues employed a descriptive approach to synthesize four large-scale evaluation studies, as a way of judging whether bilingual programs in Arizona result in positive outcomes in the areas of academic learning, L2 English learning, and L1 maintenance (Rolstad, Mahony, & Glass 2005).

As these examples indicate, then, quantitative research synthesis (including, but going beyond meta-analysis) can play a crucial role in helping researchers to evaluate study methodologies, to explore patterns in findings, to clarify how the domain defines constructs and variables, and to pursue a range of related improvements in future research.

Between systematicity and interpretation: Synthesizing qualitative research

What if a synthesist wishes to review qualitative studies systematically? How can we make sense of accumulated knowledge when the body of research to be synthesized is qualitative and may have interpretive, constructivist, or post-structuralist roots? The answers given by reviewers in this area have been diverse. Some – particularly in sociology – have applied (post)positivist methodologies to synthesize qualitative primary studies. Others – particularly educational researchers, but also some researchers in sociology and health studies – have questioned the relevance and appropriacy of such methods and have explored purposes and models for systematic review from distinct epistemological perspectives. Here, we examine some of the challenges and choices related to synthesizing qualitative research.

It is possible for synthesists to superimpose a (post)positivist lens onto a body of interpretive qualitative studies. Precisely this is what sociologist Charles Ragin set out to do in his Qualitative Comparative Analysis (QCA) (Ragin, Drass, & Davey 2003). This method is close to Yin and Heald's (1975) methodology for systematic synthesis of qualitative case studies, which is known as "case survey," but QCA has been more precisely developed into a set of formal techniques. A good illustration of QCA from sociology is Hodson's (2004) synthesis of 131 ethnographic cases of life in the workplace. Hodson hypothesized the degree of worker autonomy, among other variables, to be predictive of job satisfaction as reflected in workers' attitudes and behaviors. In a complex three-step procedure, the relevant qualitative information found across the ethnographies was transformed into quantitative variables and submitted to statistical analyses, in search of causal relationships. Clearly, the QCA approach to synthesis, although focused on qualitative ethnographic studies, subscribes to the tenets of quantitative and post-positivist research synthesis as we traditionally know it.

For many, however, a synthesis of qualitative case studies ought to preserve the epistemological premises of the primary studies it reviews. This requirement of epistemological congruence between the synthesis and individual primary studies was the persistent theme in a set of papers published in two issues of *Review of Educational Research* in 1998 and 1999. In her contribution, educational ethnographer Margaret Eisenhart (1998) likened positivist and postpositivist syntheses to building *stone walls* and interpretive reviews to crafting *groundswells* that problematize stone walls and force us to look at them as potentially other things. Good interpretive reviews (which Eisenhart argued probably did not exist) offer "provocative, empirically rich, and politically situated interpretations" of what multiple ethnographies on a similar topic seem to reveal (p. 395). Poststructuralist feminist educational researcher Patti Lather (1999) further noted that good reviews are intertextual webs in which the author comes to novel forms of knowing and self-knowing through reviewing. A good qualitative review, Lather suggested, "is gatekeeping, policing, and productive rather than merely mirroring" and it "is not exhaustive; it is situated, partial, perspectival." Reviewing pursues "a critically useful interpretation and unpacking of a problematic that situates the work historically and methodologically" (p. 3).

In terms of methodology, among the more congruent choices is to employ well-established qualitative techniques and apply them to the analysis of study themes rather than raw qualitative data. For example, in education Baumann and Duffy-Hester (2002) used the well-known constant comparative method outlined by Glaser and Strauss (1967) to synthesize themes about teacher inquiry that emerged from a purposeful sample of 34 studies of teachers in literacy-based classrooms.

Yet another possibility is to develop a set of methods specifically designed to deal with the systematic synthesis of qualitative bodies of research. Such an approach was proposed by educational researchers Noblit and Hare (1988) and is known by the name of "meta-ethnography" or "meta-synthesis." Recall that the meta-analytic tradition aims at representativeness or exhaustiveness in the sampling of studies, at resolution of long-standing research debates, and at generalizability. By contrast, meta-syntheses are usually based on small numbers of ethnographies, and the goal is to interpretively integrate and reconceptualize ethnographic knowledge about a given topic, without compromising the conceptual richness and density that is typical of the primary studies involved. What gets synthesized in meta-synthesis is not (quantitative or qualitative) raw data, but interpretations whose warrants have been carefully inspected within and across studies. A good example in the field of education is Doyle's (2003) meta-synthesis of four ethnographic book-length accounts of educational leadership which resulted in improvements in the quality of schools. The present volume includes another example, by Téllez and Waxman (Chapter 7). They apply meta-synthesis to distill best classroom practices for English language learners from the findings reported in a body of 25 qualitative studies. Beyond education, meta-synthesis has been used amply in the field of health studies (e.g., Paterson et al. 2001). For example, nursing researchers Sandelowski et al. (1997) view meta-synthesis as a means for "enlarging the interpretive possibilities of findings and constructing larger narratives or general theories" (p. 396). It requires "a complex exercise in interpretation: carefully peeling away the surface layers of studies to find their hearts and souls in a way that does the least damage to them" (p. 370).

In sum, those who seek to synthesize qualitative research will need to grapple with certain tensions: Should qualitative synthesists view research through a lens that is congruent with the epistemological affiliations of the primary studies under inspection? Is it appropriate, or even possible, to synthesize interpretive qualitative research without betraying the underlying epistemological commitments of the primary studies? Furthermore, could it be that the very task of synthesizing is a modernist enterprise in essential contradiction with interpretive (postmodern) epistemologies? In the end, in confronting the theses and antitheses at play across qualitative studies, reviewers can, at a minimum, elucidate the character of these tensions, if not transcend them to craft a synthetic (perhaps fragmented) understanding of collective emergent themes.

How do we synthesize? The case of meta-analysis

As reviewers respond to the 'will to synthesis' and engage with the array of initial considerations outlined above, they begin to move from purpose to process, articulating the methods of review to the goals of the synthesis within a targeted domain of research. Thus, for example, in our own practice, research synthesis has issued from a broadly post-positivistic rationale for clarifying exactly what quantitative studies have to say. We envision synthetic methodologies as advancing our ability to produce new knowledge by carefully building upon, expanding, and transforming what has been accumulated over time on a given topic of intense interest for the research community. However, we recognize that no knowledge is ever definitive – human understanding can never be complete, and all knowledge is bound by context and purpose; it is therefore always situated and perspectival. With this underlying tension between knowledge accumulation and requisite contextualization in mind, we have explored the application of meta-analysis for synthesizing new, more sharply defined understandings of quantitative work on L2 instruction. We have sought understandings of accumulated findings, to be sure, but also understandings of the scope within which they can be contextualized and of their relationship with methodological tendencies in the domain. In this section, in order to demonstrate how synthetic processes are mapped onto purposes such as these, we outline the use of meta-analytic practices, and we offer insights into the procedural details implied by this one synthetic approach. In doing so, we hope to model something of the 'how' of research synthesis, though we are certainly not suggesting here that all syntheses will proceed according to the precise steps of a quantitative meta-analysis.

In conducting a meta-analysis attention needs to be directed first to *problem specification*, a conceptual step which involves characterization of the research domain and demarcation within it of the research problem that the meta-analyst wishes to synthesize. In many ways, this first step is similar to the traditional literature review prior to undertaking a primary study. The main goals are to develop expertise in the substantive area and to establish a clear purpose for the meta-analysis, including the specification of research questions that are worth pursuing meta-analytically. Subsequently, meta-analysis comprises three empirical phases: sampling, coding, and analyzing. In the first phase, sampling, the meta-analyst turns to *study identification and retrieval*, which involves planning and conducting systematic bibliographic searches. Here the goal is to uncover the universe of studies that contribute potentially relevant information regarding the purposes of the meta-analysis. Once exhaustive bibliographical searches have been conducted, the meta-analyst proceeds to formulating explicit *study eligibility criteria*. This step involves an iterative process of examining the potentially relevant studies uncovered during the study identification and retrieval step, working towards clear and well-motivated criteria for inclusion and exclusion of studies. Moving to the second phase, coding, the meta-analyst first develops a *study features coding book*. Here the meta-analyst decides on a specific set of substantive, methodological, and reporting features for which all studies will be coded. As with the preceding, this step is an iterative process of designing, piloting, and revising coding categories as needed, and it should eventually lead to a well-founded coding book that can be used consistently by any trained coder. Next comes the *coding* of all studies and the documentation of intercoder reliability wherever judgment or inference is required. In the third phase, the meta-analyst is ready for the *analysis* of coding outcomes, including the aggregation of effect sizes and values for other study features, and inspection of the relationship between effect sizes and such features. Lastly, findings are interpreted and the meta-analysis is disseminated. In the following, we address some of the major concerns in these three empirical phases of meta-analysis.

Sampling of primary studies

Because quantitative synthesists aspire to produce knowledge about a research domain that is trustworthy and replicable, a key ingredient to good meta-analyses is the careful design and reporting of sampling strategies. In primary research, it is generally presumed impossible in a single study to include the entire population of reference for a given research problem. For this reason, quantitative sampling typically generates a random or representative slice of the population. By contrast, in meta-analysis (and most other forms of synthesis) it is more common to expect that the full population of 'similar-enough' studies from a research domain will be targeted. Including the complete universe of studies that focus on a given problem is expected to be a relatively manageable task, perhaps amounting to a hundred or a few hundred studies at most, and participation problems of primary research (volunteerism, subject mortality, informed consent, etc.) do not apply to publicly accessible research reports.

On the apples and oranges problem and study eligibility criteria
The first challenge in sampling primary studies for a meta-analysis is to define the relevant conceptual problem space that will be the focus of the study, characterizing the theoretical backdrop against which the purposes of a meta-analysis are illuminated. At a more mundane level, the problem is to define what makes studies "similar enough" to be included in a review, or "different enough" to be excluded, the so-called *apples and oranges* problem. Fundamentally, this stage requires the meta-analyst to establish theoretically and conceptually relevant criteria for defining "similarity" in a given research domain (just as important characteristics of participants are needed to define a population for primary studies). For example, and building on the fruit metaphor that is so popular among meta-analysts, one may well justify a comparison of apples and oranges if the definition of relevant similarity involves "round-shaped, middle size fruits." But then peaches, mangoes, and some other fruits would probably have to be included (and, conversely, melons, star fruit, bananas, and grapes would have to be excluded). Even more importantly, the meta-analyst would have to offer some theoretically compelling argument for "roundness" and "middle size" to be the key definitional criteria of the research domain.

Given a clear theoretical backdrop for, and key characteristics of a universe of studies, meta-analysts proceed to the comprehensive search and retrieval of fitting study reports. Methods for search and retrieval of available literature are relatively straightforward, and they have been facilitated considerably through electronic and web-based archiving and accession. All of the studies in the current volume report the mechanics of accessing relevant study reports. Key here is the requirement that meta-analysts explicate exactly how they ensured that study sampling was exhaustive and that sampling bias was minimized. This explicit presentation of sampling strategies, in turn, makes the synthesis replicable by others. Furthermore, meta-analyses typically include a rather lengthy section in which clear *inclusion and exclusion criteria* are spelled out (relevant variables, type of design, requisite statistics, etc.). These criteria justify membership in the specific corpus of reports from which meta-analysts work. Often, reasons for excluding particular studies that readers may associate with a given domain are given singular weight. A good example is Goldschneider and DeKeyser (2001), who, in their Table 1, provided readers with a list of 25 excluded studies and reasons for each decision. Another model is Dinsmore (Chapter 2, this volume), who first explains five specific reasons for study exclusion in his main text and then provides readers with an appendix in which 57 excluded studies are referenced, each linked to the reasons for exclusion. With such open and precise reporting of what may seem like mundane details, readers can agree or disagree with the exclusions and inclusions laid out in a given meta-analysis, and they have the full information needed to pursue a different definition of the research domain or to investigate whether sampling different studies would change the results and conclusions of the synthesist.

It would be naïve, however, to imagine that all problems are solved by carefully explicating and appending sampling decisions. Defining a research domain or problem is a theory-laden task, and therefore criteria for inclusion and exclusion of studies can always be contested. For example, in a politically charged area like bilingual education, a good number of syntheses have been conducted using vote-counting, meta-analysis, and a mixture of both approaches, but interpretation of the results is far from settled. Such syntheses typically compare data generated from programs that fit a broad category of "L2-only immersion" (i.e., programs offering no instruction in the L1) against data gleaned from programs that fit the broad category of "L1 support" (e.g., bilingual or ESL pull-out programs). One of many areas of disagreement pertains to the legitimacy of including data from studies conducted in Canadian immersion programs. Many synthesists in this domain argue that French immersion programs in Canada are fundamentally different from English immersion programs in the United States and that, therefore, it would be a serious flaw to aggregate both kinds of data together under the "L2-only immersion" category. Their rationale is that Canadian French immersion education represents an elective, additive immersion approach that serves the

linguistic majority population of Anglophones, whereas English-only education in the United States essentially condemns immigrant linguistic minorities
to sink-or-swim L2-only immersion. A few synthesists, by contrast, appear to
be convinced that L2-only immersion programs should work equally well regardless of context. The meta-analysts who exclude Canadian program data
(Greene 1997; Rolstad et al. 2005; Slavin & Cheung 2005; Willig 1985) report
small but reasonable mean effect sizes favoring bilingual education over instruction in the L2 only (sink-or-swim US programs). Specifically, Rolstad et
al. (2005) and Slavin and Cheung (2005) interpret their findings as sound proof
that bilingual education (a) certainly puts students at no risk or detriment in
acquiring their L2, (b) often helps them acquire the L2 better, and (c) definitely
promotes the maintenance of bilingual abilities. However, the synthesists who
staunchly include Canadian French immersion program data in their syntheses
produce very different results (Rossell & Baker 1996), rejecting findings that
favor bilingual education on the charge of ideological bias (Rossell & Kuder
2005). In the end, at least, by laying bare the architecture of each meta-analysis
(in the form of sampling strategies and study eligibility criteria), this discourse
is made possible and readers are provided sufficient information to judge for
themselves.

Study quality, a priori or a posteriori?
Another special challenge related to study sampling is known as the *garbage
in, garbage out* problem, referring to the quality of the studies that make up a
meta-analysis. Further building on the fruit metaphor (see also Ellis, Chapter
9, this volume), the quality of a juice or a smoothie is dependent on the felicity
of the mix of different ingredients that are blended together (the apple and
oranges problem). But it also depends on the sheer quality of each ingredient.
Just as an orange juice cannot be sweet if it was made from sour oranges, or
a smoothie will not be very tasty if curdled milk went into the mix, a research
synthesis that is based on flawed or low quality studies will yield findings that
are not trustworthy. Of course, all researchers would agree that methodological
quality is important and matters very much when evaluating what we know
about a given research question. What causes disagreement among synthesists
is what to do about it. Should we use study quality as a criterion to include
and exclude studies from our meta-analyses? Or should quality be made into
an empirical matter that is examined in the synthesis proper?

Classic Glassian meta-analysis is all-inclusive and treats methodological
quality as an a posteriori research question. Based on the principle of exhaustive (rather than random or purposeful) sampling, as proposed by Glass et al.

(1981) and espoused by many meta-analysts since then, methodological quality is not considered in decisions for exclusion or inclusion. Instead, all studies can be coded for methodological features, and the possible effects of methodological inadequacy can be tested empirically via sensitivity analyses (Greenhouse & Iyengar 1994). By contrast, a quality-first approach is espoused by educational researcher Robert Slavin. He coined the term "best evidence synthesis" to refer to a special type of meta-analysis in which individual study quality is used as a sampling criterion (Slavin 1986). That is, only studies of the highest quality available are admitted into the synthesis.

We find compelling the arguments for treating methodological quality as an empirical matter. First, research quality is not as straightforward as it may appear. Seasoned researchers and astute reviewers may disagree when evaluating the merits of a given methodology and of particular studies within that methodology. Often, judgments of methodological quality are entangled with particular theoretical and conceptual biases that reviewers bring to their task. If quality judgments are adjudicated by the synthesist alone, hidden biases can also be introduced. One strategy in this regard is adopted by some meta-analysts, who consult with a board of experts and use their quality ratings to make decisions about what studies to include and exclude, or to compare through sensitivity analyses the results gleaned from high-quality versus low-quality studies (for more suggestions, see Wortman 1994).

A second important point is that low study quality can lead to erroneous interpretations about cumulative evidence in some domains, but in others it may make no difference or the nature of the error may be unpredictable. This fact was established by Lipsey and Wilson (1993) in an oft-cited article about the typical magnitude of psychological interventions. They inspected effect sizes reported across 302 meta-analyses published in psychology journals. A subset of meta-analyses reported effect size averages separately for studies according to methodological quality: (a) studies with nonrandom versus random assignment to treatment (74 meta-analyses); (b) studies with one-group pre- and post-test designs versus control/treatment designs (45 meta-analyses); and (c) studies rated as "low-quality" versus "high-quality" (27 meta-analyses). When Lipsey and Wilson compared the results reported across these three groups of meta-analyses, they found that averages based on studies using one-group pre- and post-test designs led to an overestimation of effect by comparison to averages reported in the same meta-analyses using control/treatment designs. However, for the first and third operationalizations of quality, no pattern in average effect sizes was discernable. In the end, therefore, it would seem more cautious to assess any impact of study quality as part of the meta-analysis proper, rather than to exclude studies a priori.

We would also add a third qualification (concurring on this with Slavin; see discussion in Slavin & Cheung 2005:253). Namely, at least to some extent, methodological rigor should be defined contextually and differently for each research domain and body of literature. Sweetness and texture are key qualities of pineapples that are intended for eating, but mouth appeal and acidity level take precedence when the target is pineapple juice (and we promise that this is our last reference to fruit!). To illustrate with an example from second language acquisition, it could be argued that idiosyncratic teacher effects are more threatening to research quality when investigating the effectiveness of L2 instructional methods than when investigating interlanguage development. On the other hand, failure to report reliability of outcome measures probably does not bias results of effectiveness of instruction in systematic ways, but may well render results that purport to speak to interlanguage development uninterpretable (see discussion in Norris & Ortega 2003).

Publication bias and fugitive literature

A third major challenge in sampling study reports for meta-analyses has to do with how and why quantitative studies get published, and whether the complete universe of research is best reflected (or skewed) in the published literature. There are several arguments against and in favor of including unpublished studies (the "fugitive" literature) in systematic research syntheses. The main argument against inclusion is one of research quality. An assumption is made by those who take this position that unpublished studies are generally of lower (or untested) methodological quality than published reports. Unpublished research cannot be trusted because these studies did not go through the stringent peer review process that is typical of published reports, which ideally serves to enhance the quality of final published versions as well as to keep the least trustworthy studies from appearing in print.

Those who advocate the inclusion of unpublished studies in systematic reviews offer two important arguments that merit careful consideration. First, while it is true in general that peer reviewing enhances methodological quality, it is also the case that an unpublished study (for example, a report from a research center, or a dissertation) can be of equal or better quality than many published ones, and therefore the burden of deciding quality and relevance in the process of sampling studies should not rest solely on the type of publication. Even Slavin's (1986) selective best evidence approach treats unpublished studies the same as published ones, in that both are submitted first to stringent scrutiny for research quality before either type is counted for the given research domain. In Slavin and Cheung (2005), for example, of 17 studies that were screened into certified best evidence on the issue of bilingual reading instruction, only five were published, whereas the rest were technical reports and dissertations or theses.

Second, perhaps the most important argument in favor of including unpublished studies in meta-analysis is the established danger of *publication bias*. Simply put, it has been widely documented that published quantitative studies tend to report statistically significant findings to a larger extent than unpublished studies. Where researchers conduct studies and find "no results" (that is, where no statistically significant differences are observed), their studies tend to be put away rather than submitted to journals for review, or they are more likely to be rejected and then put away, two patterns that reflect the so-called file drawer problem (Rosenthal 1979). Thus, an inflated view favoring positive and large expected effects is created precisely when unpublished studies are not included in syntheses, and the actual patterns of findings in the domain may be dramatically skewed.

In the present volume, two of the five meta-analyses (Keck et al., Chapter 3; and Russell and Spada, Chapter 4) included only published studies, and they both provide reasons for this decision, arguing that: (a) comparisons with previous narrative reviews on their topics is enhanced, because these narrative reviews have focused exclusively on published evidence; (b) future research is better served, because published reports can be more easily retrieved by subsequent researchers wishing to replicate these meta-analyses; and (c) attempting to collect fugitive literature would be a difficult task that most likely would result in idiosyncratic, incomplete inclusions (cf. Chaudron's remarks on this last issue in Chapter 10, this volume). These reasons relate to the nature of the research domains synthesized in these two chapters (the empirical link between interaction and acquisition, and the effectiveness of error correction). Namely, both domains have been disputed, theoretically and empirically, and have also generated a good number of extant narrative reviews and empirical studies. The other three meta-analyses in this volume included unpublished studies. Of particular interest is Taylor et al. (Chapter 6), who meta-analyzed the findings gleaned from 21 reports, representing almost equally published and unpublished sources. The unpublished findings came from 9 dissertations and 2 ERIC documents. These authors also explicitly looked into the possibility that systematic differences in observed effect sizes could be caused by the inclusion of unpublished studies, thus addressing the concern that study quality in the unpublished half of the meta-analysis may have been an issue. They found no evidence to that effect (see Chapter 6, Appendix 1).

In a young field like applied linguistics, where the use of quantitative methodologies has outpaced sufficient training (Lazaraton 2000; Norris & Ortega 2003; Shohamy 2000) and where much faith is placed in the anonymous referee process, it is difficult to convince authors, reviewers, and editors that study quality cannot be assumed in refereed publications or discarded in unpublished ones, and that the file drawer problem and the concomitant threat of publication bias are real. Yet, the consensus among meta-analysts (in psychology, particularly) is that unpublished and fugitive literature should be included whenever possible, and that syntheses that are based on published studies exclusively should explicitly acknowledge the concern of publication bias. For example, this has been the policy of the *Psychological Bulletin* since Harris Cooper took over its editorship:

> Synthesists submitting manuscripts to *Psychological Bulletin* who have the goal of making summary claims about a particular relationship, hypothesis, or treatment will be expected to conduct thorough searches to locate both published and unpublished research. Deviations from the exhaustive search strategy will require convincing justification.   (Cooper 2003:6)

This position, which may seem odd to many applied linguistics readers, issues from several tenets that many meta-analysts hold and that we have discussed in this section, such as the preference for exhaustive (rather than random or purposeful) sampling, the conviction that quality is an empirical matter, and the belief the there is a publication bias that overestimates the magnitude of a phenomenon. It also reflects the widely held position that statistical significance testing has been (and continues to be) overvalued, at the expense of identifying the actual effects associated with study variables, which are never revealed by a statistical significance test (Harlow, Mulaik, & Steiger 1997). In sum, whether unpublished sources are included or not, most meta-analysts are concerned about publication bias, and they attempt to document through various graphical and statistical techniques the degree to which such a concern needs to be considered when interpreting their results. Two examples exist in applied linguistics: Ross (1998), who made use of the fail-safe statistic proposed by Rosenthal (1979), and Norris and Ortega (2000), who employed the funnel plot suggested by Greenhouse and Iyengar (1994).

Coding of primary studies

In meta-analysis, each study under review is itself studied in a way that is analogous to the elicitation of information from participants in primary research. Just as a survey instrument consists of carefully designed items and response formats, in a meta-analysis it is essential to develop a coding scheme or coding book, in which each of the "questions" we want to ask with consistency of all of our studies is spelled out (Stock 1994). These questions take the form of coding categories, which, like test or survey items, are carefully developed, piloted, and revised on the basis of both theoretical motivations for the meta-analysis and intensive interaction between the meta-analyst and the study reports under review. Requisite for trustworthy and replicable meta-analyses is inclusion of not only the rationale and development of coding categories but also the consistency with which they are applied in extracting information from study reports (i.e., by well-socialized coders).

Meta-analytic coding categories can reflect substantive features (e.g., types of instruction in Norris & Ortega 2000), methodological features (e.g., the sample size per study and per cell within a study; or the type of design, such as pre- and post-test plus control group designs, one-group pre- and post-test designs, and so on), and reporting features (e.g., which statistics were and were not reported). Whether substantive, methodological, or reporting, some of these categories will call for the recording of a numerical value on an interval scale, as is the case for the descriptive statistics that are eventually used in calculating effect sizes. Many categories are nominal, however, and in such instances a closed set of possible cases across studies needs to be developed in advance. For example, Russell and Spada (Chapter 4) coded each study for nine such nominal categories, among which "type of correction provided on oral errors" consisted of 10 possible cases, and "type of correction on written errors" consisted of 7 possible cases (see their Appendix). It is also possible to code for a study variable that is expressed as interval values in primary studies, but later recategorized into nominal values by the meta-analyst. For example, Jeon and Kaya (Chapter 5) recorded the length of treatments across studies in hours and minutes (see their Table 4) but eventually inspected effect size differences for a binary categorization of short versus long treatments (defined as less than five hours versus more than five hours of instruction; see their Tables 11 and 12). As these examples demonstrate, the diverse categories that comprise a coding book will vary from one meta-analysis to the next (i.e., there is no set of stock questions to ask of primary studies), and it is therefore imperative for the meta-analyst to explicate what is being coded, how, and why it is essential to the review.

An important initial consideration when developing a coding book is to gauge the likelihood of retrieving desired information consistently across all or most study reports. Namely, some times the meta-analyst deems it important to record a given study feature, but the feature is reported in only some primary studies, thus making the recording of the variable impossible. Likewise, for any feature that will be coded, it is important to clarify how such 'empty' cases will be recorded, clearly distinguishing between missing information that should have been reported versus information that is not reported in a given study because it is irrelevant. For example, when looking for pre-test scores across studies, the absence of this information in a study that adopts a pre-post-test design should be coded as "missing information," but the same absence in a study adopting a treatment-control post-test only design can be coded as simply "not applicable." This information on what gets reported, including what needs to be reported but is not, can prove to be of particular utility in reforming study reporting practices.

Another important dimension in determining coding categories is that they can reflect very closely those features already operationalized in the primary studies, or they may introduce added layers of abstraction beyond the individual reports. In immediate proximity to primary studies, the meta-analyst may take coding categories directly from the variables as they are reported by primary researchers, be it methodological features implemented by design across studies or substantive features that were the focus of the investigations (typically independent, dependent, and moderating variables in the primary studies). An example is Masgoret and Gardner (2003), who coded and meta-analyzed five attitude/motivation variables and their correlations with three kinds of L2 achievement measures, all eight variables issuing directly from the primary studies.

One step removed from the primary studies, meta-analysts may extract information available in the reports in order to look at relationships that were not necessarily investigated in the individual studies. For example, though duration of treatments is carefully controlled and usually reported in experimental studies, it is only at the meta-analytic level that it is typically coded for and analyzed as a potential causal variable in its own right. Of the five meta-analyses in this collection, four fit this pattern: Dinsmore (see his coding sheet in Appendix 2 in Chapter 2), Russell and Spada (see their Appendix in Chapter 4), Jeon and Kaya (see their Table 1, and also Tables 3 and 5 in Chapter 5), and Taylor et al. (see their coding variables in Tables 3 and 4 in Chapter 6).

Other meta-analytic coding categories can represent variables or constructs that were not directly examined in the primary studies; instead, they are superimposed across primary studies by the meta-analyst, who must exert considerable efforts to ground these abstract codings in the actual features of the studies as reported. Often, these categories are adopted from previous theoretical arguments, as was the case in Goldschneider and DeKeyser (2001) and Norris and Ortega (2000). In the present volume, Keck et al. (Chapter 3) provide a good example. This team investigated the impact of Loschky and Bley-Vroman's (1993) well known principle of task-essentialness on acquisitional gains derived from L2 interaction. They did so by applying definitional criteria to judge the match between the task used and the L2 form targeted (see their Table 3), thereby identifying degree of task-essentialness across primary studies. The criteria were derived from Loschky and Bley-Vroman's theoretical proposal, and the judgment was grounded on the descriptions of tasks and L2 forms that primary researchers provided. However, no primary study in the meta-analysis had investigated task-essentialness as a variable.

It should be clear, then, that the development of some coding categories can involve a great deal of theoretically motivated interpretations and decisions. In the end, a researcher will have to make choices about what information to elicit across studies based on a careful blend of theoretical and conceptual understanding of the research domain, on the one hand, and practical considerations regarding the nature of studies and reporting practices under review, on the other.

Given the complexities of meta-analytic coding, it follows that, in addition to explicating how and why coding categories were developed, the calculation and reporting of reliability of final codings is a key element of good meta-analyses (as it is of any form of empirical research where observations are systematically extracted; for a detailed discussion, see Orwin 1994; also Norris & Ortega 2003: 740–746). Achieving, maintaining, and reporting adequate coder reliability is particularly important for high-inference categories, such as the decision to label a given instructional treatment explicit or implicit (as in Norris & Ortega 2000; Jeon & Kaya, Chapter 5) or a given task design form-essential (as in Keck et al., Chapter 3).

Reliability in the coding process is generally sought through the socialization of coders into the use of a coding book and categories, often including trial runs on a handful of primary study exemplars, followed by discussion and adjudication of any disagreements or 'fuzzy' categories. Subsequent coding of a healthy portion or all of the primary studies is then undertaken by at least two coders, and their consistency is checked through the use of intercoder reliability estimates, including: (a) simple agreement calculations (the ratio of total agreements to total codings); and possibly (b) Kappa coefficients (a more conservative reliability estimate that adjusts for chance agreements between coders). Finally, to enable a complete depiction of (and to encourage) coder consistency, it is essential that reliability be considered and reported not simply overall, but rather for each category under examination (see, e.g., Keck et al., Chapter 3; also Norris & Ortega 2000: 440).

Analyzing and interpreting effects

In the final phase of meta-analysis, the synthesist engages in quantitative and logical analysis of data extracted from the studies and then interprets the findings. The fundamental goal during this phase is to discern the *magnitude* of effects or relationships that have been found, on average, across accumulated studies – primarily at stake is the size and consistency of findings, not their statistical probability. The basics of analysis are straightforward. For each primary study, one or more "effect sizes" are calculated, translating the available study findings into a standardized unit of analysis that is comparable across studies. These effect sizes may then be adjusted according to the sample size of the primary study, or the number of unique samples investigated in a single study, so as to address bias associated with small-sample and multi-sample primary studies. Effect sizes are then averaged across the studies under review, providing an indication of the overall effect or relationship in question. The error (or certainty) with which this overall effect has been observed is also estimated, through tests of the homogeneity of effect sizes, and through the calculation of standard errors and confidence intervals. More fine-tuned analyses generally ensue, with effect sizes aggregated according to distinct coded features (e.g., different kinds of treatments, measures, learner populations), and comparisons/contrasts drawn between these average effects. In the end, effect sizes are interpreted on the basis of collective meta-analytic wisdom and guidelines, and more importantly, according to theory- or practice-driven expectations and other frames of reference from the domain under review.

There are many texts that provide comprehensive treatment of the statistical details and the range of possible analyses for calculating and interpreting observed effects. Among these, we refer readers to: Cooper (1998); Cooper and Hedges (1994a); Cortina and Nouri (2000); Lipsey and Wilson (2001); and Rosenthal, Rosnow, and Rubin (2000). In addition, there are several cost-free as well as commercial meta-analytic tools, including web-based effect size calculators, downloadable Microsoft Excel macros, and the like (for a useful online compendium of resources, see Lane 2005). Finally, Chapters 2 through 6 in this volume all include clear descriptions of the calculations used in their analyses. Given these resources, our purpose here is not to offer a tutorial on meta-analytic statistical procedures. Rather, we highlight a few of the main considerations that face synthesists as they engage in the analysis and inter-pretation of effects accumulated within a domain of primary research.

Extracting effect sizes from individual studies

The first task in this phase of meta-analysis is to transform available statistical data into effect size estimates for each primary study. According to the types of relationships under investigation in the domain, the synthesist will have to select one from among a number of available equations for calculating effect sizes, including Cohen's *d*, Hedges' *g*, Pearson *r*, and others (see Lipsey & Wilson 2001). Note that, mathematically speaking, most of these statistics can be transformed into each of the others (see formulas in Rosenthal, Rosnow, & Rubin 2000); however, conceptually the different estimates may make more or less sense in interpreting the kinds of relationships observed within the domain. Thus, if the domain under investigation consists of correlational studies, then the Pearson product-moment correlation coefficient (*r*) provides a most useful indicator of the strength (magnitude) of association observed between pairs of variables in a given study. More frequently, when the domain is focused on differences between experimental or quasi-experimental conditions (e.g., in-structional treatments), then the most typical effect size estimate is Cohen's *d* (Cohen 1977). This effect size is calculated by subtracting the mean value of the control group on a dependent variable measure from the mean value of the experimental group on the same measure, and then dividing this mean differ-ence by the pooled (average) standard deviation of the two groups. The result is a "standardized mean difference" effect size, and it indicates the amount of standard deviation units that distinguishes the two groups.

Three features are critical in calculating and understanding Cohen's *d* and similar effect size estimates. First, the mean difference (the numerator in the equation) is calculated between an experimental group and a control or com-parison group, not directly between two experimental groups – what is sought here is a value that can be compared from one study to the next, hence the con-trol group is assumed to provide a common point of reference across studies, from which the average size of a treatment/experimental effect can then be dif-ferentiated. Direct comparisons between treatment conditions are not made, because they would be idiosyncratic to the particular study, and therefore not comparable with other studies that did not operationalize exactly the same two treatments. Second, d is calculated from the values on one dependent variable measure, generally the immediate post-test values from the experiment; where studies investigate change or difference with more than one measure, separate effect size estimates are calculated for each. Third, the magnitude of the difference between group means (the numerator) is obviously dependent on the scale used in the particular measure investigated (e.g., subtracting 10–9 results in a different mean difference than does 100–90). As such, in order to enable comparisons across the variety of measurement scales in different primary studies, the mean difference is standardized in much the same way as in the calculation of z-scores: the mean difference is divided by the standard deviation for the particular population on the particular measure (the denominator). Most synthesists agree that by pooling the standard deviations between the two groups under comparison, the most accurate estimate of the population variance will be achieved (for one equation, see Norris & Ortega 2000: 442).

Several additional uncertainties may come into play at this point, depending on the types of studies under investigation. For one, what happens when studies do not utilize a control group, but instead investigate pre-test to post-test differences within a single group (a repeated measures design), or when they have a mixed between-groups and within-groups design? Cohen's d can also be calculated on the basis of the mean gain from pre-test to post-test for a single group on a single measure, dividing the outcome by the pooled standard deviation on the pre- and post-test values. However, it is likely that this "standardized mean gain" will be statistically biased and not comparable with between-groups estimates, and mean gain effect sizes are therefore treated separately from "standardized mean difference" effect sizes (Lipsey & Wilson 2001; for an example, see Jeon & Kaya, Chapter 5, this volume). Further, what if the basic descriptive statistics (means, standard deviations, and sample sizes) are not reported in a given primary study? Alternative methods for calculating effect sizes are available for studies that report the exact values from statistical significance tests (such as the exact F value from ANOVA, or the exact t from t-test; see Rosenthal 1994, for formulas). By taking advantage of all mathematical possibilities available, synthesists can increase the sample of effect sizes included; unfortunately, it is frequently the case that some primary studies do not report enough statistical detail and simply must be ruled out of further analysis (or their authors hunted down and the data extracted from them directly!).

In most meta-analyses, as reflected in those collected in this volume, other judgments will be have to be made along the way in order to determine the most appropriate types of effects to calculate and incorporate into further analysis. It is essential that the synthesist explicitly delineate the types of effect sizes calculated and the contrasts upon which they were based (i.e., which values were differentiated in the numerator). For example, in Norris and Ortega (2000: 445–46) we defined 5 distinct kinds of contrasts that were utilized in estimating effect sizes in the domain of L2 instructional effectiveness studies. In the end, meaningful interpretations about the magnitude of relationships among study variables will rest on an accurate understanding of how the effect sizes themselves were estimated.

Adjusting effect sizes
Before effect sizes can be aggregated for the whole domain, or averaged and compared for sub-groups based on study features, synthesists are faced with several questions about which effect sizes to include. One question asks how many effect sizes should be contributed by any one study. Thus, where a single primary study has investigated multiple independent and dependent variables, or has incorporated multiple measurement takes, it may contribute many effect sizes. If all are included in the analysis, this one study will be weighted heavier than other studies that investigated fewer variables. Hidden features of the study or lab context where the investigations took place, or unknown characteristics of the participant sample, might 'sneak' into the analysis and have a more dramatic effect because of the disproportionate number of effect sizes contributed. Multiple effect sizes based on the same participant sample are also non-independent observations, which is a violation for subsequent inferential statistical analyses that might be applied.

For such reasons, some meta-analysts advocate strategies such as averaging all effect sizes into a single estimate for a single study, or selecting one representative (or random) effect size for a single study – that is, the study itself, rather than the effect size is adopted as the unit of analysis (Lipsey & Wilson 2001). Of course, in doing so, the most important differences among variables might be obfuscated, for example when a L2 primary researcher looks into differences in explicit versus implicit learning – clearly, averaging the associated effect sizes into one value for the single study would eliminate the main point of the investigation. There are three possible solutions to this conundrum: (a) include only one effect size per study; (b) include all effect sizes from each study, but avoid further inferential analyses of the accumulated effect sizes, focusing on cautious description rather than causal inference; or (c) utilize specially designed statistical procedures for dealing with non-independent observations (see Cortina & Nouri 2000; Gleser & Olkin 1994). Given the limitations of (a), and the technical and primary study reporting demands of (c), we would suggest that option (b) generally provides the most broadly applicable strategy for the basic interpretive demands of meta-analysis in LL&LT research. However, the other two strategies may be appropriate for exacting interpretations in some domains; the synthesist might also engage in inclusive description first and then move on to more selective inferential analyses if necessary.

A second question asks whether the effect sizes from primary studies with differing sample sizes should be trusted to the same degree. It is commonly argued that studies with larger sample sizes probably provide a more accurate estimate of whatever relationships are under investigation; that is, the larger the number of observation points in a single study, the closer it will approximate the population to which findings are being generalized. In response to this problem, meta-analysts typically "weight" the effect sizes contributed by each study, mathematically giving heavier weight to larger sample studies (see calculations in Lipsey & Wilson 2001; for examples in this volume, see Chapter 2 by Dinsmore and Chapter 4 by Russell & Spada). Of course, there are no guarantees that larger sample studies will reflect more accurately the actual effect than smaller sample studies, especially in light of the range of other factors that might be contributing to observed effects (measurement reliability, study quality, and so on). Therefore, it behooves synthesists to report unweighted as well as weighted effect size estimates for each study, and to justify which type was used in further analysis.

Prior to combining and comparing effect sizes, additional questions may ask about outliers in the distribution of observed effects, systematic biases for particular effect size estimates, reliability levels of measured variables, and other artifacts that introduce error into interpretations about the 'real' effects in the domain of studies (see useful discussion in Lipsey & Wilson 2001). Statistical adjustments can be made for any of these eventualities observed in the set of effect sizes, though synthesists should report and justify any adjustments (and they should avoid the temptation to adjust the numbers until they look like they are supposed to look, rather than what they really look like!).

Aggregating and comparing effect sizes
Once a final set of effect sizes has been calculated, the individual effects can be averaged together in order to depict the overall magnitude of relationships observed within the domain. This mean effect size provides a basis for subsequent calculations, as well as for comparisons with other meta-analyses or other domains of research. However, on its own, this average is not particularly meaningful. As with any measure of central tendency, it also requires an

estimate of dispersion (e.g., standard deviation) in order for readers to understand the extent to which collected study effect sizes differ from the mean. Perhaps more directly useful is the calculation of a confidence interval within which the mean can be assumed to occur 95% or 99% of the time. For example, in Norris and Ortega (2000), we found an average overall "standardized mean difference" effect size of 0.96 (nearly one standard deviation unit) for the full group of analyzed studies on effectiveness of L2 instructional techniques. We then calculated a 95% confidence interval for the mean (see formula in Norris & Ortega 2000:449; also see Lipsey & Wilson 2001, for formulas appropriate to different types of effect size). The resulting interval indicated that, with 95% certainty, the mean effect size in the domain could be assumed to fall somewhere between 0.78 and 1.14.

One additional analysis that is commonly applied to the full collection of study effect sizes investigates whether they form a homogeneous distribution. Assuming no systematic biases or sampling errors, the accumulated effect sizes should most likely form a relatively normal distribution around the average effect, with some bigger and some smaller effects. A homogeneity analysis (the Q-test, see Hedges & Olkin 1985) provides a probability-based statistic for determining whether the actual observed distribution falls in the expected pattern, given the number of studies included and their dispersion around the mean. Where a statistically significant value is returned, the assumption of homogeneity is violated and other reasons for the unexpected distribution must be investigated. However, for smaller samples of studies under analysis, this statistical homogeneity analysis may not be particularly trustworthy; accordingly, it is probably best for synthesists to plot effect size frequency distributions and to interpret them graphically and descriptively (the 'eyeballing' method; see Light et al. 1994 for useful suggestions). Furthermore, subsequent investigation of the potential sources for differential effect sizes nearly always ensues anyway, so the homogeneity test is not particularly necessary for authorizing such analysis (though it does return one useful piece of information).

In addition to the average effect size for a domain of studies, sub-groups of studies may be combined and contrasted with each other, based on the coded study features. Thus, it might be useful to calculate average effect sizes and 95% confidence intervals for different types of independent, dependent, and moderating variables, different lengths of study, different participant population characteristics, different researchers (looking for a so-called 'lab effect'), and so on. The basic calculations here are identical to those above for the overall group of studies, with the exception of the homogeneity analysis (which generally does not add new information at the sub-group level). Particularly useful again in making comparisons among sub-groups (e.g., between different independent variable groupings) is the calculation of 95% confidence intervals, followed by their graphic comparison (see many examples in the current collection). Where 95% intervals overlap with each other, any differences between them are not considered to be statistically trustworthy, whereas non-overlapping intervals indicate trustworthy differences. For example, in Norris and Ortega (2000:467), we found non-overlapping 95% confidence intervals for average effect sizes in comparing implicit instructional techniques (0.26 to 0.82) with explicit techniques (0.93 to 1.33).

It is also possible to engage in inferential statistical comparisons and modeling to identify the effects of different accumulated variables, and to investigate whether observed differences are systematic (often called "fixed") or random. Practices analogous to ANOVA and regression can be applied to the collected effect sizes, with study features entered as between- or within-groups factors (see details in Cooper & Hedges 1994; Cortina & Nouri 2000; Lipsey & Wilson 2001). While these additional analyses may be useful for answering some questions in some domains, and their practice is de facto in certain meta-analytic traditions, we suggest caution in their use. For one, in applied linguistics, the number of collected studies for any given domain is likely to be quite small, and associated violations of most assumptions for inferential tests are therefore also likely. Further, one of the primary purposes of meta-analysis, and research synthesis more broadly, is to help various participants in a community of research practice come to common understandings about the accumulated knowledge. Inferential statistical significance testing has proven to be particularly ineffective as a communicative practice in this regard (e.g., Carver 1978; Cohen 1994), and it may divert researchers away from the focal questions of the analysis: what is the magnitude of relationships observed between important variables, and what patterns can be discerned between study features and these effect sizes? In pursuit of directly meaningful answers to these questions, we suggest that meta-analysis should nearly always emphasize description of studies and their findings, graphic depiction of effect sizes and confidence intervals, and logical comparisons between sub-groups of studies.

Interpreting effect sizes and other analyses
So, what do the outcomes of these analyses mean, and what do they tell us about the accumulated knowledge within a given domain of research? What size of effect can be considered 'big' or 'big enough' or 'important'? Most basically, the effect size has a *mathematical meaning* that underlies other interpretations (see Lipsey & Wilson 2001, or Rosenthal, Rosnow, & Rubin 2000,

for interpretations of distinct types of effect sizes). For "standardized mean difference" effect sizes (e.g., Cohen's d), the statistic indicates the number of standard deviation units that differentiate experimental conditions from control conditions, however these have been defined in the primary research of the domain (see above). Thus, envisioning a frequency distribution, an average effect size of +1.00 would indicate that the experimental conditions produce dependent variable scores that are one standard deviation higher than scores for the control group (located at 0.00). In percentile terms, participants in the experimental conditions would on average fall around the 84th percentile, while control participants would fall around the 50th percentile (based on the properties and assumptions of normal score distributions).

Though the basic mathematical meaning of an effect size is relatively straightforward, it may not on its own enable a good understanding of findings about the accumulated effects – what is needed is *a frame of reference* for interpreting effect sizes that can be understood by readers, users, and researchers alike. The best known frame of reference is from Cohen (1962, 1977, 1988), who proposed rough rules of thumb for interpreting standardized mean difference effect sizes, based on his observations of the typical range of findings in social science research: small effects ($d \leq 0.20$), medium effects ($0.20 < d < 0.80$), and large effects ($0.80 \leq d$). Though this heuristic is helpful and has been applied frequently in the meta-analysis literature, it should not be over-interpreted. Cohen was careful to point out that these were simply his estimates based on typical observations, and that interpretations about the magnitude of effects could only be meaningful in relation to specific domains and the types of effect sizes that made some kind of apparent difference (for psychological phenomena, in his case).

Another meaningful frame of reference might be the range of effect sizes that have been found in similar domains, where possible based on preceding meta-analyses. Thus, Cooper (1998) has advocated that "...an effect size should be labeled 'small' or 'large' depending on its magnitude relative to a variety of related estimates" (p. 177). For example, Lipsey and Wilson (1993) compared average effect sizes across 302 meta-analyses in psychology, education, and behavioral research, and found an average effect of 0.50 ($SD = 0.29$) with a range from just below 0.00 to nearly 2.00.

For a similar basis of comparison closer to home in LL&LT, in Norris and Ortega (2000) we found that the average instructional treatment effect across 49 unique sample studies was 0.96. Mean effect sizes reported in this volume are congruent with this average as well. Clearly, with respect to the studies in Lipsey and Wilson (1993), L2 instructional treatment studies produce relatively large effects. This finding may, of course, be a statistical artifact related to the relatively low sample sizes of studies in L2 instruction (and the corresponding larger effect sizes required to 'achieve' statistically significant *p* values on inferential tests). On the other hand, it may be that an effect size of around one standard deviation is the magnitude at which differences between L2 instructional conditions become apparent in the outcome measures that are utilized and in the contexts under investigation. For now, at least, future LL&LT meta-analyses could relate their effect sizes to ours, and to those in Lipsey and Wilson, and they could seek to account for bigger or smaller magnitudes in their particular domains through attention to defining study features (for examples of these strategies in this volume, see Chapter 4 by Russell & Spada and Chapter 5 by Jeon & Kaya).

In addition to these relative comparisons, the ideal basis for interpreting effect sizes would be extended descriptive research that ties measurement-based observations to contextually meaningful changes in the phenomena of interest. Before we jump into the interpretation of effect sizes, we need a basis for understanding the kinds of effects that mean something *in real-world terms*. Indeed, it is imperative to interpret the real-world meaningfulness of an effect contextually in addition to mathematically and comparatively. For example, it is quite possible that even a 'small' effect could be meaningful. A well known case is the small but positive effect of aspirin on heart attack rates (see Rosenthal 1990). What numerically looked like an extremely small effect size ($r = 0.034$) translated not only into saving on average 34 lives out of every 1000 people with high risk of suffering a heart attack, but did so with something as simple and inexpensive as taking a daily aspirin (Rosenthal & DiMatteo 2001:78). Shanahan (2002) provides another telling example from reading research. When he compared tutoring sessions in reading imparted by teachers, adult volunteers, and peers, he found similar-sized effects for the three conditions. Yet these "equal effects" were associated with strikingly different contextual conditions, where the highly trained teachers tutored students with extreme reading needs and the peers tutored average-reading students. Shanahan concluded that "The effects were roughly equal, but the conditions under which they were derived require different interpretations" (p. 147). Unfortunately, in LL&LT research we have little descriptive-relational work connecting measurements to amounts of change, difference, or other outcomes that are valued in real-world terms (see discussion in Norris & Ortega 2003). One example is Ortega (2003), who compared measures of syntactic complexity in L2 writing development with foreign language curricular levels, and found corresponding relationships in how much measurement change (and of what type) related to how much curricular change (i.e., across increasing years of language instruction).

A final caution is in order here. It is tempting to interpret meta-analytic results by focusing only on the average effects observed across studies. To avoid misleading readers, it is crucial to interpret both the confidence intervals associated with any average effects and the actual distribution of individual study effects. Graphic displays are essential for conveying such patterns and should form the basis of most meta-analytic discussion (see examples in the chapters in this volume). Beyond the comparison of means and their confidence intervals, the depiction of variance observed across studies within a single analysis provides important information about the consistency of patterns in the domain. Thus, binomial effect size displays, probability of superiority estimates, success rate differences, and stem-and-leaf plots all provide useful depictions of individual study effect sizes in meaningful terms (see details in Cooper 1998; Lipsey & Wilson 2001).

In the end, it is really up to the research synthesist to make sense of meta-analytic outcomes in organic terms, that is, those that define the theory and practice of the domain. To reiterate, interpretation is not simply a matter of applying rules of thumb for small versus big effects (or applying statistical significance tests, for that matter). Instead, it is up to the synthesist to ground interpretations in the indicators, scales, and criteria that provide meaning to the domain of research work. Along these lines, it is also crucial for the synthesist to interpret with caution. Meta-analysis is always a post-hoc endeavor, and as such, variables can not be manipulated nor study quality improved. It is therefore incumbent on the synthesist to incorporate comprehensive findings about the primary study research itself into any interpretations that are put forth. To be sure, the numbers on their own do not lie, but selective attention to their genesis or decontextualization when interpreting results can certainly lead to dramatically dissimilar truths.

Thinking and acting synthetically: A research ethic

The preceding section conveys something of the painstaking and complex undertaking that comprises meta-analysis and, by extension, other forms of research synthesis. Clearly, a researcher should have a very good idea of the potential contribution to be made by such work, before engaging in it. In the last two sections of this chapter, we turn to our own broader views on the potential contributions of research synthesis. We believe that synthesis, of whatever sort, ought to help specific communities within language learning and language teaching make better sense of the research problems that interest them. In our own work, we have sought to underscore the value of research synthesis as a "cumulative context" (Norris & Ortega 2000:422) within which a variety of participants can communicate about research in mutually meaningful ways. However, in order to arrive at this cumulative context across the diverse clines of LL&LT, it is incumbent upon the individual members of each research community to begin thinking and acting synthetically.

Of course, we are not suggesting that we all need to be conducting comprehensive meta-analyses on every question or variable or domain of research, at every opportunity. Nor does a commitment to thinking and acting synthetically restrict us from thinking 'outside of the box,' asking new questions, improving on research methods, or coming up with other innovations. What it does force us to do is consider much more carefully *why* we are doing a piece of research, be it primary or secondary, by situating ourselves within (or even in contrast to) a body of existing knowledge, and by explicating how the *ends* to which we put our research efforts will contribute something of value to the same (see Ortega 2005). The synthetic ethic requires us to specify the bases for our empirical claims and theoretical arguments, and to justify any so-called 'evidence-based' actions on the grounds of the actual and complete available evidence. It encourages us to shape up our methods, and to be honest and 'go public' with the key methodological features and epistemological affiliations of our studies. It also demands that we educate ourselves and others in research methods, of whatever epistemological genus. In a world where decisions and actions are based increasingly on 'best evidence,' 'clear indications,' 'significant differences,' 'scientifically-based knowledge,' and similar research claims – claims that may be warranted or not – that is the least that can be expected of educated actors, including users of research knowledge, critics of research paradigms, and researchers themselves. The ethic of research synthesis entails, at heart, a commitment to intelligible and respectful communication: between past and present studies, across theory and research and practice divides, between research contexts or camps, and among members of each research community.

Problematizing meta-analysis and "effect"

We believe there is much to be gained in applied linguistics through the application of established (but still novel for our field) meta-analytic methodologies of reviewing. For one, its systematic approach helps generate detailed knowledge that can inform immediate practical applications (e.g., in L2 teaching) as well as future research, by identifying patterns in and relationships among findings, and by uncovering gaps and methodological weaknesses to degrees of precision and insight that traditional literature reviews can not. It also has the potential to generate novel theoretical knowledge not found in any single primary study (Miller & Pollock 1994), by resolving the extent to which theoretical tenets and constructs actually hold as increasing empirical light is shed upon them. Finally, meta-analysis emphasizes the importance of thinking in terms of the magnitude of effects, and it puts statistical significance testing into a balanced perspective. This feature alone can have a salutary effect on the field of applied linguistics, where quantitative researchers have abundantly misused and abused inferential statistics (see discussion in Lazaraton 2000; Norris & Ortega 2003).

At the same time, supporters as well as critics have warned against the real danger of technocracy in meta-analysis and other forms of systematic quantitative synthesis. Interestingly, this danger has been acknowledged by editors of the very journals that provide the foremost venues for publication of syntheses and meta-analyses. For example, when taking over the editorship of the *Psychological Bulletin*, Masters, Cantor, and Hedges (1988) remarked that "a troubling aspect of many manuscripts submitted to *Psychological Bulletin* is their excessive, uncritical, and sometimes inappropriate reliance on empirical methods, often to the virtual exclusion of theory and conceptualization" (p. 3). Similarly, Grant and Grauer (1999: 395), in their statement as new co-editors of *Review of Educational Research*, referred to quantitative research synthesis as "the traditional (cookie-cutter technical) style" of reviewing and deplored that this style had dominated that journal during the 1970s and 1980s. Other seminal voices have warned against the temptation of "high-tech statistication," as Rosenthal and DiMatteo (2001: 68) put it. Even Glass, as noted earlier, has grown cautious over the years against the technocratization of meta-analysis (Glass 1999). On the receiving end of this problem, it is not uncommon for readers of meta-analyses to experience a sense of conceptual vacuum when technical meta-analytic expertise is not coupled with deep knowledge of the theoretical and conceptual issues at stake in the research domain under review.

We do not wish to promote in our field the cookie-cutter ethos that Grant and Grauer (1999) rightly lamented. Much to the contrary, with this chapter and the contributions in the current volume, we hope to introduce readers to some of the possibilities that systematic research synthesis offers to applied linguists, and thus to encourage diversity as well as quality in reviewing practices in our field. Quantitative meta-analysis is one available option. However, we do not subscribe to the position that it is the most 'scientifically-based' form of synthesis. Quite the contrary, synthesis that strives to achieve a cumulative context for communication must be broadly aware and inclusive. Thus, as research domains emerge and evolve in response to the real-world problems of language learning and teaching, distinct approaches to knowledge are invoked, including: (a) theory generation, (b) in-depth observation and description, (c) extended exploration, (d) controlled experimentation, and other empirical practices that flesh out a domain. Synthesis should enable an articulation, rather than a disembodiment, of these distinct features with each other. Meta-analysis on its own cannot accomplish this end; thinking and acting in a broadly synthetic way can. In this sense, meta-analysts are also required to think and act synthetically beyond the combination of effect sizes across studies – they must communicate with the theories, constructs, and contexts that define the domains from which observed effects emerge. Average effects on their own may be as meaningless as statistical significance tests on their own, if they are not accompanied by a frame of reference within which they can be meaningfully interpreted.

Typical in meta-analysis is a focus on effects, as in the cause-effect relationships that are posited in theories and investigated by primary researchers in the form of independent and dependent variables. We would like to propose here a second notion of effect in relation to the synthetic ethic: the effect of a piece of research. In this second sense, effect is much more than a statistic that is extracted from an individual study or aggregated across studies; rather, it captures the extent to which any piece of research can be incorporated into improved understanding, informed action, or other kinds of knowledge utilization (see Ortega 2005). For a piece of research, primary or secondary, to be considered *effect*ive, it must facilitate communication and dialogue among the various constituencies in a given research community. This claim is grounded in recent work at the interface between research, policy, and practice, where the utilization of research-generated knowledge is treated as a matter of empirical study (e.g., Ginsburg & Gorostiaga 2003; Patton 1997). In a recent collection of such work in the field of education, Ginsburg (2003) summarized:

> Certainly, it may be easier – and, in that sense, more efficient – for researchers, policy makers, and practitioners in education to engage in action (or even in praxis) in isolation of members of the other groups. However, the decisions that are made and the actions that are pursued are likely to be less effective. This is the case not only because the quality of judgments may be lower but also because the activities of one group may detract from or cancel out those of other groups. (p. x)

Some implications for ethical practice

To encourage, enable, and sustain *effective* research in LL&LT, we suggest that it is the ethical responsibility of all of us to act synthetically, to pursue a cumulative context for communication and dialogue. Here, we outline a few implications of this ethic for the main participants in the research community.

For **secondary researchers** – those who look empirically across a body of research work and seek answers to specific research questions about the state and quality of accumulated knowledge – the components of synthetic practice should be clear from the preceding discussion. Systematic secondary reviews are well-founded in the theories and epistemologies that define a domain, they target a specific purpose that helps the domain to better understand an important problem, and they subscribe to adequate methodologies for surveying, extracting, analyzing, and reporting the state of related knowledge. We would like to underscore here three related ethical implications. First, secondary reviews do not set out to prove anything, no matter how 'significant' the apparent effects that have accumulated; the goals of any synthetic review should be to establish accurate and meaningful points of reference for interpreting existing and future research, to identify gaps in current knowledge, and to improve research practice. Second, in summarizing exactly what a given domain of research has to say about an important problem or question, anomalous findings require balanced attention and explanation. That is, synthesists do not only report the 'average' finding from a collection of studies, but also attend to any 'outliers' in the domain. Third, and related to this point, in the synthetic ethic there is no place for capricious or incomplete reviews; vendettas in the guise of research synthesis serve only to detract from, to "cancel out," the potential value of thorough-going secondary reviews.

The synthetic ethic also holds specific implications for **primary researchers**. Because the data-base for secondary research syntheses consists of collected primary research studies, their substantive focus, methodological quality, and depth of reporting will play a determining role in the extent to which knowledge can be accumulated, compared, contrasted, and trusted within a given domain. In turn, the interpretation of primary study outcomes will be greatly enhanced through consideration of the accumulated knowledge that already exists (especially the frames of reference provided by research syntheses; see previous). Responding to such concerns, in concluding Norris and Ortega (2000), we recommended nine specific practices for improving primary research in relation to the specific case of meta-analysis (pp. 497–98), and we would maintain still that L2 quantitative researchers need to take those into careful consideration. More generally, with the synthetic goal of a cumulative context for communication in mind, all primary researchers can engage in:

- Grounding primary research in a thorough understanding of the existing knowledge on a given question or problem, looking to research syntheses or other forms of secondary review, where they already exist, as good starting points for the identification of problems in need of attention by primary researchers, including replication;
- Operationalizing study procedures in ways that enable comparisons to be made across studies, which in some cases will mean the replication of specific variables and in other cases careful explication of new operationalizations by explicit description and contrast with those that have come before;
- Reporting study findings in a way that will enable synthesists to treat them as data for secondary research;
- Enabling access to primary study data, where feasible and given appropriate informed consent, for example by posting certain kinds of data to publicly accessible web sites (e.g., the CHILDES data base; see MacWhinney, 2000); and
- Interpreting study findings on the basis of (in comparison/contrast with) other related research, such that, for example, statistically significant differences or small, medium, or large effects are related to indicative points of reference in the domain under investigation.

For **editors and publishers** of research, the ethic entails major implications as well. After all, the research that appears in print is the research that will be used most by teachers, policy makers, and others, and it is the research that stands the best chance of being included in secondary reviews. Incumbent on those who make publishing decisions, then, is the responsibility to foster accurate and comprehensive reporting, to encourage the conduct and dissemination of research syntheses, and to enable a synthetic perspective on diverse domains of research. These ends may be met through practices that include the following:

- Requiring that primary study reports include sufficient descriptive data for subsequent secondary analysis;
- Publishing and regularly updating guidelines for the conduct of research in LL&LT, so as to make readers aware of the variety of methodological approaches current to the domain (e.g., Chapelle & Duff 2003);
- Establishing editorial policies that oblige contributors to engage in rigorous and improved research methods and reporting (for example, *Language*

Learning, which since 2000 requires the report of effect size estimates; Ellis 2000);

– Providing for the dissemination of extended study reports and data through new publishing formats, such as web-based publishing of appendices, measurement tools, raw data, and the like (for one application of this idea, see Kluwer's forthcoming *Encyclopedia of Language Teaching*, Hornberger, in press; for another, see the web-based journal *Language Learning & Technology*);

– Contracting, for the review of submitted manuscripts, expert referees who understand research synthesis (including the relationship between primary and secondary research); multi-stage refereeing may also enhance the value of this process, with *methodological* review preceding and independent of final publication decisions (see Kupfersmid 1988).

Finally, the **users of research knowledge** will also benefit from and contribute to the synthetic enterprise, with the following implications. Foremost, teachers, policy makers, and others who apply LL&LT research outcomes to their practices can act synthetically by seeking out opportunities to educate themselves in research methods; the more they know, the more likely they will be to rebuff researchers' erroneous or exaggerated interpretations of study findings (and resist their own). Further, they should realize (and researchers should explain) that any single study can not provide a definitive answer to a question or problem, despite a tendency of primary researchers to promote that impression in their study conclusions. By reading each piece of research with a healthy dose of caution, and by looking for contextual cues that may enable or disable generalization of study findings to their own practical concerns, users will develop their own reasonable interpretations on the basis of the actual evidence provided. In addition, users can begin to look for secondary reviews, especially systematic research syntheses, on the topics that are relevant to their practical concerns, as these will be made increasingly available over the foreseeable future and will offer comprehensive treatments of the implications of existing evidence. Lastly, those who base decisions on research knowledge can also contribute immensely to the utility of the research that occurs and the accumulation of relevant evidence, by communicating their practical needs to researchers in related domains, and by calling for and participating in opportunities for research-practitioner collaboration and action research (Crookes 1993).

The future of research synthesis in language learning and teaching

In closing, we point to themes that are most likely to define the continued development of a synthetic ethic for research in LL&LT domains. We address first a handful of immediate challenges for those who seek to conduct systematic research syntheses. We then highlight several major contributions that we anticipate research synthesis can make to research-related work in LL&LT.

Challenges

It should be apparent that anyone setting out to conduct a systematic research synthesis in one of the many LL&LT domains will be confronted with a variety of often complex problems that demand resolution in one way or another. Of these, several are in need of immediate and persistent collective attention by LL&LT research communities.

The most obvious problem for the synthesist, and the pattern that most readily emerges across the following chapters, is that of inconsistent primary study reporting. It is, quite simply, impossible to take full advantage of research synthesis, when the primary studies that define a domain provide impoverished accounts of their research methods and study findings. Key among the features that are frequently missing from reports in LL&LT are (a) basic descriptive data (e.g., descriptive statistics) essential for combining or comparing/contrasting findings across studies in consistent ways, and (b) basic contextualization (e.g., indicators of learners' L2 proficiency levels, sufficient description of instructional treatments) essential for situating and interpreting findings, and for generalizing about learning-teaching processes and their outcomes for particular populations. The roots of this problem are many. However, responsibility for its resolution is shared equally by those who publish primary research and those who produce it, and the preceding section offers suggested changes in this regard. For now, synthesists can only address what they find and utilize the evidence at hand; in this sense, it may be that a major contribution of syntheses at this point is still to raise the awareness of specific LL&LT domains about the inadequacy of their research reporting practices.

A second, related problem that is also apparent in the syntheses collected here is that of methodological infelicities in many primary studies. Where synthesists look for best evidence about a question, in the form of methodological criteria for study inclusion, they face the fact that methodological weaknesses occur in most walks of published LL&LT research, from study designs to procedures and from analyses to interpretations. For the synthesist, as we outlined earlier, the problem can be tackled as an empirical question to some extent, through the evaluation of primary study quality and the comparison of findings in bodies of work with higher or lower levels of quality. Some problems, though, mar the interpretability of virtually all studies within a domain (see discussion in Norris & Ortega 2003). As research practices continue to evolve and improve within the maturing domains of LL&LT, it will be important for synthesists to identify such areas of primary study methodology most in need of resolution.

In terms of the accumulation of existing knowledge within specific LL&LT domains, it is possible that another problem will require attention in the near future. Virtually all syntheses that have been conducted to date in LL&LT have dealt with published and fugitive literature available in English, and they have tapped a corpus of work that is accessible through relatively high-tech mechanisms of information exchange (e.g., web-based search and archival functions). However, there are, potentially, additional literatures available in certain domains. Research of some kinds is certainly being published on LL&LT in languages other than English, and there are likely to be dissertations, theses, action research projects, program evaluations, and other types of reports that never reach the light of day, publication-wise, but which contain relevant additional evidence. It is an empirical question whether (a) these additional literatures actually exist for any specific domain of work, or (b) their contributions to the body of accumulated work would make a difference in synthetic findings. Telling for future synthetic work will be the exploration of methods for the identification and retrieval of such literature, as well as its incorporation into comprehensive secondary reviews.

One last challenge that confronts synthesis in LL&LT has to do with the increasing diversity in research that is being conducted within any particular domain. Thus, researchers may pursue similar questions from distinct epistemological perspectives, producing studies that are of a quality and substantive focus worthy of inclusion in a synthesis, but that diverge in methodologies to the extent that it is unclear how their findings may be woven into a meaningful meta-narrative about the state of accumulated knowledge. Adding to this diversity is the introduction of single study mixed-methods work (see Tashakkori & Teddlie 2003; and Norris, forthcoming), which incorporates multiple investigative approaches in order to answer the kinds of complex questions that tend to occur rather frequently in the more applied reaches of LL&LT work. Simply ignoring a chunk of the literature (e.g., dismissing all positivist or all constructivist research on epistemological grounds or ruling out mixed-methods studies) is no solution, as it will result in inaccurate depiction of the actual available evidence. Possible responses to this challenge include: (a) multi-part syntheses, dealing with each distinct methodology in turn; (b) theory-driven interpretivist syntheses, which adopt qualitative procedures for mapping distinct layers of research (including quantitative studies) onto the creation of a synthesist's interpretations (see Thomas & Collier 2002); and (c) decision- or action-driven evaluative syntheses, which weigh distinct forms of evidence about a priority problem on the basis of their utility for the primary stake-holders in a particular context. Though mostly speculative at this point, these suggestions may provide initial inroads for broaching the complex, but increasingly urgent, demands of mixed-methods syntheses.

Immediate contributions

Finally, we would like to highlight several major contributions that we anticipate research synthesis can make to research-related work in LL&LT. For starters, good syntheses will help us to establish concise and meaningful expectations for the outcomes of teaching-learning processes, in research and practice alike. Rather than depending on a statistical significance test to tell us whether one instructional approach is better than another, we desperately need meaningful frames of reference that indicate how much learning occurs, of what quality, for what duration, under what circumstances. Syntheses – of qualitative and quantitative studies alike – should look to aggregate concrete, targeted L2 learning outcomes (advancement from one curricular level to the next, changes in global proficiency levels, increments in developmental stages, enhancements in fluency of speech production, increases in reading rate, decreases in reaction times, etc.) and the type, frequency, and amount of language teaching required for bringing about valued increments in the same. *Non-chance* differences are not really what we need to know for understanding and improving practice – we need to know which practices lead to *expected* differences, and these expectations in turn must be defined.

Research synthesis will make a related contribution in the use of measurement for LL&LT work. Comprehensive reviews of particular domains should reveal the actual constructs for which interpretations are sought, as well as the instruments via which these constructs have been operationalized. Careful analysis of available correlational and descriptive data across studies (to the extent that it is available) will then enable a critique of the extent to which measurement-based construct interpretations are warranted through the use of these instruments, for the specific learners and contexts under investigation. This synthetic process of "validity and reliability generalization" (see discussion in Norris & Ortega 2003; Vacha-Haase 1998) will play a major role in clarifying what measurements can and should be used for what teaching-learning constructs; it will also elucidate the array of measures in need of development.

More broadly, and perhaps most importantly, research synthesis can contribute immediately to the transcendence of LL&LT research, from a collection of disparate purposes, practices, classroom field sites, labs, methods, and the like, to a cohesive undertaking founded on effective communication. Good descriptive syntheses – that make a first pass at compiling what work has been done, how and how well it has been done, and where there seems to be agreement and discord in findings – will provide essential watershed opportunities for diverse participants in the LL&LT community to interact within a common space and with a common focus. Rather than providing accurate final answers to the simple questions of LL&LT domains, this first generation of syntheses should probably set more modest goals of staking out the territory and raising awareness. As the diverse participants in language learning and teaching research begin to coalesce in their work, perhaps the next generation of syntheses will be able to tease apart finer-grained distinctions and to inform more trustworthy claims.

References

Baumann, J. F., & Duffy-Hester, A. M. (2002). Making sense of classroom worlds: Methodology in teacher research. In M. L. Kamil, P. B. Mosenthal, P. D. Pearson & R. Barr (Eds.), *Methods of literacy research: The methodology chapters from the handbook of reading research, volume III* (pp. 1–22). Mahwah, NJ: Lawrence Erlbaum.

Brown, J. D., & Rodgers, T. S. (2002). *Doing second language research.* Oxford: Oxford University Press.

Carver, R. P. (1978). The case against statistical significance testing. *Harvard Educational Review, 48,* 378–399.

Chapelle, C., & Duff, P. (2003). Some guidelines for conducting quantitative and qualitative research in TESOL. *TESOL Quarterly, 37,* 157–178.

Chaudron, C. (1988). *Second language classrooms: Research on teaching and learning.* Cambridge, UK: Cambridge University Press.

Cohen, J. (1962). The statistical power of abnormal-social psychological research: A review. *Journal of Abnormal and Social Psychology, 65,* 145–153.

Cohen, J. (1977). *Statistical power analysis for the behavioral sciences* (rev. ed.). New York: Academic Press.

Cohen, J. (1988). *Statistical power analysis for the behavioral sciences* (2nd ed.). Hillsdale, NJ: Lawrence Erlbaum.

Cohen, J. (1994). The earth is round (p <.05). *American Psychologist, 49,* 997–1003.

Cooper, H. (1998). *Synthesizing research: A guide for literature reviews* (3rd ed.). Thousand Oaks, CA: Sage.

Cooper, H. (2003). Editorial. *Psychological Bulletin, 129*, 3–9.

Cooper, H., & Hedges, L. V. (Eds.). (1994a). *The handbook of research synthesis*. New York: Russell Sage Foundation.

Cooper, H., & Hedges, L. V. (1994b). Research synthesis as a scientific enterprise. In H. Cooper & L. V. Hedges (Eds.), *The handbook of research synthesis* (pp. 3–14). New York: Russell Sage Foundation.

Cortina, J. M., & Nouri, H. (2000). *Effect size for ANOVA designs*. Thousand Oaks, CA: Sage.

Crookes, G. (1993). Action research for second language teachers: Going beyond teacher research. *Applied Linguistics, 14*, 130–144.

Doyle, L. H. (2003). Synthesis through meta-ethnography: Paradoxes, enhancements, and possibilities. *Qualitative Research, 3*, 321–344.

Eisenhart, M. (1998). On the subject of interpretive reviews. *Review of Educational Research, 68*, 391–399.

Ellis, N. (2000). Editor's statement. *Language Learning, 50* (3), xi–xiii.

Ginsburg, M. B. (2003). Series Editor's Introduction: Dialogue isn't necessarily more efficient, but it's more democratic and, therefore, more effective. In M. B. Ginsburg and J. M. Gorostiaga (Eds.), *Limitations and possibilities of dialogue among researchers, policy makers, and practitioners* (pp. ix–xi). New York: RoutledgeFalmer.

Ginsburg, M. B., & Gorostiaga, J. M. (2003). Dialogue about educational research, policy, and practice: To what extent is it possible and who should be involved? In M. B. Ginsburg and J. M. Gorostiaga (Eds.), *Limitations and possibilities of dialogue among researchers, policy makers, and practitioners* (pp. 1–36). New York: RoutledgeFalmer.

Glaser, B. G., & Strauss, A. L. (1967). *The discovery of grounded theory: Strategies for qualitative research*. Hawthorne, NY: Aldine de Gruyter.

Glass, G. V. (1976). Primary, secondary, and meta-analysis of research. *Educational Researcher, 5*(10), 3–8.

Glass, G. V. (1999). *Meta-analysis at 25*. Unpublished manuscript of talk delivered on July 15,1999, in Washington D.C. Retrieved on March 14, 2005, from http://glass.ed.asu.edu/gene/papers/meta25.html.

Glass, G. V., McGaw, B., & Smith, M. L. (1981). *Meta-analysis in social research*. Beverly Hills, CA: Sage.

Gleser, L. J., & Olkin, I. (1994). Stochastically dependent effect sizes. In H. Cooper & L. V. Hedges (Eds.), *The handbook of research synthesis* (pp. 339–355). New York: Russell Sage Foundation.

Goldschneider, J., & DeKeyser, R. M. (2001). Explaining the "natural order of L2 morpheme acquisition" in English: A meta-analysis of multiple determinants. *Language Learning, 51*, 1–50.

Grant, C. A., & Grauer, E. (1999). (Re)viewing a review: A case history of the Review of Educational Research. *Review of Educational Research, 69*, 384–396.

Greene, J. P. (1997). A meta-analysis of the Rossell and Baker review of bilingual education research. *Bilingual Research Journal, 22*(2 & 3), no page numbers. Available at: http://brj.asu.edu/articlesv2/green.html

Greenhouse, J. B., & Iyengar, S. (1994). Sensitivity analysis and diagnostics. In H. Cooper & L. V. Hedges (Eds.), *The handbook of research synthesis* (pp. 383–398). New York: Russell Sage Foundation.

Harlow, L. L., Mulaik, S. A., & Steiger, J. H. (Eds.). (1997). *What if there were no significance tests?* Mahwah, NJ: Erlbaum.

Hedges, L., & Olkin, I. (1985). *Statistical methods for meta-analysis.* New York: Academic Press.

Henning, G. (1986). Quantitative methods in language acquisition research. *TESOL Quarterly, 20,* 701–709.

Hinkel, E. (Ed.). (2005). *Handbook of research in second language teaching and learning.* Mahwah, NJ: Lawrence Erlbaum.

Hodson, R. (2004). A meta-analysis of workplace ethnographies: Race, gender, and employee attitudes and behaviors. *Journal of Contemporary Ethnography, 33,* 4–38.

Hornberger, N. (Ed.). (in press). *Encyclopedia of language education* (2nd ed.). New York: Springer.

Hunt, M. (1997). *How science takes stock: The story of meta-analysis.* New York: Russell Sage Foundation.

Jackson, G. B. (1980). Methods for integrative reviews. *Review of Educational Research, 50,* 438–460.

Krashen, S., Long, M. H., & Scarcella, R. (1979). Accounting for child-adult differences in second language rate and attainment. *TESOL Quarterly, 13,* 573–582.

Kupfersmid, J. (1988). Improving what is published: A model in search of an editor. *American Psychologist, 43,* 635–642.

Lane, D. (2005). *Hyperstat online.* Web site. Downloaded December 10, 2005, at http://davidmlane.com/hyperstat/effect_size.html.

Lather, P. (1999). To be of use: The work of reviewing. *Review of Educational Research, 69,* 2–7.

Lazaraton, A. (2000). Current trends in research methodology and statistics in applied linguistics. *TESOL Quarterly, 34,* 175–181.

Light, R., & Pillemer, D. (1984). *Summing up: The science of reviewing research.* Cambridge, MA: Harvard University Press.

Light, R. J., Singer, J. D., & Willett, J. B. (1994). The visual presentation and interpretation of meta-analysis. In H. Cooper & L. V. Hedges (Eds.), *The handbook of research synthesis* (pp. 439–453). New York: Russell Sage Foundation.

Light, R. J., & Smith, P. V. (1971). Accumulating evidence: Procedures for resolving contradictions among research studies. *Harvard Educational Review, 41,* 429–471.

Lipsey, M. W., & Wilson, D. B. (1993). The efficacy of psychological, educational, and behavioral treatment: Confirmation from meta-analysis. *American Psychologist, 48,* 1181–1209.

Lipsey, M. W., & Wilson, D. B. (2001). *Practical meta-analysis.* Thousand Oaks, CA: Sage.

Long, M. H. (1983). Does second language instruction make a difference? A review of the research. *TESOL Quarterly, 17,* 359–382.

Long, M. H. (1990). Maturational constraints on language development. *Studies in Second Language Acquisition, 12,* 251–286.

Loschky, L., & Bley-Vroman, R. (1993). Grammar and task-based methodology. In G. Crookes & S. Gass (Eds.), *Tasks and language learning: Integrating theory and practice* (pp. 123–167). Philadelphia, PA: Multilingual Matters.

MacWhinney, B. (2000). *The CHILDES project: Tools for analyzing talk. Volume II: The database* (3rd ed.). Mahwah, NJ: Lawrence Erlbaum.

Marinova-Todd, S. H., Marshall, D. B., & Snow, C. E. (2000). Three misconceptions about age and L2 learning. *TESOL Quarterly, 34,* 9–34.

Masgoret, A.-M., & Gardner, R. C. (2003). Attitudes, motivation, and second language learning: A meta-analysis of studies conducted by Gardner and associates. *Language Learning, 53,* 123–163.

Masters, J. C., Cantor, N. E., & Hedges, L. V. (1988). Editorial. *Psychological Bulletin, 103*(1), 3–4.

Miller, N., & Pollock, V. E. (1994). Meta-analytic synthesis for theory development. In H. Cooper & L. V. Hedges (Eds.), *The handbook of research synthesis* (pp. 457–483). New York: Russell Sage Foundation.

Nicholas, H., Lightbown, P. M., & Spada, N. (2001). Recasts as feedback to language learners. *Language Learning, 51,* 719–758.

Noblit, G. W., & Hare, R. D. (1988). *Meta-ethnography: Synthesizing qualitative studies.* Newbury Park, CA: Sage.

Norris, J. M. (forthcoming). *Validity evaluation in language assessment.* New York: Peter Lang.

Norris, J. M., & Ortega, L. (2000). Effectiveness of L2 instruction: A research synthesis and quantitative meta-analysis. *Language Learning, 50,* 417–528.

Norris, J. M., & Ortega, L. (2003). Defining and measuring SLA. In C. Doughty & M. H. Long (Eds.), *Handbook of second language acquisition* (pp. 717–761). Malden, MA: Blackwell.

Ortega, L. (2003). Syntactic complexity measures and their relationship to L2 proficiency: A research synthesis of college-level L2 writing. *Applied Linguistics, 24,* 492–518.

Ortega, L. (2005). For what and for whom is our research? The ethical as transformative lens in instructed SLA. *Modern Language Journal, 89,* 427–443.

Orwin, R. G. (1994). Evaluating coding decisions. In H. Cooper & L. V. Hedges (Eds.), *The handbook of research synthesis* (pp. 139–162). New York: Russell Sage Foundation.

Paterson, B. L., Thorne, S. E., Canam, C., & Jillings, C. (2001). *Meta-study of qualitative health research: A practical guide to meta-analysis and meta-synthesis.* Thousand Oaks, CA: Sage.

Patton, M. (1997). *Utilization-focused evaluation: The new century text.* Thousand Oaks, CA: Sage.

Ragin, C. C., Drass, K. A., & Davey, S. (2003). *Fuzzy-set/qualitative comparative analysis.* Available at www.Fsqca.Com (Version 1.1). Tucson, Arizona: Department of Sociology, University of Arizona.

Reichelt, M. (2001). A critical review of foreign language writing research on pedagogical approaches. *Modern Language Journal, 85,* 578–598.

Rolstad, K., Mahoney, K. S., & Glass, G. V. (2005). Weighing the evidence: A meta-analysis of bilingual education in Arizona. *Bilingual Research Journal, 29*(1), 43–67.

Rosenthal, R. (1979). The "file drawer problem" and tolerance for null results. *Psychological Bulletin, 86*, 638–641.

Rosenthal, R. (1990). How are we doing in soft psychology? *American Psychologist, 45*, 775–777.

Rosenthal, R. (1994). Parametric measures of effect size. In H. Cooper & L. Hedges (Eds.), *Handbook of research synthesis* (pp. 231–244). New York: Russell Sage Foundation.

Rosenthal, R., & DiMatteo, M. R. (2001). Meta-analysis: Recent developments in quantitative methods for literature reviews. *Annual Review of Psychology, 52*, 59–82.

Rosenthal, R., Rosnow, R. L., & Rubin, D. B. (2000). *Contrasts and effect sizes in behavioral research*. Cambridge, UK: Cambridge University Press.

Ross, S. (1998). Self-assessment in second language testing: A meta-analysis and analysis of experiential factors. *Language Testing, 15*, 1–20.

Rossell, C., & Baker, K. (1996). The educational effectiveness of bilingual education. *Research in the Teaching of English, 30*, 7–74.

Rossell, C., & Kuder, J. (2005). Meta-murky: A rebuttal to recent meta-analyses of bilingual education. In J. Söhn (Ed.), *The effectiveness of bilingual school programs for immigrant children* (pp. 43–76). Berlin: Wissenschaftszentrum Berlin für Sozialforschung (Social Science Research Center).

Sandelowski, M., Docherty, S., & Emden, C. (1997). Qualitative metasynthesis: Issues and techniques. *Research in Nursing and Health, 20*, 365–376.

Shanahan, T. (2002). Research synthesis: Making sense of the accumulation of knowledge in reading. In M. L. Kamil, P. B. Mosenthal, P. D. Pearson & R. Barr (Eds.), *Methods of literacy research: The methodology chapters from the handbook of reading research. Volume III* (pp. 133–150). Mahwah, NJ: Lawrence Erlbaum.

Shohamy, E. (2000). The relationship between language testing and second language acquisition, revisited. *System, 28*, 541–553.

Slavin, R. E. (1986). Best evidence synthesis: An alternative to meta-analytic and traditional reviews. *Educational Researcher, 15*(9), 5–11.

Slavin, R. E., & Cheung, A. (2005). A synthesis of research on language of reading instruction for English language learners. *Review of Educational Research, 75*, 247–284.

Smith, M. L., & Glass, G. V. (1977). Meta-analysis of psychotherapy outcome studies. *American Psychologist, 32*(9), 752–760.

Spada, N. (1997). Form-focussed instruction and second language acquisition: A review of classroom and laboratory research. *Language Teaching, 29*, 1–15.

Stock, W. (1994). Systematic coding for research synthesis. In H. Cooper & L. Hedges (Eds.), *The handbook of research synthesis* (pp. 125–138). New York: Russell Sage Foundation.

Tashakkori, A., & Teddlie, C. (Eds.). (2003). *The handbook of mixed methods in social and behavioral research*. Thousand Oaks, CA: Sage.

Thomas, M. P., & Collier, V. P. (2002). *A national study of school effectiveness for language minority students' long term academic achievement: Final report*. Washington, DC: Center for Research on Education, Diversity, and Excellence.

Truscott, J. (1996). Review article: The case against grammar correction in L2 writing classes. *Language Learning, 46*, 327–369.

Truscott, J. (1999). What's wrong with oral grammar correction. *Canadian Modern Language Review, 55*, 437–456.

Vacha-Haase, T. (1998). Reliability generalization: Exploring variance in measurement error affecting score reliability across studies. *Educational and Psychological Measurement, 58,* 6–20.

Willig, A. C. (1985). A meta-analysis of selected studies on the effectiveness of bilingual education. *Review of Educational Research, 55,* 269–317.

Wittgenstein, L. (1969/1972). *Über Gewissheit [On certainty].* New York: Harper & Row Publishers [Edition by G. E. M. Anscombe & G. H. von Wright, originally published in 1969 by Blackwell].

Wortman, P. M. (1994). Research synthesis as a scientific enterprise. In H. Cooper & L. V. Hedges (Eds.), *The handbook of research synthesis* (pp. 97–109). New York: Russell Sage Foundation.

Yin, R. K., & Heald, K. A. (1975). Using the case survey method to analyze policy studies. *Administrative Science Quarterly, 20,* 371–381.

Research syntheses

Introduction to Section II

The ins and outs of research synthesis are many, its application complex and full of choices, and its methodologies demanding. In our experience, we have found that an effective means for apprehending the fundamentals of research synthesis is through extensive exposure to good examples. Section II offers models for how to approach the task of systematic research synthesis in LL&LT domains. Further, we hope this section demonstrates something of the wide variety of purposes and approaches, even epistemologies, that motivate syntheses in this field. We are convinced, and we hope to convince other applied linguists, that it is most fruitful to acknowledge the need for such diversity rather than to confine ourselves to one solitary approach.

Most of the contributions in this section are implicitly motivated by positivist or postpositivist stances towards systematic research synthesis. Five of the empirical chapters are quantitative meta-analyses. Dinsmore in Chapter 2 and Taylor et al. in Chapter 6 focus on providing best answers about, respectively, the magnitude of differences between native and non-native speakers in their grammatical intuitions, and the effectiveness of training L2 learners in the use of reading strategies. These synthesists formulate their answers via quantitative summaries of primary findings available to date on their topics; thus, the two chapters represent what we might call canonical meta-analyses. The three meta-analyses by Keck et al., Russell and Spada, and Jeon and Kaya (in Chapters 3 through 5) go beyond the quantitative summary of main and moderating effects. While they also provide summative answers, these synthesists are more intent on developing a rich picture of exactly how research has occurred in the domains of: (a) native-speaker non-native speaker interaction, (b) provision of negative feedback in speaking and writing, and (c) instruction of pragmatics, respectively. Indeed, readers who are primary researchers in these domains will find critical and explicit guidance for future (improved) research praxis in these three chapters.

The remaining two empirical contributions are Chapter 7 by Téllez and Waxman and Chapter 8 by Thomas. They are not meta-analyses; rather, they illustrate two distinct approaches to research synthesis: meta-synthesis and historiography. In the first, a meta-synthesis of qualitative studies on approaches to the instruction of English Language Learners (ELLs), interpretive and constructivist motivations are apparent in the synthetic methodologies adopted. In the second, Thomas demonstrates how historiographical analysis of L2 proficiency measurement practices can highlight research methodological developments within a domain and underscore critical gaps in the same. Both of these contributions reflect the practical utility of diverse synthetic applications, with Téllez and Waxman identifying practices of immediate utility for ELL teachers in U.S. schools, and with Thomas stressing the immediate demand for specific improvements in L2 measurements used by primary researchers. Neither of these ends would have been amenable to canonical meta-analysis in the domains under review.

CHAPTER 2

Principles, parameters, and SLA

A retrospective meta-analytic investigation into
adult L2 learners' access to Universal Grammar

Thomas H. Dinsmore
University of Cincinnati – Clermont College

The purpose of this investigation was to meta-analyze the results of primary
research studies which examined the relationship between Universal
Grammar (as postulated in the Principles and Parameters version) and
second language acquisition, in order to discern which extreme of the three
primary positions – full, mediated, or no access – best represented the way in
which second language adults access Universal Grammar. Primary research
studies were retrieved through a multiple channel approach, using a
combination of manual and computer searches. A set of criteria was
established to determine which of the retrieved studies would be included in
this meta-analysis, leading to the final inclusion of sixteen primary research
studies published between 1981 and 1999. Theses studies together
investigated the grammaticality knowledge of 942 second language
participants. Using Cohen's d index as the measure of the outcome of each
primary study's sample(s), 69 effect sizes were generated. Each of these effect
sizes was weighted and averaged to produce an overall effect size for this
meta-analysis. The overall mean effect size produced was 1.25, a very large
effect size. A confidence interval was also calculated on the mean effect size,
yielding a lower limit of 1.12, and an upper limit of 1.31. The fact that the
confidence interval test does not contain zero further supports the conclusion
that these adult second language learners' performance on various kinds of
grammatical knowledge tasks was "fundamentally different" (Bley-Vroman
1989) from the performance of native speaker groups. Based on the premise
that the mean effect size would approach zero if second language learners did
have full access to Universal Grammar, the present results indicate that
they do not.

Introduction

Current generative grammar focuses on the investigation of two fundamental issues: how to characterize the speaker's knowledge of a language, and how such knowledge is acquired and used by language learners. The first issue is concerned with the devising of grammars which represent the underlying system of rules which has been internalized in a speaker's mind, and the second is concerned with the characterization of the processes involved in language acquisition.

Many structures of human language are so complex and abstract that it is difficult to believe that children unconsciously learn language solely on the basis of the evidence they are exposed to – otherwise known as input data (Chomsky 1965). The mismatch between what children actually hear and what they eventually attain, which is referred to as the "logical problem" or the "projection problem" in the linguistics literature, can be overcome by assuming that children are born with a specific set of cognitive structures which control and guide the way children handle all the aspects of the language that is to be acquired (see, e.g., Chomsky 1986; Fodor 1983). This structure is known as Universal Grammar (UG). The Principles and Parameters version of UG that was developed in the 1980s defined possible human languages and consisted of a set of principles which constrained the types of hypotheses that children could entertain about their language. These UG principles applied uniformly to all grammars of all human languages. Along with these principles, this model of UG also made available to children a set of parameters which accounted for some of the differences among the world's languages. The speaker's knowledge of a language was described in terms of those principles and parameters.

During the 1980s and into the 1990s, many researchers sought to develop a representation of the relationship of Universal Grammar, as postulated in the Principles and Parameters version of this theory, to second language acquisition (SLA). This evolved into a dominant metaphor of "access" to UG that was articulated into three primary positions: full access, mediated access, and no access. In addition, there was an age restriction placed on these three positions – it was generally assumed that children always have access to UG, while there was a question as to whether adolescents and adults did (for further discussion see Flynn & Manuel 1991; White 1989b). In more recent years, a new metaphor of "constraint" has evolved and has begun to displace the older access research program (interested readers will find good discussions of this disciplinary change in Hawkins 2001; Thomas 2003; White 2003). The research community is also engaged in an exploration of wider notions of what knowledge of Universal Grammar might mean for L2 learners (e.g., Hawkins 2001). The research reported in this chapter was originally conducted for my doctoral dissertation, completed in 1999 at the University of Cincinnati, at a time when the access metaphor was current and the three positions were being developed and researched. Hence, the present meta-analysis is retrospective in nature, in that it takes stock of a research tradition that has now begun to shift into newer theoretical directions. I hope this chapter will inspire future meta-analytic research on similar, but reframed questions about the relationship between UG and SLA with studies conducted since 1999. The level of reporting in this chapter is explicitly designed to make this possible for future researchers interested in the research domain of Universal Grammar in SLA. Before delving into the meta-analysis proper, however, and particularly for the benefit of applied linguistics readers who may work in other research traditions, it will be useful to briefly define Principles and Parameters through some illustrations and to outline the access issue that is the focus of the present synthesis.

Principles and parameters illustrated

One of the primary components of the Principles and Parameters (PP) version of UG is that of the Binding Principles (see Chomsky 1986, for a full discussion), which determine which noun phrases in a sentence can serve as coreferents for one another. That is, these principles explain how nouns and pronouns are interpreted within sentences. For example, in the following English sentence *John* and *himself* refer to the same person:

(1)   Bill said John saw a picture of himself

It is impossible for *himself* to refer to Bill because of Binding Principle A, for this principle controls the way in which reflexive pronouns are understood and interpreted. The reason English speakers know the pronoun, *himself*, and the noun, *John*, are the same person is due to the parameter settings specified for English. It is the parameter settings of this Binding Principle which tell English speakers the *himself* is only to refer to *John*. It is impossible for it to refer to *Bill*. On the other hand, if the above sentence is modified to read as in (2) below, it is now impossible for *John* and *him* to be the same person:

(2)   Bill said that John saw a picture of him

In this case, it is possible for the pronoun to refer to the noun, *Bill*, because of Binding Principle B. This principle controls the way in which English speakers interpret and understand the personal pronoun in this sentence. Binding Principle B tells English speakers that *Bill* and *him* could be the same person.

Other languages allow for greater variation than English among parametric settings of these Binding Principles, especially Binding Principle A, which indicates how close a reflexive must be to the noun to which it refers. Principle A has the possibility to take five different parameter settings. For example, one could consider the following English sentence, taken from Yoshikawa (1993: 45):

(3)   John said that Tom is asking that Bill persuade Ken to consider Jack fond of himself

The most restrictive of the parameter setting occurs in a language like English; *himself* can only refer to *Jack*. In a language like Italian, *himself* can refer to either *Jack* or *Ken*. In a language like Russian, *himself* can refer to *Bill, Ken,* or *Jack*. In a language like Icelandic, *himself* can refer to *Tom, Bill, Ken,* or *Jack*. And finally, the least restrictive of the parameter occurs in a language like Japanese, where *himself* can refer to *John, Tom, Bill, Ken,* or *Jack*.

Other examples are the Subjacency Principle and the Empty Category Principle (ECP). Haegeman (1994) states that both are related to syntactic movement. These principles allow English speakers to form questions. Specifically, Subjacency specifies how far elements of a sentence can be moved to form a question, and the ECP specifies whether or not subjects or objects can be moved out of complementizer phrases. For example, consider the following sentence for analysis:

(4)   I think Tom saw Mary

If a hearer of the above sentence did not understand the speaker, he or she could ask:

(5)   Who do you think that Tom saw?

The hearer is able to replace *Mary* with *who*, and because of Subjacency, he or she is then able to move *who* to the front of the sentence, thus producing this question. In the same manner, the hearer could produce the following question:

(6)   You think that who saw Mary?

But the following question is impossible:

(7)   *Who do you think that saw Mary?

The sentence is ungrammatical because it violates both Subjacency and the ECP. Subjacency prevents the hearer from moving *who* to the front of the sentence, and the ECP does not permit the subject position of the that-complementizer to be empty in English.

The three positions in the UG access problem

The question of parameter-setting in second language (L2) acquisition is of considerable research interest because L2 learners can be faced with a situation where a principle differs in regard to its parameter-setting value in the first language (L1) and the L2. In this case, L2 learners already have one type of parameter-setting for their L1. Then the question is what kind of influence the L1 parameter-setting will exert on L2 acquisition. If UG principles were available to L2 learners exactly as in L1 acquisition, they would simply focus on the target language, apply the principles of UG to the L2 data, and then eventually – just as the acquisition of the first language does not occur instantaneously, neither does the acquisition of a second language – set the parameter to its L2 value. On the other hand, if L2 learners were affected by their L1 parameter-setting, they might transfer their L1 setting to the L2. Thus, in the 1980s this became a question of what type of access is available to adolescent and adult L2 learners. Three types of access to UG were proposed: full, none, or partial. White (1989b, as quoted in Thomas 2003) provides a summary of the positions:

- the 'pure UG hypothesis', which anticipates that L2 acquisition exactly recapitulates UG-driven L1 acquisition without impediment or support from the L1;
- the proposal that 'UG is dead' and cannot be recruited to overcome any logical problem of L2 acquisition; and
- several sub-varieties of the notion that 'UG is partially available' to L2 learners wherein, in instances where L1 and L2 differ, access to UG is blocked either permanently, or only temporarily due to an initial controlling influence of the L1, or where access to UG is mitigated in other ways and by other factors yet to be defined. (Thomas 2003: 362–363)

In response to the above, over the two decades of 1980s and 1990s, generative SLA researchers conducted primary research studies in an attempt to discover which of the above three positions best explained the type of access to UG that L2 learners had (White 2003).

Discovering the operation of UG in L2 acquisition

If both the L1 and L2 have the same principle, with the same parameter settings, it would be impossible to determine whether L2 learners attain such knowledge as a result of the operation of a UG principle or because of the role the learners' L1 plays in the attainment of that particular parameter setting. Thus, in investigating the effects of UG principles in L2 acquisition, researchers turned to ask whether or not L2 learners applied a certain UG principle in a situation where that principle did not exist in their L1. Not all principles operate in the same way in all languages. For example, the Subjacency Principle does not operate in languages that do not have syntactic movement. It can also be observed that a principle, in any particular language, can be realized with different parameter settings, as in the head-initial/head-final parameter. Thus researchers could investigate whether L2 learners whose L1 does not exhibit syntactic movement acquire the principle independently of their L1. In this case, if L2 learners successfully demonstrated knowledge of that principle, the researcher had good reason to conclude that UG principles were still available to adult L2 learners. In addition, it could be extended that if the L2 learners could successfully reset the parameter in question, the researcher had good reason to conclude that UG principles were still available. On the other hand, if the L2 learners systematically failed to acquire the principle or could not successfully reset the parameter in question, the researcher had good reason to conclude that UG principles were no longer accessible to L2 learners and that UG principles are only realized through the L1 instantiations or that some other cognitive structures control and guide the acquisition of the L2.

A fundamental methodological question in researching the acquisition of a second language is whether the types of measurements that are used are valid and reliable. In L2 studies of UG access, two types of tests have been widely used: elicited imitation tasks and grammaticality judgment tasks. In an elicited imitation task, the participants are asked to repeat a prompt sentence, which has been designed to test the L2 learner's underlying competence in the target language. It is assumed that the participants will repeat the grammatical structure they hear, using their internal grammar of the target language. Bley-Vroman and Chaudron (1994) raise a number of concerns relating to this task type because of the processing stages involved (perception, retention in echoic memory, parsing and analysis, and production; see p. 258). Thus, they do not advocate this type of test since the participants' production relies not only on their internal grammar but also on many other factors.

On the other hand, in a grammaticality judgment task, the L2 learner is presented with sentences which contain grammatical and ungrammatical items and are asked to determine whether or not the sentence is grammatical. One primary objection to the use of grammaticality judgment tasks is that the researcher does not know whether the participants are relying on translation and formal prescriptive grammar or linguistic intuition (Munnich, Flynn, & Martohardojno 1994).

Other types of tests are possible but their use presents certain weaknesses as well. For example, there is controversy surrounding the use of multiple choice comprehension tasks. Lakshmanan and Teranishi (1994) suggest that this type of methodology is flawed because it limits the number of options that are available to the participant. That is, they suggest that this type of procedure is only testing the preferences of the participant, since there is a limited set of possibilities. Lakshmanan and Teranishi (1994) also critique a methodology that uses a picture identification task. They suggest that a non-grammatical strategy could be adopted for choosing the picture that correctly identifies the grammatical item (for example, the use of the Binding Principle) because they are identifying the action (because of lexical familiarity or not) and not particularly the item being researched.

Meta-analysis

Numerous empirical studies during the first two decades of generative SLA research have been conducted in an attempt to discover the ways in which L2 learners resolve the conflicts between their L1 and the L2. These researchers have attempted "to prove" empirically the relationship of Universal Grammar to Second Language Acquisition, typically by comparing native and nonnative speaking performance on various kinds of tasks that purport to tap knowledge of grammaticality in the L1 and the L2. Since numerous empirical studies have accumulated by now, addressing the question of "access," and given that we find ourselves at a watershed point in the development of this research domain (Hawkins 2001; White 2003), the time seems ripe for a retrospective view on the accumulated research and for a synthesis of the primary studies contributed by the first two decades of generative SLA research. But why choose the methodology of meta-analysis?

Jackson (1980) states that "[r]eviews of research are a fundamental activity in the behavioral sciences" (p. 348). Reviews play an essential role in synthesizing the knowledge in research, discovering new developments in the research fields, and identifying unsolved problems or needs. In addition, they test and evaluate existing theories, introduce new theories, and provide direction for further research (Bangert-Drowns 1986; Cooper 1998; Jackson 1980). However, not all approaches equally meet the requirements of a scientifically sound review.

Traditional literature review methods are narrative in nature. Because of this, they are subjective and liable to biases. They have also been criticized for a series of weaknesses in methodology. Cook and Leviton (1980) summarize three major problems with the traditional method, the "box count." This method entails the review of studies simply by putting them into categories, which are typically based on the statistical significance or non-significance of the findings, and then basing a conclusion on the frequency counts generated from that categorization. Cook and Levinton claim that the box count method ignores important information on the relationship and direction of cause and effect, typically relies on a narrow literature search, and overlooks statistical interaction effects. Light and Pillemer (1982) also point out that the narrative review is subjective and not scientifically sound because there are not many defined rules for reviewers to follow while conducting the review process. Thus, this does not seem to be an efficient method.

By contrast, meta-analysis meets the need to synthesize the primary studies scientifically. The word "meta-analysis" was coined by Glass (1976: 3), who defined it as an "analysis of analysis." The purpose of meta-analysis is to integrate the findings of individual primary research studies through rigorous statistical analyses, in order to draw an overall conclusion about the research effort (Glass 1976). Glass' call for a systematic and integrative method of review in the social and behavioral sciences sparked the interest of other researchers. Rosenthal (1978) developed a combined probability method. In addition many other researchers have continued to refine meta-analytic techniques (Cooper 1998; Hedges 1981, 1982a, 1982b, 1982c; Hedges & Olkin 1985; Hedges, Shymansky, & Woodworth 1989).

Even though there are several methods for performing a meta-analysis, the method initiated by Glass is the most commonly used. Glassian meta-analysis synthesizes the individual studies by using an effect size as the representation of the outcome. An effect size is obtained by dividing the difference between the treatment-group mean and the control-group mean by the standard deviation of the control group. It is also possible to use the pooled standard deviation of both treatment and control groups in the denominator. Some researchers prefer the second method because it is "slightly more stable" (Hedges, Shymansky, & Woodworth 1989: 24). For interpreting these standardized effect size outcomes, Cohen (1988) defined a magnitude around 0.20 as small, around 0.50 as medium, and greater than 0.80 as large.

Several features of meta-analyses help increase systematicity and reduce bias. First, they do not rely on significance values of a single statistical test or a few statistical performed on a limited number of participants. Second, they employ an extensive literature search which selects both published and unpublished studies and follow well-defined criteria for each step of this process. Since the criteria are well defined, replication of the same meta-analysis is also possible. In keeping with the ideals of systematicity, reduced bias, and replicability, the procedure for doing the present meta-analysis will be reported in detail. Each and every step involved in the production of this meta-analysis is reported in the appropriate sections of this article with the intention that a replication of this study be possible.

The meta-analytical research process

Meta-analyses not only follow the basic scheme of any other exploratory research but also include unique features and procedures. In general, reviewers follow these steps: formulate the problem, decide the criteria for relevance, locate research studies, develop a coding sheet, refine the coding sheet, code the studies, establish the intercoder reliability of coding, decide the unit of analysis, analyze the data, interpret the data, and finally report the findings (Cooper 1998; Hedges, Shymansky, & Woodworth 1989).

Hall, Rosenthal, Tickle-Degen, and Mosteller (1994) write that a research synthesis can accomplish two fundamental tasks: "learning from combining studies and learning from comparing studies" (p. 18). *Learning from combining studies* refers to finding, summarizing, and describing the already existing results of research. *Learning from comparing studies* refers to additional analyses that shed new light on variations in the phenomenon under study and on theoretical issues of causation, explanation, and construct validity. Thus the synthesist can sometimes make inferences that go well beyond the original results.

Research synthesis extends our knowledge through the combination and comparison of primary studies. As with primary research, there are boundaries to how much we can learn from research synthesis. These boundaries can be identified by the following questions:

1. Cause and effect: How confident can we be that the independent variable actually affects the dependent or outcome measure?

2. Generalization: How confident can we be that the findings can be generalized beyond a small subset of populations, settings and procedures?
3. Theory development: Does the research advance the theoretical understanding of the phenomenon?

Research questions

The present study investigates the extent of the availability of Universal Grammar to adolescent and adult second language learners. In order to examine the relationship between Universal Grammar and Second Language Acquisition, the present study addresses the following question: Was Universal Grammar operating, and if so, to what extent, in adults and adolescents learning a second language? Thus, the theory that will be tested is whether or not adult/adolescent L2 learners had full access to Universal Grammar in studies that investigated the Principle and Parameters version.

As mentioned earlier, three types of access to UG were hypothesized in the primary research literature: direct, indirect/partial, or none. If UG were available in its entirety, post-Critical Period L2 learners would react the same way as native speakers do when presented with data from the target language. That is, the magnitude of the effect size (i.e., the degree to which the L2 learners differ from the native speakers in their responses to tasks) would be small to zero. In the same manner, it follows that if UG were only available to L2 learners through the mediation of their L1, or were entirely inaccessible and in its place some other cognitive structure was involved, L2 learners would react differently from native speakers when presented with data from the target language. Therefore, the magnitude of the effect size would more likely be moderate to large. Unfortunately, the results of this meta-analysis do not allow for a distinction between the two positions of indirect versus no access, since both of them would be assumed to produce results where the effect size is moderate to large. However, it is possible in this study to investigate the role that the type of measurement has in assessing whether or not UG is available to post Critical Period L2 learners, an interesting question given the controversial nature of the measurement methods typically employed. That is, in addition to investigating the overall effect for studies in this domain, this meta-analysis compares the results across primary studies depending on the types of tasks used to measure the availability of UG.

Method

Retrieval of relevant studies

The literature search for this meta-analytic study was guided by the theoretical concept of UG (Principles and Parameters) that first appeared in 1981 (Chomsky 1981) and its relationship to second language acquisition. Therefore, the time span that was covered was 1981 to March 1999, the time of the writing of my dissertation. In order to retrieve the maximum amount of studies, a multiple channel approach was employed: a combination of computer and manual searches. That is, I searched computer databases and conducted both an ancestry search and a hand search.

The first method for retrieving relevant studies was to conduct a literature search of the relevant databases provided by OhioLink. This is a centralized catalogue, which permits the user to access the individual catalogues of its 74 participating institutions. For the most part, these institutions are public and private colleges and universities in the state of Ohio. OhioLink also contains 67 computer databases. The relevant databases that were searched are the OhioLink versions of Educational Resource Information Center (ERIC) (1966 – present), PsychInfo (1967 – present), the ProQuest version of Dissertation Abstracts (1861 – present), and the OCLC version ProceedingsFirst (1993 – present). In addition the Linguistics and Language Behavior Abstracts (the WebSpirs Silver Platter version; 1973 – present), which is not available through OhioLink, was searched at Ohio University.

The above research databases were searched using a keyword search, a strategy that provides the most broad type of searching. This enabled the search to find citations which may have not been in the Subject Thesaurus of each of the databases. It searches the title and abstract of each entry. The following search terms were used in the keyword searches: *Generative Grammar* (GG), *Universal Grammar* (UG), and *Second Language Acquisition* (SLA). Table 1 presents the results of the research databases. (For those research databases that do not have an abbreviation above, the following will be used: PsychInfo (PI), Dissertation Abstracts (DA), and ProceedingsFirst (PF).)

The empty cells in Table 1 are due to the search strategies that were used. That is, if the database permitted searching for the individual keyword expression and then subsequent combining, that method was used. If the database did not permit the former method, the search terms were entered simultaneously as indicated in the table.

Table 1. Database Search Results

	ERIC	PI	DA	PF	LLBA
UG	230	183			973
GG	1761	206			2943
SLA	4728	590		14	2888
UG & SLA	49	50	24		196
GG & SLA	72	20	3		29

Note. *Government and Binding* and *Principles and Parameters* are included under the search terms of *Universal Grammar* and *Generative Grammar*. That is, the hits produced by the former search terms were also retrieved by the latter terms.

The citation abstracts were examined for the combinations of UG & SLA and GG & SLA. Forty-seven abstracts were kept for review because they showed promise for relevant data for this meta-analysis, and those studies were retrieved. Subsequently, the bibliographies of the retrieved studies were examined to see if this would produce additional studies. This produced an additional nineteen studies for examination. In order to ensure that additional studies not identified via the above two methods were also found, a hand search was conducted of the following journals: *Annual Review of Applied Linguistics, Applied Linguistics, Behavioral and Brain Sciences, International Review of Applied Linguistics, Journal of Psycholinguistic Research, Language, Language Learning, Linguistic Inquiry, Second Language Research,* and *Studies in Second Language Acquisition.* This method produced an additional seven studies.

In total, seventy-three potentially relevant studies were retrieved for this meta-analysis and were subjected to the inclusion criteria discussed below.

Inclusion criteria for the relevant studies

Cooper (1998) provides three methods for determining which of the studies should be included in the analysis:

1. the threats to validity approach;
2. the methods-criteria approach; and,
3. the mixed-criteria approach.

In the threats to validity approach, the researcher checks the experimental design against a list of threats to the external validity of the design. Some of the threats include, but are not limited to, history, experimenter bias, and so on. In the methods-criteria approach, the reviewer exhaustively codes the objective characteristics of each study's methods, as they are described by the primary researchers. Finally, in the mixed-criteria approach the first two approaches are combined.

Examining the credibility of experimental manipulations and measurements requires a description of the procedures that the primary researchers used to create independent variables and measure dependent variables. With regard to manipulated independent variables, reviewers can code the number and type of empirical realizations used: How many ways was the independent variable manipulated? How was the manipulation achieved? Similarly, the reviewer can record the presence or absence of controls to keep the experimenter blind to treatment conditions, and whether or not deception or misdirection was used to lead the participant away from guessing the hypothesis.

Distinctions in measurement techniques can be codified by recording: (a) the number of measurements used; (b) whether they were verbal, written, or behavioral judgments; (c) whether they were standard, informal, or experimenter constructed; and (d) their relative reliability, if such estimates are available. It has also been suggested that the reviewer can record any restrictions on the types of individuals sampled in the primary studies, when and where the studies were conducted, and when the dependent variable measurements were taken in relation to the manipulation or measurement of the independent variables. Finally, the reviewer needs to assess a study's statistical power by recording the number of participants, whether a between- or within-subjects design was used, the number of other factors (sources of variance) extracted by the analyses, and the statistical test used.

In order to proceed with the present meta-analysis, a set of criteria were established for selecting the studies that are to be included. The criteria originated from the Government and Binding (Principles and Parameters) version of Universal Grammar. That is, the relevant studies had to investigate that particular version of UG. The primary studies included in the meta-analysis also had to satisfy the following criteria. First, the study had to test a principle or parameter. Those studies that offered criticisms of the present theoretical framework or reviewed the research of other primary researchers (theoretical or design criticisms) were excluded. Second, the studies had to be quantitative in nature and include at least one experimental and at least one target language control group. Studies that based conclusions on the mere comparing of percentages were excluded (i.e., no inferential statistic test was used – the researchers assumed that if one group scored a higher percentage of correct answers, that showed a significant difference between the groups), as were studies that presented longitudinal data on non-native speakers. Third, all of the quantitative studies needed to provide sufficient statistical information for an effect size to be calculated. In addition, the statistics presented needed to compare the target language control group and experimental group. Fourth, the participants of the primary studies had to be adolescents or adults. That is, studies that made comparisons to children, or used children as their research sample were excluded. This was done because it is generally believed (by those who adhere to a Universal Grammar position) that children do have full access to UG, and thus these studies would add confusion to the present meta-analysis since there seems to be no question on their access status. Finally, if the same study appeared as a published conference proceeding and a journal article, and the data were the same, the journal article was used because it is believed that the journal article goes through a more rigorous review process.

The above criteria were applied to the seventy-three studies retrieved for this study. Of those studies, sixteen satisfied all of the criteria above (they are marked with an asterisk in the reference list). The other fifty-seven studies were excluded for violating one or more of the criteria above. Interested readers will find a complete list of the excluded studies and the reasons for exclusion in Appendix 1.

Characteristics of the coding sheet

Another important step in conducting this meta-analysis was the designing of a coding sheet. The rationale behind the coding sheet was to collect sufficient information common to many of the included studies so that further analysis could be conducted to examine the underlying relationship between the studies' characteristics and their corresponding effect sizes.

In order to design a comprehensive coding sheet, a draft was constructed and piloted on several studies to ensure that the coding sheet included the information that might be relevant to this review. After piloting several versions of the coding sheet, a final one was developed, which consisted of four categories (see Appendix 2 for the complete Coding Sheet).

Publication Characteristics was the first category on the coding sheet. It included the background information for the study, such as author name, title, and so on. In addition, this category included the subcategories of publication type (journal article, dissertation, etc) and source of the reference (ERIC, etc.). *Participant Characteristics* contained the background information of the participants, such as age, native language and so on. *Design Characteristics* contained the information pertinent for the description of the study's design (e.g., sample size, sampling strategy, etc.). The measurement type (for example, Grammaticality Judgment task, Multiple Choice Comprehension task, and so on) was also recorded under this category. Finally, *Statistical Information* recorded all the statistical information contained in the studies, including means, standard deviations of each group, the *F*, *t*, or χ^2 statistic, the *p* value and whether or not each test was significant. Additionally, the results of each test were recorded individually.

Reliability of the coding

The coding sheet was pilot-tested several times, and it was revised accordingly before the final version was produced. Fifty percent of the studies were again coded by someone who is knowledgeable and currently active in the field of Second Language Acquisition and is familiar with the Principles and Parameters version of Universal Grammar.[1] The coding sheets of the independent rater were compared with those of this researcher. An inter-rater reliability (agreement rate, henceforth AR) was calculated using the following formula from Orwin (1994: 147):

$$AR = \frac{\text{number of observations agreed upon}}{\text{total number of observations}}$$

The resulting number from the above equation was then multiplied by 100 to produce a percentage. The agreement between the two coders was 87%. Most discrepancies in the coding were due to the nature in which the statistical information was presented. That is, it was not always obvious what information went on a particular line of the coding sheet. All discrepancies was resolved through discussion about the items in question.

Identification of units of analysis

Cooper (1998) states that it is also important for the researcher to decide what the unit of analysis is going to be. He gives the following five units:

–   laboratories – that is, the research group conducts testing on a particular hypothesis (research question) multiple times with the same or different participants;
–   studies – that is, the hypothesis is tested on multiple groups within the same study;
–   samples – that is, studies can contain more than one distinct group of participants (for the present study, the sixteen studies yielded twenty-two samples);

- hypothesis tests – that is, there are instances where a sample participates in multiple tasks (for the present study, a hypothesis test is an Elicited Imitation task, Grammaticality Judgment task, and so on); and
- shifting units – that is, a combination of the units above.

The laboratory is considered to be the most conservative and the hypothesis test the least. The shifting unit is considered to be a compromise. The unit of analysis for this meta-analysis is the shifting unit of analysis, using the sample unit and hypothesis units of analysis. The first unit of analysis is the sample. For the most part, the studies included in this meta-analysis did not conduct inferential tests on more than one sample. In four instances, however, the samples of L2 learners were grouped independently by their native language or age (i.e. adult or adolescent), and the results of the varied tests were presented independently within the study. The rationale behind choosing the sample as the first unit of analysis is that it is important to distinguish between the different native language samples (when it is possible), since languages vary in respect to their particular parameter-settings of the various principles. Thus, the overall effect size reported in this meta-analysis uses the sample as the unit of analysis.

The second unit of analysis is the hypothesis test (i.e., the type of measure used for testing the given hypotheses in each study). The rationale behind choosing it as the second unit of analysis is that the issue of the choice of test type is itself controversial. In this part of the analysis, it will be possible to examine the individual effect sizes of each type of test.

Method for computing and reporting of overall effect size estimates

The procedure used for computing and combining effect sizes across studies is not one that is based on the significance level of the results (e.g., $p < 0.05$), but one that is based on the combination of effect sizes of the treatments (for this study, the treatment consists of exposure to language tasks). The rationale for this use of effect sizes is explained by Cooper (1998):

> If an ample number of participants are available or if a sensitive research design is employed, a rejection of the null hypothesis often is not surprising. This state of affairs becomes even more apparent in a meta-analysis that includes a combined significance level, in which the power is great to detect even very small relations. A null hypothesis rejection, then, does not guarantee that an important social insight has been achieved. (pp. 125–26)

Consequently, an effect size is calculated for each study under review, and the effect sizes are then compared. Cohen (1988) defines an effect size as follows:

Without intending any necessary implication of causality, it is convenient to use the phrase 'effect size' to mean 'the *degree* to which the phenomenon is present in the population,' or 'the degree to which the phenomenon confirms the null hypothesis is false.' By the above route it can readily be clear that when the null hypothesis is false, it is false to some specific degree, i.e., *the effect size (ES) is some specific non-zero value in the population.* The larger this value, the greater the *degree* to which the phenomenon under study is manifested. (pp. 9–10, emphases in the original)

In terms of the present study, the effect size represents the degree of difference between the native speakers' and non-native speakers' responses to the language task.

The "*d*-index" (the effect size that is usually associated with *t*-tests or *F*-tests based on a comparison of two treatment levels) was calculated for each of the studies under review. It was calculated using the following formula:

$$d = \frac{X_1 - X_2}{SD_1 + SD_2/2}$$

where

X_1 and X_2 = the two group means; and
SD_1 and SD_2 = the pooled standard deviation for the two groups (Cooper 1998: 101–102).

In the event that the effect could not be determined by the previous method because the group means and standard deviations were not presented in the study, the effect was computed from the test statistic (e.g., χ^2, t, or F) that was reported (see Cooper 1998, for the appropriate conversion formulae).

Expected outcomes and contributions of the study

Cooper and Hedges (1994) maintain that precision in literature searches improves dramatically if one uses meta-analytic methods. It is no longer acceptable to string together paragraph descriptions of studies, with a focus on significance tests, and then conclude that the data are inconsistent but appear to indicate that X influences Y (or not). Thus, they envision the role of the synthesist as being able to provide: "(a) confidence intervals around effect size estimates (b) for separate parts of a literature distinguished by both methodological and theoretical criteria (c) calculated several different ways of using different ways using different assumptions about the adequacy of the literature search and coding scheme, and alternative statistical models" (p. 523).

Regarding the above, this meta-analysis includes a 95% confidence interval in order to test the null hypothesis associated with overall combined effect sizes. That is, in lieu of combining significance levels, this meta-analysis examines this interval to determine if the null hypothesis holds true: there is no difference in the native and non-native speakers' group means since they reacted in the same manner when presented with the language tasks. If the interval does not contain zero, the null hypothesis can be rejected (Cooper 1998).

When individual studies are combined and effect size estimates are computed, it is important to test whether there is homogeneity of variance. In meta-analyses, it is assumed that variance in effect sizes is generally due to sampling error, if it is not attributable to differences in study variables. Cooper (1998: 146) provides a formula for determining the homogeneity of variance statistic (Q_t). This statistic has a chi-square distribution with N-1 degrees of freedom. After determining this statistic, the meta-analyst then refers to table containing chi-square values. If the calculated statistic is greater than the critical value listed in the table, the meta-analyst then must reject the hypothesis that the variance is due to sampling error alone. If heterogeneity exists, the meta-analyst then explores the possible causes for the excess variation. Following the suggestions of Hedges, Shymansky, and Woodworth (1989), the relationship between study characteristics is analyzed in the present meta-analysis using each value of a particular study characteristic as independent variables, and the effect sizes associated with each study characteristic as the dependent variable, in subsequent analysis of variance tests. Put differently, in these further analyses the categories from the Coding Sheet are treated as the independent variables and the effect sizes as the dependent variable.

Results

Effect size analysis

As stated earlier, this meta-analysis includes 16 studies which yielded 22 samples (unique groups being investigated). From these samples, 69 effect sizes were calculated, based on the performances of each sample on each of the tasks conducted across the studies. Subsequently, each of these 69 individual effect sizes was weighted by multiplying the mean effect size by the inverse of the total weighting factor (the weighting factor is computed from the number of observations or sample size in each group; see Cooper 1998). This weighting was done in an attempt to minimize the skewing effect due to size of the sample. Table 2 presents the individual unbiased (weighted) effect sizes, one each for each study sample on each dependent variable test task. In addition, at the bottom of the table, the overall mean effect size is displayed. According to Cohen (1988), an effect size of 0.20 is considered small, 0.50 a medium effect size, and 0.80 a large effect size, though these recommendations are merely rules of thumb. It can be seen in Table 2 that the mean effect for this analysis can be considered (very) large, thus implying that the L2 participants performed clearly differently from the native speaking groups across these studies. This finding is compatible with the position that UG is not fully accessible during L2 learning by adolescents or adults. If the L2 learners had full access to UG, the mean effect size would approach zero, since they would perform the same way as the control group on the dependent variables (the language test tasks).

In turn, each of the 69 individual effect sizes was then matched with the sample from the study from which it was drawn, and the mean for the matched individual effect sizes was calculated for each unique sample. For example, the Bennet (1994) study produced four individual effect sizes (i.e., four tasks were performed) for a single sample. These four effect sizes were then added together, and the mean was calculated for that sample. This process was performed for all the samples, which yielded a mean effect size for each of the 22 samples comprising the 16 studies. Table 3 presents the study from which each sample was obtained, the number of individual effect sizes (i.e., one per dependent variable test task), the mean effect size for each of the samples (i.e., across tasks), and the standard error associated with each of those means.

Using study sample as the unit of analysis, a mean effect size and 95% confidence interval was calculated on the 22 unbiased (weighted) mean effect sizes shown in Table 3. The mean effect size was 1.25, with an upper 95% confidence limit of 1.31 and a lower limit of 1.12. This interval does not contain zero, clearly. Thus, it can be concluded that the null hypothesis of no difference between the L2 samples and L1 groups (on their average test task performances) can be rejected. In terms of this meta-analysis, this finding implies that Universal Grammar was not fully operating (full access) in the adolescent and adult second language learners who participated in these studies.

When individual units of analysis are combined and effect size estimates are computed, it is important for the analyst to test whether the assumption of homogeneity of variance is met. As mentioned earlier, in meta-analyses, it is assumed that the variance of effect size estimates is due to sampling error. If any variance is found in excess of sampling error, it is thought to be contributed systematically by variables associated with certain primary study characteris-

Table 2. Individual weighted effect sizes

ID	d	ID	d
BEN94a	0.56	MAT94h	1.46
BEN94b	0.47	UZI93a	0.56
BEN94c	0.13	WHI88a	0.97
BEN94d	0.94	WHI88b	0.97
BLV88a	2.49	WHI88c	0.58
FLY87a	1.03	WHI88d	0.57
FLY87b	1.54	WHI88e	1.52
FLY87c	1.66	WHI88f	0.30
FLY87d	0.70	WHI88g	0.74
HAW97a	1.62	WHI88h	0.70
KOE93a	1.23	WHI88i	1.08
KOE93b	0.88	WHI88j	1.48
KOJ93a	1.85	WHI88k	0.48
KOJ93b	2.64	WHI88l	0.57
KLN95a	1.02	WHI88m	1.88
KLN95b	1.17	WHI89a	1.41
LEA92a	1.88	WHI89b	2.00
LEA92b	2.54	WHI89c	2.00
LEA92c	0.90	WHI89d	0.55
LEA92d	1.33	WHI89e	1.55
LEB92a	1.16	WHI98a	0.80
LEB92b	1.22	WHI98b	1.13
LEB92c	1.76	WHA97a	2.15
LEB92d	0.72	WHA97b	1.48
LEC92a	1.89	WHB97a	1.74
LEC92b	0.54	WHB97b	0.91
LED92a	1.09	WHJ98a	1.48
LED92b	0.55	WHJ98b	1.56
MAT94a	2.53	YIN99a	0.51
MAT94b	1.78	YIN99b	0.42
MAT94c	2.69	YUA98a	0.18
MAT94d	2.81	YUA98b	0.10
MAT94e	1.64	YUB98a	2.46
MAT94f	0.44	YUB98b	1.26
MAT94g	0.71		
Mean d	*SD*	min d	max d
1.25	0.68	0.10	2.81

Note. For study abbreviation key, please see Table 3.

Table 3. Effect sizes for study samples

Study for the samples	Number of effect sizes (1 per DV)	Mean effect size for the sample	Standard error
Bennett (1994) (BEN 94)	4	0.53	0.33
Bley-Vroman et al. (1988) (BLV88)	1	2.49	n/a
Flynn (1987) (FLY87)	4	1.23	0.44
Hawkins & Chan (1997) (HAW97)	1	1.62	n/a
Kinoshita$_1$ (1993) (KOE93)	2	1.06	0.24
Kinoshita$_2$ (1993) (KOJ93)	2	2.24	0.56
Klein (1995) (KLN95)	2	1.09	0.10
Lee$_1$ (1992) (LEA92)	4	1.66	0.71
Lee$_2$ (1992) (LEB92)	4	1.22	0.42
Lee$_3$ (1992) (LEC92)	2	1.22	0.96
Lee$_4$ (1992) (LED92)	2	0.82	0.38
Matsumura (1994) (MAT94)	8	1.76	0.89
Uziel (1993) (UZI93)	1	0.56	n/a
White (1988) (WHI88)	13	0.91	0.47
White (1989a) (WHI89a)	5	1.70	0.28
White (1998) (WHI98)	2	0.97	0.23
White et al.$_1$ (1997) (WHA97)	2	1.82	0.47
White et al.$_2$ (1997) (WHB97)	2	1.33	0.59
White and Juffs (1998) (WHJ98)	2	1.52	0.06
Ying (1999) YIN99	2	0.47	0.06
Yuan$_1$ (1998) YUA98	2	0.14	0.06
Yuan$_2$ (1998) YUB98	3	1.60	0.75

Note. n/a=not applicable since only one sample was featured in the study. The repetition of a study name indicates a separate sample used for the analyses. DV = Dependent Variable.

Table 4. Homogeneity of variance test

Unit of analysis	Q_t Value	Significance
Study Sample ($n = 22$)	102.93	$p = 0.00$
Test Task ($n = 69$)	344.22	$p = 0.00$

tics. Table 4 presents the results of homogeneity of variance tests (Q_t) for each of the units of analysis, calculated following Cooper (1998).

The overall Q_t value for the sample unit of analysis (i.e., the different groups of participants taken from each study in this meta-analysis) indicates that a homogeneity of variance assumption was violated, which, in turn, indicates the source of the variation is potentially due to some moderating variable or variables – potentially the differing study characteristics as recorded in the categories of the Coding Sheet. In addition, when the same homogeneity statistic was computed for the 69 effect sizes derived from each different test (task) used across the 16 studies (hypothesis unit of analysis), the results similarly indicated that the homogeneity of variance assumption was violated.

Because of the heterogeneity of variance of the effect size estimates, further analysis was necessary to explore the possible cause(s) for the excess variation. Following the suggestions of Hedges, Shymansky, and Woodworth (1989), the relationships between the various characteristics of the sample and hypothesis units of analysis and their respective effect sizes were analyzed using the study characteristics (i.e. the categories from the Coding Sheet) as the independent variables and the corresponding effect sizes as the dependent variables. These results are reported in the next two sections.

Analysis of variance by coding characteristics for the sample unit of analysis

Since the variance was not due to sampling error alone, seventeen analysis of variance procedures were performed in order to explore where potential relationships might be found between study characteristics and observed effect sizes. It should be emphasized that, due to the very low n of 22 samples, and the repeated use of ANOVA comparisons, statistical significance outcomes should be interpreted with extreme caution; here, they are used for exploratory purposes only. The coding characteristics (listed in the column entitled "Subcategory" in Table 5) served as the independent variables (each level of the variable listed in the column entitled "Values"), and the related mean effect sizes served as the dependent variables. A statistically significant finding in these analyses (with the alpha-level set at $p < 0.05$) would suggest that certain study characteristics may be the source of the excess variation. Table 5 presents the frequency distributions of the coding characteristics. A more general narrative is presented below, where each potential moderating variable examined is mentioned and results are discussed for those variables that yielded results of interest.

None of the seven independent variables drawn from the Publication and Participant Characteristics yielded significant results. Of the ten independent variables in the Design Characteristics category (see Appendix 2), two yielded results that merit some discussion.

The findings for sample size suggest that this may be a moderator variable of importance when interpreting primary L2 studies of UG access. This independent variable has three levels: studies with sample sizes of 0–50, 51–99, and 100+ participants. Table A3.1 in Appendix 3 presents the results of the cor-

Table 5. Coding characteristics for the study samples

Category	Subcategory	Value	*n*	mean	*sd*
Publication Characteristics					
	Year	1981–1991	4	1.58	0.67
		1992–1999	18	1.24	0.56
	Type	Journal	12	1.26	0.71
		Dissertation	6	1.37	0.51
		Edited Volume	3	1.38	0.41
		Book	1	1.23	n/a
Participant Characteristics					
	Control Group Age	Adolescent	2	1.07	0.77
		Adult	20	1.33	0.58
		Mixed	0	n/a	n/a
	Experimental Group Age	Adolescent	3	0.86	0.35
		Adult	18	1.36	0.60
		Mixed	1	1.72	n/a
	Number of Native Languages	Single	18	1.32	0.61
		More than one	4	1.22	0.51
	Native Language–Control Group	Chinese	3	0.73	0.77
		English	17	1.35	0.51
		Japanese	1	2.24	n/a
		Spanish	1	1.23	n/a
	Target Language Learning Conditions	Foreign Language Setting	7	1.24	0.65
		Second Language Setting	1	1.09	n/a
Design Characteristics					
	Sample Size	0–50	8	0.97	0.57
		51–99	9	1.36	0.44
		> 100	5	1.74	0.62
	Conditionally Robust	yes	13	1.26	0.60
		no	9	1.37	0.59
	Criteria for Inclusion–Control Groups	Participation in a Course	5	1.11	0.83
		Other	17	1.36	0.51

Table 5. (*continued*)

Category	Subcategory	Value	*n*	mean	*sd*
	Criteria for Inclusion– Experimental Group	Standardized Test	9	1.42	0.62
		Participation in a Course	9	1.24	0.67
		Other	4	1.18	0.32
	Type Course– Experimental Group	Intensive Target Language	6	1.54	0.48
		Regular Curriculum Course	9	1.23	0.76
		Other	7	1.20	0.41
	Principle Being Tested	Binding	12	1.19	0.57
		Subjacency and the ECP	6	1.36	0.68
		Case Theory	1	1.70	n/a
		Morphological Uniformity	2	1.65	0.84
		X' Theory	1	1.23	n/a
	Target Language Being Tested	Chinese	3	0.73	0.77
		English	18	1.35	0.49
	Control Group Language	Same as Target Language	21	1.31	0.60
		Similar Parameter Setting to Target Language	1	1.23	n/a
	Test (Task) Formats	One Type of Task	10	1.29	0.72
		Two or More	12	1.31	0.48

responding ANOVA which used sample size as the independent variable and effect size of the sample as the dependent. Although the *p*-value does exceed the level of significance, it does so just barely. Thus, it appears that the Sample Size of the primary study might be a cause for some of the excess variation of the Q_t -Statistic.

The Target Language Being Tested is the only Design Characteristics variable that yielded statistically significant results. This independent variable has three levels: English, Chinese, and Japanese. Table A3.2 in Appendix 3 presents the results of the corresponding ANOVA. The resulting p-value is 0.0229, suggesting that the target language that is being tested may be a cause for the heterogeneity of variance observed in this group of 22 study samples.

Hypothesis analysis

For the hypothesis analysis, the *Type of Test* (or task) served as the independent variable. Unlike the analyses presented so far, which were based on average effect sizes representing each study sample, the effect size from each type of task, regardless of whether it was drawn from the same or a different sample, contributed independently to this analysis. For example, the sample from Bennett (1994) contributed one effect size for the Sample Analysis (cf. Table 3); but for this analysis, that same sample contributed 4 effect sizes (cf. Table 2). The types of task were separated into the following levels: Grammaticality Judgment Task; Comprehension Task, and Other (Elicited Imitation, Prompt Modification, Picture Identification, etc.). Table 6 presents the frequency and mean effect size for these three levels.

The information in Table 6 was then entered into another exploratory analysis of variance with the type of task as the independent variable. Table A3.3 in Appendix 3 presents the results from the ANOVA. No statistically significant effect was found for type of test task. Thus, it appears that the type of task does not contribute substantially to the heterogeneity of variance identified in the Q-Statistic. Therefore, it seems reasonable to suggest that the type of task is not a source of systematic variance with which researchers need to concern themselves when conducting future primary studies in this research domain. Nevertheless, the fact that the average effect sizes did differ between each task type, and that large standard deviation values were found within each type, also suggests that there is considerable variability across studies which utilized similar types of tasks.

Table 6. Descriptive statistics for type of test task

Task	n	mean	sd
Grammaticality Judgment	31	1.29	0.58
Comprehension	22	1.34	0.88
Other	16	1.06	0.57

Discussion

With an overall mean effect size of 1.25 and a standard deviation of 0.68, the findings of this meta-analysis indicate that L2 learners perform noticeably different from native speaking baseline or control groups when asked to demonstrate their intuitive grammatical knowledge of the L2. The 95% confidence interval test also confirms this finding. Not only did the confidence interval not contain zero, but it fell well above it, with a lower limit of 1.12 standard deviation units. Thus, there is a clear and large difference between the control group and experimental group for each of the sample units of analysis investigated in this meta-analysis. However, the effect size estimates calculated for each of the samples did turn out to be heterogeneous – that is, the homogeneity of variance assumption was violated as shown by the significance of the Q_t-Statistic – which consequently implies that the differences in the effect size estimates are not solely due to sampling error but likely relate to something else. The characteristics of each study was recorded and separated for the differences in Publication, Participant, and Design characteristics. For the most part, these divisions did not seem to be clearly associated with differences in effect sizes, except in two cases: the target language that was being tested, and, more tentatively, the number of participants in any given sample.

Which target language researchers tested across the 22 study samples meta-analyzed – English, Japanese or Chinese – seemed to be the moderating variable that most heavily accounted for the heterogeneity of variance on the Q_t-Statistic. However, this result should be interpreted with caution. Eighteen of the samples used English as the target language, and only four used either Chinese or Japanese as the target. According to Stevens (1996) the population variances are conditionally robust "if group sizes are equal or approximately equal – largest/smallest < 1.5" (p. 238). Using this definition as a criterion, the results for Target Language Being Tested were most likely biased, since these data did not meet the conditions for conditional robustness: the larger group (English) is more than 1.5 times bigger than either of the smaller groups (Chinese and Japanese). This imbalance, rather than any substantive reason related to participants' L1 background, could be the cause of excess of variance. Nevertheless, all researchers recognize that the nature of the particular L1-L2 differences is important when investigating the representation of Universal Grammar in SLA, and that there is a great need for further studies in languages other than English. For example, Binding Principle A has the possibility of five different parameter settings across languages, with English exhibiting the most restrictive case and Japanese the least restrictive (see Chomsky 1986). Moreover, the preceding example is not the only case where Japanese and English differ greatly. Japanese does not have syntactic movement; therefore, native speakers have no need to activate Subjacency and the Empty Category Principle (see Haegeman 1994). Thus, it is imperative for researchers to test target languages other than English if the relationship of Universal Grammar and second language acquisition is to be more fully investigated.

The analysis of variance with sample size as the independent variable did not yield significant results at the 0.05 alpha, but the p-value was not much larger, suggesting that the number of participants may have affected the heterogeneity of variance found in the Q-Statistic. Clearly, sample size may play an important role in determining outcomes observed in primary research. Thus, for example, one of the underlying assumptions of statistical techniques, such as an ANOVA, is the so-called "homogeneity of variance" assumption, which states that the samples associated to the independent variables of the test in question should have the same degree of variability with respect to the dependent variable (see Huck & Cormier 1996, for a full discussion of these assumptions). Gravetter and Wallnau (1996) state that if the sample size is small, there is a chance that the homogeneity of variance requirement has not been met. Although they do not suggest that larger sample sizes will automatically meet the requirement for this assumption, the researcher does have a better chance of meeting this requirement if the sample size is larger. Thus, researchers who employ inferential statistics in their studies need to be concerned with small sample size and its potential to lead to a violation of the homogeneity of variance assumption. In terms of the present meta-analysis, the primary studies used to calculate the mean effect sizes may not have met the "homogeneity of variance" assumption, particularly the eight studies that had smaller number of participants. Therefore, future generative SLA researchers employing inferential statistics to compare the performance of groups of L2 and L1 speakers ought to be concerned with the number of their sample sizes and check that the assumption of homogeneity of variance is met in their samples.

One noticeable finding emerged from the systematic process of literature retrieval and study coding that has not been mentioned yet. Namely, the statistical information reported in many of the studies was sorely incomplete in most cases. Because of the lack of statistical information, it was not possible to compute an effect for the comparison in question in thirty-one studies, and these had to be excluded for this reason alone (see Appendix 1). Had these studies been included, the results of this present meta-analysis may have been different. Therefore, the need for better reporting practices in this research domain, particularly when it comes to providing sufficient statistical information, should be brought to the attention of editorial boards (whether it be a journal, edited volume, or book) and dissertation committee members. Future quantitative studies should provide not only the means and standard deviations, but also group size(s), sum of squares, F and t statistic values, and exact p value of significant and non-significant results, so that they can be included in future meta-analyses.

Conclusion

The results of this meta-analytic investigation clearly indicate that post-Critical Period second language learners' performance on various kinds of grammatical knowledge tasks is "fundamentally different" (Bley-Vroman 1989) from the performance of native speaker groups. Based on the premise that the mean effect size would approach zero if second language learners behaved close enough to native speakers, the results are congruent with the view that Universal Grammar does not fully operate in adult/adolescent L2 learning. This conclusion, which is based on the careful inspection of main and moderating effects observed across 16 studies, 22 samples, and the pooled performance of 942 L2 participants, can be reasonably generalized to the numerous empirical studies that have accumulated during the first two decades of generative SLA research. This research was inspired by the access to UG metaphor and premised on the direct comparison of native and nonnative speaker performance on various kinds of tasks that purport to tap knowledge of grammaticality in the L1 and the L2. Over these first two decades, much has been accomplished. Much has also begun to be reframed and reconceptualized (Hawkins 2001; White 2003). The research community has gradually moved from a metaphor about access to UG to another about constraints (Thomas 2003). We may now be ready to reconsider the comparative approach, which never completely broached the problem of the comparative fallacy (Bley-Vroman 1983), and to turn towards an exploration of wider notions of what knowledge of Universal Grammar might mean for L2 learners. I hope this meta-analysis inspires other researchers to embark on other systematic syntheses of findings in newer studies and pursuing similar questions about UG and SLA from other relevant perspectives.

Notes

1. I would like to thank Stephanie Gilbertson, a fellow doctoral candidate at the time, for all her help with the coding.

* References proceded with an asterisk are the studies that were included in this meta-analysis.

References

Bangert-Drowns, R. (1986). Review of developments in meta-analysis. *Psychological Bulletin, 99,* 388–399.

*Bennett, S. (1994). Interpretation of English reflexives by adolescent speakers of Serbo-Croatian. *Second Language Research, 10,* 125–156.

Bley-Vroman, R. (1983). The comparative fallacy in interlanguage studies: The case systematicity. *Language Learning, 33,* 1–18.

Bley-Vroman, R. (1989). What is the logical problem of foreign language acquisition? In S. M. Gass & J. Schachter (Eds.), *Linguistic perspectives on second language acquisition* (pp. 41–68). Cambridge, UK: Cambridge University Press.

Bley-Vroman, R., & Chaudron, C. (1994). Elicited imitation as a measure of second-language competence. In E. E. Tarone, S. M. Gass & A. D. Cohen (Eds.), *Research methodology in second-language acquisition* (pp. 245–261). Hillsdale, NJ: Lawrence Erlbaum.

*Bley-Vroman, R., Felix, S., & Ioup, G. (1988) The accessibility of Universal Grammar in adult language learning. *Second Language Research, 4,* 1–32.

Chomsky, N. (1965). *Aspects of the theory of syntax.* Cambridge, MA: MIT Press.

Chomsky, N. (1981). *Lectures on government and binding.* Dordrecht: Foris.

Chomsky, N. (1986). *Knowledge of language: Its nature, use, and origin.* New York: Praeger.

Cohen, J. (1988). *Statistical power analysis for the behavioral sciences* (2nd ed.). Hillsdale, NJ: Lawrence Erlbaum.

Cook, T., & Leviton, L. (1980). Reviewing the literature: A comparison of traditional methods with meta-analysis. *Journal of Personality, 48,* 449–472.

Cooper, H. (1998). *Synthesizing research: A guide for literature reviews* (3rd ed.). Newbury Park, CA: Sage.

Cooper, H., & Hedges, L., V. (1994). Potentials and limitations of research synthesis. In H. Cooper & L. V. Hedges (Eds.). *The handbook of research synthesis* (pp. 521–29). New York: Russell Sage Foundation.

*Flynn, S. (1987). *A parameter-setting model of L2 acquisition: Experimental studies in anaphora.* Boston: D. Reidel.

Flynn, S., & Manuel, S. (1991). Age-dependent effects in language acquisition. In L. Eubank (Ed.), *Point counterpoint. Universal Grammar in the second language.* Amsterdam: John Benjamins.

Fodor, J. A. (1983). *The modularity of the mind.* Cambridge, MA: MIT Press

Glass, G. (1976). Primary, secondary, and Meta-analysis of research. *Educational Researcher,* *5* (10), 3–8.

Gravetter, F. J., & Wallnau, L. B. (1996). *Statistics for the behavioral sciences.* (4th ed.) Los Angeles: West Publishing Company.

Haegeman, L. (1994). *Introduction to Government and Binding theory.* (2nd ed.) Oxford: Blackwell.

Hall, J., Rosenthal, R., Tickle-Degen, L., & Mosteller, F. (1994). Hypotheses and problems in research synthesis. In H. Cooper & L. V. Hedges (Eds.). *The handbook of research synthesis* (pp. 17–28). New York: Russell Sage Foundation.

Hawkins, R. (2001). The theoretical significance of universal grammar in second language acquisition. *Second Language Research, 17,* 345–367.

*Hawkins, R., & Chan, C. (1997). The partial availability of Universal Grammar in second language acquisition: The 'failed functional features hypothesis.' *Second Language Research, 13,* 187–226.

Hedges, L. (1981). Distribution theory of Glass's estimator of effect size and related estimator. *Journal of Educational Statistics, 6,* 107–128.

Hedges, L. (1982a). Estimation of effect size from a series of independent experiments. *Psychological Bulletin, 92,* 490–499.

Hedges, L. (1982b). Fitting categorical models to effect sizes from a series of experiments. *Journal of Educational Statistics, 7,* 119–137.

Hedges, L. (1982c). Fitting continuous models to effect size data. *Journal of Educational Statistics, 7,* 245–270.

Hedges, L., & Olkin, I. (1985) *Statistical methods for meta-analysis.* Orlando: Academic Press.

Hedges, L., Shymansky, J., & Woodworth, G. (1989). *Modern methods of meta-analysis.* Washington, DC: National Science Teachers Association.

Huck, S. W. & Cormier, W. H., (1996) *Reading statistics and research* (2nd ed.). New York: Harper Collins.

Jackson, G. (1980). Methods for integrative reviews. *Review of Educational Research, 50,* 438–460.

*Kinoshita, K. (1993). *Defectively working Universal Grammar and Prodrop Parameter resetting in adult second language acquisition.* Unpublished doctoral dissertation. Georgetown University.

*Klein, E. (1995). Evidence for a 'wild' L2 grammar: When PPs rear their empty heads. *Applied Linguistics, 16,* 85–117.

Lakshmanan, U., & Teranishi, K. (1994). Preferences versus grammaticality judgements: Some methodological issues concerning the Governing Category Parameter in second language acquisition. In E. Tarone, S. Gass, & A. Cohen (Eds.). *Research methodology in second language acquisition* (pp. 227–243). Hillsdale, NJ: Lawrence Erlbaum.

*Lee, D. (1992). *Universal Grammar, learnability and the acquisition of L2 English reflexiv6e binding by L1 Korean speakers.* Unpublished doctoral dissertation. University of Southern California.

Light, R., & Pillemer, D. (1982). Numbers and narrative: Combining their strengths in research reviews. *Harvard Educational Review, 52,* 1–26.

*Matsumura, M. (1994). Japanese learners' acquisition of the locality requirement of English reflexives: Evidence for retreat from overgenralization. *Studies in Second Language Acquisition, 16,* 19–42.

Munnich, E., Flynn, S., & Martohardjono, G. (1994) Elicited imitation and grammaticality judgment tasks: What they measure and how they relate to each other. In E. Tarone, S. Gass, & A. Cohen (Eds.). *Research methodology in second language acquisition* (pp. 227–243). Hillsdale, NJ: Lawrence Erlbaum.

Orwin, R. (1994). Evaluating coding decisions. In H. Cooper & L. V. Hedges (Eds.). *The handbook of research synthesis* (pp. 139–162). New York: Russell Sage Foundation.

Rosenthal, R. (1978) Combining results of independent studies. *Psychological Bulletin, 85,* 185–193.

Stevens J. (1996). *Applied multivariate statistics for the social sciences* (3rd ed.). Mahwah, NJ: Lawrence Erlbaum.

Thomas, M. (2003). Two textbook representations of second language acquisition and Universal Grammar: 'access' and 'constraint.' *Second Language Research, 19,* 359–376.

*Uziel, S. (1993). Resetting Universal Grammar parameters: Evidence from second language acquisition of Subjacency and the Empty Category Principle. *Second Language Research, 9,* 49–83.

*White, L. (1988). Island effects in second language acquisition. In S. Flynn & W. O'Neil (Eds.). *Linguistic theory in second language acquisition.* (pp. 144–172). Boston: Kluwer Academic Publishers.

*White, L. (1989a). The principle of adjacency on second language acquisition. In S. Gass & J. Schachter (Eds.). *Linguistic perspectives on second language acquisition* (pp. 134–158). Cambridge, UK: University Press.

White, L. (1989b). *Universal Grammar and second language acquisition.* Amsterdam: John Benjamins.

*White, L. (1998). Second language acquisition and Binding Principle B: Child/adult differences. *Second Language Research, 14,* 425–439.

White, L. (2003). On the nature of interlanguage representation: Universal Grammar in the second language. In C. J. Doughty & M. H. Long (Eds.). *The handbook of second language acquisition* (pp. 19–42). Malden, MA: Blackwell.

*White, L., Bruhn-Garavito, J., Kawasaki, T., Pater, J., & Prévost, P. (1997). The researcher gave the subject a test about himself: Problems of ambiguity and preference in the Investigation of reflexive binding. *Language Learning, 47,* 145–172.

*White, L., & Juffs, A. (1998). Constraints on wh-movement in two different contexts of nonnative language acquisition: Competence and processing. In S. Flynn, G. Martohardjono, & W. O'Neil (Eds.). *The generative study of second language acquisition* (pp. 111–129). Mahwah, NJ: Lawrence Erlbaum.

*Ying, H. (1999). Access to UG and language transfer: A study of L2 learners interpretation of reconstruction in Chinese. *Second Language Research, 15,* 41–72.

Yoshikawa, T. (1993). *The acquisition of English reflexives by L2 learners.* Unpublished doctoral dissertation. Indiana University.

*Yuan, B. (1998). Interpretation of binding and orientation of the Chinese reflexive *ziji* by English and Japanese speakers. *Second Language Research, 14,* 324–340.

Appendix 1: Bibliography of excluded studies

The following is a bibliography of studies excluded from this meta-analysis. The number before each entry indicates the reason for exclusion. The following list gives the reasons for exclusion:

1. This study did not test a UG principle or parameter: reviewed or criticized the work(s) of other primary researchers; or discussed theoretical implications or relevance.
2. This study was not quantitative in nature: case study or comparison of percentages.
3. This study did not provide sufficient statistical information for the calculation of an effect size: missing standard deviations, missing degrees of freedom, missing inferential statistic (t, F, or χ^2) information, etc.
4. This study investigated the presence of UG operation in children.
5. This study was later published in a journal article.

[3]Ayoun, D. (1997). The subset principle in second language acquisition. *Applied Psycholinguistics, 17*, 185–213.

[3]Beck, M-L. (1998). L2 acquisition and obligatory head movement: English-speaking learners of German and the Local Impairment Hypothesis. *Studies in Second Language Acquisition, 20*, 311–348.

[1]Birdsong, D. (1986). Empirical impediments to theories of second language acquisition. Paper presented at *Kentucky Foreign Language Conference*, Lexington, KY. (ERIC Reproduction Service No. ED 276 259).

[1]Bley-Vroman, R., & Chaudron, C. (1990). Second language processing of subordinate clauses and anaphora–first language and universal influences: A review of Flynn's research. *Language Learning, 40*, 245–285.

[3]Boe, D. (1996). *Parameter resetting in adult second language acquisition: Inflectional richness and the null subject parameter (adult learners).* Unpublished doctoral dissertation. Indiana University.

[3]Broselow, E., & Finer, D. (1991). Parameter setting in second language phonology and syntax. *Second Language Research, 7*, 35–59.

[3]Bruhn-Garavito, J. (1995). L2 acquisition of verb complementation and binding principle B. In F. Eckman, D. Highland, P. Lee, J. Mileham, & R. Weber (Eds.), *Second Language Acquisition Theory and Pedagogy* (pp. 79–99). Mahwah, NJ: Lawrence Erlbaum.

[3]Bruhn-Garavito, J., & Montrul, S. (1996). Verb movement and clitic placement in French and Spanish as a second language. In A. Stringfellow, D. Cahana-Amitay, E. Hughes, & A. Zukowski (Eds.), *Proceedings of the 20th Boston University Conference on Language Development (Vol. 1)* (pp. 123–134). Sommerville, MA: Cascadilla Press.

[3]Davies, W. (1996). Morphological uniformity and the null subject parameter in adult SLA. *Studies in Second Language Acquisition, 18*, 475–493.

[3]Dekydtspotter, L., Sprouse, R., & Anderson, B. (1998). Interlanguage A-bar dependencies: Binding construals, null prepositions and Universal Grammar. *Second Language Research, 14*, 341–358.

[3]Downey-Vanover, J. (1994). *Adult access to universal grammar in second language acquisition.* Unpublished doctoral dissertation. University of Maryland.

[2]Eckman, F. R. (1994). Local and long-distance anaphora in second-language acquisition. In E. Tarone, S. Gass, & A. Cohen (Eds.). *Research methodology in second language acquisition* (pp. 207–225). Hillsdale, NJ: Lawrence Erlbaum.

[3]Emberson, J. (1986). *The Pro Drop parameter in the acquisition of Spanish as a second language.* Unpublished doctoral dissertation. University of Texas at Austin.

[3]Eubank, L. (1989). Parameters in L2 learning: Flynn revisited. *Second Language Research, 5,* 43–73.

[3]Felix, S. (1988). UG-generated knowledge in adult second language acquisition. In S. Flynn & W. O'Neil (Eds.), *Linguistic theory in second language acquisition* (pp. 277–294). Boston: Kluwer.

[3]Finer, D. (1991). Binding parameters in second language acquisition. In L. Eubank (Ed.), *Point Counterpoint: Universal Grammar in the second language* (pp. 351–374). Amsterdam: John Benjamin.

[3]Finer, D. & Broselow, E. (1986). Second language acquisition of reflexive binding. In S. Berman, J-W. Choe, & J. McDonough (Eds.), *Proceedings of NELS 16* (pp. 154–168). Amherst, MA: GLSA, UMass/Amherst.

[3]Finney, M. (1997). Markedness, operator movement and discourse effects in the acquisition of purpose clause constructions in a second language. *Second Language Research, 13,* 10–33.

[4]Flanigan, B. (1995). Anaphora and relativization in child second language acquisition. *Studies in Second Language Acquisition, 17,* 331–351.

[5]Flynn, S. (1987). Contrast and construction in a parameter-setting model of L2 acquisition. *Language Learning, 37,* 19–62.

[1]Flynn, S. (1988). Nature of development in L2 acquisition and implications for theories of language acquisition in general. In S. Flynn & W. O'Neil (Eds.), *Linguistic theory in second language acquisition* (pp. 76–89). Boston: Kluwer.

[3]Flynn, S. (1996). A parameter setting approach to second language acquisition. In W. Ritchie & T. Bhatia (Eds.), *Handbook of second language acquisition* (pp. 121–158). San Diego: Academic Press.

[3]Flynn, S., & Espinal, I. (1985). Head-initial/head-final parameter in adult Chinese L2 acquisition of English. *Second Language Research, 1,* 93–117.

[3]Hamilton, R. (1998). Underdetermined binding of reflexives by adult Japanese-speaking learners of English. *Second language Research, 14,* 292–320.

[2]Hartford, B. (1995). Zero anaphora in nonnative texts: Null-object anaphora in Nepali English. *Studies in Second Language Acquisition, 17,* 245–261.

[3]Hawkins, R., Towell, R., & Bazergui, N. (1993). Universal Grammar and the acquisition of French verb movement by native speakers of English. *Second Language Research, 9,* 189–223.

[2]Hilles, S. (1986). Interlanguage and the pro-drop parameter. *Second Language Research, 2,* 33–52.

[2]Hilles, S. (1991). Access to Universal Grammar in second language acquisition. In L. Eubank (Ed.), *Point Counterpoint: Universal Grammar in the second language* (pp. 305–338). Amsterdam: John Benjamin.

[3]Hirakawa, M. (1990). A study of L2 acquisition of English reflexives. *Second Language Research, 6,* 60–85.

[2]Hulk, A. (1991). Parameter setting and the acquisition of word order in L2 French. *Second Language Research, 7*, 1–34.

[2]Hulk, A. (1996). Parameter setting and the acquisition of *wh*-questions in L2 French. In P. Jordens & J. Lalleman (Eds.), *Investigating Second Language Acquisition* (pp. 237–259). New York: Mouton de Gruyter.

[2]Jordens, P. (1988). The acquisition of verb categories and word order in Dutch & German: evidence from first and second language acquisition. In J. Pankhurst, M. Sharwood Smith, & P Van Buren (Eds.), *Learnability and second languages: A book of readings* (pp. 132–166). Dordrecht: Foris.

[1]Jordens, P. (1989). Linguistic knowledge in second language acquisition. Paper presented at the *Annual Second Language Research Forum*, Los Angeles, CA, (ERIC Reproduction Service No. 306 777).

[3]Kanno, K. (1997). The acquisition of null and overt pronominals in Japanese by English speakers. *Second Language Research, 13*, 265–287.

[4]Lakshmann, U. (1995). Child second language acquisition of syntax. *Studies in Second Language Acquisition, 17*, 301–329.

[1]MacLaughlin, D. (1993). The responsibility of linguistic theory to second language acquisition data. Paper presented at the *Workshop on Language Acquisition and Linguistic Theory* as part of the *Boston University of Applied Linguistics Colloquium Series*, Boston, MA (ERIC Reproduction Service No. 362 023).

[1]MacLaughlin, D. (1996). Second language acquisition of English reflexives: Is there hope beyond transfer? In A. Stringfellow, D. Cahana-Amitay, E. Hughes, & A. Zukowski (Eds.), *Proceedings of the 20th Boston University Conference on Language Development (Vol. 2)* (pp. 453–464). Sommerville, MA: Cascadilla Press.

[3]Martohardjono, G., & Gair, J. (1993). Apparent UG inaccessibility in second language acquisition: Misapplied principles or principled misapplications. In F. Eckman (Ed.), *Confluence: Linguistics, L2 acquisition and speech pathology* (pp. 79–103). Amsterdam: John Benjamins.

[4]Mazurkewich, I. (1988). The acquisition of infinitive and gerund complements by second language learners. In S. Flynn & W. O'Neil (Eds.), *Linguistic theory in second language acquisition* (pp. 127–143). Boston: Kluwer.

[2]Platt, E. (1993). Parameter-resetting in second language acquisition: A study of adult Spanish and Vietnamese learners of English. In F. Eckman (Ed.), *Confluence: Linguistics, L2 acquisition and speech pathology* (pp. 105–134). Amsterdam: John Benjamins.

[3]Polio, C. (1995). The use of zero pronouns by nonnative speakers of Chinese and the implications for the acquisition of nominal reference. *Studies in Second Language Acquisition, 17*, 353–377.

[3]Register, N. (1990). Influences of typological parameters of L2 learners' judgements of null pronouns in English. *Language Learning, 40*, 369–385.

[1]Schachter, J. (1989). A new look at an old classic. *Second Language Research, 5*, 30–42.

[3]Sheppard, K (1991). *At sea in SLA: Evidence of UG in the acquisition of French and English verbs*. Unpublished doctoral dissertation. City University of New York.

[3]Thomas, M. (1989). The interpretation of English reflexive pronouns by non-native speakers. *Studies in Second Language Acquisition, 11*, 281–303.

[3]Thomas, M. (1991). Reflexives in a second language. *Language, 67*, 211–239.

[1]Thomas, M. (1993). *Knowledge of reflexives in a second language.* Amsterdam: John Benjamins.

[3]Thomas, M. (1995). Acquisition of the Japanese reflexive *zibun* and movement of anaphors in Logical Form. *Second Language Research, 11,* 206–234.

[3]Tomiyama, M. (1988). *The acquisitions of restrictions on backward anaphora by adult English as a second language learners: Linguistic theory and the relevance of second language acquisition data.* Unpublished doctoral dissertation. Pennsylvania State University.

[1]Wakabayashi, S. (1996) The nature of interlanguage: SLA of English reflexives. *Second Language Research 12,* 266–303.

[3]White, L. (1985). The acquisition of parameterized grammars: Subjacency in second language acquisition. *Second Language Research, 1,* 1–17.

[3]White, L. (1985). The "pro-drop" parameter in adult second language acquisition. *Language Learning, 35,* 47–62.

[2]White, L. (1987). Markedness and second language acquisition: The question of transfer. *Studies in Second Language Acquisition, 9,* 261–286.

[5]White, L. (1998). Second language acquisition and binding principle B: Child/adult differences. In *Proceedings of the 1997 Generative approaches to second language acquisition conference: Special issue of the McGill working Papers in linguistics (Vol. 13)* (pp. 220–229).

[2]Yoshikawa, T. (1993). *The acquisition of English reflexives by L2 learners.* Unpublished doctoral dissertation. Indiana University.

[3]Yuan, B. (1997). Asymmetry of null subjects and null objects in Chinese speakers' L2 English. *Studies in Second Language Acquisition, 19,* 467–497.

[5]Yuan, B. (1998). Acquisition of the Chinese reflexive *Ziji* by English- and Japanese-Speaking learners. In *Proceedings of the 1997 Generative approaches to second language acquisition conference: Special issue of the McGill working Papers in linguistics (Vol. 13)* (pp. 209–220).

[2]Zobl, H. (1988). Configurationality and the subset principle: The acquisition of V by Japanese learners of English. In J. Pankhurst, M. Sharwood Smith, & P Van Buren (Eds.), *Learnability and second languages: A book of readings* (pp. 116–131). Dordrecht: Foris.

Appendix 2: Coding sheet

ID No._____

Coding Sheet

1. Publication Characteristics

Author(s):_____

Title:_____

Journal:_____ or

Edited Volume:_____

Year_____ Volume_____ Pages_____

Type of Publication
_____Journal Article _____Dissertation
_____Edited Volume _____Conference Proceeding
Source of the reference
_____ERIC _____DAI _____LLBA _____PsychInfo
_____Hand-Search _____Ancestry Search

2. Participant Characteristics
Age
Control Group
mean age_____ and sd_____ or
_____Adolescent _____Adult _____Mixed
Experimental Group
mean age_____ and sd_____ or
_____Adolescent _____Adult _____Mixed
Native Language (Experimental Group)
_____ Chinese_____ English _____ Hebrew
_____ Italian _____ Korean _____ Japanese
_____Serbo-Croatian _____French _____ Mixed
Native Language (Control Group)
_____ Chinese_____ English _____ Japanese
Target Language Learning Conditions
_____Foreign Language Setting/Avg. Length of Time_____(years) _____(months)
_____Second Language Setting/Avg. Length of Time_____(years) _____(months)
_____Both conditions
Length of Time in Target Language Country (Experimental Group)
_____years _____months (average)

3. Design Characteristics
Sample Size
Total_____
_____ No. of experimental groups (i.e. Target Language)
No. in each _____ _____ _____
_____ No. of control groups (i.e. Native Language)
No. in each _____ _____ _____
Criteria for inclusion in the study
Control Group
_____Participation in a course
_____Other: Name_____
Experimental Group
_____Standardized Test Name_____
_____Participation in a course
_____Other: Name_____
Type of Course the Experimental Group was drawn from
_____Intensive Target Language Course
_____Adult/Continuing Education

_____Regular Curriculum Course
_____Other
UG Principle and or Parameter being tested
Name:_____(principle)
Name:_____(parameter)
Target Language Being Tested
_____ Chinese _____ Japanese _____ English
Control Group Native Language
_____Same as the target language
_____Similar parameter settings to the target language
Test Format(s)
Type_____
Type_____
Type_____
Type_____

4. Statistical Information (fill in all applicable spaces)
Type_____
Control Group _____no of participants _____means _____sd
Experimental Group _____no of participants _____means _____sd
statistical test used (supply values)
_____t-test _____anova _____chi square
_____df numerator _____df denominator
_____ p value sig or non-sig (circle one)
Type_____
Control Group _____no of participants _____means _____sd
Experimental Group _____no of participants _____means _____sd
statistical test used (supply values)
_____t-test _____anova _____chi square
_____df numerator _____df denominator
_____ p value sig or non-sig (circle one)
Type_____
Control Group _____no of participants _____means _____sd
Experimental Group _____no of participants _____means _____sd
statistical test used (supply values)
_____t-test _____anova _____chi square
_____df numerator _____df denominator
_____ p value sig or non-sig (circle one)
Type_____
Control Group _____no of participants _____means _____sd
Experimental Group _____no of participants _____means _____sd
statistical test used (supply values)
_____t-test _____anova _____chi square
_____df numerator _____df denominator
_____ p value sig or non-sig (circle one)

Appendix 3: Coding characteristics results

Table A3.1. Analysis of variance with sample size as the independent variable

Source	df	SS	MS	F	p
Between	2	27.2742	13.6371	3.42	.0537
Within	19	75.6568	3.9819		
Total	21	102.9311			

Table A3.2. Analysis of variance with target language being tested as the independent variable

Source	df	SS	MS	F	p
Between	2	33.7541	16.8757	4.63	0.0229
Within	19	69.1797	3.6410		
Total	21	102.9311			

Table A3.3. Analysis of variance with type of task as the independent variable

Source	df	SS	MS	F	p
Between	2	12.2805	6.1402	1.24	0.2961
Within	67	331.9357	4.954		
Total	69	344.216			

CHAPTER 3

Investigating the empirical link between task-based interaction and acquisition

A meta-analysis

Casey M. Keck, Gina Iberri-Shea,
Nicole Tracy-Ventura, and Safary Wa-Mbaleka
Northern Arizona University

Despite the seemingly rich context that task-based interaction provides for acquisition and the large amounts of research fueled by the Interaction Hypothesis (Long 1996), oft-cited findings to date appear to be conflicting. While some studies (e.g., Ellis, Tanaka & Yamazaki 1995; Mackey 1999) demonstrate that task-based interaction can facilitate acquisition of specific linguistic features, others (e.g., Loschky 1994) support no such relationship. This has prompted a variety of SLA researchers to question whether interaction can be empirically linked to acquisition. Over the past decade, however, and perhaps motivated by this criticism, the study of direct links between interaction and acquisition has gained momentum. The present meta-analysis was undertaken to synthesize the findings of all experimental, task-based interaction studies published between 1980 and 2003 which aimed to investigate the link between interaction and the acquisition of specific grammatical and lexical features. Results from 14 unique sample studies that satisfied stringent inclusion and exclusion criteria show that experimental groups substantially outperformed control and comparison groups in both grammar and lexis on immediate and delayed posttests. In addition, consistent with Loschky and Bley-Vroman's (1993) proposal, tasks in which use of the target feature was essential yielded larger effects over time than tasks in which use of the target form was useful, but not required. Initial support was also found for Swain's (1985, 2000) arguments that opportunities for pushed output play a crucial role in the acquisition process. Drawing upon these findings, and the synthesis of study design features, we propose specific recommendations for future interaction research.

Introduction

Since Long first proposed his Interaction Hypothesis in 1980, much research in second language acquisition (SLA) has investigated the role that interaction plays in the development of learners' interlanguage systems. Early descriptive accounts of native speaker and non-native speaker (NS-NNS) conversations suggested that interaction could provide learners with important opportunities (a) to negotiate meaning, thus making input comprehensible (Doughty & Pica 1986; Gass & Varonis 1985; Long 1983; Pica 1988; Pica & Doughty 1985), (b) to notice gaps between their interlanguage and the target language (Schmidt 1990), and (c) to modify their output so that they can be understood (Pica, Holliday, Lewis, & Morgenthaler 1989; Swain 1985). Two oft-cited studies (Gass & Varonis 1994; Pica, Young, & Doughty 1987) tested the first of these hypotheses – that interaction could facilitate second language (L2) comprehension – by comparing interactionally modified input (i.e., input plus opportunities for learners to ask questions and negotiate meaning) with pre-modified input (i.e., simplified input without opportunities for interaction). Both studies found that learners comprehended input better when they had opportunities to negotiate meaning with their interlocutors. Based on the assumption that comprehensible input was necessary (though perhaps not sufficient) for L2 learning (Krashen 1985; Long 1983), these findings suggested that there was at least an "indirect causal relationship" between interaction and acquisition (Long 1996:449).

Findings suggesting that conversational interaction could provide rich contexts for L2 acquisition prompted many to advocate the use of communication tasks in L2 language classrooms, and many empirical studies of interaction and L2 acquisition ensued (see, e.g., Crookes & Gass's edited volumes 1993a and 1993b). Drawing upon previous conceptions of task in the L2 literature (e.g., Nunan 1989), Pica et al. (1993) defined communication tasks as activities which engage two or more learners in work toward a particular goal (i.e., the learners carry out the task, rather than the teacher), and which "promote teachers' objectives for their students' efficient language learning and provide researchers with insight into the learning process" (p. 12). Pica et al.'s typology of communication task types (e.g., jigsaw, information gap) highlighted a number of important task design features that can impact the extent to which a communication task promotes L2 comprehension, L2 production, feedback on production, and modified output in response to feedback. These task design features involve the nature of the interactant relationship (two-way or one-way information flow), the interaction requirement (whether interaction is required or not), goal orientation (whether the task is convergent or not), and the number of outcome options (one or more) (see Pica et al. 1993: 18–27; for a more recent discussion, see Pica 2005).

Also focusing on communication tasks, Loschky and Bley-Vroman (1993) emphasized the importance of two additional task design features: (a) the extent to which the task requires accurate comprehension and/or production of particular linguistic features, and (b) whether the task involves planned feedback in response to learners' target feature accuracy. Loschky and Bley-Vroman argued that tasks designed so that learners must attend to the target feature in order to complete the task successfully (i.e., the target feature is task-essential) are more effective in promoting acquisition, as are tasks in which feedback on target feature accuracy is provided.

Following Pica et al. (1993) and Loschky and Bley-Vroman's (1993) recommendations regarding the use and design of communication tasks, a number of experimental studies over the past decade have investigated whether task-based interaction can be directly, rather than just indirectly, linked to L2 learners' acquisition of specific lexical and grammatical features. The earliest of these studies, Loschky (1994), investigated the impact of negotiated input (unmodified input with opportunities to interact and negotiate meaning) on not only comprehension, but also the acquisition of lexical and grammatical features. While Loschky (1994) found that negotiated input resulted in superior comprehension, this task-based interaction did not result in superior performance on acquisition measures. Rather, all three groups (unmodified input with interaction, premodified input with no interaction, unmodified input with no interaction) demonstrated similar learning gains. Loschky concluded that other task-design features (e.g., task essentialness), rather than the absence or presence of interaction alone, might have played a more central role in promoting the L2 acquisition of target features.

For many, this study called into question whether task-based interaction could directly promote L2 acquisition. Despite the subsequent publication of Ellis, Tanaka, and Yamazaki's (1995) studies, in which learners participating in negotiated input showed greater gains in vocabulary acquisition than learners exposed to premodified input, a number of researchers expressed doubt as to whether an empirical link between interaction and L2 acquisition could be established (e.g., Alcon 1998; Gass 1997; Long 1996; Mitchell & Myles 1998; Skehan 1996). In *Input, Interaction, and the Second Language Learner*, Gass (1997) wrote, "Many studies in the SLA literature have been influenced in their description of what occurs in negotiation routines. Few, however, have established a link between actual negotiation and subsequent learning, opera-

tionally defined as change in linguistic knowledge" (p. 126). Even as recently
as 2002, researchers (see de la Fuente 2002; see also Skehan & Foster 2001;
Tarone 2000) have pointed to the lack of clear evidence demonstrating the
interaction-acquisition link.

And yet, since Loschky (1994) and Ellis et al. (1995), a number of experimental studies have examined the impact of task-based interaction on
L2 learners' acquisition of specific lexical and grammatical features. These
studies investigate whether task-based interaction is more effective in promoting acquisition of particular linguistic features than tasks which do not
provide opportunities for interaction (de la Fuente 2002; Garcia & Asención
2001; He & Ellis 1999; Inagaki & Long 1999; Long, Inagaki, & Ortega 1998;
Mackey 1999). Some have also explored the extent to which features of task
design impact the effectiveness of interaction tasks, while others have begun
to pay attention to the role of pushed output in promoting the acquisition
of linguistic features (de la Fuente 2002; Mackey 1999; He & Ellis 1999).[1]
These experimental, task-based interaction studies have involved a variety of
learner populations (e.g., L1s of Japanese, English, Korean, Spanish), educational settings (e.g., secondary, university, adult education), and target languages (e.g., ESL, EFL, Spanish as a Foreign Language, Japanese as a Foreign
Language); and they have employed a range of task types (e.g., jigsaw, information gap, narrative), task design features (e.g., types of feedback), and
target structures. Taken together, these studies not only address the broad
question of whether interaction promotes L2 acquisition, but also have the
potential to deepen our understanding of the ways in which various features
of task design impact the magnitude and duration of task-based interaction
effects.

Because the link between task-based interaction and acquisition has cap-
tured the attention of SLA researchers for over two decades, we feel that
the accumulating research in this domain warrants a comprehensive synthesis of study findings. The present study employs the methodologies of research synthesis and meta-analysis to summarize and compare experimental, task-based interaction research methods and results. Research synthesis,
through the systematic description of research practices within a domain, allows for the quantitative synthesis of primary research findings by standard-
izing the results across studies and comparing effect sizes (Light & Pillemer
1984; Lipsey & Wilson 2001; Norris & Ortega 2000). Meta-analysis, then, allows us to identify the various approaches that experimental task-based interaction studies have taken in investigating the interaction-acquisition link.
The rationale for using this type of methodology is that it provides a replica-

ble, statistically sound summary of research findings (Norris & Ortega 2000). What is more, by synthesizing the available experimental research in the field,[2] meta-analysis allows us to investigate broader research questions than those of the original studies (Miller & Pollock 1994). For example, while individual studies may not isolate particular task design features as independent variables (e.g., task-essentialness of target structures), meta-analysis allows us to investigate the impact of such task features on task effectiveness through the systematic coding of these features and comparisons of the effects they produce.

In this chapter, we synthesize the primary research investigating the impact of task-based interaction on the acquisition of grammatical and lexical L2 features. The research domain was defined as all experimental or quasi-experimental task-based interaction studies published since Long's (1980) interaction hypothesis, until 2003, the time this meta-analysis was conducted. We focus our analysis on the following research questions:

1. Compared to tasks with little or no interaction, how effective is task-based interaction in promoting the acquisition of grammatical and lexical features?
2. Is the effectiveness of interaction tasks related to whether the target feature is grammatical or lexical?[3]
3. Are certain task types (e.g., information gap) more effective than others in promoting acquisition?
4. How long does the effect of task-based interaction last?
5. To what extent do the following task design features impact the extent to which interaction tasks promote acquisition: (a) the degree of task-essentialness of target features and (b) opportunities for pushed output?

To investigate the above research questions, we categorized studies according to target feature, task type, and task design features. For each of these variables, average effect sizes and confidence intervals were calculated so that the impact of task features on interaction task effectiveness could be assessed. The overall effects of task-based interaction on acquisition – and the duration of these effects – were also evaluated.

Method

The literature search

In order to fully identify the population of research studies for the current meta-analysis, we performed an exhaustive search of the literature. We searched ERIC (EBSCO), Linguistic and Language Behavior Abstracts, Psych-Info, and Academic Search Premier databases for review articles and empirical studies on interaction since 1980. Search terms included combinations of the following: (a) interaction, (b) negotiation, (c) feedback, (d) communicative, (e) input, (f) output, (g) intake, (h) uptake, (i) review of the literature, (j) empirical, (k) results, and (l) second language acquisition (and learning).[4]

In addition, we conducted both manual and electronic searches of nine journals in the field (*Applied Linguistics, Applied Psycholinguistics, Canadian Modern Language Review, Language Learning, Language Teaching Research, Modern Language Journal, Second Language Research, Studies in Second Language Acquisition,* and *TESOL Quarterly*) and reviewed textbooks in second language acquisition (Ellis 1994: 243–291; Larsen-Freeman & Long 1991: 114–152; 266–286; Mitchell & Myles 1998: 122–143). Once review articles and empirical studies were identified, the references of these sources were searched for additional studies.

Most meta-analysts (e.g., Rosenthal 1994) argue that, in addition to collecting published studies, reviewers should also make efforts to search the so-called "fugitive literature," that is, unpublished studies such as conference presentations and dissertations. Ignoring such literature runs the risk of publication bias, a well-documented phenomenon in most research fields. Namely, a much greater proportion of studies reporting statistically significant results are accepted for publication than studies reporting non-significant findings. As a result, the population of published studies represents a biased view of the research domain. Including fugitive literature in the meta-analysis can help to address this problem.

The current meta-analysis does not, however, include unpublished studies. There are two main reasons for this. First, although a number of reviews of interaction research (e.g. Ellis 1999: 3–31; Gass 1997; Gass, Mackey, & Pica 1998; Long 1996; Pica 1994) have been conducted, these have typically taken the form of either a narrative or vote-counting review of the literature. Focusing our meta-analysis on published studies allows readers to compare our empirical findings to these narrative research syntheses also based on published studies. Furthermore, though some narrative reviews (e.g., Alcon 1998; Gass

1997; Long 1996) pointed to the scarcity of direct research on the interaction-acquisition link, we feel that enough primary studies in this domain have now accumulated in the published research forum to warrant a systematic synthesis of their findings. Second, because unpublished studies are difficult to locate, we felt it would be almost impossible to reliably retrieve the entire population of unpublished interaction studies. While Dissertation Abstracts International indexes a number of unpublished dissertations, and published studies occasionally include unpublished manuscripts in their references, using these resources alone would not identify the entire body (or even most) of the fugitive literature on the topic. Locating all eligible studies would require contacting researchers and graduate students and asking for unpublished manuscripts. To avoid collecting an idiosyncratic and biased sample of fugitive literature, we decided to focus our analysis on published studies.

Inclusion/exclusion criteria

Over 100 studies concerned with the link between interaction and acquisition were identified through our literature search. These studies were then reviewed to determine whether they were relevant to our research questions. Studies included in the meta-analysis met the following criteria. (These studies are marked with an asterisk in the reference list.)

1. The study was published between 1980 and 2003. This time frame was chosen because we believed that it encompassed the relevant and comparable research on interaction following Long's dissertation in 1980, up to the time the meta-analysis was conducted. Studies published after 2003 could not be included (e.g., Gass & Alvarez Torres 2005; McDonough 2004).
2. The study measured the acquisition of a second or foreign language by adolescents or adults (age 13 and over). Because it is unclear whether age affects task-based interaction processes, we decided to avoid introducing age as another variable in the analysis by limiting the age of participants to post-pubertal (adolescent or adult) L2 learners.
3. The study used communication tasks which were (a) used as the treatment in the study or (b) used to create contexts for application of the treatment (e.g., recasts), as in many studies of feedback (e.g., Inagaki & Long 1999; Han 2002) and pushed output (e.g., He & Ellis 1999). (See Footnote 1.)
4. The tasks used in the study were face-to-face, dyadic or group, oral communication tasks.

5. The task and/or treatment was designed to foster the acquisition of specific grammatical and/or lexical features.
6. The study was experimental or quasi-experimental in design and either (a) measured gains made by one group after the treatment using a pre-post-test design, or (b) compared gains made by treatment groups with control or comparison groups.
7. The study adequately described the tasks employed in the study, so that these could be coded for task characteristics.
8. The dependent variable(s) (post-tests) measured the acquisition of specific grammatical or lexical structures targeted by the treatment.

Typically, studies were excluded from the analysis for one of more of the following reasons:

1. Studies used descriptive or correlational designs (e.g., Pica 1988; Oliver 2002; Shehadeh 2001).
2. In addition to the interaction treatment, participants received treatments that did not meet the inclusion criterion number 2 above, such as written feedback on use of the target structure (e.g., Ayoun 2001; Doughty & Varela 1998).
3. Interaction tasks were computer-based (e.g., Izumi 2002; Linnell 1995). As with the variable of age, we did not wish to introduce an additional variable of computer-mediated versus face-to-face interaction.
4. Specific grammatical or lexical forms were not targeted in the interaction treatment, and/or dependent variables did not measure the acquisition of specific grammatical or lexical forms. This criterion resulted in the exclusion, for example, of studies that investigated the impact of interaction on comprehension only (e.g., Pica, Young, & Doughty 1987; Polio & Gass 1998), and studies that compared interaction and non-interaction groups by describing learners' performance on tasks, such as their incorporation of feedback in subsequent output (e.g. Gass & Varonis 1994; Philp 2003).

Studies were coded for methodological variables so that (a) the range of research practices in the domain could be described, and (b) the effect of research methodology on study outcomes could be investigated. Thirteen study reports, from the over 100 studies initially identified, met all the inclusion and exclusion criteria and were included in the meta-analysis. These 13 study reports contained 14 unique study samples[5] which contributed effect sizes to the meta-analysis. These studies, and the task codings for each treatment group, are presented in the Appendix.

Coding procedures and reliability

After retrieving and selecting the studies that met our inclusion criteria, we proceeded to code and classify the 14 unique sample studies according to different features. Table 1 summarizes the substantive and methodological features coded for the research synthesis and meta-analysis. Definitions for both substantive features (which were to be examined as independent variables in our meta-analysis) and methodological features (e.g., sample size) were established in advance of coding. Low-inference variables (e.g., sample size, duration of treatment) were coded independently by at least two of the four researchers, and conflicts were resolved through discussion. One substantive feature – degree of task-essentialness of the target feature (see following sections) – was considered a high inference variable. In this case, a number of steps were taken to enhance reliability of coding (these are reported in detail below).

Substantive features

For the purpose of the current study, the coding of substantive features focused on those independent variables that were investigated in the primary studies. Because operationalization and/or naming of variables differed considerably across studies, we created two overarching generic categories, and several levels

Table 1. Substantive and methodological features coded

Substantive features	Methodological features
Task type	Research design and reporting
Jigsaw	Group assignment
Information gap	Proficiency assessment
Problem-solving	Dependent measures
Decision-making	
Information-exchange	Learner characteristics
	L1
Degree of task-essentialness	Proficiency level
Task-essential	
Task-useful	Treatment setting
Task-natural	Target language
	Educational context
Opportunity for pushed output	
–Pushed output	Statistical Analyses
+Pushed output	Procedures used
	Statistics reported

within each: (a) task types (e.g., jigsaw, information gap), and (b) task design features (degree of task-essentialness and opportunity for pushed output).

Task type. Tasks completed by treatment groups were classified using six task type categories. Table 2 provides a brief description of each task type, along with an example. The first five task type categories were operationalized using the criteria provided by Pica, Kanagy, and Falodun (1993). Tasks were coded as jigsaw tasks if (a) information flowed two ways (each participant held a piece of information needed by other group members), (b) all learners were required to participate in the interaction, and (c) all participants shared the same goal, with only one outcome possible. Tasks were considered information gap if they met the jigsaw criteria (b) through (c), but information flowed only one way. Tasks coded as problem-solving differed from jigsaw and information gap in that all participants had access to the same information. Thus, while participants shared a common goal and worked toward one outcome, all participants were not required to interact in order to complete the task successfully. Decision-making tasks shared all but one of the characteristics of problem-solving tasks: in decision-making tasks, multiple outcomes were

Table 2. Task type descriptions and examples[a]

Task type	Info exchange	Interaction	Goal orientation	Outcome options	Example
Jigsaw	2 way	Required	Convergent	1	Spot the difference (Iwashita 2003)
Information gap	1 way	Required	Convergent	1	Object placement (e.g., He & Ellis 1999; Leeman 2003)
Problem-solving	2 way	Not required	Convergent	1	Sharing notes to prepare for an exam (Garcia & Asención 2001)
Decision-making	2 way	Not required	Convergent	1+	Not used by studies in present meta-analysis; see Pica & Doughty 1985 for an example
Opinion exchange	2 way	Not required	Divergent	1+	Discussing a topic of group's choice (Iwashita 2003)
Narrative	2 way	Required	Divergent	1+	Telling a story based on a picture (Han 2002; Takashima & Ellis 1999)

[a] adapted from Pica et al. (1993:19)

possible. If participants did *not* share a common goal, the task was coded as opinion-exchange. In opinion-exchange tasks, interaction among all participants was not required; it was possible for group members to either dominate the conversation or refrain from participation.

The sixth task type category listed in Table 2, narrative, is not discussed by Pica et al. (1993), but was the chosen task of 2 studies included in the meta-analysis. Tasks were coded as narrative if participants interacted by telling a story (based on a picture), and received feedback in the form of recasts or requests for clarification. All group members participated (each tells a story), but participants did not work towards a common goal.

Degree of task essentialness. In coding for task-essentialness, we considered the extent to which the use of the target feature(s) was required by the design of the task. Our definitions, which were adapted from Loschky and Bley-Vroman (1993), are shown in Table 3. The coding of degree of task-essentialness was based on the information about target feature and task design reported by

Table 3. Features of task-essential, task-useful, and task-natural tasks[a]

Definition	Features of task
Task-essential: Participants must comprehend or produce the target structure accurately in order to complete the task successfully	– The task is convergent – groups/dyads work together to complete a common goal. – The task is designed to create obligatory contexts for the target feature. – A participant's incorrect use/avoidance of the target feature, or inability to understand the target feature when used by others, makes it impossible for the group to achieve the shared goal.
Task-useful: Participants do not need to comprehend or produce the target feature accurately in order to complete the task successfully, but task completion is facilitated by correct use of target feature.	– The task may be convergent or divergent. – The task is designed to create obligatory contexts for the target feature. – The task can be completed despite incorrect use or avoidance of the target feature because (a) incorrect use/avoidance does not impede communication or (b) the task can be completed in spite of communication breakdown because there is no shared goal.
Task-natural: Participants can easily complete the task without using the target feature.	– The task is not designed to create obligatory contexts for the target feature.

[a] developed based on Loschky and Bley-Vroman (1993)

primary researchers, rather than on actual participant performance. This was because knowledge of whether participants actually used (or needed) the target features during the task requires access to transcripts of participant interactions, or counts of features used by participants during the task, and this information was not available in most studies included in the meta-analysis. Thus, we considered both the particular target feature (e.g., morphological and syntactic functions), and the design of the task (e.g., how the task created contexts for comprehension and/or production of the target feature). If, for example, a task used in a study was designed so that the target features would be task-essential, the task itself was coded having the task design feature of task-essentialness.

To begin the coding process, two of the authors coded 3 study reports independently, following the coding definitions established at the onset of the study. We then discussed any disagreements and refined the original coding definitions. Following these revised definitions, we independently coded all 14 studies. An overall agreement ratio of .88 was reached (Cohen's kappa = .77) and any disagreements were resolved through discussion[6] .

Features of each task were used to guide the coding of task essential, task useful, and task natural variables. Tasks were considered to be *task-essential* if participants were required to comprehend or produce the target structure accurately in order to complete the task successfully. Tasks coded as task-essential were convergent, and were designed in such a way as to create obligatory contexts for the target feature. The design of task instructions and/or goals suggested to participants that, if they did not correctly use or comprehend the target features, they could not achieve their group's shared goal. For example, in the object placement tasks of He and Ellis (1999), participants were instructed to place various utensils on a picture of a kitchen. These kitchen utensils were the target features of the study; thus, participants needed to comprehend the meaning of the target words in order to select and place objects correctly.

Tasks were coded as *task-useful* if comprehending or producing the target structure was not required, but made the completion of the task much easier. Tasks coded as task-useful differed from task-essential tasks in one of two ways: (a) despite the task being convergent, groups could still achieve their shared goal because incorrect use or avoidance of the target feature would not impede communication; or (b) groups did not share a common goal (i.e., the task was divergent), and thus correct use or comprehension of the target feature was not essential to the successful completion of the task. An example of a convergent task that was coded as task-useful is Inagaki and Long's (1999) recast treatment for the target feature of adjective ordering in Japanese. In this task, the participant and NS interlocutor shared a common goal – the researcher was to locate an object identified by the participant. However, incorrect use of the target feature (e.g., a violation of the "size-shape-color-NP" word order), would not necessarily impede communication, as the researcher could still identify the object described. Han's (2002) narrative task was also coded as task-useful. In this case, however, there was no explicit, shared goal among group members. Group members did not work together, for example, to re-create the order of story events – no features of the task suggested that storytellers needed to use tense consistency in order to help their listeners understand their story. Listeners also did not need to comprehend the storyteller's use of tense in order to fulfill their role as passive listeners. Thus, while tense consistency could certainly aid in the telling and understanding of the narratives, it was not essential to the completion of Han's treatment task.

Tasks were considered to be *task-natural* if participants could easily complete the task using the target structure; that is, no efforts were made to create obligatory contexts for the target feature. No studies included in the meta-analysis designed task-natural treatments. Iwashita (2003) selected a task-natural design for her comparison group, which engaged in an opinion exchange on a topic of their choice. However, because this group served as the baseline comparison for interaction treatments, it could not be included in the analysis of main effects.

Opportunity for pushed output. Tasks were also classified as without opportunities for pushed output (–PO) or with opportunities for pushed output (+PO). Table 4 offers definitions and examples. Tasks coded as –PO typically involved negotiated input tasks. In these tasks, a NS interlocutor (e.g., researcher, teacher) acted as the information holder in a one-way task, providing oral instructions either to one participant or to a large group of participants. Participants were encouraged to interact with their interlocutors when they needed to negotiate meaning or clarify aspects of the input. While participants' *comprehension* of target forms may have been required, their attempted *production* of these forms was not. Though many participants likely attempted to negotiate meaning as instructions were being given, they could potentially avoid trying to produce target features by (a) negotiating meaning without them and/or (b) choosing to listen to other participants as they negotiated meaning with the NS interlocutor. A slightly different case was Garcia and Asención's (2001) problem-solving task, which was also coded as –PO. In this study, participants were asked to work with one another in small groups in or-

Table 4. Features of –pushed output and +pushed output tasks

Definition	Examples
–pushed output: Participants are *not* required to attempt production of target features during the inter-action	– Interactionally modified input treatments of Ellis, Tanaka, & Yamazaki (1995); He & Ellis (1999); and Loschky (1994) – Group interaction task of Garcia & Asención (2001)
+pushed output: Participants *are* required to attempt production of target features during the interaction	– Reciprocal information gap tasks used with de la Fuente's (2002) Negotiation of Input Plus Output (NIPO) group – Picture drawing, picture sequencing, and story completion tasks used in Mackey (1999)

der to compare notes taken during a dictation. Participants could, but were not required, to produce utterances using target forms.

In *+PO* tasks, participants *were* required to attempt production of target features in addition to questions they might ask in the negotiation of meaning. In most tasks coded as *+pushed output*, the participants had the opportunity to play the role of information-holder in jigsaw, information gap, or narrative tasks. For example, participants could provide their interlocutor with oral task directions (e.g., de la Fuente 2002), or tell a story to an audience of participants (Han 2002; Takashima & Ellis 1999). Task directions and narratives were designed to create contexts for *production* of the target feature. In the Interactor treatments of Mackey and colleagues (Mackey 1999; Mackey & Philp 1998), participants were not the holders of information, but were instructed to attempt the production of target question forms in order to elicit the information held by their interlocutors. In other words, attempted production of the target feature was not optional (as in the negotiated input information gap tasks) but a required element of the participant's task role.

Methodological features

Methodological features were coded in order to describe the range of features across studies and to analyze the extent to which primary researchers adequately reported this information. These methodological features included: (a) research design and reporting, (b) learner characteristics, (c) treatment setting, and (d) statistical analyses.

To describe the range of research designs within the study population, studies were coded for features of group assignment, proficiency assessment, and pre- and post- testing. Studies were classified into 5 assignment categories: *random-random* if participants were randomly selected and randomly assigned to different groups; *volunteer-random* if participants volunteered for the study but were randomly assigned to groups; *intact-random* if participants were part of an intact class that was randomly split into different groups; and *nonrandom* if both selection and assignment were non-random.

Following Thomas (1994), we used 4 categories to classify the type of proficiency assessment used in each of the studies. Studies were coded as *impressionistic judgment* if reported proficiency levels were based on the researcher's own subjective evaluation, and as *institutional status* if reported proficiency was based on participants' enrollment in a language class (e.g., participants labeled as beginner because they are enrolled in Spanish 101). If the researcher used locally developed and administered tests, the study was coded as *in-house assessment*. Studies making use of established proficiency assessments, such as the TOEFL, were coded as reporting *standardized test scores*. In addition to coding for measures of proficiency, we also coded the following features of the dependent measures: the number of pre- and post-tests administered, the time delay of each post-test, reported reliability of dependent measures, and dependent measure types. To code for type of dependent measure, we adopted Norris and Ortega's (2000: 439–441) classification of outcome measures: metalinguistic judgment, selected response, constrained constructed response, and free constructed response.

In order to document the variety of learner characteristics and treatment settings found across studies, the following study features were coded: (a) L1 of participants, (b) reported proficiency level of participants, (c) age of participants, (d) target language of study, and (e) educational context (e.g., university). To describe the statistical analyses used to interpret and compare group gains, studies were coded for choice of statistical procedure (e.g. ANOVA, MANOVA), as well as for their reporting of the following: a priori alpha, exact *p*, multiple *p*, inferential statistics table, strength of association, standard error (SE), confidence intervals, and effect size.

The quantitative meta-analysis

In order to synthesize the findings of studies investigating task-based interaction and second language acquisition, we carried out a quantitative meta-analysis of the identified study population. In estimating the effect sizes, a number of calculations were adopted depending on the statistics that were reported in each study. To compare the effect of treatment against control/comparison groups, as well as group change between pretests and posttest, we used Cohen's d (adopted from Norris & Ortega 2000:442). These calculations were possible only if a study reported means and standard deviations. One study (Inagaki & Long 1999) did not report descriptive statistics but reported raw scores, and we calculated means and standard deviations based on the individual scores given. If a study did not report descriptive statistics or individual raw scores, but did report a t or F value, we adopted the following equations (adopted from Lipsey & Wilson 2001:198):

$$Es_{sm} = t\sqrt{\frac{n_1 + n_2}{n_1 n_2}}$$

where t is the value of t-test and n the sample sizes for each group, and

$$Es_{sm} = \sqrt{\frac{F(n_1 + n_2)}{n_1 n_2}}$$

where F-ratio (F) comes from a one-way ANOVA and the samples sizes (n) for each group.

Finally, for one study (Mackey 1999) that reported proportions only (i.e., the percentage of group members that experienced gains), we adopted a transformation procedure described by Lipsey and Wilson (2001:188). In order to compare proportions to interval data, the proportions must be transformed into probit, logit, or arcsine values. Lipsey and Wilson (2001) recommend using arcsine transformations because these produce the most conservative estimate of effect size. An arcsine table, which provides arcsine values for each corresponding proportion, is found in Lipsey and Wilson (2001:204, Table B14). Using this table, effect sizes for proportional data were calculated using the following equation:

$$E_S = \arcsin e_{treatment} - \arcsin e_{control}$$

In summary, we calculated effect sizes for all studies that reported (a) samples sizes and means and standard deviations, (b) raw scores on posttests for all study participants, (c) t or F values (with df numerator equal to 1), or (d) percentage of participants achieving a pre- to post-test gain.

Defining contrasts for effect size calculations. Norris and Ortega (2000) argue that, from the perspective of meta-analysis, "the ideal primary research design is one in which a single experimental condition is contrasted with a single control condition on a single dependent variable" (p. 445). Data from such a design would make the calculations of effect sizes easy, and they would precisely demonstrate the effect of a treatment. In the task-based interaction research domain, however, this is not always the case. Most research designs did not use a true control group, but instead compared treatment groups to a comparison group which participated in some type of interaction task. Many studies did not report the pretest scores needed to calculate the pre- to post-test gain effect sizes. Finally, multiple interaction treatments were often included in the same study. To address these difficulties, contrasts for effect sizes calculations were defined in the following manner:

1. For studies with a true control, effect sizes were calculated by comparing each treatment group with the control group.
2. For studies using a comparison group, effect sizes were calculated by comparing each treatment group with the comparison group.
3. If studies had neither a control or comparison group, but post-test scores were reported for multiple treatment groups, a baseline (least interactive) group was chosen. All other treatment groups were compared against the baseline group.

Combining and comparing effect sizes. We calculated effect sizes for each separate treatment group on immediate and delayed post-tests, such that it was possible for one study to yield multiple effect sizes. For studies that compared multiple independent variables (i.e., several interaction treatments), separate effect sizes were calculated for each treatment type. If studies investigated the acquisition of multiple grammatical features, separate effect sizes were calculated for each feature.

It should be noted that some meta-analysts recommend combining within-study effect sizes in order to extract one average effect size from each study (Light & Pillemer 1984) to avoid the problem of non-independence of effect size values (see discussion by Lipsey & Wilson 2001:98–104). However, we feel our strategy was preferable because it allowed us to collect information about the way in which task characteristics and type of linguistic feature impact the effect of interaction treatment. First, one important aim of our meta-analysis was to investigate whether different task types yield different effects on acquisition. This becomes impossible when the effects of different interaction treatment types are averaged. Second, as Norris and Ortega (2000) argue, it is possible that type of structure also greatly impacts the degree of treatment effectiveness. Third, non-independence of values is less of a concern for meta-analyses like ours, in which only descriptive statistics, but no inferential tests, are employed to investigate accumulated effects.

In sum, we calculated the following effect sizes:

(a) Overall average effect size for interaction treatment.
(b) Average effect size for target feature (i.e., grammar vs. lexis)
(c) Average effect size for each task type: jigsaw, information gap, problem-solving, decision-making, opinion sharing, and narrative.
(d) Average effect size for each task design feature: (1) degree of task-essentialness and (2) opportunity for pushed output.
(e) Average pre to post gain for treatment and control/comparison/baseline groups.
(f) Average effect size for treatment on delayed post-tests.

We also calculated 95% confidence intervals in order to evaluate the trustworthiness of mean effect sizes and differences among groups. Confidence intervals help us to assess the possible range of values for a given effect of treatment. (See Lipsey & Wilson 2001; Norris & Ortega 2000; Rosenthal 1995, for more discussion of the use of confidence intervals in meta-analysis.)

Results

The research synthesis

This section synthesizes and compares several study features in order to provide a fuller picture of methodological and reporting features of the task-based interaction research domain.

Research publication. Fourteen experimental studies on task-based interaction published between 1980 and 2003 met the criteria for inclusion in the current meta-analysis. As shown in Figure 1, the first of these studies was published in 1994. The number of experimental studies investigating the interaction-acquisition link increased between 1994 and 1999, but dropped slightly since then, to 2003. Seventy-nine percent of the studies collected in this synthesis appeared in 5 refereed journals: *Canadian Modern Language Review, Language Learning, Modern Language Journal, Studies in Second Language Acquisition,* and *TESOL Quarterly.* The remaining 21% were published as book chapters in edited collections.

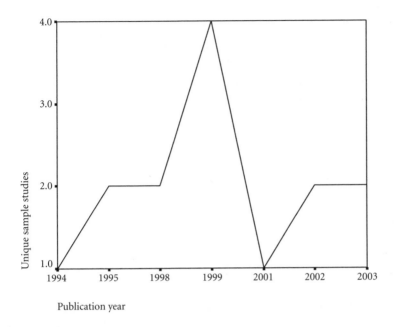

Figure 1. Publication frequency of empirical research on L2 task-based interaction.

Research setting. The studies included in the current synthesis reported a variety of learner characteristics, educational settings, and task types. Fifteen different L1s were reported; 12 of the 14 studies reported the exact number of participants from each language background. The target language contexts included English as a Second Language (29%), English as a Foreign Language (21%), Spanish as a Foreign Language (29%), and Japanese as a Foreign Language (21%). The majority of studies took place in university contexts (71%); 14% took place in high school settings, and 14% in adult school settings other than university. Table 5 summarizes these study features.

Ages of participants ranged from 15 to 44; however, it should be noted that 57% of the studies did not report an age range or mean age for their sample. Reported proficiency levels were beginner (36%) and intermediate (29%). Two studies used both beginner and intermediate learners, and 3 studies did not report any proficiency level. Proficiency levels were determined largely by institutional status (64%), with only 5 studies using standardized assessments (e.g., the TOEFL) or in-house proficiency measures. Two among these 5 considered developmental readiness in their designs as well (Mackey 1999; Mackey & Philp 1998). This pattern is consistent with the preference found by Thomas (1994) for institutional proficiency assessment among empirical studies conducted

Table 5. Learner characteristics in research domain

L2	n^a	L1	n	Reported Proficiency	n	Proficiency Assessment	n	Setting	n
English SL	4	Japanese	6	Beginner	5	Institutional status	9	University	10
English FL	3	English	5	Intermediate	4	In-house assessment	3	High School	2
Spanish FL	4	Chinese	5	Multiple	2	Standardized test	2	Other	2
Japanese FL	3	Korean	4	Not reported	3				
		Spanish	3						
		Czech	2						
		Thai	2						
		French	2						
		Swiss-German	2						
		Indonesian	2						
		Other[b]	5						

[a] number of unique sample studies reporting of $N = 14$
[b] The following L1s were reported in one study each: Russian, Portuguese, Malay, Tagalog, Arabic.

between 1988 and 1992 and again between 2000 and 2004 (see Thomas, this volume). Though this is slightly preferable to impressionistic assessment, as Thomas points out, what "beginner" means can differ greatly across programs. A consistent criterion for interpretation of proficiency levels is still lacking.

Research design. There was a high degree of variety in the designs employed by studies in the research domain. The majority of studies reported using either intact classes with random assignment to treatment groups (35%), or nonrandom assignment (35%). A few of the studies (29%) reported using volunteers and random assignment; none of the studies described here utilized random sampling. In several of the studies, researchers reported to have issued a pretest, but only 57% reported a description of the test and any results. Those studies that did describe a pretest used free (50%) or constrained constructed response (36%) to measure knowledge of the target feature. Sample sizes in the domain ranged from 8 to 127 ($M = 48.93$). Number of treatment groups ranged from 2 to 5, and treatment group sample size ranged from 4 to 42 ($M = 15.44$). Most of the studies used a comparison group (64%), and only 4 studies provided a true control (Mackey 1999; Mackey & Philp 1998; and the two studies in Long, Inagaki, & Ortega 1998).

Interaction treatment task types included jigsaw (9%), information gap (81%), problem-solving (3%), and narrative (6%). Decision-making and opinion-exchange tasks were not used for treatment groups. Treatment was delivered in one or several task sessions that ranged each from 20 minutes to

Table 6. Study characteristics in research domain

Characteristic	Mean	SD	Range	n^a
Sample size	48.93	29.72	8–127	14
Treatment group sample size	14.44	11.56	4–42	14
Length of treatment session (hrs)	.78	.20	.33–1.00	12 (2 nr)
Number of treatments	2.14	1.91	1–8	14
Timing of immediate post-test	1.86	2.57	0–7	14
Timing of delayed post-test 1 (days)	15.80	11.11	7–34	10
Timing of delayed post-test 2 (days)	39.29	16.57	21–60	7

[a] number of unique sample studies reporting of N = 14; nr = not reported

one hour in length ($M = .78$ hours). Frequency of treatment ranged from 1 to 8 treatment sessions ($M = 2$), with over half of the studies (57%) consisting of only 1 treatment session. Two of the studies failed to report the length of treatment. All of the studies reported an immediate post-test, which was administered 0–7 days after treatment. Six of the studies conducted a delayed post-test of 7–29 days after treatment, and 5 studies conducted a delayed post-test 30–60 days after treatment. Unfortunately, none of the research reports included any measure of reliability for their dependent variables. Many of the authors cited previous research using similar measures as support for their choices, but there were no indications as to whether reliability had ever been established. Table 6 displays design characteristics of the study population.

Statistical Analysis. The statistics and data reported in the domain of studies were inconsistent, making it difficult to objectively decipher many of the original findings. As a result, there was no way of verifying many of the interpretations made in the original studies. Thirteen of the 14 studies used inferential statistics to interpret their results. Studies used ANOVA (52%), *t*-tests (21%), chi square (14%), ANCOVA (7%) and MANOVA (7%) to conduct comparisons among groups. Interestingly, Lazaraton (2000) also found that ANOVA is by far the preferred inferential test of choice in applied linguistics. All of the studies reported significance, though 62% of the studies failed to set an a priori acceptable probability level, and less than half of the studies (43%) reported an exact *p* value. In fact, of the 13 studies using inferential statistics, 50% reported significant findings at multiple probability levels. Despite the problems apparent in these procedures, results were interpreted primarily through statistical significance. No studies provided confidence intervals or standard error of the mean, nor did any studies report effect sizes.

Quantitative meta-analysis

The quantitative meta-analysis combined effect sizes from 14 unique sample studies to determine an average effect of task-based interaction treatment. Effect sizes were also combined in order to: (a) evaluate the impact of target feature type (lexis vs. grammar) on treatment effectiveness; (b) compare the relative effectiveness of different task types and task design features; and (c) investigate the extent to which the effects of interaction treatments were sustained over time. Tables 7 through 9 summarize the meta-analytic findings by displaying mean effect sizes, confidence intervals, and the number of study reports and study effect sizes contributing to each effect size calculation. The Appendix displays the task types and task design features used by each unique sample study, along with the effect sizes contributed by each treatment group.

Table 7. Interaction treatment effect sizes

IV	n^a	k^b	Mean d	SD d	95% CI lower	95% CI upper
All interaction treatments (immediate post)	12	24	.92	.68	.68	1.16
Target Feature						
Grammar	7	16	.94	.67	.65	1.23
Lexis	5	8	.90	.75	.40	1.40
Task types (immediate post)						
Jigsaw	1	3	.78	.10	.15	1.41
Information gap	8	18	.91	.67	.53	1.29
Problem-solving	1	1	–	–	–	–
Narrative	2	2	1.60	1.27	–4.08	7.28
Task-essentialness (immediate posttest)						
Task-essentialness	6	9	.83	.74	.37	1.29
Task-utility	6	15	.98	.66	.68	1.28
Task-essentialness (delayed posttest)						
Task-essential	3	6	1.66	.71	1.08	2.24
Task-utility	3	9	.76	.38	.52	1.00
Opportunity for pushed output (immediate posttest)						
–pushed output	5	7	.61	.69	.10	1.12
+pushed output	7	17	1.05	.66	.77	1.33
Opportunity for pushed output (delayed posttest)						
–pushed output	3	4	1.08	1.10	–.22	2.38
+pushed output	5	11	1.14	.55	.84	1.44

[a] number of unique sample studies contributing to effect sizes
[b] number of interaction treatments

Overall effectiveness of task-based interaction. The average effect size computed across all treatment groups ($d = .92$) shows that treatment groups differed substantially from control/comparison groups on immediate post-tests, although there was substantial variation across treatments in terms of magnitude of effects ($SD = .68$). Cohen (1988) suggests that effect sizes of .80 or higher should be considered large effects; thus, it can be said that groups receiving interaction treatment far outperformed groups exposed to control/comparison conditions. It is important to point out, however, that only 8% of the contrasts contributing to this effect size involved a true control group. Seventy-eight percent of the contrasts were based on differences between treatment and comparison groups, and in one comparison, a baseline group was chosen. Comparison groups and baseline groups did participate in communication tasks. For example, Iwashita's (2003) comparison group participated in an opinion sharing task; He and Ellis's (1999) baseline group participated in a narrative task, but received no focused feedback on the accuracy of their target form use. Treatment groups, then, represent groups exposed to what researchers felt were ideal interaction conditions, while comparison/baseline groups received less than ideal interaction conditions (e.g., interaction with no focused feedback). The 95% confidence interval for this effect is fairly narrow (.24 standard deviation units). Thus, we can be relatively confident that the effect of interaction treatment ranges from .68 to 1.16 – a medium to large effect. This suggests that interaction treatment groups substantially outperform control/comparison groups on immediate post-test measures.

In addition to calculating the average main effects for different types of interaction treatments, the effectiveness of task-based interaction can also be evaluated by comparing the pre to post-test gains made by treatment groups to those made by control/comparison groups. For the small subset of studies ($n = 5$) that reported both pre- and post-test scores, effect sizes were calculated for pre to immediate post gains (see Table 8 and Figure 2). Treatment groups ($d = 1.17$) made much greater gains than control/comparison groups ($d = .66$) (though confidence intervals overlap). Still, the control/comparison

Table 8. Magnitude of change from pre-test to post-test

IV	n^a	k^b	Mean d	SD d	95% CI lower	95% CI upper
All interaction treatments	5	16	1.17	.87	.79	1.55
Control/comparison	5	8	.66	.55	.29	1.03

[a] number of unique studies contributing to effect sizes
[b] number of interaction treatments

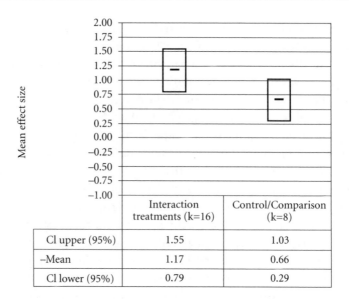

Figure 2. Magnitude of change from pre- to immediate post-test

gain is somewhat substantial (see Norris & Ortega 2000, for similar findings). This may be partially explained by the fact that 6 of the control/comparison groups participated in communication tasks. However, confidence intervals for control/comparison conditions include the small effect of .29. In contrast, the range of pre to post-test gains for treatment groups dips no lower than .79. Thus, we can be confident that task-based interaction results in substantial pre- to immediate post-test gains.

Effectiveness of interaction for lexis versus grammar. Treatments focusing on grammatical and lexical acquisition achieved similar main effects, .94 and .90 respectively. Interaction treatments proved to be effective for both types of features. Upper and lower CI limits suggest that task-based interaction results in medium to large effects for grammatical acquisition (.65 to 1.23). The confidence interval for lexical acquisition is much wider, ranging from .40 to 1.40 (see Figure 3), due to the low number of observations available. Thus, more studies investigating the impact of interaction on lexical acquisition are needed in order to make this effect more interpretable.

Task type. Mean effect sizes from each of the different task types ranged from 1.6 (narrative) to .78 (jigsaw). (No treatments used decision-making or

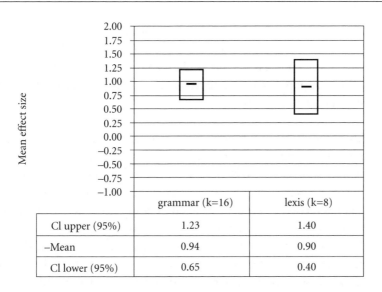

Figure 3. Mean effect sizes for studies investigating grammatical and lexical acquisition

opinion-sharing tasks, and only one treatment group used a problem-solving task. Thus, mean effect sizes for these task types could not be calculated.) The mean effect sizes for each task type must be interpreted with caution, how-

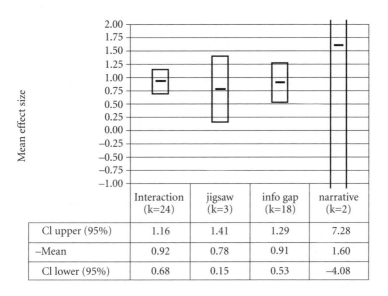

Figure 4. Average effect of interaction task types

ever, considering the small number of groups included in the analyses and the overlap of confidence intervals for each task type (see Figure 4). In addition, comparisons among these task types could not be made beyond the immediate post-test, because only one narrative group and no jigsaw groups were assessed using delayed post-test measures.

Durability of the effect of treatment. To investigate the durability of the effect of the interaction treatments over time, delayed post-tests were divided into two categories: short delay (8–29 days, $k = 15$) and long delay (30–60 days, $k = 6$), and the main effect of interaction treatment was calculated for both groups. Task-based interaction treatments resulted in large effects ($d = .92$) that were not only maintained but slightly grew through short delayed ($d = 1.12$) and long delayed post-tests ($d = 1.18$), as shown in Table 9 and depicted in Figure 5. However, whereas the confidence interval for mean effect size on short delayed posttests was relatively narrow (.31 standard deviation units), a wide confidence interval for the mean effect size on long delayed posttests (.83 standard deviation units) suggests that this last long-term effect (30–60 days after the interaction treatments took place) cannot be interpreted as trustworthy until more observations are available.

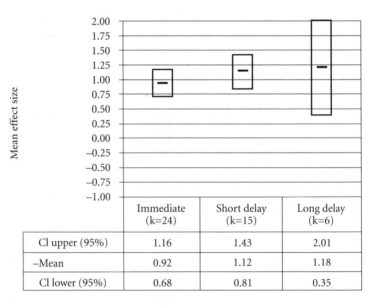

	Immediate (k=24)	Short delay (k=15)	Long delay (k=6)
Cl upper (95%)	1.16	1.43	2.01
–Mean	0.92	1.12	1.18
Cl lower (95%)	0.68	0.81	0.35

Figure 5. Mean effect of treatment for immediate, short delayed, and long delayed post-tests

Table 9. Mean effect for immediate, short delayed, and long delayed post-tests

IV	n^a	k^b	Mean d	SD d	95% CI lower	95% CI upper
Immediate post	12	24	.92	.68	.68	1.16
Short delay (8–29 days)	5	15	1.12	.69	.81	1.43
Long delay (30–60 days)	5	6	1.18	1.01	.35	2.01

Task essentialness and pushed output. Task design features (i.e., degree of task essentialness, opportunity for pushed output) were compared by calculating mean effect sizes of each design feature on immediate and short delayed posttests (see Table 7). Tasks in which use of the target feature was essential ($d = .83$) produced slightly smaller effects on immediate posttests than tasks in which use of the target form was useful, but not required ($d = .98$), though Figure 6 clearly shows that confidence intervals overlap. (No interaction treatments were designed as task-natural.) However, on short delayed posttests, the mean effect size for task-essential designs was much larger ($d = 1.66$) than task-useful designs ($d = .76$). The 95% confidence interval for task essentialness ($CI = 1.08 - 2.24$) shows that we can be fairly certain of its sustained effect on acquisition (see Figure 6). The narrower confidence interval for task utility (.24 standard deviation units) and the location of upper and lower limits suggest

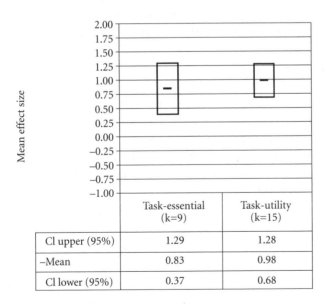

Figure 6. Mean effect sizes for task-essentialness and task-utility on immediate posttest

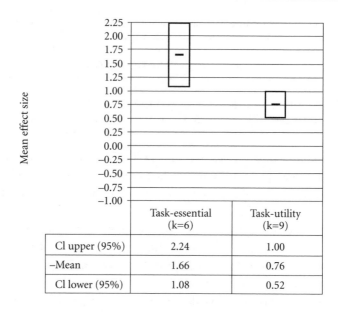

	Task-essential (k=6)	Task-utility (k=9)
Cl upper (95%)	2.24	1.00
–Mean	1.66	0.76
Cl lower (95%)	1.08	0.52

Figure 7. Mean effect sizes for task-essentialness and task-utility on delayed posttest

that the probable effect is consistently smaller, ranging from medium (0.52) to large (1.00). As Figure 7 shows, the confidence intervals around the mean effect sizes for task-essentialness and task-utility on delayed post-tests do not overlap. Thus, the observed difference in effects can be considered trustworthy (see Figure 7).

Tasks involving opportunities for pushed output (d = 1.05) produced larger effects than tasks without pushed output (d = .61) on immediate post-tests. As shown in Figure 8, the confidence interval for +PO tasks suggests these effects are robust (CI = .77–1.33). On the other hand, the effectiveness of –PO is less clear, as the confidence interval (.10–1.12) approaches zero. Differences between +PO and –PO treatments should, however, be interpreted with caution, as confidence intervals overlap and the number of observations available for –PO cases is small.

On short delayed posttests, the difference between +PO (d = 1.14) and –PO (d = 1.08) tasks was much smaller (only .06 standard deviation units), and confidence intervals, depicted in Figure 9, largely overlapped. The robust effects of +PO tasks still hold, however, with a confidence interval range of .84 to 1.44. The wide confidence interval for –PO (–.22 – 2.38) can be explained by the small number of treatment groups (k = 4) that contributed to the analysis, which makes the effect of –PO tasks on delayed post-tests difficult to interpret.

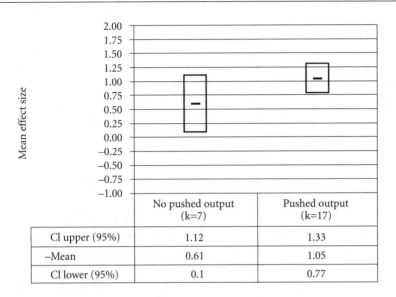

	No pushed output (k=7)	Pushed output (k=17)
Cl upper (95%)	1.12	1.33
–Mean	0.61	1.05
Cl lower (95%)	0.1	0.77

Figure 8. Mean effect sizes for –pushed output and +pushed output on the immediate posttest

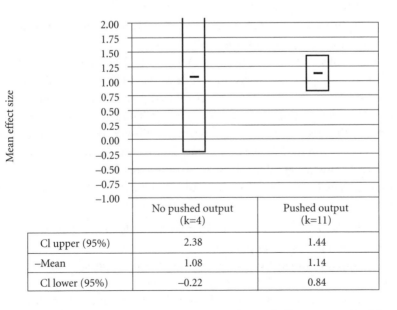

	No pushed output (k=4)	Pushed output (k=11)
Cl upper (95%)	2.38	1.44
–Mean	1.08	1.14
Cl lower (95%)	−0.22	0.84

Figure 9. Mean effect sizes for –pushed output and +pushed output on the delayed posttest

Discussion

We conclude this chapter with a summary and discussion of the main findings contributed by the present meta-analysis. We also offer some cautionary re-marks regarding the interpretation of our study findings, and suggest further directions for research on the empirical link between task-based interaction and L2 acquisition.

Research question 1: Compared to tasks with little or no interaction, how effective is task-based interaction in promoting the acquisition of grammatical and lexical features?

In our analysis of the results relevant to research question one, the null hypothesis would be that there is no effect of task-based interaction on the ac-quisition of grammatical and lexical features. Our findings lead us to reject the null hypothesis and instead posit that interaction does in fact promote acqui-sition. When comparing control/comparison/baseline and interaction groups, the mean effect size for task-based interaction across studies was .92, a large effect (Cohen 1988). With a lower confidence interval boundary of .68 (well above zero), we can be confident that within the domain included in this meta-analysis, studies show that task-based interaction is more effective in promoting acquisition than tasks with little or no interaction.

Research Question 2: Is the effectiveness of interaction tasks related to whether the target feature is grammatical or lexical?

Both tasks that focused on grammar ($d = .94$) and tasks that focused on lexis ($d = .90$) produced large main effects. Confidence intervals were fairly wide for lexis (0.40–1.40), however, perhaps due to the small number of study effect sizes ($n = 8$) contributing to the analysis. Though previous research sug-gests that the type of linguistic feature impacts the effectiveness of instructional intervention, comparison of specific linguistic features could not be conducted, for target features varied greatly across studies. Replication of studies on spe-cific linguistic features is needed in order to investigate the impact of type of linguistic feature on interaction treatment effectiveness.

Research Question 3: Are certain task types (e.g., information gap) more effective than others in promoting acquisition?

Jigsaw and information gap tasks were the most popular task types used within the research domain (together they made up 90% of treatment group tasks). This pattern likely reflects the belief expressed in the literature that jig-saw and information gap tasks are superior because they require the interaction of all participants (Pica et al. 1993). The meta-analysis does reveal that both jigsaw ($d = .78$) and information gap ($d = .91$) tasks are more effective than control/comparison conditions, and that the differences between these two task types are not trustworthy. However, the accumulation of more studies employing all six task types will be necessary before interpretations can be made about relative magnitude of effects associated with a wider range of task types.

Research Question 4: How long does the effect of task-based interaction last?

The effects of task-based interaction were evaluated and compared at two points in time: 8–29 days (short delay) and 30–60 days (long delay). The large effect for interaction at the short delay ($d = 1.12$; CI = .31 standard deviation units) suggests that the effects of interaction treatment are sustained for approximately 8 to 29 days. Beyond one month, however, it is unclear whether the effects of interaction treatment hold. The lower confidence interval for effect of treatment on 30–60 day delayed post-tests (.35) is not far from zero. However, only 6 study effect sizes contributed to this effect size calculation. More studies that include long delayed posts are needed to confidently evaluate the duration of interaction treatment effectiveness.

Research Question 5: To what extent do the task design features of degree of task-essentialness and opportunity for pushed output impact the success of interaction tasks?

On immediate post-tests, tasks with the characteristic of essentialness ($d = .83$) were found to have slightly smaller effects that task-utility designs ($d = .98$); however, confidence intervals were largely overlapping. A more trustworthy and larger difference between the effectiveness of task essential ($d = 1.66$) and task useful ($d = .76$) designs was observed for short delayed post-tests. When the effects were measured up to 29 days after the interaction treatment, the mean effect of task essentialness was .90 standard deviation units greater than task utility, and confidence intervals did not overlap. This finding suggests that the effects of interaction may not be observable immediately. Rather, as Gass and Varonis (1994) and Mackey (1999) have proposed, learners may need time to process the input and feedback they have received. Certainly, it will be important to continue to assess the long-term benefits of task-based interaction. These findings also support claims made by Loschky and Bley-Vroman (1993), Loschky (1994), and Doughty and Varela (1998): task-essentialness likely exerts an important influence on interaction effects, and thus is an important variable to consider in task design.

Treatment tasks which were designed to create opportunities for pushed output ($d = 1.05$) resulted in larger effects than tasks without pushed output ($d = .61$). Over time, the effects of pushed output tasks were maintained, with a short delayed post-test mean effect ranging from .84 to 1.44 standard deviation units. Because few treatment groups ($k = 4$) contributed to the analysis of –*pushed output* tasks on delayed post measures, it was difficult to interpret the durability of –*PO* design effects. The robust +*PO* findings lend support to arguments made by Swain (1985, 2000) that opportunities for pushed output play a crucial role in the acquisition process. However, because confidence intervals for –*PO* and +*PO* groups overlapped, observed differences between the two may not be trustworthy, and statements about the relative effectiveness of +PO versus –PO tasks should not be made until more data are available.

The available research data to date suggests that interaction has indeed been linked to L2 acquisition gains. In general, interaction tasks result in substantial pre- to post- gains ($d = 1.17$), and participants exposed to interaction treatments outperform control and comparison groups on post-test measures ($d = .92$). The effects of interaction on acquisition are large for both lexical ($d = .90$) and grammatical features ($d = .94$), and the effects of interaction are maintained on delayed post-test measures, for as long as 8 to 29 days ($d = 1.12$) and 30–60 days ($d = 1.18$) after the interaction treatment has been experienced.

Though the operationalization of interaction varied across studies, the majority (90%) chose to engage participants in either jigsaw ($d = .78$) or information gap ($d = .91$) tasks, both of which resulted in larger gains than control/comparison groups. The findings concerning information gap and jigsaw task types do not, however, tell us whether these task types are superior to others (e.g., problem-solving). This hypothesis, put forth by Pica et al. (1993), has yet to be tested empirically, as the effects of problem-solving, decision-making, opinion exchange and narrative tasks have not yet been sufficiently investigated in the research domain.

The research to date does, however, provide strong evidence that specific features of task design impact task effectiveness. While both task-essential ($d = .83$) and task-useful ($d = .98$) designs resulted in large immediate post-test effects, task-essentialness led to much greater effects over time, with a mean effect of 1.66 on delayed post-tests. Analysis of task design features also suggests that tasks which include opportunities for pushed output result in robust effects on immediate ($d = 1.05$) and delayed post measures ($d = 1.14$). Differences observed between task designs with and without pushed output, however, cannot be interpreted with confidence. More quantitative studies of pushed output tasks are needed to evaluate their effectiveness in promoting the L2 acquisition of linguistic features. When coupled with descriptive accounts of learner interaction and noticing during output tasks (e.g., Storch 2001; Swain & Lapkin

2001, 2002), such studies could provide rich information concerning the role that pushed output plays in the L2 acquisition process.

Looking forward: Recommendations for future research

Because the number of studies contributing to the present meta-analysis was small ($n = 14$), the findings presented here should be interpreted as *suggestive* rather than definitive. Certainly, more research is needed to deepen our understanding of the role that interaction, and related task design features, plays in L2 acquisition. We conclude with a number of caveats regarding our findings, as well as recommendations for future research within the interaction domain:

1. The 14 unique sample studies that were included in the meta-analysis focused primarily on university settings ($n = 10$), and have studied the acquisition of English ($n = 7$), Spanish ($n = 4$), and Japanese ($n = 3$) as a second or foreign language. Findings to date concerning the effect of interaction on L2 acquisition may not apply to educational settings, learner populations, and target languages that, as of 2003, were unrepresented in the research domain.

2. In the majority of unique sample studies (85%), interaction treatments involved native-speaker interlocutors (e.g., researchers, teaching assistants), who were trained to carry out specific task designs. In only three studies (Garcia & Acensión 2001; He & Ellis 1999; Takashima & Ellis 1999) did participants interact with other participants. Some primary researchers (de la Fuente 2002; Han 2002) noted that their treatment tasks would be difficult to reproduce in classroom settings. Thus, caution should be exercised when deriving pedagogical implications from the present meta-analysis. Replication of treatment designs in classroom settings, with learner-learner groups, is needed in order to understand what role student interaction might play in classroom language learning.

3. As observed in Norris and Ortega (2000), the majority of unique sample studies ($n = 10$) did not utilize a true control group in their design. Thus, it is difficult to interpret to what extent variables not controlled for (e.g., pre-test practice) contributed to the effects observed. The control/comparison group demonstrated a sizable pre- to post- gain of $d = .66$. Furthermore, though 13 of the 14 studies reported statistically significant findings, 29% did not report descriptive statistics, and none provided effect sizes. Because this research domain is concerned mainly with the extent to which interaction promotes

acquisition and the relative effectiveness of various task design features, information about magnitude of effect is just as, if not more, important than statistical significance. The reporting of this information in future interaction studies (as required, for example, by the journal *Language Learning* since 2000) would greatly benefit the research domain. At a minimum, better reporting of basic descriptive statistics is sorely needed, so as to enable other researchers to synthesize findings in future meta-analyses of this research domain.

4. Findings concerning the impact of task design features (task-essentialness, pushed output) were based on task *design*, rather than actual participant performance. Descriptions of group interactions could greatly enrich quantitative findings concerning the role that interaction plays in the acquisition process. Some studies provided both quantitiative and descriptive data, such as extensive analysis of transcripts (Han 2002; Iwashita 2003) and counts of linguistic features used (Garcia & Asención 2001; Mackey 1999; Mackey & Philp 1998). Inclusion of such data in future investigations of interaction may provide important insights into *how* and *why* certain interaction tasks did or did not promote the acquisition of lexical and grammatical features.

We hope that this study has succeeded in summarizing empirical findings and research practices in the task-based interaction research domain. We also hope that future primary studies explore further some of the variables (task type, degree of task-essentialness, pushed output) that we have identified as important to our understanding of task-based interaction effects. Cumulative findings do provide evidence of an empirical link between interaction and L2 acquisition, and they suggest that task design features can moderate the magnitude of the learning benefits fostered by task-based interaction. While much has been done thus far to investigate, specifically, the use of information gap tasks in university settings, the effectiveness of a variety of tasks types across multiple populations and settings deserves further exploration. It will also be important to establish consistent constructs for interaction and related task design features, so that the effectiveness of treatment tasks can be reliably compared across studies. Based on the cumulative findings of interaction research thus far, it appears that what now demands our attention is not whether interaction makes a difference or not, but rather, to what extent specific features of task design impact the magnitude and duration of interaction treatment effects.

Acknowledgement

We would like to thank Alison Mackey and an anonymous reviewer for their comments on an earlier version of this chapter. We are also indebted to Lourdes Ortega and John Norris for their guidance and support throughout this project.

Notes

1. Many of these recent studies have also examined the effectiveness of interactional feedback (Inagaki & Long 1999; Leeman 2003; Long, Inagaki, & Ortega 1998; Iwashita 2003; Mackey & Philp 1998). See Russell and Spada, this volume, for a meta-analysis that focuses on this topic.

2. Because a meta-analytic study can only compare findings of experimental studies, a number of influential interaction studies could not be included in the present analysis, such as the descriptive research program developed by Pica and her students (see Pica 2005), and the descriptive classroom studies conducted by Oliver and her colleagues (e.g., Oliver 1995; Mackey, Oliver, & Leeman 2003), among others.

3. It would have been of interest to investigate the ways in which interaction effects might vary across specific linguistic features (e.g., past tense -ed versus reflexive pronouns). Unfortunately, it was not possible to include target structures as a variable in the analysis because studies investigated a wide range of L2 features with little accumulation for any given one.

4. As an anonymous reviewer pointed out, many readers may note that the word "task" is not included in our list of search terms. This is because, at the onset of our study, we aimed to synthesize the broad domain of interaction research. As a result of the search process, we found that the available *experimental* studies in this domain all investigated task-based interaction specifically.

5. Thirteen study reports and 14 actual studies (or unique samples) were included in the present meta-analysis. Ellis, Tanaka, and Yamazaki (1995) is one article reporting on 2 separate studies (Saitama & Tokyo; see Appendix). Although Long, Inagaki, and Ortega (1998) also contains two studies in the same report, we extracted the data for the Spanish recast study from this article and the data for the Japanese recast study from Inagaki and Long (1999). This strategy allowed us to recover the individual scores to calculate effect sizes for the Japanese study sample.

6. Perhaps due to space limitations, many studies offered few details about target features and task designs, and this may explain the rather low inter-rater reliability coefficient for the variable of task-essentialness. In order for this variable to be coded more reliably in the future, studies will need to provide descriptions of (a) in what contexts native speakers consistently use the target feature and (b) in what ways the treatment task attempts to recreate these obligatory contexts. Though some studies offered detailed descriptions of both the target feature and the treatment task (e.g., Iwashita 2003; Inagaki & Long 1999; Mackey 1999),

others did not explain in what contexts the target feature was typically used, and/or offered only names of treatment tasks (e.g., story completion) without explanation or example.

References

Alcon, E. (1998). Input and input processing in second language acquisition. *International Review of Applied Linguistics, 36*, 343–362.

Ayoun, D. (2001). The role of negative and positive feedback in the second language acquisition of the passe compose and imparfait. *Modern Language Journal, 85*, 226–243.

Cohen, J. (1988). *Statistical power analysis for the behavioral sciences* (2nd ed.). Hillsdale, NJ: Lawrence Erlbaum.

Crookes, G., & Gass, S. (1993a). *Tasks and language learning.* Philadelphia: Multilingual Matters.

Crookes, G., & Gass, S. (1993b). *Tasks in a pedagogical context.* Philadelphia: Multilingual Matters.

*de la Fuente, M. J. (2002). Negotiation and oral acquisition of L2 vocabulary: The roles of input and output in the receptive and productive acquisition of words. *Studies in Second Language Acquisition, 24*, 81–112.

Doughty, C., & Pica, T. (1986). "Information gap" tasks: Do they facilitate second language acquisition? *TESOL Quarterly, 20*, 305–325.

Doughty, C., & Varela, E. (1998). Communicative focus on form. In C. Doughty & J. Williams (Eds.), *Focus on form in classroom second language acquisition* (pp. 114–138). Cambridge, UK: Cambridge University Press.

Ellis, R. (1994). *The study of second language acquisition.* Oxford: Oxford University Press.

Ellis, R. (1999). *Learning a second language through interaction.* Amsterdam: John Benjamins.

*Ellis, R., Tanaka, Y., & Yamazaki, A. (1995). Classroom interaction, comprehension, and the acquisition of L2 word meaning. In B. Harley (Ed.), *Lexical issues in language learning* (pp. 187–228). Amsterdam: John Benjamins.

*Garcia, P., & Asención, Y. (2001). Interlanguage development of Spanish learners: Comprehension, production, and interaction. *Canadian Modern Language Review, 57*, 377–402.

Gass, S. M. (1997). *Input, interaction, and the second language learner.* Mahwah, NJ: Lawrence Erlbaum.

Gass, S. M. & Alvarez Torres, M. J. (2005). Attention when? An investigation of the ordering effect of input and interaction. *Studies in Second Language Acquisition, 27*, 1–31.

Gass, S. M., Mackey, A., & Pica, T. (1998). The role of input and interaction in second language acquisition: Introduction to the special issue. *Modern Language Journal, 82*, 299–305.

Gass, S. M., & Varonis, E. M. (1985). Variation in Native Speaker Speech Modification to Non-Native Speakers. *Studies in Second Language Acquisition, 7*, 37–57.

Gass, S., & Varonis, E. (1994). Input, interaction, and second language production. *Studies in Second Language Acquisition, 16*, 283–302.

*Han, Z.-H. (2002). A study of the impact of recasts on tense consistency in L2 output. *TESOL Quarterly, 36*, 543–572.

*He, X., & Ellis, R. (1999). Modified output and the acquisition of word meanings. In R. Ellis (Ed.), *Learning a second language through interaction* (pp. 115–132). Amsterdam: John Benjamins.

*Inagaki, S., & Long, M. H. (1999). Implicit negative feedback. In K. Kanno (Ed.), *The acquisition of Japanese as a second language* (pp. 9–30). Amsterdam: John Benjamins.

*Iwashita, N. (2003). Negative feedback and positive evidence in task-based interaction: Differential effects on L2 development. *Studies in Second Language Acquisition, 25*, 1–36.

Izumi, S. (2002). Output, input enhancement, and the noticing hypothesis: An experimental study on ESL relativization. *Studies in Second Language Acquisition, 24*, 541–577.

Krashen, S. (1985). *The input hypothesis: Issues and implications*. London: Longman.

Larsen-Freeman, & Long, M. (1991). *An introduction to second language acquisition*. London: Longman.

Lazaraton, A. (2000). Current trends in research methodology and statistics in applied linguistics. *TESOL Quarterly, 34*, 175–181.

*Leeman, J. (2003). Recasts and second language development. *Studies in Second Language Acquisition, 25*, 37–63.

Light, R., & Pillemer, D. (1984). *Summing up: The science of reviewing research*. Cambridge, MA: Harvard University Press.

Linnell, J. (1995). Can negotiation provide a context for learning syntax in a second language? *Working Papers in Educational Linguistics, 11*, 83–103.

Lipsey, M. & Wilson, D. (2001). *Practical meta-analysis*. Thousand Oaks, CA: Sage.

Long, M. H. (1980). *Input, interaction, and second language acquisition*. Unpublished doctoral dissertation. University of California, Los Angeles.

Long, M. H. (1983). Native speaker/non-native speaker conversation and the negotiation of comprehensible input. *Applied Linguistics, 4*, 126–141.

Long, M. H. (1996). The role of the linguistic environment in second language acquisition. In W. Ritchie & T. Bhatia (Eds.), *Handbook of second language acquisition* (pp. 413–468). New York: Academic Press.

*Long, M. H., Inagaki, S., & Ortega, L. (1998). The role of implicit negative feedback in SLA: Models and recasts in Japanese and Spanish. *Modern Language Journal, 82*, 357–371.

*Loschky, L. (1994). Comprehensible input and second language acquisition: What is the relationship? *Studies in Second Language Acquisition, 16*, 303–323.

Loschky, L., & Bley-Vroman, R. (1993). Grammar and task-based methodology. In G. Crookes & S. Gass (Eds.), *Tasks and language learning* (pp. 123–167). Clevedon, UK: Multilingual Matters.

*Mackey, A. (1999). Input, interaction, and second language development: An empirical study of question formation in ESL. *Studies in Second Language Acquisition, 21*, 557–587.

*Mackey, A., & Philp, J. (1998). Conversational interaction and second language development: Recasts, responses, and red herrings? *Modern Language Journal, 82*, 338–356.

Mackey, A., Oliver, R., & Leeman, J. (2003). Interactional input and the incorporation of feedback: An exploration of NS-NNS and NNS-NNS adult and child dyads. *Language Learning, 53*, 35–66.

McDonough, K. (2004). Learner-learner interaction during pair and small group activities in a Thai EFL context. *System, 32*, 207–224.

Miller, N., & Pollock, V. E. (1994). Meta-analytic synthesis for theory development. In H. Cooper & L. V. Hedges (Eds.), *Handbook of Research Synthesis* (pp. 457–483) New York: Russell Sage Foundation.

Mitchell, R., & Myles, F. (1998). *Second language learning theories*. London: Arnold.

Norris, J. M., & Ortega, L. (2000). Effectiveness of L2 instruction: A research synthesis and quantitative meta-analysis. *Language Learning, 50*, 417–528.

Nunan, D. (1989). *Designing tasks for the communicative classroom*. Cambridge, UK: Cambridge University Press.

Oliver, R. (1995). Negative feedback in child NS/NNS conversation. *Studies in Second Language Acquisition, 17*, 459–481.

Oliver, R. (2002). Age differences in negotiation and feedback in classroom and pairwork. *Language Learning, 50*, 119–151.

Philp, J. (2003). Constraints on "noticing the gap": Nonnative speakers' noticing of recasts in NS-NNS interaction. *Studies in Second Language Acquisition, 25*, 99–126.

Pica, T. (1988). Interlanguage adjustments as an outcome of NS-NNS negotiated interaction. *Language Learning, 38*, 45–73.

Pica, T. (1994). Research on negotiation: What does it reveal about second language learning conditions, processes and outcomes? *Language learning, 44*, 493–527.

Pica, T. (2005). Classroom learning, teaching, and research: A task-based perspective. *Modern Language Journal, 89*, 339–352.

Pica, T., & Doughty, C. (1985). Input and interaction in the communicative language classroom: A comparison of teacher-fronted and group activities. In S. Gass & C. Madden (Eds.), *Input in second language acquisition* (pp. 115–1132). Rowley, MA: Newbury House.

Pica, T., Young, R., & Doughty, C. (1987). The impact of interaction on comprehension. *TESOL Quarterly, 21*, 737–758.

Pica, T. Kanagy, R., & Falodun, J. (1993). Choosing and using communication tasks for second language instruction and research. In G. Crookes & S. Gass (Eds.), *Tasks and language learning: Integrating theory and practice* (pp. 9–34). Clevedon, UK: Multilingual Matters.

Pica, T., Holliday, L., Lewis, N., & Morgenthaler, L. (1989). Comprehensible output as an outcome of linguistic demands on the learner. *Studies in Second Language Acquisition, 11*, 63–90.

Polio, C., & Gass, S. M. (1998). The role of interaction in native speaker comprehension of nonnative speaker speech. *Modern Language Journal, 82*, 308–320.

Rosenthal, R. (1994). Parametric measures of effect size. In H. Cooper & L. Hedges (Eds.), *Handbook of research synthesis* (pp. 231–244). New York: Russell Sage Foundation.

Rosenthal, R. (1995). Writing meta-analytic reviews. *Psychological Bulletin, 118*, 183–192.

Schmidt, R. (1990). The role of consciousness in second language learning. *Applied Linguistics, 11*, 129–158.

Shehadeh, A. (2001). Self- and other-initiated modified output during task-based inter-action. *TESOL Quarterly, 35,* 433–457.

Skehan, P. (1996). A framework for the implementation of task-based instruction. *Applied linguistics,* 17, 38–62.

Skehan, P. & Foster, P. (2001). Cognition and tasks. In P. Robinson (Ed.), *Cognition and second language instruction* (pp. 183–205). Cambridge, UK: Cambridge University Press.

Storch, N. (2001). How collaborative is pair work? ESL tertiary students composing in pairs. *Language Teaching Research, 5,* 29–53.

Swain, M. (1985). Communicative competence: Some roles of comprehensible input and comprehensible output in its development. In S. Gass & C. Madden (Eds.), *Input in second language acquisition* (pp. 235–253). Rowley, MA: Newbury House.

Swain, M. (2000). The output hypothesis and beyond: Mediating acquisition through collaboration. In J. P. Lantolf (Ed.), *Sociocultural theory and second language learning.* Oxford: Oxford University Press.

Swain, M., & Lapkin, S. (2002). Talking it through: Two French immersion learners' response to reformulation. *International Journal of Educational Research, 37,* 285–304.

Swain, M., & Lapkin, S. (2001). Focus on form through collaborative dialogue: Exploring task effects. In M. Bygate, P. Skehan, & M. Swain (Eds.), *Researching pedagogic tasks* (pp. 99–118). New York: Longman.

*Takashima, H., & Ellis, R. (1999). Output enhancement and the acquisition of the past tense. In R. Ellis (Ed.), *Learning a second language through interaction* (pp. 173–188). Amsterdam: John Benjamins.

Thomas, M. (1994). Assessment of L2 proficiency in second language acquisition research. *Language Learning, 44,* 307–336.

Appendix

Table A. Summary table of unique sample studies[a]

Study report/ Treatment groups	n	Task Type	Task Essen	Pushed Output	Target Feature	Imm Post	Delay (8–29)	Delay (30–60)
Iwashita 2003								
Locative word order	41	jigsaw	U	+	G	0.81	.	.
Locative particle use	41	jigsaw	U	+	G	0.87	.	.
Verb morpheme (-te)	41	jigsaw	U	+	G	0.67	.	.
Leeman 2003								
Recast – gender	18	Info gap	U	+	G	1.3	0.82	.
Recast – number	14	Info gap	U	+	G	1.87	1.33	.
Negative evidence – gender	18	Info gap	U	+	G	0.66	0.32	.
Negative evidence – number	17	Info gap	U	+	G	0.03	0.66	.
Enhanced salience – gender	18	Info gap	U	+	G	1.47	0.95	.
Enhanced salience – number	18	Info gap	U	+	G	0.9	1.03	.
Mackey & Philp 1998[b]								
Recast ready	9	Info gap	E	+	G	.	.	.
Recast unready	8	Info gap	E	+	G	.	.	.
Interactor ready	6	Info gap	E	+	G	.	.	.
Interactor unready	6	Info gap	E	+	G	.	.	.
Han 2002	4	narrative	U	+	G	2.5	.	3.14
Inagaki & Long 1999								
Recast adjective	4	Info gap	U	+	G	1.3	.	.
Recast locative	4	Info gap	U	+	G	0.39	.	.
Ellis, Tanaka, & Yamazaki 1995								
Saitama study	24	Info gap	E	–	L	1.37	.	1.02
Tokyo study	42	Info gap	E	–	L	0.64	.	0.46
Garcia & Asención 2001	18	prob solve	E	–	G	0.22	.	.
de la Fuente 2002								
NIPO	11	Info gap	E	+	L	1.81	2.28	.
NIWO	8	Info gap	E	–	L	1.69	2.63	.
Loschky 1994								
Vocabulary	13	Info gap	E	–	L	0.06	.	.
Grammar	13	Info gap	E	–	G	–0.18	.	.
Mackey 1999[c]								
Interactors	7	Info gap	E	+	G	.	1.24	.
Interactor unreadies	7	Info gap	E	+	G	.	1.61	.
Scripteds	7	Info gap	U	–	G	.	0.06	.
Observers	6	Info gap	U	–	G	.	0.94	.

Table A. (*continued*)

Study report/ Treatment groups	*n*	Task Type	Task Essen	Pushed Output	Target Feature	Imm Post	Delay (8–29)	Delay (30–60)
Long, Inagaki, & Ortega 1998								
Object topicalization	6	Info gap	U	+	G	0	.	.
Adverb placement	6	Info gap	U	+	G	1.27	.	.
He & Ellis 1999								
Negotiated output	16	Info gap	E	+	L	1.34	1.56	1.19
Interactionally modified input	16	Info gap	E	–	L	0.49	0.64	0.37
Takashima & Ellis 1999	27	narrative	U	+	L	0.71	0.72	0.94

[a] E = task-essential; U = task-useful + = with pushed output; – = without pushed output G = grammar; L = lexis.

[b] Only pre-to-post effect sizes were computed for Mackey & Philp because they did not report descriptive statistics for their control group.

[c] Mackey (1999) reported proportion values that reflected a developmental stage increase as demonstrated on 2 of the 3 post-test measures. Since a stage increase would necessarily involve performance on both the immediate post-test measure and a second or third post-test measure (both given less than 30 days after treatment), the effect size values were obtained from the reported proportions using Lipsey & Wilson's arcsine equation and were assigned to the short delay category.

CHAPTER 4

The effectiveness of corrective feedback for the acquisition of L2 grammar

A meta-analysis of the research

Jane Russell and Nina Spada
University of Toronto

In this chapter, we report on a meta-analysis of research that investigated the effects of corrective feedback (CF) on second language (L2) grammar learning. We describe the rationale for undertaking this research and the steps taken in the collection and coding of 56 primary studies in preparation for the meta-analysis. Of these 56 studies, 31 were considered suitable for the meta-analysis and 15 provided sufficient data to calculate effect sizes. Due to this small number, a broadly inclusive approach was taken in meta-analyzing their findings. We report the results in terms of the overall effectiveness of corrective feedback for L2 learning.

Introduction

Investigations have been undertaken to explore a variety of factors that may influence the effectiveness of corrective feedback (CF) for second language (L2) grammar learning. These include the type of feedback (e.g., explicit or implicit) (e.g., Carroll & Swain 1993; Lyster & Ranta 1997), the amount of feedback (e.g., Havranek 1999), the mode of feedback (i.e., oral or written) (e.g., Doughty & Varela 1998), the source of feedback (e.g., Van den Branden 1997), learner proficiency level (e.g., Iwashita 2003; Lin & Hedgcock 1996; Mackey & Philp 1998), learners' attitudes towards feedback (e.g., Semke 1984), learners' aptitude, motivation, and anxiety (e.g., DeKeyser 1993), learner noticing and interpretation of feedback (e.g., Mackey, Gass, & McDonough 2000; Morris 2002; Ohta 2000), and learners' age (e.g., Havranek 1999).

Below, we present a narrative review of some relevant studies that are illustrative of the varied foci for corrective feedback research and those that are particularly relevant to this meta-analysis. Only those studies that clearly isolate the results of grammar-based feedback from other types of corrective feedback are included, and only those studies that isolate corrective feedback from instruction. This narrative review is not intended to be comprehensive; rather, it is intended to provide a brief summary of some of the relevant findings of research examining the relationship between CF and the development of L2 grammatical accuracy.

Before examining this empirical work, it is important to note two central features in the CF literature: how corrective feedback is defined and how 'effectiveness' of corrective feedback is measured. In this paper, the term *corrective feedback* will refer to any feedback provided to a learner, from any source, that contains evidence of learner error of language form. It may be oral or written, implicit or explicit. For the purposes of this research, corrective feedback does not refer to feedback focused on any aspect of language other than grammatical form. The measurement of 'effectiveness' in the CF literature also varies considerably. For example, dependent variables in studies have included measures of uptake,[1] improvement on receptive tests of the target structure, improvement in productive use of the target structure, and improvement on general proficiency tests. For the purposes of this review, 'effectiveness' will be based on any of the above measures.

Feedback on oral production

Considerable research of both a descriptive and experimental nature has been done to examine the effects of CF on oral production. One of the earliest descriptive studies was carried out by Chaudron (1977), who investigated the different types of CF provided to French immersion students by their teachers. He observed that while a great deal of teacher feedback went unnoticed, some types of CF (e.g., repetition with emphasis) led to more immediate reformulations on the part of learners than others (e.g., repetition without emphasis).

In a descriptive classroom study with adult learners of French as a foreign language, Doughty (1994) also observed a variety of different types of teacher feedback and found that the most frequent were clarification requests, repetitions and recasts.[2] An examination of learners' responses to the feedback revealed that learners did not respond frequently to any of the oral CF types but that when they did, it was most often to a recast. Recasts have been the focus of considerable research on the effects of corrective feedback on oral production. Other descriptive classroom studies (Havranek 1999; Lochtman 2000;

Lyster & Ranta 1997; Panova & Lyster 2002) investigating different corrective feedback types have also observed that the most frequently used was the recast. However, in these studies recasts were found to be the least likely to lead to learner uptake. Instead, uptake was more likely to occur in response to other CF types (e.g., elicitation, clarification requests, or metalinguistic cues).[3] It is important to note that all of the above studies examined learners' immediate responses to feedback rather than its effects on learning over time.

An increasing number of experimental studies on the effects of different CF types on oral production have been carried out in both laboratory and class-room contexts. Doughty and Varela (1998) examined the use of CF within the context of a middle school content-based ESL science class and found that students who received CF (via "corrective recasts") from their teacher on specific language forms exhibited greater oral accuracy and development[4] than students who did not receive CF. Advantages for CF in the form of recasts have also been observed in experimental laboratory studies (Iwashita 2003; Long, Inagaki, & Ortega 1998; Mackey 1999; Mackey & Philp 1998; Philp 2003).

The different findings across descriptive and experimental CF studies may be related to the explicit/implicit nature of the corrective feedback type, the extent to which type of feedback is dependent on context (i.e., laboratories versus classrooms) and the intensive/extensive nature of the CF. Nonetheless, there is growing evidence that CF can be helpful for L2 learning. Despite this, there are L2 theorists who argue either that corrective feedback is not useful at all (Truscott 1996, 1999) or that it is only useful in effecting superficial and temporary changes to L2 learners' performance, not to their underlying competence (Schwartz 1993). This is consistent with the claim that CF may be useful for monitored production (i.e., writing) but not for spontaneous oral production (Krashen 1982). In the section below, we present some of the research on CF and written production.

Feedback on written production

Some researchers have found CF to be effective for written errors. For example, Fathman and Whalley (1990) conducted an experimental classroom study on the effects of type of feedback (in this case feedback on form versus feedback on content) on intermediate ESL college students' writing and found both to be equally effective. Ashwell (2000) also found clear support for the use of CF for developing grammatical accuracy in written compositions. He conducted an evaluation of feedback on adult learners' written essays in which feedback involving underlining or circling grammatical, lexical, or mechanical errors, as well as content-related suggestions for improvement, was provided on the first and second drafts of a composition. He found that when revising their essays, students took into account three fourths of the feedback they received on form. In addition, the results showed that students relied more on the form feedback than on the content feedback.

Contrary to Ashwell's and Fathman and Whalley's findings, however, Kepner (1991) found no significant effects of either type of feedback on language form in the compositions of L2 college students. Kepner concluded that feedback on written compositions is ineffective for developing students' grammatical accuracy. It should be noted, however, that in contrast to Ashwell's (2000) study, the students in Kepner's sample were not required to revise their essays, and the measures used in the study represent students' scores on the sixth assignment of a semester after having received or not received feedback on the previous five (different) assignments (see Chandler 2003, for further discussion of these different findings).

Fazio (2001) also did not find support for the use of CF in an experimental study of the effects of feedback on form and content in student writing. In her study, students were in grade 5 at a French-language school in Montreal, where both French L1 speakers and French L2 speakers were in mixed classes. Fazio found that neither feedback on form nor content affected students' accuracy in their writing, for either the L1 or L2 students.

Source of corrective feedback

Traditionally, CF research has focused mainly on teacher feedback in classroom settings or on native-speaker feedback outside the classroom. This is undoubtedly due to the widely held assumption that non-native speaking L2 learners are not considered to be linguistically equipped to provide effective CF. Some empirical evidence to support this comes from an early study by Long and Porter (1985), who observed that while learners can offer each other genuine communicative practice, including the negotiation of meaning, they cannot always provide each other with accurate and reliable grammatical input.

Chaudron (1984) studied the effects of both teacher and peer feedback on written compositions and found that there were no significant improvements on student essays between the draft and final versions, regardless of the source of the CF. The results also indicated that learners had less positive attitudes towards the value of peer feedback than towards native-speaking teacher feedback. However, other research has reported positive benefits of peer feed-back on L2 writing. In an examination of university-level ESL learners' written compositions before and after receiving CF from a peer, Villamil and De Guerrero (1998) found that 74% of the peer-aided revisions were incorporated into the students' final versions, and of the total revisions made on the final versions only 7% were incorrect. Villamil and De Guerrero concluded that the peer-aided revision sessions were an effective method of providing feedback for revising essays.

Other research investigating peer-feedback on oral production has also provided evidence that learners can help each other with accuracy and form. This has been reported during negotiation of form practice (Lyster 1994, 2001), grammatical consciousness-raising tasks (Fotos & Ellis 1991), meta-talk activities (Swain & Lapkin 1998) and other tasks in which learners have been observed to successfully provide each other with accurate and useful CF (Bruton & Samuda 1980; Samuda & Rounds 1993).

Explicitness – implicitness

According to Schmidt's (1990) "noticing hypothesis", in order to learn anything that is new (including grammatical forms in a second language), noticing is essential. For this reason, the degree of explicitness of CF that is necessary to promote noticing, without detracting from the communicative focus of instruction, is a core theme in current research on CF (see, e.g., Lyster 1998a, 1998b). Carroll and Swain (1993) define explicit feedback as "any feedback that overtly states that a learner's output was not part of the language-to-be-learned" (p. 361), and implicit feedback as including, "… such things as confirmation checks, failures to understand, and requests for clarification (because learners must infer that the form of their utterance is responsible for the interlocutor's comprehension problems)" (p. 361). Ellis (2001) describes different types of corrective feedback as falling along a continuum between implicit and explicit feedback. Towards the more implicit end are recasts – defined by Ellis (2001) as "reformulations of all or part of the learners' deviant utterance" (p. 24). Slightly more explicit is negotiation of form, whereby confirmation checks and clarification requests are used to elicit a more accurate utterance from the learner. Two types of CF that fall towards the more explicit end of the continuum are identified by Lyster and Ranta (1997) as: (a) 'explicit correction' – when it is clearly expressed that an error has been made and the correct form is given; and (b) 'meta-linguistic feedback' – when a metalinguistic explanation of the underlying grammatical rule is given.

In an experimental laboratory study, Carroll and Swain (1993) investigated the effectiveness of several different types of oral CF on adult second language learners' ability to learn a particular grammatical structure and to generalize their learning to novel items. They compared 'explicit hypothesis rejection' (in which subjects were told they had made an error and were given an explicit metalinguistic explanation); 'explicit utterance rejection' (in which subjects were told only that they had made an error); 'modeling plus implicit negative feedback' (in which errors were recast; subjects had been told beforehand that they would receive correction if they made errors); 'indirect metalinguistic feedback' (in which subjects were asked if they were sure of their response when they made an error, having been told beforehand that they would be asked this if they made errors); and no feedback of any kind. All CF groups outperformed the no feedback control group. In addition, the 'explicit hypothesis rejection' group, which received the most explicit feedback, performed statistically significantly better than all other groups.

Notwithstanding these results, some positive effects for less explicit types of CF, specifically recasts, have been reported in a growing number of experimental laboratory studies investigating the effects of CF on different language features. Mackey and Philp (1998) report that learners who were "developmentally ready" responded positively to recasts, while less developmentally advanced learners did not. Similarly, Iwashita (2003) reports that learners who were less advanced needed more explicit negative feedback than the more advanced learners. In Philp's (2003) study, learners responded most positively to recasts that were developmentally appropriate, short, and similar to the learners' original utterances.

According to Nicholas, Lightbown, and Spada (2001), the positive effects for recasts in the laboratory studies:

> ...may be due to the dyadic nature of the laboratory interactions, which may help learners recognize the interlocutor's feedback as corrective. In addition, in the L2 laboratory studies, only one or two features have received the feedback focus, and this consistency may have helped learners recognize the intention of the feedback. (p. 749)

In the descriptive classroom studies, however, teachers have been observed using different CF strategies as they respond to a variety of learners' errors in the midst of everything else that goes on in normal classroom life.

In the classroom study by Lyster and Ranta (1997), not only was there less support for recasts, but other types of CF (e.g., elicitations, clarification requests, metalinguistic cues and repetition) led to learner uptake more frequently, and they were also more effective in leading to student-generated repair (Lyster & Ranta 1997). Lyster (1998a) argues that implicit feedback in the form of recasts is not an effective type of feedback because it can be easily misinterpreted as alternative positive evidence or repetition. In his re-analysis of the Lyster and Ranta (1997) data, Lyster (1998a) observed that the teachers used recasts in the same way as and in equal distribution to non-corrective repetition. Also, recasts were often used as alternative ways of expressing the same meaning or as signs of approval, thus revealing the extent of ambiguity in the intent of teacher recasts to learner output. Lyster concludes that implicit recasts are not a source of useful negative evidence for L2 learners in content-based/communicative classrooms.

However, in another descriptive classroom study which examined students' private speech in class (speech directed to the self only), Ohta (2000) reports that the use of recasts appeared to be effective, not only for the students who made the errors, but also for other students present. Although this study used measures of students' private speech in response to recasts as the dependent variable, rather than directly measuring student learning, the findings suggests that recasts may be noticed by at least some students present and that traditional methods of measuring student noticing of recasts may not be sufficiently sensitive. A rather different interpretation of these results is that because the foreign language students in Ohta's study were accustomed to an emphasis on language forms and corrective feedback in their regular classroom instruction, they may have been particularly sensitive to all types of CF and thus interpreted recasts as overt correction (Nicholas, Lightbown, & Spada 2001).

Summary and research questions

In this selected review of empirical studies of CF and L2 learning, it is evident that the studies address diverse questions, consider a variety of types of corrective feedback, study different populations, employ different measures, and apply different methodologies. Consequently, each study produces results that often differ from others with respect to their conclusions and interpretations. Each study also involves a small sample size, which makes it difficult to generalize beyond the particular sample considered in any one study. In light of the findings from individual studies concerning the effectiveness of CF, it would be useful to determine whether there are beneficial effects for CF when the studies are combined and examined as a whole. Therefore the primary research question addressed in this study is:

1. *How effective is Corrective Feedback in general for L2 learning?*

Additionally, two research questions related to methodological features of the primary studies are examined since these are potentially important variables in assessing the effectiveness of CF. The first identifies the extent to which different features have been included in the studies, such as contextual factors (laboratory or classroom), treatment conditions (e.g., type of feedback) and methodological approaches (e.g., experimental or descriptive). The second investigates the effects that these features might have on the results of the studies. The two related questions are:

2. *What features/variables have been included in the CF primary research to date?*

3. *Do the effects of CF vary in terms of the methodological features of the primary studies?*

Below, we describe the steps taken in the data collection, coding, and meta-analysis of the primary studies investigating the effects of CF. Findings are presented in the form of two phases: (a) the first describes the analysis of several important study characteristics of the 56 studies included in the final pool of studies examined; and (b) the second describes the analysis of the 15 studies which met the criteria for inclusion in the meta-analysis.

Data collection

For this meta-analysis, the data were collected by searching the online ERIC database, tables of contents of journals, and reference lists from other review articles in the field of second language acquisition (SLA). Suitable studies were selected from the pool of all published empirical studies examining the effects of corrective feedback.

To qualify for the analysis, studies had to meet specific inclusion criteria. They had to: (a) include empirical data; (b) be published in English; (c) include a measure of form-focused corrective feedback of grammar as an independent variable; (d) include a measure of learning as a dependent variable; (e) clearly isolate the corrective feedback from other forms of instruction that may have been included; and (f) clearly isolate corrective feedback in response to errors in grammatical form from corrective feedback in response to other types of errors (e.g., sociolinguistic, discourse, phonological). Similar to Norris and Ortega (2000), we chose to exclude unpublished research papers, theses, dissertations, research reports available only for a fee, and conference presentations. Despite the potential 'file-drawer problem', the decision to exclude unpublished research papers and those not freely offered was made because such studies are not readily available to most researchers, making replication of the present meta-analysis implausible. Computer Assisted Language Learning (CALL) studies were also excluded because they go beyond the scope of this research, and because the majority of studies that have examined CF and L2 learning have implemented more traditional varieties of CF. Studies that re-used the same data from a study already included in the selection were also excluded, to avoid inflating sample sizes (Matt & Cook 1994; Norris & Ortega 2000).

The process of searching the ERIC database for relevant studies involved cross-referencing the following search terms: Publication Type: 'research' AND Keyword: 'second language' AND Keyword: 'feedback' OR Keyword: 'negative evidence' OR Keyword: 'recast'. The search had no posterior cut-off date, therefore any study published up to and including February 2004 was eligible. Those journals that were identified in the ERIC search as having published at least two relevant articles were examined further by scanning their tables of contents for other potentially relevant studies. Thus, the journals selected for this search were *Canadian Modern Language Review*, *Foreign Language Annals*, *Journal of Second Language Writing*, *Language Awareness*, *Language Learning*, *Modern Language Journal*, *Second Language Research*, *Studies in Second Language Acquisition*, and *TESOL Quarterly*. The earliest study that was selected from our ERIC search was published in 1982, with the majority of studies published in the 1990s or later. Only the journals' tables of contents for the years 1975 to February 2004 were scanned. Selecting 1975 as the anterior cut-off date prevented wasting time on an ineffectual pursuit, yet it still allowed for other potential studies that may have been published prior to 1982 to emerge from the search. Through these combined search procedures, a set of 56 appropriate studies was established. This initial group included observational/descriptive and experimental/quasi-experimental studies. These are identified in the Appendix.[5]

The analysis of these primary studies took place in two phases. The first phase involved coding all 56 studies in the database according to the categories described below. This analysis, which included both descriptive and experimental studies, enabled us to synthesize and compare the existing CF research in terms of a wide range of characteristics. The purpose of this phase was to organize the data in preparation for the meta-analysis and, in the process, to identify the extent to which these characteristics have been studied to date. The second phase involved the meta-analysis itself. Below, the analyses and results of the two phases are presented.

Analysis and results: Phase 1

Each of the 56 studies was coded according to several categories. Some were valuable for determining a study's suitability for inclusion in the meta-analysis (i.e., research design, basis for sample size), others for assessing the type of treatment conditions that have been examined in the literature to date (i.e., research context, mode of errors and CF, source and focus of CF, and type of CF).[6] In addition, we coded the year of publication, as it is a common variable of interest in interpreting the results of meta-analyses (Greenhouse & Iyengar 1994; Lipsey & Wilson 2001). The results of Phase I are presented in Tables 1 through 5. (The coding of the 56 individual studies is presented in the Appendix.)

Table 1 indicates that 38 (almost 70%) of the 56 CF studies examined in this research were published between the years 1995 and 2003. This suggests that CF research is a relatively young field of inquiry and that it is gaining momentum. The remaining 18 CF studies were published over a thirteen-year period with most of them appearing in the literature between 1990–1994.

Table 2 indicates that of the 56 studies, 41 are experimental or quasi-experimental, while 15 are descriptive/observational. Due to the requirements of quantitative meta-analyses, only experimental or quasi-experimental studies can contribute data to the analysis. Table 2 also shows that the studies are almost evenly divided between those that were conducted in classrooms (31) and laboratories (25).

Table 1. Publication dates of primary CF studies

Year of publication	No. of publications
2000–2003	20
1995–1999	18
1990–1994	9
1985–1989	6
1977–1984	3

Note. N = 56.

Table 2. Research design and context

Research design and context		No. of studies	(%)
Design of study			
	Experimental/quasi-experimental	41	(73)
	Observational/descriptive	15	(27)
Context of study			
	Laboratory	25	(45)
	Classroom	31	(55)
Basis for sample[a]			
	Individual participants	38	(68)
	Dyads of participants	2	(4)
	Language Events	17	(30)

Note. N=56.

[a]One study, Van den Branden (1997), used a combination of individual participants and language events as the basis for the sample in analyses; therefore, this study is counted towards both of these categories.

In order for the studies to be comparable in a meta-analysis, they must use the same unit as the basis for sample size in their analyses. As shown in Table 2, 38 of the 56 studies used individual participants as the unit on which sample size was based, making these studies comparable. Another two studies used dyads of participants and 17 used language events as the basis for sample size, rendering these studies incomparable to the first group. Although no particular unit of analysis is inherently preferable over others, to synthesize the studies empirically, they must all utilize the same unit of analysis. Due to the small number of studies using 'dyads' as the unit of analysis, we could not meta-analyze them. Should there be more studies of this kind in the future, it may be possible to do so. Similarly, studies that use 'language events' as the unit of analysis are only potentially comparable with one another. A problem does arise when the language events of interest are not the same across studies, as is the case here. Since the 'language events' measured in these studies were not the same, they are not comparable. For example, Braidi (2002) used the number of native-nonnative speaker (NS-NNS) negotiation interactions falling into the specified pattern of 'NNS errorful utterance – NS response – NNS reaction' as the unit on which analyses were based, while Qi and Lapkin (2001) used the number of instances of participants' 'noticing' of their own errors as the unit of analysis in their study. While each of these is a valid unit of analysis, they are not comparable. In the future, if more studies are conducted that examine the same type of language event as the unit of analysis, those studies may be combined meta-analytically. Therefore, of the 56 studies, only the 38 that used individual participants as the unit of analysis were suitable for synthesizing further.

Table 3. Mode of errors and mode of corrective feedback

Language modality		No. of studies	(%)
Mode of errors			
	Oral	33	(59)
	Written	22	(39)
	Both oral and written	1	(2)
Mode of CF			
	Oral	34	(61)
	Written	18	(32)
	Both oral and written	4[a]	(7)

Note. N=56.

[a] In Doughty & Varela (1998), the experimental group received both oral and written CF corresponding to the mode of their errors. In Hedgcock & Lefkowitz (1992) one experimental group received oral CF while another received written CF, both in response to written errors. In Tomasello & Herron (1988, 1989), the experimental group received both oral and written CF on oral errors.

Table 3 indicates that most of the studies (n = 33) focused on learners' oral errors, while 20 focused on written errors. Only one study (Doughty & Varela 1998) focused on both. In terms of the mode of CF provided, 34 of the studies included oral CF, 18 included written CF and four included both.

An analysis of the 56 primary studies in terms of the source of CF revealed that teachers and/or researchers usually provided the CF. Studies investigating peer (and other) sources of feedback were less numerous. These results are presented in Table 4. Also presented in Table 4 are the results related to the focus of CF; that is, whether the CF was form-specific or form-general. In 33 of the studies, CF was provided on a variety of forms, while in 23 of the studies CF was directed to a specific feature. It has been argued that CF focussed on a specific form is more intensive and thus may be more effective than CF that is more general in nature (Ellis 2001; Lyster 1998b).

Table 5 presents the results of the different types of CF provided in the primary studies. With regard to oral CF, recasts have been investigated more than any other type, with 20 studies including them. The next most frequently investigated CF types are clarification requests and confirmation checks (in 12 studies) and metalinguistic feedback (in 9 studies). With respect to the different types of written feedback investigated, the most frequently used were indicating the location of errors (11 studies), providing direct correction (9 studies), and coding error types (7 studies).

Table 4. Source and focus of CF in primary studies

Source and focus of CF		No. of studies	(%)
Source of CF[a]			
	Teacher only[b]	16	(29)
	Teacher as researcher [b]	13	(23)
	Researcher only	16	(29)
	Peer (NNS)	9	(16)
	Other NS	10	(18)
Focus of CF			
	General	33	(59)
	Specific	23	(41)

Note. N=56.

[a] Studies may be counted towards more than one category if applicable.

[b] Three studies are counted toward both 'Teacher-as-Researcher' and 'Teacher only' because for at least one treatment group the teacher was also one of the researchers, while for at least one treatment group the teacher was not one of the researchers.

Table 5. Type of corrective feedback

Type of corrective feedback		No. of studies	(%)
Type of CF: Oral[a, b]			
	Recast	20	(53)
	Confirmation check	12	(32)
	Clarification request	12	(32)
	Metalinguistic	9	(24)
	Direct correction	7	(18)
	Elicitation	6	(16)
	Repetition (with corrective intent)	5	(13)
	Explicit indication of existence of error only	4	
	Cues (Zone of Proximal Development)	2	
	Not reported	1	
Type of CF:Written[a, c]			
	Indication of location of error	11	(50)
	Direct correction	9	(41)
	Code	7	(32)
	Indication of existence of error only	3	(14)
	Metalinguistic	2	(9)
	Reformulation	2	(9)
	Not reported	2	(9)

[a] Studies may be counted towards more than one category if applicable.

[b] N=38

[c] N=22

Analyses and results: Phase 2

For the second phase of the research, the meta-analysis itself, it was necessary to first eliminate those studies that were not methodologically appropriate for inclusion in the analysis. There were two essential criteria that the primary studies needed to meet in order to be included in the meta-analysis: (a) the use of individual participants as the unit for the basis of sample size for analyses; and (b) the existence of an appropriate comparison group (i.e., treatment/control[7] or pre/post-test) (Lipsey & Wilson 2001). After eliminating those studies that did not meet these criteria, there were 31 studies remaining.

There are different approaches to the synthesis of research. While some researchers advocate that strict 'quality' criteria must be met to ensure the integrity of the synthesis (Slavin 1986), other researchers promote a more inclusive approach (Lipsey & Wilson 2001). Similar to Norris and Ortega (2000), we took a broadly inclusive approach to the suitability of studies for the meta-analysis. That is, although we coded for study characteristics generally considered important quality criteria for meta-analyses (e.g., prior equivalence between treatment groups, random assignment) (Cooper & Hedges 1994; Lipsey & Wilson 2001), we did not eliminate studies on the basis of these characteristics.[8] A previous attempt to do so resulted in an insufficient number of studies that met such criteria (Russell 2003).

The next step in the process was to calculate effect sizes for the 31 studies. To do this, we used Wilson's (2001) *Effect Size Determination Program* to calculate Cohen's *d* values. As is usually the case (Cooper & Hedges 1994; Lipsey & Wilson 2001), not all of the studies contained sufficient data to enable effect size calculations. Thus, it was possible to calculate effect sizes for only 20 of the 31 studies.

In carrying out meta-analyses, effect sizes based on continuous variables should not be analyzed together with effect sizes based on dichotomous variables (Lipsey & Wilson 2001). Because five of the 20 studies permitted effect sizes based only on dichotomous variables, they could not be included with the 15 other studies.[9] Effect sizes based on treatment/control comparisons should also be meta-analyzed separately from those based on pre/post comparisons (Lipsey & Wilson 2001). However, because all effect size calculations were based on treatment/control group comparisons for the 15 remaining studies, there was no need to conduct a separate meta-analysis for pre/post comparisons.

Some of the studies contained multiple comparisons. Since only one effect size per study should be included in the meta-analysis (Lipsey & Wilson

2001), it was necessary to decide which comparison to include. To do this, we followed a series of steps suggested by Lipsey and Wilson (2001). We first evaluated whether there was one comparison that was more suitable than the others for the focus of this meta-analysis.[10] If so, that comparison was used to calculate the effect size for that study. If there was not one that was most relevant, we determined whether or not it was possible to take the average of the effect sizes for all relevant comparisons without inflating the sample size. This is possible only if no participants are overlapped in the study groups. If this was not feasible either, we randomly selected one of the relevant comparisons.

The effect sizes for each of the 15 studies, after they were all weighted by sample size, are presented in Table 6 along with the calculation type used and the sample size for the groups compared. Table 7 presents the descriptive statistics for post-test comparisons for all the studies. The effect sizes (d) range from 0.09 (virtually no effect) to 2.18 (a large effect). The mean weighted effect size is 1.16 (a large effect).

General guidelines for interpreting Cohen's d effect sizes state that a d-value between 0.2 and 0.5 is considered a small effect, a d-value between 0.5 and 0.8 is considered a medium-sized effect, and a d-value of more than 0.8 is considered a large effect (Cooper & Hedges 1994; Lipsey & Wilson 2001). Thus, the majority of effect sizes for this group of studies were well above the minimum level for large effects. Figure 1 shows that for the 15 studies, there were 2 in which the CF treatment had no effect, 1 in which the CF treatment had a small effect, 2 in which the CF treatment had a medium-sized effect, and 10 in which the CF treatment had a large effect.

In a study by Lipsey and Wilson (1993), it was found that the typical range of effect sizes for psychological, educational and behavioral treatment meta-analyses was between –0.2 and 1.6 with a median of 0.5. The findings of this study differ in that most of the effect sizes were large with the weighted mean being 1.16. This is consistent with the findings of Norris and Ortega (2000), who report a weighted mean effect size of 0.96. One explanation for this could be the fact that all studies included in this meta-analysis were published, and it is well documented that published studies are more likely to have found significant positive effects for treatments. In an attempt to investigate other possible explanations, we examined the data in terms of different methodological features of the studies, including the analyses carried out within them and differences in the treatments implemented in the individual studies. Since year of publication is often considered as a variable of interest in meta-analyses, as research methods arguably improve over the years (Cooper & Hedges 1994; Lipsey & Wilson 2001), we examined this factor first. Figure 2 shows the distri-

Table 6. Effect sizes for post-test comparisons: Individual studies

Study	Effect Size Basis	Total N	N (exp)	n (ctrl)	d-value (weighted)	r-value[a]
Herron & Tomasello 1988	Mean & t-test	32	16	16	0.86	0.40
Tomasello & Herron 1989	Mean & t-test	32	16	16	1.00	0.45
Fathman & Whalley 1990	Frequency Positive Outcome	28	14	14	1.25	0.53
Herron (3) 1991	t-test (p-value only)	25	n/r	n/r	1.47	0.59
Kepner 1991	Mean & SD	60	30	30	0.39	0.19
Carroll & Swain 1993	Mean & SD	40	20	20	1.18	0.51
DeKeyser 1993	Mean & SD	35	16	19	0.15	0.07
Lee 1997	Mean & SD	99	50	49	2.18	0.74
Long et. al (1) 1998	Independent t-test (no mean)	14	8	6	0.09	0.05
Long et. al (2) 1998	Mean & SD	24	12	12	1.20	0.51
Ashwell 2000	ANOVA (k>2)	25	13	12	1.98	0.70
Muranoi 2000	Mean & SD	20	10	10	0.92	0.42
Fazio 2001	Mean & SD	30	15	15	0.74	0.35
O'Relly, Flaitz & Kromrey 2001	Mean & SD	30	16	14	0.53	0.26
Leeman 2003	Mean & SD	28	14	14	1.74	0.66

Note. n/r = not reported.

[a] The r-value represents the Pearson Product Moment Correlation. Similar to Cohen's d, this statistic is also commonly used in meta-analyses. The r-value can easily be converted to a Cohen's d-value and vice versa. It is presented here because some readers may prefer to interpret the results from the r-values.

Table 7. Descriptive statistics for effect sizes of post-test comparisons: All studies

Weighted Mean	1.16
Standard Error	0.16
Standard Deviation	0.62
Skewness	0.22
Minimum	0.09
Maximum	2.18
Confidence Interval (95%)	Upper: 1.38 Lower: 0.70

Note. $N = 15$; unweighted mean effect size was $d = 1.04$.

bution of effect sizes for the 15 studies, presented in order of year of publication. There appears to be no noticeable patterns in the distribution, suggesting that the year of publication is not particularly related to the effect sizes found

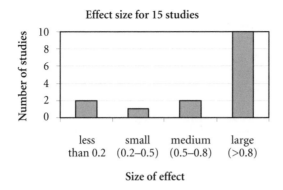

Figure 1. General magnitude of effects for post-test comparisons

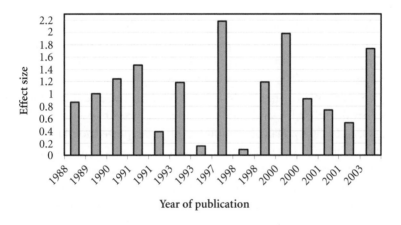

Figure 2. Distribution of effect sizes for post-test comparisons, by year of publication

here. This may be due in part to the fact that all of the studies are relatively recent, with the earliest from 1988.

In our analysis of methodological features of the studies, we considered the basis of effect size calculation, group sample size, prior equivalence of treatment groups, and method of assignment of participants to groups as possible explanatory factors. No patterns emerged in relation to any of these variables, and mean effect sizes were consistently large. When we considered reliability and validity of measures, however, a possible pattern did emerge. Figure 3 shows the distribution of effect sizes based on primary studies' reporting of

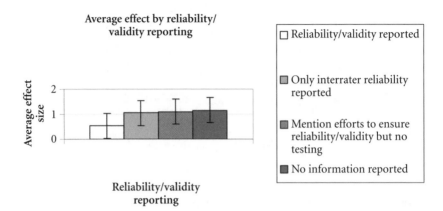

Figure 3. Effect sizes of post-test comparisons relative to reliability/validity reporting

reliability and validity of measures. Of the 15 studies, three studies reported the reliability and validity of measures used; four studies reported inter-rater reliability only; three studies mentioned efforts made to increase the reliability and/or validity of the study without reporting such testing; and six studies made no mention of reliability or validity of measures. The three studies that did report the reliability and validity of the measures (DeKeyser 1993; Muranoi 2000; and O'Relly, Flaitz & Kromrey 2001) all reported good reliability and validity coefficients. The small number of studies precludes any strong conclusions, but the pattern appears to suggest that the studies that reported both reliability and validity of measures ($n = 3$) resulted in more modest effects ($d = 0.53$ – a medium-sized effect), while those studies that were less stringent in their reporting of reliability and validity of measures resulted in greater effects (d-values ranging from 1.05 to 1.16 – all large effects). However, these findings must be cautiously interpreted because of the overlap in confidence intervals surrounding these effect size estimates.

The next step was to look for possible explanations for the results within the CF treatments. Unfortunately, due to the small number of studies in the different treatment groups, it was not feasible to conduct statistical comparisons of any subgroups based on the characteristics of the studies outlined in Phase 1 (e.g., context, type of feedback, mode of feedback). However, we did examine the data to look for potential patterns. Of the 15 studies, nine were conducted in classrooms, while six were conducted in laboratories, but both contexts appeared to yield similar-sized effects (for classroom research, the mean effect size was 1.12, while for laboratory research the mean effect size was 0.93 – both large effects). Mode of errors and mode of CF resulted in similar patterns, which is not surprising since most of the studies were overlapped in each of these categories. Those studies that examined oral errors were the same studies that investigated the use of oral CF ($n = 10$). These studies yielded a mean effect size (d) of 0.91. Those that examined written errors ($n = 5$) yielded a mean effect size (d) of 1.31, while those that investigated the use of written CF ($n = 6$) yielded a mean effect size (d) of 1.26. While the oral errors and oral CF effect sizes are slightly smaller overall than the written errors and written CF effect sizes, again, all of these are large mean effects.

Those studies for which the treatment and control group participants carried out the same task ($n = 12$) yielded larger effects overall than those studies for which the treatment and control group participants carried out different tasks ($n = 3$), with the 'same task' group averaging a large effect of 1.13 and the 'different task' group averaging a medium-sized effect of 0.72. The target structure focus of CF (either general or specific forms) did not appear to make a difference to the effects of the CF, with both yielding large effects ($d = 1.19$ for general forms, $n = 5$; $d = 0.97$ for specific forms, $n = 10$). Again, all of these results must be interpreted with caution due to the small number of studies involved.

Consistent with meta-analytic procedures, the effect sizes were calculated separately for delayed post-tests. Of the 15 studies, five involved delayed post-test comparisons. To see if a different pattern might appear with delayed post-test results, effect sizes were also calculated for the corresponding treatment-control delayed post-test comparisons for these five studies. Tables 8 and 9 below display the effect sizes for these comparisons and their descriptive statistics, all weighted for sample size. As shown in the tables, of the five effect sizes based on delayed post-test comparisons, three are medium-sized effects and

Table 8. Effect sizes for treatment/control delayed post-test comparisons of 5 studies

Study	Effect Size Basis	Total N	n (exp)	n (ctrl)	d-value (weighted)	r-value	Delay Length
Tomasello & Herron 1989	Mean & *t*-test	32	16	16	0.77	0.36	~17days
Herron (3) 1991	*t*-test (*p*-value only)	25	?	?	1.61	0.63	~15days
Carroll & Swain 1993	Mean & *SD*	40	20	20	0.71	0.33	1 week
Muranoi 2000	Mean & *SD*	20	10	10	0.66	0.31	5 weeks
Leeman 2003	Mean & *SD*	28	14	14	1.32	0.55	1 week

Table 9. Descriptive statistics for delayed post-test comparisons

Weighted Mean	0.98
Standard Error	0.19
Standard Deviation	0.42
Skewness	0.83
Minimum	0.65
Maximum	1.61
Confidence Interval (95%)	Upper: 1.54
	Lower: 0.48

Note. $N = 5$; unweighted mean effect size was $d = 1.01$.

two are large. Therefore, although the sample size is too small to permit firm conclusions, it seems that the effects of CF have not been considerably reduced over time. Neither is there evidence in this small sample that year of publication is related to differences in the magnitude of effect size.

Discussion and conclusion

The findings are discussed in relation to the three research questions that motivated this research. We begin with the first question: *How effective is CF in general for L2 learning?*

The meta-analysis of the 15 studies that met the criteria for inclusion produced a mean effect size of 1.16, a very large effect. Indeed, large effect sizes were found for the majority ($n = 10$) of the primary studies analyzed, including studies investigating the effects of CF on oral and written performance. This finding provides support for the effectiveness of CF in general for L2 grammar learning. Even when one considers that the methodological quality of the studies, particularly in terms of reliability and validity, may have contributed to inflated effect sizes, those studies that *did* report reliable and valid measures yielded medium-sized effects on average, suggesting that CF has a substantial effect on L2 acquisition. Furthermore, the findings suggest that the benefits of CF are durable. That is, all CF studies that included delayed post-tests in their design also indicate medium or large effect sizes. This result needs to be interpreted more cautiously, however, because only a small number of studies were involved in the delayed post-test analysis ($n = 5$). Furthermore, a comparison of the effect sizes for immediate and delayed post-test results within individual studies indicates stronger effect sizes for the former.

The finding that CF is beneficial, in this meta-analysis, probably comes as no surprise to most L2 educators and researchers. However, there are some dissenting voices. Perhaps the strongest voice against the benefits of CF in the recent literature is that of Truscott (1996, 1999). In his 1999 article on oral correction, he states that:

> ...research evidence points to the conclusion that oral correction does not improve learners' ability to speak grammatically. No good reasons have been advanced for maintaining the practice. For these reasons, language teachers should seriously consider the option of abandoning oral grammar correction altogether. (p. 437)

According to the results of the present research, 21 studies had focused on oral CF prior to the time Truscott wrote those words. Although only seven of them met the criteria for inclusion in the meta-analysis, all of those yielded medium or large effect sizes for groups who received CF. Empirical findings like these do not support Truscott's arguments against the benefits of oral CF feedback.[11] Furthermore, since 1999, three additional studies of oral CF that met the criteria for this meta-analysis also revealed medium and large effects of CF. Similar arguments against the benefits of written CF (Truscott 1996) are not consistent with the findings of this study either.

While the results from this meta-analysis indicate that CF (oral and written) is useful overall, it was not possible to determine whether particular CF variables make a difference. This is discussed in relation to the next two research questions: *What features/variables have been included in the primary research to date?* and *Do the effects of CF vary in terms of the methodological features of the primary studies?*

This study has confirmed that a wide range of CF variables have been investigated in the instructed SLA literature. It has produced a synthesis of the number of studies that have investigated different CF variables. In the 56 studies examined, five major treatment variables have been examined: type of CF; source of CF; mode of CF; mode of errors; and focus of CF. These variables have been investigated in experimental/quasi-experimental and descriptive studies in laboratory and classroom contexts.

When considering the role of context and CF, it has been argued that the nature and characteristics of the laboratory setting (e.g., dyadic interaction between the learner and the researcher/interviewer) create greater learner sensitivity and noticing of CF than do those of the classroom (Nicholas, Lightbown, & Spada 2001). Of the 15 studies for which effect sizes could be calculated, 9 were conducted in classrooms and 6 in laboratories. The effect sizes obtained for all of them were large, indicating that CF was more effective than no CF in both contexts. However, because the small number of studies in each group prevented a comparison of the effect sizes across contexts, it was not possible to confirm or disconfirm the claim that CF is more effective in the laboratory than the classroom. More studies to investigate the contributions of CF in both contexts are needed before a meta-analysis of this context variable in CF research can be conducted.

An ongoing debate in the SLA literature is whether a particular type of implicit CF (i.e., recasts) is beneficial for L2 learning and how this compares with other types of CF. In this research, effect sizes could only be calculated for three studies that investigated more implicit types of CF (including recasts) compared with no CF, and these all yielded medium to large effects for implicit CF. An effect size was also calculated for one study that compared the effects of implicit versus explicit feedback types on L2 learning (Carroll & Swain 1993). This yielded a large effect size for the group receiving explicit CF. These seemingly conflicting findings are difficult to interpret and, once again, due to the small number of studies that have investigated type of feedback and that met the criteria for inclusion in the meta-analysis, it was not possible to compare effect sizes across studies. Thus, there is insufficient evidence to date to claim benefits for one particular type of feedback over another. Some recent experimental classroom studies (Ammar 2003; Ammar & Spada in press; Lyster 2004) report that learners benefit from CF types that push them to be more accurate in their output (e.g., repetitions, metalinguistic clues, clarification requests and elicitation) than they do from CF that provides them with the correct model (i.e., recasts). More research to directly compare varying degrees of explicit and implicit types of CF on L2 learning is needed, particularly in the classroom setting.

The question as to whether CF is more effective when it is targeted to particular errors rather than more broadly to a wider range of errors is another area of research. This issue has also been raised with regard to the advantages reported for CF in laboratory versus classroom settings. That is, it has been argued that L2 learners are more likely to notice implicit forms of CF, such as recasts, in a laboratory study because in such a setting the CF is typically provided for one or two features. In the classroom setting, however, CF is usually provided for a variety of features and, therefore, may go unnoticed, particularly if the CF is implicit in nature. In this research, the effect sizes that could be calculated were all quite large, suggesting no differences in terms of a general or specific focus of CF. But again, the number of studies is far too small to arrive at any firm conclusions, pointing to the need for more research to investigate the general versus specific CF focus.

There is some discussion in the CF literature that students may respond differently to CF depending on whether the teacher or another student provides it. That is, some L2 learners may perceive CF feedback from their teacher as more valuable because they are native or near-native speakers of the target language and thus possess more knowledge about the L2 than do their peers. Also, some students may not consider their peers to have the "authority" to correct their mistakes and when it happens, it may lead to conflict between them (see Morris 2002). On the other hand, students may be less inhibited making mistakes when working one-on-one with a peer in activities that are designed to help them provide each other with CF. In this research, most of the studies examined CF provided by the teacher or researcher. In only nine of the 56 studies the CF was given by a peer, and not one of those studies met the criteria for inclusion in the meta-analysis. That is, all the studies that yielded large size effects supporting the benefits of CF for L2 learning were ones in which the teacher or researcher was the source of CF. This is another area where more studies are needed to confirm or disconfirm arguments for or against the benefits of peer feedback and L2 learning.

There are other variables that have been identified in the CF literature and referred to in the introduction to this chapter that have not been systematically investigated or examined in a sufficient quantity of studies to be able to synthesize the overall results. For example, few studies have investigated the impact of individual learner factors in relation to CF. These include motivation, proficiency level, and age. Compelling arguments have been made for the important role they play in relation to CF and L2 learning (DeKeyser 1993; Havranek 1999; Mackey & Philp 1998). However, until more studies are done to isolate these variables and investigate them in a series of studies in classrooms and laboratories, they remain compelling arguments without adequate supporting evidence.

A variable that was not examined in this study, but is a potentially important factor in interpreting the results of the CF studies individually and collectively, is the type of task used to measure L2 learning in the CF studies. That is, while the meta-analysis of the 15 studies in this research indicated that CF was beneficial overall, the question as to whether this finding holds for analytic, metalinguistic outcome measures, as well as for spontaneous "unmonitored" language measures, remains unexplored. In their meta-analysis of the effectiveness of L2 instruction, Norris and Ortega (2000) report that effect sizes were greater in studies that used more controlled, test-like outcome measures and that smaller effects were observed on both free response and grammaticality judgment outcome measures.

To conclude, the findings of this meta-analysis support a beneficial role for CF overall. The results also indicate that while the accumulated knowledge of previous research on CF has laid the foundation for work in this area, much more work needs to be done. It is evident that without a sufficient accumulation of studies on any one of these variables and without researchers' attention to the constellation of moderating variables that could make a difference regarding CF effectiveness, we will not be able to establish clear patterns across studies. Thus, there is a need not only for a greater volume of studies on CF, but also for studies that investigate similar variables in a consistent manner. Currently, the wide range of variables examined in CF research is spread rather thin; more work is needed to consolidate efforts and focus on those CF variables that appear to be particularly fruitful for future investigation (e.g., context, type of CF, focus of CF).

What is particularly encouraging in looking at the evolution of studies on CF over the past 15 years or so is that most of the recently published studies met the criteria for inclusion in a meta-analysis. This suggests that, over time, research on CF is adhering to higher research standards. This bodes well for future attempts to synthesize the CF literature.

Notes

1. 'Uptake' is defined as "a student's utterance that immediately follows the teacher's feedback and that constitutes a reaction in some way to the teacher's intention to draw attention to some aspect of the student's initial utterance" (Lyster & Ranta 1997:49). This uptake may or may not include repair of the error, and does not necessarily indicate learning. Furthermore, although uptake is not a definite indication of students' understanding of the feedback, a study by Mackey, Gass, and McDonough (2000) examining learner perceptions of feedback found that when uptake occurs, learners are likely to have correctly perceived the intention of the feedback.

2. The following definitions of different CF types are from Lyster and Ranta (1997:46–49): Clarification requests indicate to the students either that their utterance has been misunderstood or that their utterance is ill-formed in some way and that a repetition or reformulation is required; Repetitions refer to the teacher's repetition, in isolation, of the student's erroneous utterance; Recasts involve the teacher's reformulation of all or part of a student's utterance minus the error [and] are generally implicit.

3. One of the reasons learners did not frequently respond to recasts in these studies may be that there was no opportunity for learners to do so. In an observational study of the interactions between native and non-native English speaking children Oliver (1995), eliminated

turns in her data where there was no opportunity to respond to the recast and her results showed a much higher rate of uptake.

4. Doughty and Varela also investigated the effects of corrective recasts on written production.

5. Many of these studies overlap with those included in the Norris and Ortega (2000) meta-analysis of the effects of L2 instruction.

6. Given that the focus of this research was on the effectiveness of different CF treatments, studies that examined the effects of additional independent variables were not of direct interest to this research (e.g., motivation). Comparisons that examined the effects of such independent variables were deemed 'irrelevant comparisons'.

7. Here we refer to a control group that is relevant to the research questions of this meta-analysis (i.e., a control group that does not receive CF of form), which may or may not be the group designated as 'control' by the primary researchers, depending on the focus of the primary study.

8. See Russell (2003) for the coding of these studies according to these and other criteria.

9. Due to the small number of studies that used dichotomous variables (n = 5), we did not meta-analyse them. However, effect sizes were calculated and they are similar to those found for the continuous variables group. The exception is Ferris and Roberts (2001). The effect size for this study was zero. However, it should be noted that this study had only 3 participants in each group.

10. For example, in Fazio (2001) it made the most sense to compare the 'Combination' treatment group and the 'Comments' control group. The 'Combination' group received CF on both form and content, while the 'Comments' group received the same CF on content, but none on form; therefore, these two groups were the most similar except for the variable of interest here (i.e., CF of form).

11. See Lyster, Lightbown and Spada (1999) for a response to Truscott (1999).

* References marked with asterisks indicate studies included in the analysis. One asterisk indicates that the study was included in the 56 studies coded in Phase I, while two asterisks indicates that the study was one of the 15 studies meta-analyzed in Phase II.

References

Ammar, A. (2003). *Corrective feedback and L2 learning: Elicitation and recasts.* Unpublished doctoral dissertation. McGill University, Montreal, Quebec, Canada.

Ammar, A., & Spada, N. (in press). One size fits all? Recasts, prompts and the acquisition of English possessive determiners. *Studies in Second Language Acquisition, 28* (4).

*Ashwell, T. (2000). Patterns of teacher response to student writing in a multiple-draft composition classroom: Is content feedback followed by form feedback the best method? *Journal of Second Language Writing, 9,* 227–257.

*Blain, S. (2001). Study of verbal peer feedback on the improvement of the quality of writing and the transfer of knowledge in Francophone students in grade 4 living in a minority situation in Canada. *Language, Culture and Curriculum, 14*(2), 156–170.

*Braidi, S. (2002). Reexamining the role of recasts in native-speaker/non-native speaker interactions. *Language Learning, 52*, 1–42.

Bruton, A., & Samuda, V. (1980). Learner and teacher roles in the treatment of oral error in group work. *RELC Journal, 11*, 49–63.

*Carroll, S., & Swain, M. (1993). Explicit and implicit negative feedback: An empirical study of the learning of linguistic generalization. *Studies in Second Language Acquisition, 15*, 357–386.

*Carroll, S., Swain, M., & Roberge, Y. (1992). The role of feedback in adult second language acquisition: Error correction and morphological generalizations. *Applied Psycholinguistics, 13*, 173–198.

*Chandler, J. (2003). The efficacy of various kinds of error feedback for improvement in the accuracy and fluency of L2 student writing. *Journal of Second Language Writing, 12*, 267–296.

*Chaudron, C. (1977). A descriptive model of discourse in the corrective treatment of learners' errors. *Language Learning, 27*, 29–46.

Chaudron, C. (1984). The effects of feedback on students' composition revisions. *RELC Journal, 15*, 1–14.

Cooper, H., & Hedges, L. V. (1994). *Handbook of research synthesis.* New York: Russell Sage Foundation.

*DeKeyser, R. (1993). The effect of error correction on L2 grammar knowledge and oral proficiency. *Modern Language Journal, 77*, 501–514.

Doughty, C. (1994). Fine-tuning of feedback by competent speakers to language learners. In J. Alatis (Ed.), *Strategic interaction and language acquisition: Theory, practice, and research. GURT 1993* (pp. 96–108). Washington, DC: Georgetown University Press.

*Doughty, C., & Varela, E. (1998). Communicative focus on form. In C. Doughty & J. Williams (Eds.), *Focus on form in classroom second language acquisition* (pp. 114–138). Cambridge, UK: Cambridge University Press.

Ellis, R. (2001). Introduction: Investigating form-focused instruction. *Language Learning, 51*(Supplement 1), 1–46.

*Fathman, A. K., & Whalley, E. (1990). Teacher response to student writing: Focus on form versus content. In B. Kroll (Ed.), *Second language writing: Research insights for the classroom* (pp. 178–190). Cambridge, UK: Cambridge University Press.

*Fazio, L. (2001). The effect of corrections and commentaries on the journal writing accuracy of minority- and majority-language students. *Journal of Second Language Writing, 10*, 235–249.

*Ferris, D. R. (1997). The influence of teacher commentary on student revision. *TESOL Quarterly, 31*, 315–339.

*Ferris, D., & Roberts, B. (2001). Error feedback in L2 writing classes: How explicit does it need to be? *Journal of Second Language Writing, 10*, 161–184.

Fotos S. & Ellis, R. (1991). Communicating about grammar: A task-based approach. *TESOL Quarterly, 25*, 605–628.

Greenhouse, J. B., & Iyengar, S. (1994). Sensitivity analysis and diagnostics. In H. Cooper & L. V. Hedges (Eds.), *Handbook of research synthesis* (pp. 383–398). New York: Russell Sage Foundation.

*Havranek, G. (1999). The effectiveness of corrective feedback: Preliminary results of an empirical study. *Acquisition et Interaction en Langue Etrangere, 2*, 189–206.

*Hedgcock, J., & Lefkowitz, N. (1992). Collaborative oral/aural revision in foreign language writing. *Journal of Second Language Writing, 1*, 255–276.

*Herron, C. (1991). The Garden Path correction strategy in the foreign language classroom. *French Review, 64*, 966–977.

*Herron, C., & Tomasello, M. (1988). Learning grammatical structures in a foreign language: Modeling versus feedback. *French Review, 61*, 910–922.

*Hyland, F. (1998). The impact of teacher written feedback on individual writers. *Journal of Second Language Writing, 7*, 255–286.

*Iwashita, N. (2003). Negative feedback and positive evidence in task-based interaction: Differential effects on L2 development. *Studies in Second Language Acquisition, 25*, 1–36.

*Iwashita, N. (2001). The effect of learner proficiency on corrective feedback and modified output in NN-NN interaction. *System, 29*, 267–287.

*Kepner, C. G. (1991). An experiment in the relationship of types of written feedback to the development of second language writing skills. *Modern Language Journal, 75*, 305–313.

Krashen, S. (1982). *Principles and practice in second language acquisition*. Oxford: Pergamon Press.

*Lalande, J. F., II. (1982). Reducing composition errors: An experiment. *Foreign Language Annals, 17*(2), 109–117.

*Lapkin, S., Swain, M., & Smith, M. (2002). Reformulation and the learning of French pronominal verbs in a Canadian French immersion context. *Modern Language Journal, 86*, 485–507.

*Lee, I. (1997). ESL learners' performance in error correction in writing: Some implications for teaching. *System, 25*, 465–477.

*Leeman, J. (2003). Recasts and second language development: Beyond negative evidence. *Studies in Second Language Acquisition, 25*, 37–63.

*Lin, Y.-H., & Hedgcock, J. (1996). Negative feedback incorporation among high-proficiency and low-proficiency Chinese-speaking learners of Spanish. *Language Learning, 46*, 567–611.

Lipsey, M. W., & Wilson, D. B. (1993). The efficacy of psychological, educational, and behavioral treatment: Confirmation from meta-analysis. *American Psychologist, 48*, 1181–1209.

Lipsey, M. W., & Wilson, D. B. (2001). *Practical meta-analysis*. Thousand Oaks, CA: Sage.

Lochtman, K. (2000). The role of negative feedback in experiential vs. analytical foreign language teaching. Paper presented at the *Conference on Instructed Second Language Learning*. Brussels, Belgium.

Long, M. H. & Porter, P. (1985). Group work, interlanguage talk, and second language acquisition. *TESOL Quarterly, 19*, 27–56.

*Long, M., Inagaki, S., & Ortega, L. (1998). The role of implicit negative feedback in SLA: Models and recasts in Japanese and Spanish. *Modern Language Journal, 82*, 357–371.

Lyster, R. (1994). The effect of functional-analytic teaching on aspects of French immersion students' sociolinguistic competence. *Applied Linguistics, 15,* 263–287.

*Lyster, R. (1998a). Negotiation of form, recasts, and explicit correction in relation to error types and learner repair in immersion classrooms. *Language Learning, 48,* 183–218.

Lyster (1998b). Recasts, repetition, and ambiguity in L2 classroom discourse. *Studies in Second Language Acquisition, 20,* 51–81.

Lyster, R. (2001). Negotiation of form, recasts, and explicit correction in relation to error types and learner repair in immersion classrooms. *Language Learning, 51,* 265–301.

Lyster, R. (2004). Differential effects of prompts and recasts in form-focussed instruction. *Studies in Second Language Acquisition, 26,* 399–432.

Lyster, R., & Ranta, L. (1997). Corrective feedback and learner uptake: Negotiation of form in communicative classrooms. *Studies in Second Language Acquisition, 19,* 37–66.

Lyster, R., Lightbown, P. M. & Spada, N. (1999). A response to Truscott's "What's wrong with oral grammar correction. *Canadian Modern Language Review, 55,* 546–467.

*Mackey, A. (1999). Input, interaction, and second language development: An empirical study of question formation in ESL. *Studies in Second Language Acquisition, 21,* 557–587.

*Mackey, A., Gass, S., & McDonough, K. (2000). How do learners perceive interactional feedback? *Studies in Second Language Acquisition, 22,* 471–497.

*Mackey, A., & Oliver, R. (2002). Interactional feedback and children's L2 development. *System, 30,* 459–477.

*Mackey, A., & Philp, J. (1998). Conversational interaction and second language development: Recasts, responses, and red herrings? *Modern Language Journal, 82,* 338–356.

*Makino, T.-Y. (1993). Learner self-correction in EFL written compositions. *ELT Journal, 43,* 337–341.

Matt, G. E., & Cook, T. D. (1994). Threats to the validity of research synthesis. In H. Cooper & L. V. Hedges (Eds.), *Handbook of research synthesis* (pp. 503–520). New York: Russell Sage Foundation.

*Morris, F. A. (2002). Negotiation moves and recasts in relation to error types and learner repair in the foreign language classroom. *Foreign Language Annals, 35,* 395–404.

*Muranoi, H. (2000). Focus on form through interaction enhancement: Integrating formal instruction into a communicative task in EFL classrooms. *Language Learning, 50,* 617–673.

*Nabei, T., & Swain, M. (2002). Learner awareness of recasts in classroom interaction: A case study of an adult EFL students' second language learning. *Language Awareness, 11,* 43–63.

*Nassaji, H., & Swain, M. (2000). A Vygotskian perspective on corrective feedback in L2: The effect of random versus negotiated help on the learning of English articles. *Language Awareness, 9,* 34–51.

Nicholas, H., Lightbown, P. M., & Spada, N. (2001). Recasts as feedback to language learners. *Language Learning, 51,* 719–758.

*Nobuyoshi, J., & Ellis, R. (1993). Focused communication tasks and second language acquisition. *ELT Journal, 47*(3), 203–210.

Norris, J. M., & Ortega, L. (2000). Effectiveness of L2 instruction: A research synthesis and quantitative meta-analysis. *Language Learning, 50,* 417–527.

Ohta, A. S. (2000). Re-thinking recasts: A learner-centered examination of corrective feedback in the Japanese language classroom. In J. K. Hall & L. Verplaeste (Eds.), *The construction of second and foreign language learning through classroom interaction* (pp. 47–71). Mahwah, NJ: Lawrence Erlbaum.

*Oliver, R. (1995). Negative feedback in child NS-NNS conversation. *Studies in Second Language Acquisition, 17*, 459–481.

*O'Relly, L. V., Flaitz, J., & Kromrey, J. D. (2001). Two modes of correcting communicative tasks: Recent findings. *Foreign Language Annals, 34*(3), 246–257.

Panova, I., & Lyster, R. (2002). Patterns of corrective feedback and uptake in an adult ESL classroom. *TESOL Quarterly, 36*, 573–595.

*Paulus, T. M. (1999). The effect of peer and teacher feedback on student writing. *Journal of Second Language Writing, 8*, 265–289.

*Philp, J. (2003). Constraints on 'noticing the gap': Nonnative speakers' noticing of recasts in NS-NNS interaction. *Studies in Second Language Acquisition, 25*, 99–126.

*Pica, T. (1988). Interlanguage adjustments as an outcome of NS-NNS negotiated interaction. *Language Learning, 38*, 45–73.

*Pica, T., Lincoln-Porter, F., Paninos, D., & Linnell, J. (1996). Language learners' interaction: How does it address the input, output, and feedback needs of L2 learners? *TESOL Quarterly, 30*, 59–84.

*Qi, D. S., & Lapkin, S. (2001). Exploring the role of noticing in a three-stage second language writing task. *Journal of Second Language Writing, 10*, 277–303.

*Robb, T., Ross, S., & Shortreed, I. (1986). Salience of feedback on error and its effect on EFL writing quality. *TESOL Quarterly, 20*, 83–95.

Russell, J. M. (2003). *Synthesizing the corrective feedback literature: Challenges for meta-analyses.* Unpublished master's thesis, Ontario Institute for Studies in Education of the University of Toronto. Toronto, Ontario, Canada.

Samuda, V. & Rounds, P. (1993). Critical episodes: Reference points for analyzing a task in action. In G. Crookes & S. Gass (Eds.), *Tasks in a pedagogical context: Integrating theory and practice* (pp. 125–138). Clevedon: Multilingual Matters.

Schmidt, R. (1990). The role of consciousness in second language learning. *Applied Linguistics, 11*, 129–158.

Schwartz, B. (1993). On explicit and negative data effecting and affecting competence and linguistic behavior. *Studies in Second Language Acquisition, 15*, 143–145.

*Semke, H. D. (1984). Effects of the red pen. *Foreign Language Annals, 17*(3), 195–202.

Slavin, R. E. (1986). Best evidence synthesis: An alternative to meta-analysis and traditional reviews. *Educational Researcher, 15*(9), 5–11.

Swain, M. & Lapkin, S. (1998). Interaction and second language learning: Two adolescent French immersion students working together. *Modern Language Journal, 83*, 320–337.

*Sze, C. (2002). A case study of the revision process of a reluctant ESL student writer. *TESL Canada Journal, 19*(2), 21–36.

*Tomasello, M., & Herron, C. (1988). Down the Garden Path: Inducing and correcting overgeneralization errors in the foreign language classroom. *Applied Psycholinguistics, 9*, 237–246.

*Tomasello, M., & Herron, C. (1989). Feedback for language transfer errors: The Garden Path technique. *Studies in Second Language Acquisition, 11*, 385–395.

Truscott, J. (1996). The case against grammar correction in L2 writing classes. *Language Learning, 46*, 327–369.

Truscott, J. (1999). What's wrong with oral grammar correction. *The Canadian Modern Language Review, 55*, 437–455.

*Van den Branden, K. (1997). Effects of negotiation on language learners' output. *Language Learning, 47*, 589–636.

*Villamil, O. S., & De Guerrero, M. C. M. (1998). Assessing the impact of peer revision on L2 writing. *Applied Linguistics, 19*, 491–514.

Wilson, D. B. (2001). *Effect size determination program.* (Version dated 07/25/2001) [Computer software]. University of Maryland, College Park: Author.

*Zobl, H. (1985). Grammars in search of input and intake. In S. M. Gass & C. G. Madden (Eds.), *Input in second language acquisition* (pp. 329–344). Rowley, MA: Newbury House.

Appendix

Table A.

Study	1	2	3	4	5	6	7	8	9
Ashwell 2000	E	P	C	W	W	t	G	–	L
Blain 2001	E	L	C	W	O	P	G	M	–
Braidi 2002	O	L	L	O	O	N	G	R CC Cl Ex	–
Carroll & Swain 1993	E	P	L	O	O	R	S	M R E Ex	–
Carroll, Swain & Roberge 1992	E	P	L	O	O	R	S	Cr	–
Chandler, Study 1 2003	E	P	C	W	W	t	G	–	L
Chandler, Study 2 2003	E	P	C	W	W	t	G	–	Cr Cd L
Chaudron 1977	O	L	C	O	O	T	G	R Rp	–
DeKeyser 1993	E	P	C	O	O	T	G	Cr	–
Doughty & Varela 1998	E	P	C	B	B	t	S	R Rp	Cr L
Fathman & Whalley 1990	E	P	C	W	W	T	G	–	L
Fazio 2001	E	P	C	W	W	N	S	–	Cr L
Ferris 1997	O	L	C	W	W	T	G	–	M
Ferris & Roberts 2001	E	P	C	W	W	T t	G	–	Cd L
Havranek 1999	O	L	C	O	O	T	G	R E	–
Hedgcock & Lefkowitz 1992	E	P	C	W	B	T P	G	M	?
Herron Study 3 1991	E	P	C	O	O	T t	S	M Cr	–
Herron & Tomasello 1988	E	P	L	O	O	T t	S	Q	–
Hyland 1998	O	L	C	W	W	T P	G	–	Cr Cd L
Iwashita 2003	O	D	L	O	O	N	S	R CC Cl	–
Iwashita 2001	O	D	C	O	O	P	G	CC Cl	–
Kepner 1991	E	P	C	W	W	R	G	–	M Cr
Lalande 1982	E	P	C	W	W	T	G	–	Cd
Lapkin, Swain, & Smith 2002	E	L	L	W	W	N	S	–	R
Lee 1997	E	P	C	W	W	R	G	–	Ex L
Leeman 2003	E	P	L	O	O	R	S	R Ex	–
Lin & Hedgcock 1996	O	P	L	O	O	N	G	?	–
Long, Inagaki & Ortega Study 1 1998	E	P	L	O	O	R	S	R	–
Long, Inagaki & Ortega Study 2 1998	E	P	L	O	O	R	S	R	–
Lyster 1998a	O	L	C	O	O	T	G	M R Cl E Cr Rp	–
Mackey 1999	E	P	L	O	O	N	S	CC Cl	–
Mackey, Gass, & McDonough 2000	O	L	L	O	O	N	G	R CC Cl E	–
Mackey & Oliver 2002	E	P	L	O	O	R	S	R CC Cl	–
Mackey & Philp 1998	E	P	L	O	O	R	S	R CC Cl	–
Makino 1993	E	P	C	W	W	T	G	–	Ex L
Morris 2002	O	L	C	O	O	P	G	R CC Cl Cr Rp	–
Muranoi 2000	E	P	C	O	O	t	S	R CC Cl	–
Nabei & Swain 2002	O	L	C	O	O	T	G	R	–
Nassaji & Swain 2000	E	P	L	W	O	t	S	Q	–

Table A. (*continued*)

Study	1	2	3	4	5	6	7	8	9
Nobuyoshi & Ellis 1993	E	P	L	O	O	T	S	Cl	–
Oliver 1995	O	L	L	O	O	N	G	R	–
O'Relly, Flaitz & Kromrey 2001	E	P	L	O	O	N	S	CC Cl	–
Paulus 1999	E	P	C	W	W	tP	G	–	?
Philp 2003	E	P	L	O	O	R	S	R	–
Pica 1988	O	P	L	O	O	R	G	CC	–
Pica, Lincoln-Porter, Paninos & Linnell 1996	O	L	L	O	O	PN	G	CC Cl E	–
Qi & Lapkin 2001	E	L	L	W	W	R	G	–	R
Robb, Ross & Shortreed 1986	E	P	C	W	W	T	G	–	Cr Cd Ex L
Semke 1984	E	P	C	W	W	R	G	–	Cr Cd
Sze 2002	E	L	L	W	W	t	G	–	Cd
Tomasello & Herron 1989	E	P	C	O	B	t	S	M Cr	Cr
Tomasello & Herron 1988	E	P	C	O	B	t	S	M Cr	Cr
Van den Branden 1997	E	P	L	C	O	O RP	G	M CC E Ex Rp	–
Villamil & DeGuerrero 1998	E	L	C	W	O	P	G	M	–
Zobl, Study 2 1985	E	P	L	O	O	R	S	R	–
Zobl, Study 3 1985	E	P	L	O	O	R	S	R	–

1. *Type of study*: E = Experimental/Quasi-Experimental; O = Observational/Descriptive

2. *Unit of Analysis*: P = Individual Participant; D = Dyad; L = Language Event

3. *Context*: C = Classroom; L = Laboratory

4. *Mode of Errors*: O = Oral; W = Written; B = Both

5. *Mode of CF*: O = Oral; W = Written; B = Both

6. *Source of CF*: T = Teacher Only; t = Teacher as Researcher; R = Researcher only; P = Peer; N = Other NS

7. *Focus of CF*: G = General Forms; S = Specific Forms

8. *Type of Oral CF* (if applicable): R = Recast; CC = Confirmation Check; Cl = Clarification Request; M = Metalinguistic; Cr = Direct Correction; E = Elicitation; Rp = Repetition; Ex = Explicit Indication of Existance of Error Only; Q = Cues (Zone of Proximal Development); ? = Not Reported

9. *Type of Written CF* (if applicable): L = Indication of Location of Error Only; Cr = Direct Correction; Cd = Code; Ex = Indication of Existance of Error Only; M = Metalinguistic; R = Reformulation; ? = Not Reported

CHAPTER 5

Effects of L2 instruction on interlanguage pragmatic development

A meta-analysis

Eun Hee Jeon and Tadayoshi Kaya
Northern Arizona University

Burgeoning interest in the development of L2 pragmatics in classroom settings has resulted in the accumulation of a small body of studies that look at the effects of direct teaching on the acquisition of pragmatic knowledge and abilities. The present study employed a meta-analytic approach to investigate the role of instruction in the development of interlanguage pragmatics (ILP), by synthesizing studies of the effectiveness of common pragmatic instructional techniques. Following Cooper and Hedges's (1994) and Norris & Ortega's (2000) meta-analytic methodology, a literature search located 34 potentially relevant studies. Thirteen studies with quantitative data suitable for a meta-analysis were selected for the final analysis. Each study was independently coded for relevant features such as study features (e.g., instructional setting, sample size, participants' proficiency level), nature of instruction (e.g., implicit vs. explicit instruction), types of outcome measures (e.g., discourse completion tasks, role-play, interview), and length of instruction. Effect size estimates for the included studies were subsequently calculated. Results of the meta-analysis revealed that direct instruction made a notable difference over no instruction, and that explicit instruction was in some cases more beneficial than implicit instruction. Further analysis yielded suggestive but inconclusive evidence that the type of outcome measure may influence the observed learning benefits, and that compared to short-term pragmatic instruction (i.e., less than five hours), long-term instruction (i.e., more than five hours) is likely to result in larger instructional effects. We interpret these findings in light of the methodological and substantive features of the studies we meta-analyzed, and we offer suggestions for improved research practices in future investigation into instructed L2 pragmatics. We also compare the present results with those of Norris and Ortega (2000), a meta-analysis which synthesized L2 instruction studies that primarily targeted grammatical forms. With this first meta-analysis on the role of instruction in the development of ILP, we hope to contribute to a better understanding of ILP development in instructional contexts and to offer a model for future meta-analyses of the domain.

Introduction

The field of interlanguage pragmatics (ILP) concerns itself with "the study of how people accomplish their goals and attend to interpersonal relationships while using language" (Kasper & Rose 2001:2), when the individuals studied are second or foreign language (henceforth, L2) learners. In its inception, ILP was marked by a comparative research program, in which the pragmatic intuitions and behaviors of L2 learners from a given first language (L1) background were closely described, and pragmatic differences and similarities between these L2 learners and native speakers of both the L1 and the L2 under study were compared (e.g., Cordella 1991; Hinkel 1994). Second language pragmatics research then gradually broadened its scope to include a more developmental motivation (Kasper & Schmidt 1996; Bardovi-Harlig 1999), but it has only recently begun to investigate instructional concerns in and of themselves (e.g., Kasper & Rose 2001).

Two early studies investigated the effect of instruction on development of L2 pragmatic competence in the 1980s, one by House and Kasper (1981) and the other by Wildner-Bassett (1984, 1986). Despite these early beginnings, little sustained instructional research was produced during the 1980s. Even today, the teaching of L2 pragmatics is viewed as peripheral to the teaching of other areas of the L2. It is telling, for example, that no chapter on pragmatics instruction was included in the most recent *Annual Review of Applied Linguistics* volume devoted to Advances in Language Pedagogy (McGroarty 2004). During the decade of the 1990s, however, classroom research on pragmatics with a pedagogical focus became more frequent (Kasper 2001), and a small body of interventional pragmatics studies has accumulated since then (for reviews, see Fukuya & Zhang 2002; Kasper & Roever 2005; Kasper & Rose 2002). In 2003, when the present study was at its earliest planning stage, we encountered two contrasting claims regarding the state of this research domain. Kasper and Rose (2002) asserted that "a quantitative meta-analysis ... would be out of the question at this time – there are simply not enough studies to consider" (p. 239). In contrast, Fukuya and Zhang (2002) noted that two dozen such studies had been produced since the mid-1990s. These contrasting claims motivated us to take an empirical approach towards the question of whether the accumulated research on instruction of L2 pragmatics was indeed 'meta-analyzable'. Therefore, we embarked on the present study.[1]

L2 pragmatics instruction: Four guiding questions

In this section, we review the body of instructional L2 pragmatics research, with particular attention directed to the ways in which pragmatics instruction and specific instructional techniques have been theoretically motivated and empirically operationalized across individual studies. We structure our review around four fundamental questions which will guide the present meta-analysis.

Is teaching of L2 pragmatics at all necessary?

Of the issues under investigation in the area of pragmatics instruction, the most fundamental is whether teaching of L2 pragmatics is at all necessary. Kasper and Schmidt (1996) strongly supported the necessity of pragmatics instruction by noting that unlike syntax, parents and peers "actively" instruct the appropriate use of language to a child. In other words, even in L1 acquisition, pragmatic competence is commonly treated as a special entity which develops through informal instructional events, such as caretakers' provision of negative feedback, and even of explicit statements about sociopragmatic rules or pragmalinguistic resources, in response to children's pragmatic infelicities (Schieffelin & Ochs 1986, cited in Kasper & Schmidt 1996). In line with this position, Kasper and Rose (2002) later argued that "pragmatic functions and relevant contextual factors are often not salient to learners and so not likely to be noticed despite prolonged exposure" (p. 237).

The claim that mere exposure, without direct pragmatics instruction, is not sufficient for complete L2 pragmatic development finds empirical support in Bardovi-Harlig and Hartford (1993). In this semester-long observational study, 10 international graduate students of advanced proficiency (with TOEFL scores of 573 or higher) were seen to improve their sociolinguistic knowledge about status congruent behavior just from participating in faculty advising sessions. However, they failed to develop native-like competence in pragmalinguistic areas such as the use of mitigators, which are crucial to success in these institutional encounters. Bouton (1996) also furnished evidence that mere L2 exposure, in his case operationalized as length of stay, is no panacea for the development of all L2 pragmatics areas. In this study, Bouton reported on two longitudinal investigations that focused on international students' interpretation of irony and the maxim of relevance. The first study was conducted in 1986–1991 and the second in 1990–1993. At the time of arrival, the international students who participated in the first study produced interpretations similar to those of the native speaking comparison group 79.5% of the time. Four and a half years later, when the same international students were retested, they responded in ways similar to the native speaker responses 92% of the time. The improvement was at best modest, considering the length of time elapsed, and the difference between the international students and the native speakers of English remained statistically significant. Nonnative speakers were still unable to interpret eight out of 28 items in ways similar to those of their native speaking counterparts. In the second longitudinal study, Bouton compared the interpretation of implicature by native speakers to that of three groups of nonnative speakers who had been living in the U.S. for 17 months, 33 months, and 4 to 7 years, respectively. He found that although the mean scores of the 17-month and 33-month groups were statistically significantly higher than the means produced when the two groups of students had just arrived, the performance of all three nonnative speaker groups was still statistically significantly different from that of the native speaker group. The seven test items which were reported to be most difficult to learn, even after a lengthy stay in the target speech community, involved the relevance maxim, the POPE question, a sequence of events, irony, and indirect criticism. For these items, nonnative speakers and native speakers' interpretations differed greatly, between 14 percentage points and 24 or more depending on the item. The author concluded that the interpretation of formulaic implicature seems to remain difficult even after a period of 17 months to 4 or more years. Subsequently, he conducted an interventional study targeting the POPE Q implicature, indirect criticism, and a sequence of events (also reported in Bouton 1996). As a result of the instruction, the experimental group made a statistically significant improvement in interpreting implicature, while the performance of the control group remained the same.

The empirical documentation of these more difficult-to-learn areas of L2 pragmatics, which are apparently impervious to lengthy exposure to target speech norms, bolsters the argument for L2 pragmatic instruction. The need is all the more compelling in foreign language (FL) settings, where exposure to target pragmatic norms and practice opportunities outside classroom are often minimal. Classroom instruction and input materials supplied by teachers therefore are left as one of the most crucial influences in shaping L2 pragmatic competence in FL settings (although unfortunately the target pragmatic norms represented by textbooks in use today are not without problems, as Bardovi-

Harlig 2001, discusses). A good number of studies to date, beyond the ones reviewed above, attest to the value of providing formal instruction on L2 pragmatics (e.g., House & Kasper 1981; LoCastro 2000; Olshtain & Cohen 1990; Rose & Kwai-fong 2001; Wildner-Bassett 1984, 1986). In short, the necessity of pragmatics instruction can be summarized in two statements: (a) pragmatics instruction facilitates more efficient acquisition of certain areas of L2 pragmatics which are difficult to learn only through exposure; and (b) in a foreign language setting, L2 pragmatics instruction is a crucial response to scarce opportunities for exposure to target pragmatic norms and an impoverished environment for practice.

What are effective ways to teach L2 pragmatics?

With the rise of a broad consensus on the necessity for instruction of L2 pragmatics when advanced to native-like levels of attainment are the goal, the next question on the agenda is: "what are effective ways to teach L2 pragmatics?" A body of interventional studies on L2 pragmatics set out to answer this question (e.g., Armstrong 1995; Bouton 1996; Fukuya & Zhang 2002; House 1996; Tateyama 2001; Wildner-Bassett 1984, 1986; Wishnoff 2000). A cursory review of such interventional L2 pragmatics studies to date reveals that they are largely motivated by the theories and frameworks built by second language acquisition (SLA) research. Of the SLA theories suggested for the past two decades, consciousness raising (Fotos 1993), the Noticing Hypothesis (Schmidt 1995), and the Output Hypothesis (Swain 1995) seem to have been the three frameworks most-commonly adopted by interventional L2 pragmatics researchers.

In her illustration of consciousness raising instruction, Fotos (1993) argued that the external manipulation of learning conditions can trigger noticing, which in turn can facilitate L2 learning. Schmidt (1995), however, argued that noticing is an act which only happens internally, and thereby pointed out its potential invulnerability to the external manipulation of learning condition. Ellis (1994, 1997) also noted that consciousness raising is only directed to explicit knowledge and does not guarantee that the object of instruction will turn into intake. In this regard, the body of instructed pragmatics studies to date can be seen as laboratory ground where researchers attempt to prove or refute the effects of external manipulation of learning conditions and particularly implicit vs. explicit condition on the acquisition of L2 pragmatic competence.

Despite the at first sight dichotomous nature of explicit vs. implicit instruction, the actual treatment conditions of instructed pragmatics studies often reflect a point on a continuum between the absolutely explicit and the absolutely implicit extremes. Many interventional pragmatics studies feature techniques on the most explicit end of the continuum, and typically include teacher fronted instruction on pragmalinguistic forms or sociopragmatic rules sanctioned by the target speech community (e.g., Billmyer 1990; Bouton 1994, 1996; Fukuya 1998; Fukuya et al. 1998; King & Silver 1993; Olshtain & Cohen 1990; Spada 1986; Takahashi 2001; Wishnoff 2000). This condition is often characterized by a complete disclosure of the goal of the lesson (e.g., LoCastro 1997; Mollering & Nunan 1995), frequent use of metalanguage and metapragmatic information (e.g., House 1996; Takahashi 2001), unidirectional information flow (from teacher to learners) (e.g., Kubota 1995; Robinson et al. 2001), and structural exercises (e.g., Lyster 1994).

On the adjoining point of the continuum toward the implicit end is instruction employing consciousness raising activities. This treatment condition, which is often labeled as the "implicit condition" by authors, is largely characterized by learners' induction or self-discovery of target features from given input. This discovery happens through film in Fukuya (1998) and Tateyama et al. (1997), through analysis of native speaker output in a spoken or written form in Rose and Kwai-fong (2001) and Wishnoff (2000), or via directions, as in the explicit oral direction to find the "rules" of language use employed in Kubota (1995) to guide learners' exploration of target features, or through the directions given for analysis of worksheets employed in Fukuya (1998).

In other consciousness raising activities, learners are encouraged to participate in collaborative activities such as group discussion or pair work, which intend to facilitate their focal attention to the target of instruction and to foster the discovery of language use patterns through interaction. These group-based consciousness raising activities are also used for purposes other than induction of target features, namely as an advance organizer preceding exposure to input (e.g., film and native speaker data in Tateyama et al. 1997) in order to maximize the intake from the input, as well as to focus learners' attention on the intended target features (e.g., Tateyama et al. 1997; Tateyama 2001). Another interesting consciousness raising activity which has been increasingly adopted by recent instructed pragmatics studies is retrospective analysis of self-elicited data, a clear reflection of Swain's Output Hypothesis, which supports the exploitation of learner reflection using metalinguistic resource and collaborative learning tasks (Swain 1995, 2000). In these tasks, learners are often asked to listen to or view the audio- or video-recordings of their own production activities (e.g., pair conversational exercise, role-play, writing task), and to analyze their own performance referring back to the instructed target features, or to the contents of previous group discussion (e.g., Billmyer 1990; Bouton 1994, 1996; Fukuya 1998; House 1996; Robinson et al. 2001; Spada 1986; Takahashi 2001).

As Fukuya and Zhang (2002) have pointed out, only a handful of studies exist on the next point of the continuum, which more closely reflects the principles of implicit instruction. Wildner-Bassett (1984) adopted the method of Suggestopedia in her study, which investigated learning of agreement and disagreement gambits. In order to implicitly raise learners' attention to the target forms, typical features of Suggestopedia, such as relaxation in the learning environment and aural input enhancement (e.g., exaggerated intonation of the target features), were utilized without any explicit prompts to guide learners' focal attention to language forms of interest. In their own study, Fukuya and Zhang (2002) assessed the effect of recast, an implicit instructional technique, on the learning of request behavior.

Instructed pragmatics studies at the very end of the implicit pole hardly involve external manipulation of learners' attention to target forms. Most often realized as the implicit counterpart of the explicit experimental conditions in type-of-instruction studies, purely implicit instruction conditions are largely characterized by sole exposure to authentic language data (e.g., film footages, native speaker oral or written samples), no direction to guide learners' attention to language form of interest, no use of metalanguage, and absence of any type of consciousness raising activities (e.g., the comparison groups in Fukuya et al. 1998; House 1996; House & Kasper 1981; Wildner-Bassett 1984).

As we hope to have shown, the number of classroom pragmatics studies that look at the effects of direct teaching in L2 pragmatics exhibits a wide variety of instructional techniques. The present meta-analysis sought to identify any patterns of instructional efficacy associated with the corresponding range of different treatment conditions.

What are the outcome measures commonly employed in instructed L2 pragmatics studies, and is there a measurement method effect?

A variety of measurement methods have been employed in instructed pragmatics studies (see Chapter 3 in Kasper & Rose 2002, for a detailed discussion). Kasper and Dahl (1991) compared and contrasted findings resulting from different data types employed in Rintell and Mitchell (1989), Eisenstein and Bodman (1986), and Beebe and Cummings (1985). In all three studies, a written discourse completion task was adopted along with one or two types of language elicitation techniques such as role play, field notes, or audio recordings of authentic conversation. Kasper and Dahl uncovered a consistent picture across the three studies. Namely, the data collected via open-ended methods, such as oral role play or authentic conversation, were considerably longer, more complex, and richer in pragmatic strategies than the data yielded by written discourse completion tasks. The question is then whether this difference in quantity, complexity, and range of pragmatic strategies is associated with any kind of systematic test method effect.

Brown (2001) and Hudson (2001) directly addressed this question. In a study investigating requests, refusals, and apologies in an English as a second language context, Hudson (2001) reported that among the three types of data collected (i.e., written discourse completion task, role play, and language lab discourse completion task), the role play data were rated the highest and also had the smallest within group variance. These findings are reminiscent of those noted earlier by Kasper and Dahl. Hudson speculated that raters may have been more lenient when they graded live performance of the test takers than when they graded pre-recorded performances such as language lab or written discourse completion test data. In a similar vein, Brown (2001) offers evidence for test method effects in a study in which he conducted two factor analyses on scores of six different instruments administered to an EFL group and a Japanese as a second language group.[2] For each group, a best-fitting, two-factor solution was found. However, the variables contributing to each factor were different for each sample. For the test data of the EFL group, the six variables loaded on the first and the second factor in a balanced fashion, with the first factor apparently related to an underlying productive-language construct and the second factor seemingly related to an underlying receptive-language construct. For the test data yielded by the Japanese as a second language group, all variables, with the exception of the multiple-choice discourse completion task, loaded most heavily on Factor 1, while only the written discourse completion task and the multiple-choice discourse completion task loaded on Factor 2. The first and second factors were thus each labeled as an oral test factor and a paper-and-pencil factor. Simply put, these different groups of subtests were measuring different constructs in the EFL and the Japanese as a second language groups, thus revealing an important construct validity issue to be examined when selecting appropriate assessment tools in instructed pragmatics studies. The present meta-analysis sought to address the issue of test method effects based on the instructed pragmatics studies included.

What is the appropriate length of L2 pragmatics instruction?

The relationship between length of stay in a target speech community and pragmatic development has been frequently investigated by researchers. Out of this literature, the consensus emerges that there is a positive relationship between the length of residency in the target speech community and pragmatic development, operationalized as approximation of the target pragmatic norm (Bardovi-Harlig & Hartford 1993; Bouton 1996; Olshtain & Blum-Kulka 1985). When it comes to the length of treatment, however, the limited available evidence is less clear. To our knowledge, no interventional L2 pragmatics studies have been conducted with length of treatment as a single independent variable where all other variables have been controlled. Kasper (2001) addressed the question of "what is the appropriate length of treatment?" by briefly inspecting three interventional studies (Bouton 1994; Kubota 1996; Tateyama et al. 1997) out of 15 included in her review. Kasper pointed out that two studies with short treatments of approximately the same length (20 minutes for Kubota 1996; and 25 minutes for Tateyama et al. 1997) yielded contrasting results. She attributed this difference in outcome to the level of cognitive demand and complexity involved in the instructional targets. In the same review, Kasper further compared the outcomes of Bouton (1994) with those of Kubota's (1996) replication of the same study. She concluded that treatment length was one of the variables to account for the relative success of Bouton (1994) over Kubota (1996). However, as acknowledged by Kasper, a difference in treatment length was only one of several variables (e.g., level of proficiency, EFL vs. ESL teaching context) which varied across the two studies. Thus, it is premature to posit any causal relationship between treatment length and degree of success in acquisition of an instructional pragmatics target for these two or any other studies. However, meta-analysis makes it possible to inspect the issue via a correlational question, even when the individual studies may not have investigated length of treatment as a variable in their designs.

Research questions

In response to the issues raised in the narrative review of the research domain presented above, the following research questions were addressed in the present meta-analysis:

(1) Has instruction on pragmatic features been effective in ILP development?

(2) What is the relative effectiveness of different types of instruction (i.e., explicit vs. implicit) employed across L2 pragmatics studies?

(3) Is there a systematic relationship between the type of outcome measure (e.g., natural language data vs. elicited language data) and observed instructional effectiveness?

(4) What is the relationship between the length of treatment and the effects of instruction?

In addition, whenever possible and relevant, we compare our answers to these four research questions to the findings reported for effectiveness of L2 grammar instruction by Norris and Ortega (2000).

Method

The literature search

Exhaustive electronic and manual bibliographical searches were conducted to locate accessible reviews and empirical studies on instructed pragmatics published until 2003, the year in which we conducted the final data analysis for the present study. In order to empirically assess the validity of two contrasting claims, the former of which stated that research investigating the instructional effects on L2 pragmatics was overly scarce (Kasper & Rose 2002; cf. 15 interventional studies included in Table 3 of Kasper 2001) and the latter of which noted that two dozen such studies had been produced since the mid-1990s (Fukuya & Zhang 2002), an exhaustive and inclusive literature search was undertaken. All accessible instructed L2 pragmatics studies were collected without screening on the basis of participants' L1, target of instruction, or type of publication (e.g., articles in refereed journals, books, fugitive literature). Despite concerns regarding the quality of unpublished study reports (Bardovi-Harlig, October 2003, personal communication), fugitive literature was also included in the present meta-analysis in order to overcome the well known problem of publication bias (Light & Pillemer 1984).

The electronic databases of ERIC, LLBA, and PsycINFO were searched in order to obtain related studies for the present meta-analysis. Since articles in the databases are listed hierarchically, from major topics to minor topics, we first used broader key- and subject-terms in Boolean combinations in order to capture all the possible related studies (e.g., pragmatics, sociolinguistics, pragmalinguistics, interlanguage). This method reduces the possibility of missing articles described by minor and narrower terms. However, to be thorough, all the likely narrower terms (e.g., politeness, refusal, implicature, downgrader, indeixicality, mitigation) were also checked in the databases. In addition, sixteen applied linguistics periodicals were manually searched (see Appendix 1), and footnotes and citations in studies and literature reviews were probed for relevant references. Finally, additional searches were conducted by consulting with colleagues and experts of ILP, as well as by searching websites of oft-cited authors in ILP and by examining syllabi of L2 pragmatics-related courses at U.S. academic institutions, bibliographies, and handouts. This exhaustive, principled, and replicable search process resulted in the identification of 34 potentially relevant studies, all marked by one or two asterisks in the references.

Study eligibility criteria

Of the 34 potentially relevant studies that were located in the initial review, 13 studies screened through the following inclusion and exclusion criteria. (They are marked by two asterisks in the reference list and summarized in a tabular form in Appendix 2.) The inclusion and exclusion criteria were constructed based on the research questions guiding the present study. In order to be included:

(1) The study had to employ systematic quantitative data suitable for a meta-analysis.
(2) The study had to involve instructional effects on learning of any pragmatic feature (e.g., speech acts, implicature, or sociopragmatically appropriate language).
(3) The independent variables in the primary studies needed to include some type of reasonably well described classroom-based instruction of L2 pragmatic features.
(4) The dependent variables in the primary studies had to involve the measurement of participants' performance on the pragmatic feature(s) targeted by instruction.
(5) The target language of instruction was either a second or a foreign language for the study participants.
(6) The study investigated participants of secondary or post-secondary school age.

Conversely, there were four main reasons for excluding studies from the meta-analysis:

(1) Studies providing only qualitative analysis with no statistical reports or with unsuitable quantitative data for a meta-analysis were excluded. This resulted in the exclusion of 17 studies: Armstrong (1995); Bouton (1996); Brice and Absalom (1997); House (1996); King and Silver (1993); Kondo (2001); LoCastro (1997); Mollering and Nunan (1995); Olshtain and Cohen (1990); Pearson (2001);[3] Robinson et al. (2001);[4] Rueda (2004); Takahashi (2001);[5] Tateyama et al. (1997); Tochon and Dionne (1994); Wishnoff (2000); and Yoshimi (2001).

(2) A study written in languages other than English was excluded: House and Kasper (1981).

(3) Two studies based on the same sample (Rose & Kwai-fong 1999/2001; Wildner-Bassett 1984/1986) appeared in more than one journal or book and therefore each was counted only once as a unique sample study.

(4) Regrettably, despite our persistent effort, the following potentially synthesizable studies were not located by the time of final analysis: Morrow (1996) and Wijeyewardene (2001).

It is important to note that since instructed pragmatics studies commonly adopt qualitative data interpretation, a considerable number of qualitative studies had to be excluded from the current meta-analysis (cf. studies listed under reason number 1 for exclusion). As such, the findings of the present study are not a representation of the entire domain of instructed L2 pragmatics research, and therefore should not be unduly interpreted or generalized beyond the legitimate boundaries defined by our inclusion and exclusion criteria. That is, our meta-analytic findings only reflect accumulated evidence from instructed L2 pragmatics studies with quantitative data suitable for a meta-analysis. However, it must also be noted that, even if we assumed that the two unretrievable studies (Morrow 1996; Wijeyewardene 2001) were meta-analyzable, the present meta-analysis includes a majority (87%) of instructed L2 pragmatic studies suitable for a meta-analysis. On the other hand, in the event that the two aforementioned studies were not synthesizable, our meta-analysis arguably represents the entire domain of meta-analyzable L2 instructed pragmatics studies. Thus, although the present meta-analysis is not representative of the domain of instructed L2 pragmatics research in its entirety, it is indeed representative of the domain of such research with a data type suitable for a meta-analysis.

Table 1. Study coding scheme

Substantive features	Methodological features
Research question(s)	Publication date
Target feature(s) of instruction	Publication type
Type of input condition	Participants' first language
Type of instruction (implicit, explicit)	Participants' proficiency level
Features of treatment (five categories,	Sample size
e.g., consciousness raising)	Post-test timeline
	Presence/absence of pre-test, interim test, post-test, and delayed posttest
	Independent and dependent variables
	Type of outcome measures
	Reliability estimates of assessment instrument (e.g., inter-rater reliability and internal consistency)
	Descriptive statistics
	Type of inferential statistics used

Coding of study reports

A coding scheme was developed for a detailed profiling of each study (see Stock 1994). The items included in our coding scheme are summarized in Table 1.

In operationalizing the coding scheme, each study was assigned to two different independent coders.[6] The results of a first round of coding were then compared, and disagreements were discussed until both coders reached an agreement. Once the coding scheme was refined in this way, final intercoder reliability estimates were calculated for the two categories which were deemed to involve high levels of coder judgment: (a) type of instruction and (b) features of treatment (see Table 3 for results). The simple percent agreement on these two categories after a second round of coding was 97% for type of instruction and 94% for features of the treatment.

Calculation of effect sizes

To address the research questions about the effectiveness of instruction on pragmatic features, the results from the 13 collected research studies were aggregated by calculating Cohen's d (effect size), which can be interpreted as the magnitude of an observed difference between two groups in standard deviation units (Norris & Ortega 2000). Calculating Cohen's d requires group sample sizes, dependent variable means, and standard deviations of the two groups that are being contrasted. We followed the procedure for calculating Cohen's *d* that is explained in detail by Lipsey and Wilson (2001).

Defining Contrasts for Cohen's d Calculation. From a meta-analytic perspective, an ideal study is one in which one experimental group is contrasted with one control group on a single dependent variable (Norris & Ortega 2000:445). However, the research design adopted by the majority of 13 studies represented a wide range of designs beyond this scope. As such, a set of decisions regarding sub-categorization of studies depending on their research design was made in order to calculate Cohen's *d*. These decisions are summarized as follows:

(1) For studies reporting data on one experimental group and a true control group and documenting the equivalency among groups prior to treatments on a pre-test, Cohen's *d* was calculated by contrasting these two groups on the immediate post-test (Fukuya & Zhang 2002).

(2) For studies reporting data on two or more experimental groups and a true control group and documenting the equivalency among groups prior to treatments on a pre-test, Cohen's *d* was calculated by contrasting each experimental group with the control group on the immediate post-test (Fukuya & Clark 2001; Fukuya et al. 1998).

(3) For studies that had an experimental-control group design but that did not test the equivalency among groups prior to treatments, the data for control groups were not contrasted with those of experimental group(s). Instead, Cohen's *d* was calculated by contrasting the pre-test and post-test data for each experimental group (Bouton 1994; Kubota 1995; Lyster 1994; Rose & Kwai-fong 2001).

(4) For studies that had an experimental-control group design, but provided no pre-test data, Cohen's *d* was calculated by contrasting the experimental and control groups on the immediate post-test directly, since comparison between pre-tests and post-tests was impossible (Billmyer 1990; Witten 2000).

(5) For studies that did not involve control or comparison groups, but reported pre-test and post-test values of a treatment group (or groups) on a dependent variable, Cohen's *d* was calculated by contrasting the pre-test and post-test data for each treatment group (Fukuya 1998; Spada 1986[7]; Tateyama 2001; Wildner-Bassett 1984).

Combining Effect Sizes. Effect sizes were calculated using the *Cohen's d* formula and following the aforementioned decisions which sub-categorized 13 studies into five sources for contrasts. However, it is important to note that one single study can produce more than one effect size in this way, depending on the number of independent and dependent variables that were examined within the given study. This is considered to be problematic, for when effect sizes are averaged, one study can weigh more than other studies with fewer contrasts (Light & Pillemer 1984). Therefore, at times, it was necessary to combine more than one effect size so that the weight of each study would be equivalent. In the present study, effect sizes obtained from the same study were combined in the following manner:

(1) If the subjects were the same in two or more effect sizes of different measures (tests), averaged effect sizes were calculated to yield a unique *d* value to represent that study in the final calculation of the mean effect size in question.

(2) If the groups in a study consisted of different members, they were considered to be unique samples from the same study, and effect sizes were not combined.

As a result of the aforementioned decisions, 23 unique sample effect sizes were obtained out of the 13 study reports (that is, some of the studies had more than one subject group in their design). Of these 23 effect sizes, seven were derived from experimental-versus-control contrasts and another 16 were calculated from pre-to-post contrasts. An experimental-versus-control effect size provides an estimate of the degree to which an experimental group differed from its control group on the immediate post-test administered in a study, whereas a pre-to-post effect size gives an estimate of the extent to which post-test scores of a given treatment group differed from pre-test scores.

Calculating Confidence Intervals. In order to improve statistical trustworthiness of averaged effect sizes, 95% confidence intervals (CI) were also calculated. We employed the formula for CI provided by Norris and Ortega (2000: 505).

Results

The research synthesis

A set of tallies across studies was obtained regarding the various methodological and substantive features of each study report (e.g., publication dates, type of instruction). The purpose was to produce an overall profile synthesizing study features across the 13 studies.

Synthesis of methodological study features

In 20 years (between 1984 and 2003) only 13 instructed L2 pragmatics studies using systematic quantitative data suitable for meta-analysis were found. The rate of publication shows noticeable gaps, as no instructed L2 pragmatic studies included in the current meta-analysis were published in 1985, 1987–1989, 1991–1993, 1996–1997, 1999, and 2003. In addition, it should be noted that one author (Y. Fukuya) was involved in the conduct of four studies, indicating a cluster of authorship in the instructional L2 pragmatics research of this kind, and a potential 'lab-specific' effect on the outcomes.

As can be seen in Figure 1, half of the studies included in the meta-analysis (7 of 13 studies) were published in a traditional forum: in a refereed journal (Lyster 1994, in *Applied Linguistics*; Spada 1986, in *Studies in Second Language Acquisition*), in a book (Wildner-Bassett 1984) or book chapters (Rose and Kwai-fong 2001; Tateyama 2001), or in conference monographs (Bouton 1994, and Fukuya & Clark 2001, in *Pragmatics and Language Learning Monograph Series*). While these seven studies were relatively easy to obtain from major academic sources (e.g., library holdings and interlibrary loan services), the rest of the studies included in the meta-analysis were considered to be low-circulation fugitive literature: four studies were published in low-circulation or in-house periodicals (Billmyer 1990 in *Penn Working Papers in Educational Linguistics*; Fukuya & Zhang 2002 in *Second Language Studies*; Kubota 1995 in *IRLT Bulletin*; Witten 2000 in *Texas Papers in Foreign Language Education*), and two studies were available only through ERIC Document Reproduction Service (Fukuya 1998; Fukuya et al. 1998). These publication patterns clearly point at the relative scarcity of quantitative instructed pragmatics studies and are suggestive of the somewhat peripheral status (vis-à-vis applied linguistics) and small size of the research community of instructed pragmatics scholars (cf. Appendix 1).

An interesting picture emerged regarding participants' L1 across study reports, as summarized in Figure 2. Four studies dealt with participants with mixed L1s and another six involved participants whose L1 was an Asian language. Only three studies focused on participants whose mother tongue was a European language besides English. This pattern signals a concentration of research interest in EFL/ESL Asian learner populations. Moreover, among the Asian language speakers, Chinese, Japanese, and Korean L1 speakers were the three most popular L1 groups in instructed L2 pragmatic studies. Of the 13 studies, seven were conducted in a foreign language (FL) environment while six

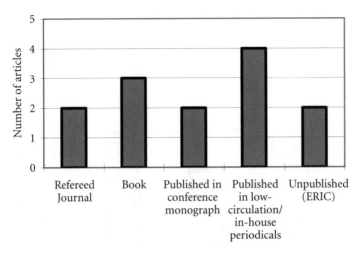

Figure 1. Studies grouped according to type of publication

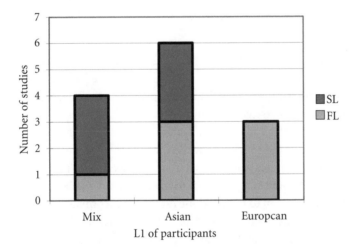

Figure 2. L1 of participants in the previous studies

were carried out in a second language (SL) environment, indicating a balance between the two different settings.

The studies were grouped under four categories depending upon their method for reporting participants' L2 proficiency, modified from Thomas (1994): (a) standardized test scores, (b) level of education (the operational-

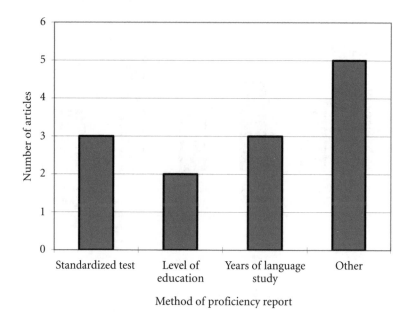

Figure 3. Proficiency measures reported

ization in this domain of what Thomas calls "institutional status"), (c) years of language study, and (d) other (e.g., participants' residence in a country of target language, description of participants' ordinary use of target language, etc). The results are summarized in Figure 3.

Only two out of 13 studies (Tateyama 2001; Witten 2000) involved learners of beginning level proficiency, while the reported level of L2 proficiency of the remaining 11 studies was deemed to have ranged from intermediate to advanced. This judgment was based on the standardized TOEFL scores reported, which ranged from 410 to 600, and the reported years of L2 instruction, which spanned 6 to 8. Intermediate to advanced university levels of education and daily use of L2 in the work place were also described in the five individual study reports classified as "other" in Figure 3. In sum, the patterns regarding study participants' proficiency levels support Bardovi-Harlig's (1999:680) claim that L2 pragmatics research has concentrated on investigating relatively advanced nonnative speakers rather than learners at all levels of proficiency. These patterns also hint at the possibility that, within the instructed L2 pragmatics research community, it is implicitly believed that a linguistic threshold is required for the acquisition of L2 pragmatics (although see recent findings in Takahashi 2005, that challenge this assumption).

Table 2. Sample size across studies and groups

Statistics	Total ($n = 13$)	Experimental ($n = 23$)	Control ($n = 10$)
Mean	54.62	22.00	20.40
Median	36.00	16.00	12.00
SD	43.81	13.92	14.70
Range	147.00	61.00	101.00
Min	17.00	8.00	8.00
Max	164.00	62.00	109.00
Total	710.00	561.00	152.00

Table 2 shows the descriptive statistics for number of participants across study reports. Among the most notable findings is the wide range of N-size across studies, with a minimum of 17 and a maximum of 164 participants in a single study. A second point is that almost one-third (four studies) of the studies did not have a control group in their design. Although it is assumed that the inclusion of a control or comparison group was often unfeasible in classroom-based research, in an effect-of-instruction study the lack of a control group is a serious drawback, for the comparison of control group and instructed group is the only way to measure the absolute effectiveness of the instruction under investigation.

Synthesis of substantive features: Design of pragmatic instruction

As shown in Figure 4, six out of the 13 studies targeted a speech act (e.g., compliments, requests) or a speech act in association with certain language forms (e.g., conditional clause in requests, progressive aspect in requests) as the object of instruction, indicating a concentration of research interest in speech act realization in a second language. The target features of the remaining seven studies included syntactic-semantic features (e.g., formulaic politeness expressions, gambits), a mixture of syntactic-semantic structure and sociopragmatic features (e.g., formulaic expressions for formal and informal contexts), and implicature (e.g., Pope questions, indirect questions). An interesting note here is that the target features of studies tended to be more formulaic and form-driven when the participants' L2 proficiency was lower (e.g., beginning level speakers learning formulaic expressions in Tateyama 2001; low-intermediate level speakers learning pre-fabricated downtoners and understaters in Fukuya 1998), while advanced level speakers were asked to engage in more function-driven instructional targets, such as speech acts or conversational implicatures (e.g., Fukuya et al. 1998; Kubota 1995; Rose & Kwai-fong 2001).

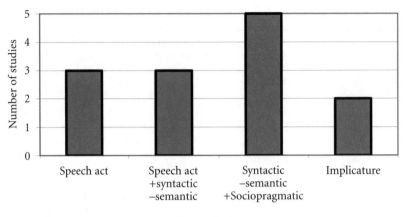

Figure 4. Target pragmatic features of instruction

The instructional treatments employed in the 13 studies were categorized under one umbrella framework for type of instruction, namely explicit vs. implicit instruction, as defined by Norris and Ortega (2000). This was done because, although each study adopted different categorical terms such as focus on forms and focus on form, or deductive and inductive, and in spite of the wide variety of details regarding treatment conditions, a close examination of each characterization of treatments revealed that, ultimately, these categories were conceptually compatible with the chosen framework and could be consistently classified as either explicit or implicit. This decision notwithstanding, it is important to underscore that many of the treatments fell within the more explicit end of the L2 explicit-implicit instructional continuum, since they frequently included delivery of declarative pragmatic information, provision of explicit instructions to attend to pragmatic rules, or both. Implicit pragmatic instructional techniques, on the other hand, appear to be scarce in the research domain. Thus, in order to obtain a more detailed picture of treatment features across study reports, treatment conditions of each study were subsequently coded for the following five subset of features: (a) presence of explicit rule explanation, (b) built-in focus on meaning, (c) built-in interaction, (d) inclusion of consciousness raising activities, and (e) use of self-initiated data collection/observation of target forms.

Table 3 shows the assignment to explicit or implicit instruction of each instructional treatment (and control or comparison condition) across studies, and the presence or absence in these conditions of the five additional treatment features identified above. Although these additional characterizations could not be used for the quantitative synthesis, because there is insufficient accumulation for each feature thus far in the research domain, the plus and minus signs help show the extent to which each condition across studies made use of explicit or implicit elements of instruction. We hope the presentation of our coding in Table 3 offers useful information for the principled design of instructional types in future individual ILP studies.

A wide range of treatment lengths was found across the 13 studies, with a minimum of 20 minutes (Kubota 1995) and a maximum of 150 hours (Spada 1986). However, more than half (8 out of 13) of the studies featured long-term treatments of more than five – often times six or many more – hours. This is in stark contrast with the length of treatment typical of the instructional studies synthesized in Norris and Ortega (2000: 474), who reported that the majority (81%) of their unique samples received brief (i.e., less than one hour) to medium-length (i.e., less than 6 hours) treatments. It would seem as if, for pragmatic instruction at least, there is consensus among researchers that lengthy treatments are needed before instructional effects can be achieved. The treatment length for each instructed pragmatics study is presented in Table 4.

Major trends employed in the assessment procedures across the 13 studies were also synthesized. Seven studies included both a pre-test and a post-test. In six of these seven studies, the post-test was administered immediately after the treatment, while in one study (Fukuya et al. 1998) the post-test was administered ten days after the treatment. Only in three of these seven studies (Kubota 1995; Lyster 1994; Spada 1986) was a delayed post-test included in addition to a pre-test and an immediate post-test. Two studies (Fukuya & Clark 2001; Witten 2000) employed a post-test only design. Finally, one study (Billmeyer 1990) reported what we call "process" tests, consisting of an aggregate of weekly or biweekly interim test results as a post-test result. The overall pattern clearly indicates two prevalent methodological shortcomings of instructed L2 pragmatic studies, namely, infrequent use of delayed post-tests (which are the only way to measure the lasting effects of instruction), and even more infrequent use of a process test, a measure which could provide a rich description of developmental transitions.

The different types of outcome measure employed are summarized in Table 5. The single most popular measure type was Discourse Completion Tests (henceforth DCTs), which were used in 11 studies, with either open ended or multiple choice items. Performance-based production tasks, such as role-play, pair conversation, and letter-writing, were also frequently used (in 6 studies). Surprisingly, researchers seldom discussed the reliability of their outcome

Table 3. Design of ILP instruction across 13 studies

Study	Groups	Explicit vs. implicit	Explicit rule expl.	Focus on meaning	Interaction	Consciousness raising	Self-initiate data
Billmyer (1990)	ExG1	Explicit	+	−	+	+	+
	Control		−	−	−	−	−
Bouton (1994)	ExG1	Explicit	+	−	+	+	+
	Control		−	−	−	−	−
Fukuya (1998)	ExG1	Explicit	+	+	+	+	+
Fukuya & Clark (2001)	ExG1	Explicit	+	−	−	−	−
	ExG2	Implicit	−	−	−	+	−
	Control		−	−	−	−	−
Fukuya et al. (1998)	ExG1	Explicit	+	−	+	−	−
	ExG2	Implicit	−	+	+	−	−
	Control		−	−	−	−	−
Fukuya & Zhang (2002)	ExG1	Implicit	−	+	+	+	−
	Control	Implicit	−	+	+	−	−
Kubota (1995)	ExG1	Explicit	+	−	−	−	−
	ExG2	Implicit	−	−	+	+	−
	Control		−	−	−	−	−
Lyster (1994)	ExG1	Explicit	+	+	+	+	+
	ExG2	Explicit	+	+	+	+	+
	ExG3	Explicit	+	+	+	+	+
	Control1		−	−	−	−	−
	Control2		−	−	−	−	−
Rose & Kwai-fong (2001)	ExG1	Explicit	+	−	−	−	−
	ExG2	Implicit	−	−	−	+	−
	Control		−	−	−	−	−
Spada (1986)	ExG1	Explicit	+	+	−	−	−
	ExG2	Implicit	−	+	+	−	−
	ExG3	Implicit	−	−	−	−	−
Tateyama (2001)	ExG1	Explicit	+	+	+	−	−
	ExG2	Implicit	−	−	−	+	−
Wildner-Bassett (1984)	ExG1	Implicit	−	−	−	+	−
	ExG2	Explicit	+	−	+	−	+
Witten (2000)	ExG1	Explicit	+	−	−	+	+
	Control		−	−	+	−	−

Note. Simple percent agreement between two independent coders was 97% for explicit vs. implicit type of instruction and 94% for five features of the treatment.

Table 4. Treatment length for 13 studies

Study Sample	Hours
Billmyer (1990)	6 hrs
Bouton (1994)	6 hrs
Fukuya (1998)	6 hrs
Fukuya & Clark (2001)	1 hr 36 min
Fukuya et al. (1998)	3 hrs 30 min
Fukuya & Zhang (2002)	5 hrs 50 min
Kubota (1995)	20 min
Lyster (1994)	12 hrs
Rose & Kwai-fong (2001)	3 hrs
Spada (1986)	150 hrs
Tateyama (2001)	1 hr 20 min
Wildner-Bassett (1984)	40 hrs
Witten (2000)	9 hrs

measures. Thus, of the ten studies which involved some form of open-ended production measure, only five furnished interrater reliability information of any kind (simple percent agreement, *kappa*, etc.). Similarly, none of the seven studies which used a selected response measure reported reliability estimates of their test instruments (e.g., in the form of internal consistency coefficients). It can be said with fairness that this lack of information about the reliability of assessment instruments is a prevailing weakness of measurement practice within instructed pragmatic research that mirrors a similar shortcoming in instructional research and in quantitative research within second language acquisition more generally (Norris & Ortega 2000, 2003).

The quantitative meta-analysis

It will be remembered that 23 unique samples were contributed by the 13 study reports included in the meta-analysis. Of the resulting 23 effect sizes, seven involved experimental-versus-control contrasts and another 16 involved pre-to-post-test contrasts. These are fundamentally different kinds of contrasts. The mean experimental-versus-control effect size provides an estimate of the degree to which experimental groups differed from their control group counterparts on the immediate post-test, whereas the mean pre-to-post effect size gives an estimate of the extent to which all treatment groups changed on average from pre-test to post-test. Consequently, values can only be meaningfully aggregated for each kind separately. For this reason, all research questions are answered by inspection of the 7 effect sizes derived from experimental-versus-

Table 5. Outcome measures

Studies	Elicited Language Data				Natural Language Data	
	DCT		LANGUAGE TEST		TASK/ACTIVITY	
	DCT with multiple choice response	DCT with open ended response	Multiple choice language test	Standardized proficiency test	Task/activity to elicit and analyze language forms	Task/activity given to raters for holistic judgment
Billmyer (1990)	–	–	–	–	(conversation meetings)	–
Bouton (1994)	(k = 22)	–	–	–	–	–
Fukuya (1998)	–	(k = 8)	–	–	(role play, k = 3)	–
Fukuya & Clark (2001)	(k = 24)	–	–	–	–	–
Fukuya et al. (1998)	–	(k = 24)	–	–	–	–
Fukuya & Zhang (2002)	–	(k = 14)	–	–	–	–
Kubota (1995)	(k = 6)	–	–	–	–	–
Lyster (1994)	(k = 18)	+	–	–	(letter writing, k = 2)	–
Rose & Kwai-fong (2001)	–	(k = 18)	–	–	–	–
Spada (1986)	–	–	(discourse and sociolinguistic)	(Michigan Test)	–	(written task)
Tateyama (2001)	(k = 10)	–	–	–	(role play k = 2)	–
Wildner-Bassett (1984)	(k = 20)	–	–	–	(role play, group discussion k = 1)	–
Witten (2000)	(k = 32)	(k = 4)	–	–	–	–

Note. k: number of test items or scenarios

control, on the one hand, and the 16 effect sizes derived from pre-to-post-test contrasts, on the other.

Research question 1: How effective is pragmatics instruction overall?

Our first research question concerns the overall effectiveness of pragmatics instruction on the acquisition of L2 pragmatic competence, as evinced in the results across the 13 studies. Table 6 displays the seven experimental-versus-control effect sizes and the associated average effect size of $d = 0.59$, suggesting a medium-magnitude superiority of experimental over control groups on the immediate post-test. Table 7 shows the 16 pre-to-post-test effect sizes and the associated average effect size of $d = 1.57$, suggesting a large average change between pre-test and post-test performance by any given experimental group. The confidence intervals associated with each mean are also shown in Tables 6 and 7.

If one interprets relative magnitude following Cohen's (1988) recommendation for psychology studies (i.e., an effect be considered large if the average d is 0.80 or higher), then it is clear that the average effect size for the seven experimental-versus-control contrasts was medium ($d = 0.59$). It is more difficult to interpret the average effect size for the 16 pre-to-post-test contrasts ($d = 1.57$). This difficulty arises from two reasons.[8] First, Cohen's recommendation was made for experimental-versus-control effect sizes only. Second, the scales of the two types of contrasts are not directly comparable, in that pre-to-post-test effect sizes tend to be larger than experimental-versus-control effect

Table 6. Effect sizes of studies with experimental and control condition comparisons

Study Sample	Contrasts	Effect Size
Billmyer (1990)	Exp-Cont	1.22
Fukuya & Clark (2001)	Exp-Cont	0.14
	Exp-Cont	−0.43
Fukuya et al. (1998)	Exp-Cont	1.06
	Exp-Cont	0.89
Fukuya & Zhang (2002)	Exp-Cont	0.85
Witten (2000)	Exp-Cont	0.39
Average Effct Size	Exp-Cont	**0.59**
95% CI Lower	Exp-Cont	0.05
95% CI Upper	Exp-Cont	1.13
k		7
SD		0.59

Table 7. Effect sizes of studies with pre-test to post-test comparisons

Study Sample	Contrasts	Effect Size
Bouton (1994)	Pre-Post	1.92
Fukuya (1998)	Pre-Post	−0.10
Kubota (1995)	Pre-Post	1.27
	Pre-Post	1.58
Lyster (1994)	Pre-Post	5.93
	Pre-Post	4.80
	Pre-Post	2.69
Rose & Kwai-fong (2001)	Pre-Post	−0.05
	Pre-Post	0.33
Spada (1986)	Pre-Post	2.07
	Pre-Post	2.06
	Pre-Post	1.94
Tateyama (2001)	Pre-Post	0.09
	Pre-Post	-0.26
Wildner-Bassett (1984)	Pre-Post	0.41
	Pre-Post	0.45
Average Effct Size	Pre-Post	**1.57**
95% CI Lower		0.63
95% CI Upper		2.51
k		16
SD		1.76

sizes, because of the attenuation in the variance of the pre-to-post-test contrast, which is based on two means contributed by one sample with similar associated standard deviations. Thus, in order to interpret the relative magnitude of the effects reported in Tables 6 and 7 more fully, a comparison with those found by Norris and Ortega (2000) for L2 instructional studies is helpful. The experimental-versus-control average of $d = 0.59$ shown in Table 6 can be judged to be a medium-sized effect, not only according to Cohen's (1988) rule of thumb interpretation, but also by comparison to the clearly larger effect in Norris and Ortega, who reported a mean effect size for 98 such contrasts of $d = 0.96$. On the other hand, when change from pre-test to post-test is considered, the reported mean effect size for 43 pre-to-post-test contrasts of $d = 1.66$ in Norris and Ortega's meta-analysis is very similar to the pre-to-post effect of $d = 1.57$ found in the present study.

Several remarks are in order, all of which are related to the problems created by the small number of available studies and contrasts. These problems are particularly acute for the group of experimental-versus-control effect sizes (see Table 6). First, there is a striking dispersion of results in Table 6, clearly indicated in a large standard deviation ($sd = 0.59$), in fact as large as the value of the mean. A few anomalous effect sizes played a major role in decreasing the mean effect size for this contrast (i.e., a negligible effect size of 0.14 and a negative effect size of -0.43, both contributed by Fukuya & Clark 2001; and a small effect size of 0.39 contributed by Witten 2000). Unfortunately, with such low numbers of individual studies available for meta-analysis, the undue weight that these outliers exert on the observed average in Table 6 cannot be avoided, and any systematic sources for the dissonance that they might contribute to the overall pattern are difficult to unmask. Small sample size also helps explain the very wide confidence interval reported in Table 6. Namely, the small number of experimental-versus-control contrasts ($k = 7$) leads to large amounts of error (reflected in the wide confidence interval) and is insufficient for trustworthy observations (as the lower limit of the confidence interval approaches close to zero).

For the pre-to-post-test effect sizes displayed in Table 7 as well, the dispersion of data is striking. This is shown in the very large standard deviation, undoubtedly caused by the negligible or negative effect sizes contributed by Fukuya (1998), Rose and Kwai-fong (2001), and Tateyama (2001), the two modest effect sizes yielded by Wildner-Bassett (1984), and the three disproportionately large effect sizes derived from Lyster (1994).[9] However, the number of pre-to-post-test contrasts available ($k = 16$) is large enough to produce trustworthy observations. Namely, the confidence interval for the mean pre-to-post-test effect size shows that the average difference between pre- and post-test performance is statistically significant and that the true effect is far from zero, falling anywhere between medium and very large (between 0.63 and 2.51).

To summarize our answer to the first research question, it can be concluded that the effectiveness of L2 pragmatic instruction was large ($d = 1.57$) and trustworthy (the true effect falling anywhere between 0.63 and 2.51 standard deviation units) in terms of average change by treatment groups from pre-test to post-test, and that, based on a small number of seven data points, experimental groups on average outperformed their control group counterparts on immediate post-tests by slightly over half a standard deviation unit ($d = 0.59$).

Research question 2: What is the relative effectiveness of implicit and explicit pragmatics instruction?

Effect sizes were aggregated according to type of instruction so that the effectiveness of explicit and implicit instructional treatments could be compared.

Tables 8 and 9 show the average effect sizes for explicit and implicit treatment conditions for experimental-versus-control contrasts and pre-to-post-test contrasts, respectively. On average, explicit instruction yielded clearly larger effects (mean $d = 0.70$ for the experimental-versus-control contrasts, and 1.91 for the pre-to-post-test contrasts) than implicit instruction (mean $d = 0.44$ and 1.01, respectively). It should be noted, however, that the available data are very limited and this results in large amounts of error reflected in the very wide confidence intervals associated with all means (cf. Tables 8 and 9). In addition, the confidence intervals for all means include zero values, except for the mean effect size of explicit treatments based on pre-to-post-test contrasts (shown in Table 9), which has a lower boundary of 0.42. This difference is likely to be explained by a combination of two facts: (a) the number of observations for explicit pre-to-post contrasts, which is slightly larger than for the other averages ($k = 10$), and (b) the three effect sizes from Lyster (1994), which largely inflated the average effect size for these contrasts. Thus, although this pattern of results is in principle consistent with the overall findings reported in Norris and Ortega (2000), the similarity of findings should not be taken at face value. What at surface may look like evidence for the superiority of explicit pragmatic instruction needs to be interpreted with caution.

Another way to understand whether explicit or implicit treatments show any instructional superiority is to inspect the effect size results within the seven primary studies which directly compared explicit and implicit treatment conditions in their design (cf. Table 3). When one does so, the indeterminate pattern already suggested by the largely overlapping confidence intervals in Tables 8 and 9 is further reinforced. Thus, the difference, albeit in favor of the explicit condition, was so small as to be truly negligible for three studies: only 0.17 standard deviation units in Fukuya et al. (1998), 0.13 and 0.12 standard deviation units in Spada (1986), and 0.04 in Wildner-Bassett (1984). In essence, these three studies showed equally strong (Fukuya et al. 1998; Spada 1986) or equally modest effects (Wildner-Bassett 1986) for pragmatic instruction regardless of condition. Oddly, Fukuya and Clark's (2001) explicit rule explanation group outperformed the control group to a larger extent than the implicit consciousness raising group did, not because the explicit treatment resulted in large benefits (with a very small positive $d = 0.14$), but because the implicit treatment appears to have been somewhat detrimental (with a moderate negative $d = -0.43$). This pattern was also attested in terms of pre-to-post effect size results in Tateyama (2001), who similarly compared an explicit rule explanation condition ($d = 0.09$) to what appeared to be a slightly detrimental implicit consciousness raising condition ($d = -0.26$). Finally, the reverse pat-

Table 8. Type of instruction effects for experimental-versus-control groups comparisons

Study Sample	Explicit/Implicit	Effect Size
Billmyer (1990)	Explicit	1.22
Fukuya & Clark (2001)	Explicit	0.14
	Implicit	−0.43
Fukuya et al. (1998)	Explicit	1.06
	Implicit	0.89
Fukuya & Zhang (2002)	Implicit	0.85
Witten (2000)	Explicit	0.39
Average Effect Size	Explicit	**0.70**
95% CI Lower		−0.12
95% CI Upper		1.53
k		4
SD		0.52
Average Effect Size	Implicit	**0.44**
95% CI Lower		−1.43
95% CI Upper		2.30
k		3
SD		0.75

tern was observed for two other studies. Both Kubota (1995) and Rose and Kwai-fong (2001) showed slightly larger pre-to-post-test gains by the implicit, rather than the explicit, conditions (and the observed gains were large in both groups for the former but only modest for the latter study).

Considering all the evidence, drawing a definitive conclusion for the second research question seems to be an unrealistic expectation at the present time. As we mentioned in the literature review, within the domain of instructed pragmatics studies instructional techniques often lean towards the explicit end of the explicit-implicit continuum, and direct comparisons with the explicit-implicit continuum implemented in general L2 instruction studies may not be possible at this point. Additionally, there may be too much variation in the details of how each study to date has operationalized explicit or implicit pragmatic instruction to be able to ascertain any stable patterns yet. We hope our meta-analysis, and the coding of five substantive instructional features provided earlier in Table 3, will be useful in guiding more systematic comparisons of L2 pragmatic instruction within and across future ILP studies.

Table 9. Type of instruction effect for pre-test to post-test comparisions

Study Sample	Explicit/Implicit	Effect Size
Bouton (1994)	Explicit	1.92
Fukuya (1998)	Explicit	−0.10
Kubota (1995)	Explicit	1.27
	Implicit	1.58
Lyster (1994)	Explicit	5.93
	Explicit	4.80
	Explicit	2.69
Rose & Kwai-fong (2001)	Explicit	−0.05
	Implicit	0.33
Spada (1986)	Explicit	2.07
	Implicit	2.06
	Implicit	1.94
Tateyama (2001)	Explicit	0.09
	Implicit	−0.26
Wildner-Bassett (1984)	Implicit	0.41
	Explicit	0.45
Average Effct Size	Explicit	1.91
95% CI Lower		0.42
95% CI Upper		3.39
k		10
SD		2.08
Average Effct Size	Implicit	1.01
95% CI Lower		−0.01
95% CI Upper		2.03
k		6
SD		0.97

Research question 3: Does type of outcome measure exhibit any systematic relationship with observed instructional effectiveness?

Our next research question asked whether type of outcome measure exhibited a systematic relationship with the effect sizes observed across the 13 studies included in the meta-analysis. More specifically, it was possible that studies employing highly structured methods for data collection (e.g., multiple-choice tests and DCTs), led to results that were in some way different from those reported in studies where naturalistic data were collected (e.g., interviews, group discussions, role plays). All the studies involving natural language data also included elicited language data, with the single exception of Billmyer (1990), who employed naturally elicited data exclusively. For this reason, effect sizes were aggregated in order to compare studies that used elicited data only with studies that employed elicited plus natural data, and Billmyer (1990) was excluded from the analysis.

As with the other research questions, contrasts based on experimental-versus-control means had to be averaged separately from contrasts based on pre-test versus post-test means. As it turned out, however, experimental-versus-control contrasts could be calculated for only four studies in the elicited language data group and for no studies in the elicited plus natural language data group. This fact left us with insufficient data points to calculate the experimental-versus-control contrast average. Consequently, evidence for this question was inspected only for pre-test versus post-test results. The corresponding average effect sizes and 95% confidence intervals are presented in Table 10.

As Table 10 indicates, a large difference in average pre-to-post-test effect size was observed in favor of comparisons using elicited plus natural language data (mean $d = 1.83$) over comparisons employing elicited language data only (mean $d = 1.01$). This finding is reminiscent of a pattern suggested in previous pragmatics literature. For example, Beebe and Cummings (1985, reviewed in Kasper & Dahl 1991) investigated refusals using two different data collection methods, authentic telephone conversation and DCT. They noted that despite the use of the same words and expressions, the range of strategies adopted by their study participants in conversation tasks was much wider than that of DCT, with DCT performance being characterized by "less negotiation, less hedging, less repetition, less elaboration, less variety and ultimately less talk" (Beebe & Cummings 1985:4).

Two important caveats need to be raised here, however. The first is that the confidence intervals around the elicited plus natural language data mean and the elicited language data only mean are overlapping and thus the observed difference, although large, is not statistically trustworthy. This no doubt is partly related to the low numbers of observations available within each case (11 and 5, respectively). A second and even more important caveat is that the elicited plus natural category in the present meta-analysis had more study samples associated with explicit instruction than the elicited language data group (three out of five study samples in the elicited data category and seven out of eleven study samples in the elicited plus natural data category). In light of this imbalance, it is impossible to confirm whether the difference between the average effect sizes of the two groups of study samples was indeed systematically related to the type of outcome measure employed (that is, elicited data vs. elicited plus

Table 10. Type of outcome measure effect for pre-test to post-test comparisons

Measure	Condition	Study	ES
Elicited	Explicit	Bouton (1994)	1.92
	Explicit	Kubota (1995)	1.27
	Explicit	Rose & Kwai-fong (2001)	−0.05
	Implicit	Rose & Kwai-fong (2001)	0.33
	Implicit	Kubota (1995)	1.58
Elicited+Natural	Explicit	Fukuya (1998)	−0.10
	Explicit	Lyster (1994)	5.93
	Explicit		4.80
	Explicit		2.69
	Explicit	Spada (1986)	2.07
	Explicit	Tateyama (2001)	0.09
	Explicit	Wildner-Bassett (1984)	0.45
	Implicit	Spada (1986)	2.06
	Implicit		1.94
	Implicit	Tateyama (2001)	−0.26
	Implicit	Wildner-Bassett (1984)	0.41
Average Effect Size		Elicited	**1.01**
95% IC Lower			−0.03
95% IC Upper			2.38
k			5
SD			0.84
Average Effect Size		Elicited+Natural	**1.83**
95% IC Lower			0.46
95% IC Upper			3.19
k			11
SD			2.04

natural data), or merely to the dominant presence of the explicit conditions in the elicited plus natural language data group.

In sum, the third research question was answered in the affirmative on the surface level, but clearly requires caution in its interpretation. Indeed, it would probably be unreasonable to make any firm claims about the relationship between magnitude of pragmatic instructional effectiveness and the nature of outcome measures employed in the research domain. Further investigation on the relationship between observed instructional effect in L2 instruction studies and the type of language data used to measure such effects is called for in future research.

Research question 4: What is the relationship between the length of treatment and the effects of instruction?

Our final research question concerned the relationship between the length of L2 pragmatics instruction and effects of instruction at the point of an immediate post-test. (The scarcity of delayed post-tests in the design of the 13 studies made it impossible to look at delayed post-test effects.) After converting reported length of instruction of all 13 studies into hours and minutes, the study samples were dichotomously coded for short (less than five hours of instruction) and long treatment conditions (more than five hours of instruction). This cut-off point of five hours was arbitrarily chosen so that the number of studies in the short and the long groups within each contrast type would be balanced. As Tables 11 and 12 indicate, for both types of contrast, the average effect sizes of the unique study samples that experienced interventions lasting more than five hours were large (0.82 and 2.22), whereas the mean effect sizes obtained for the samples that experienced less than five hours of instruction were small (0.42 and 0.49). These results clearly contrast with the findings of Norris and Ortega (2000), who reported larger effects of brief to short-treatment (lasting between less than 1 hour and 3 hours, p. 474) over long treatment (lasting more than 7 hours). It might be indeed reasonable to speculate that L2 pragmatics instruction requires considerably longer treatment periods than other target of L2 instruction (i.e., grammar-related features) in order to attain desirable effects. However, as with our answers to research question 3, and for the same reasons, caution is necessary in interpreting the present results. First, the confidence intervals around the two means are overlapping and thus the observed difference, although large, is not statistically trustworthy, possibly due to the extremely low number of cases available within each group (3 and 4, respectively). Second, explicit conditions make up the majority in the long treatment category, and this is true for both kinds of contrasts: two out of three study samples in the experimental-vs.-control condition comparison and seven out of ten study samples in the pre-test vs. post-test result comparison. Thus, since type of instruction and length of treatment are confounded, an answer to our fourth research question remains only tentative.

Conclusions, limitations, and future research directions

The most conspicuous benefit of a meta-analysis is that it enables a summary of the individual study results of the domain of interest while systematically

Table 11. Treatment length effects for treatment versus control comparisons

Length	Studies	Condition	Hours	ES
Long	Billmyer (1990)	Explicit	6 hrs	1.22
	Witten (2000)	Explicit	9hrs	0.39
	Fukuya & Zhang (2002)	Implicit	5hrs 50min	0.85
Short	Fukuya & Clark (2001)	Explicit	I hr 36min	0.14
	Fukuya et al. (1998)	Explicit	3hrs 30min	1.06
	Fukuya & Clark (2001)	Implicit	I hr 36min	−0.43
	Fukuya et al. (1998)	Implicit	3hrs 30min	0.89
Average Effect Size	Long			**0.82**
95% IC Lower				−0.21
95% IC Upper				1.85
k				3
SD				0.42
Average Effect Size	Short			**0.42**
95% IC Lower				−0.68
95% IC Upper				1.51
k				4
SD				0.69

reducing the bias that is introduced by an author's judgment in traditional narrative reviews of the literature. We hope to have convinced readers that we accomplished this end through the careful reporting of our literature search process and our developed inclusion and exclusion criteria. Through the consistent application of a coding scheme that probed comparisons on a number of useful study features, the present meta-analysis also enabled us to offer a detailed profile of substantive and methodological approaches to designing and conducting research in this domain.

For example, we determined that in studies of L2 pragmatics instruction there is a concentration of interest on Asian EFL/ESL populations and on learner populations of a relatively advanced level of L2 proficiency. We also noted that the most popular L2 targets of instruction are speech acts in isolation or in combination with related L2 forms, and that there is a tendency to choose more formulaic or form-driven pragmatic features if the L2 learner samples investigated fall toward the low-intermediate proficiency end. In terms of methodological features, we found that the single most popular measure to gauge L2 pragmatic learning effects is the DCT; that pre-test scores documenting the equivalency of treatment and control groups at the onset of a study are

Table 12. Treatment length effects for pre-test to post-test comparisons

Length	Studies	Condition	Hours	ES
Long	Bouton (1994)	Explicit	6 hrs	1.92
	Fukuya (1998)	Explicit	6 hrs	−0.10
	Lyster (1994)	Explicit	12hrs	5.93
		Explicit	12hrs	4.80
		Explicit	12hrs	2.69
	Spada (1986)	Explicit	150hrs	2.07
	Wildner-Bassett (1984)	Explicit	40hrs	0.45
	Spada (1986)	Implicit	150hrs	2.06
		Implicit	150hrs	1.94
	Wildner-Bassett (1984)	Implicit	40hrs	0.41
Short	Kubota (1995)	Explicit	20min	1.27
	Rose & Kwai-fong (2001)	Explicit	3hrs	−0.05
	Tateyama (2001)	Explicit	1hr 20min	0.09
	Kubota (1995)	Implicit	20min	1.58
	Rose & Kwai-fong (2001)	Implicit	3hrs	0.33
	Tateyama (2001)	Implicit	1hr 20min	−0.26
Average Effect Size	Long			**2.22**
95% IC Lower				0.85
95% IC Upper				3.58
k				10
SD				1.90
Average Effect Size	Short			**0.49**
95% IC Lower				−0.30
95% IC Upper				1.28
k				6
SD				0.75

often not reported; that control groups are often not included; and that delayed post-tests are rare.

In terms of substantive patterns for what counts as theoretically motivated pragmatic instruction, we believe our coding of study features also contributed important insights. A systematic review of instructional conditions revealed a considerable influence of SLA theoretical frameworks and constructs on the current research of instructed L2 pragmatics, particularly instantiated in instruction rationales related to noticing (Schmidt 1995), pushed output (Swain 1995), and metalinguistic collaborative consciousness raising principles (Fotos 1993; Swain 1998, 2000). Consistent with the definition of explicit instruction employed by Norris and Ortega (2000), we established that explicit conditions frequently include delivery of declarative pragmatic information, provision of explicit instructions to attend to pragmatic rules, or both. In addition, we found that implicit pragmatic instructional techniques are scarce, and that many of the treatments fall within the more explicit end of the L2 explicit-implicit instructional continuum. Finally, we found that treatments in L2 pragmatic instruction studies are lengthier than for other targets of instruction, such as grammar, and often involve five hours or much longer.

The evidence garnered in the meta-analytical part of the study through the calculation and aggregation of 23 effect sizes contributed by the 13 studies offered the following insights. First, we inspected evidence for overall effectiveness of L2 pragmatic instruction. A large and statistically significant mean effect size for 16 pre-to-post-test contrasts indicated that on average groups experiencing L2 pragmatic instruction changed from pre-test to post-test by one and a half standard deviation units, a large change by any standard. Probably because only five studies employed a real control group proven to be equivalent to other experimental group(s) prior to treatments, the gap in the data for experimental-versus-control contrasts led to a moderate effect size for instructed groups over control groups of slightly over half a standard deviation unit. Thus, the overall effectiveness of L2 pragmatic instruction was indicated in the present meta-analysis, and effect sizes are predicted to range from medium (around half a standard deviation unit) to large (over one standard deviation unit) in future studies.

We then inspected the evidence for systematic associations between: (1) magnitude of instructional effects and type of pragmatic instruction; (2) magnitude of instructional effects and type of outcome measure; and (3) magnitude of instructional effects and length of instruction. As it turned out, the many gaps in the data limited our ability to answer with confidence these other research questions. Explicit L2 pragmatic instructional treatments exhibited larger effect sizes than implicit L2 pragmatic instructional treatments. However, the mean effect sizes observed were trustworthy only for explicit techniques tested on the basis of pre-to-post-test contrasts (for which the number of observations available, ten, was apparently sufficient to somewhat reduce error). All other evidence pointing at putative differences between explicit and implicit conditions was weak. Studies that measured effects of pragmatics instruction through a combination of natural and elicited language data yielded larger average effect sizes than studies that relied on elicited language data exclusively, but the difference was not statistically significant. Finally, longer pragmatic treatments of more than five hours resulted in much larger gains than those observed for shorter treatments of less than five hours, but again the difference was not statistically significant. In addition, explicit types of instruction were overrepresented in all winning comparisons regarding outcome measure and instructional length, suggesting a possible confounding influence. Thus, regarding three of our four research questions, we can only put forth tentative interpretations as hypotheses for future exploration.

Our answer to the question of overall effectiveness of L2 pragmatic instruction is consistent with the main findings reported by Norris and Ortega (2000) for studies targeting mostly L2 grammar forms. By contrast, the tentative answers gleaned for the three other research questions run counter to the analogous findings reported in Norris and Ortega for L2 grammar instruction. First, the inconclusive evidence regarding effectiveness of type of L2 pragmatic instruction is inconsistent with the clear overall superiority of explicit over implicit L2 instruction reported in Norris and Ortega (2000). Second, the tentative evidence that a combination of natural and elicited language measures may lead to larger observed average effect sizes resonates with previous suggestions in the L2 pragmatics literature, but contrasts with Norris and Ortega, who reported larger effects for more controlled types of outcome measures (specifically, selected and constrained constructed-response measures over the ones tested via meta-linguistic judgment and free constructed-response measures; see p. 486). Third, the suggestive larger gains obtained for pragmatic treatments of more than five hours by comparison to shorter treatments of less than five hours runs counter to the larger effect sizes for briefer treatments lasting one to three hours reported by Norris and Ortega for studies targeting mostly L2 grammar forms.

Whether or not these differences between the two meta-analyses originate from a substantive difference in the nature of L2 pragmatics learning versus grammar learning (which was the predominant target in the studies synthesized by Norris and Ortega) is an interesting question requiring future investigation. In light of the fact that instructional techniques in the domain of instructed pragmatic studies often lean towards the explicit side of the explicit-implicit continuum, we are inclined to think that direct comparisons of types of L2 pragmatic instruction with the explicit-implicit continuum implemented in L2 grammar instruction studies may not be possible. Nevertheless, such comparisons might make sense if what counts as explicit or implicit pragmatic instruction is more carefully and systematically elucidated through future scholarly discussions. Alternatively, the possibility remains that other variables (for example, the nature of the instructional targets) may exert a more important influence than the explicitness issue in the design of instruction of L2 pragmatics, as opposed to L2 grammar. In the area of outcome measures and length of instruction, as well, future research may be well directed to investigate the possibility that determining how long effective instruction should be and how the effects can be best measured may depend on whether instruction targets L2 pragmatic versus grammatical competence. It might well be that L2 pragmatics instruction requires considerably longer treatment periods than other targets of L2 instruction (i.e., grammar-related features) in order to attain desirable effects. And, indeed, the long-term treatments of more than 5 hours employed in more than half of the studies meta-analyzed (cf. Table 4) suggest that researchers who focus on pragmatic instruction may be more willing to let this realization inform their designs than are researchers who focus on grammar instruction. Similarly, it is theoretically reasonable to speculate that the benefits of L2 pragmatic instruction may be most faithfully measured when researchers inspect naturally occurring discourse rather than when they elicit more contrived L2 performance only. However, because we maintain that the findings of the present meta-analysis should not be taken as definitive but only as indicative of hypotheses to be tested in future ILP studies, these issues cannot be settled with the available data, and instead deserve further investigation.

The value of a meta-analysis is dependent on the soundness of the research practices in a given research domain that precede synthesis of that domain. The shortcomings of the present study can be seen as an inevitable result of weaknesses in the practices that predominate in the domain of L2 pragmatic instructional research to date. In spite of the persistent and extensive search for relevant research studies, only 13 studies were found to be viable subjects for a meta-analysis. Once the coding of study features was completed, it turned out that only five of the 13 studies allowed for direct comparisons of instructional benefits between an experimental and a control group, and that the bias towards investigating explicit instruction techniques across studies (14 of 23 unique samples experienced an explicit treatment) overwhelmed the evidence that could be garnered for type of outcome measure and length of instruction, two of our moderating variables of interest. Thus, for a meta-analysis of this research domain to reach more valid and robust conclusions, it is imperative that more instructional pragmatic studies in the future adopt true (quasi-)experimental designs with control groups and pre-tests, and that theoretically motivated instructional techniques reflecting the variety of options offered by implicit instruction be designed and investigated by ILP researchers. More ILP instructional studies equipped with a sophisticated design, sound processing of data, and thorough reports on procedures and results are necessary in order to obtain a more complete picture of pragmatic instruction and its effects on L2 learning.

As much as we must acknowledge that the present meta-analysis fell short in delivering definitive answers for several of the proposed research questions, it must also be noted that as long as the research domain under analysis is still growing, no meta-analysis can provide a conclusive picture of the domain in question. In other words, all meta-analyses are inherently formative in nature and should be regarded to have achieved their goal if they successfully provide a developmental picture of the domain in the most unbiased manner possible. In this regard, our meta-analysis fulfilled its goal by analyzing and assessing the present research practices of instructed L2 pragmatics both in terms of theoretical and methodological aspects and by providing guidance for sound research in the future. A series of meta-analyses such as the present one conducted at reasonable time intervals would yield information invaluable to the field of L2 pragmatic research and instruction. The present meta-analysis, we hope, is the first step in this tradition.

Notes

1. We would like to thank our colleagues Elif Demirel and Jerry Kurjian for their contributions in the early stages of this study. We are indebted to Lourdes Ortega for her guidance on this project during a doctoral seminar at Northern Arizona University in the spring of 2003 and for her input during the writing of this chapter. Finally, we thank an anonymous reviewer for helpful comments.

2. The use of factor analysis is recommended with at least 300 cases, depending on the number of independent and dependent variables in a given design (Tabachnick & Fidell 2001). The reliability of estimation of the correlation coefficients offered by Brown (2001) is therefore not without question.

3. This dissertation did not report standard deviation of any of the tests. It only reported mean scores.

4. We would like to thank Peter Robinson, who generously responded to our request and furnished more detailed data for the findings reported in Robinson et al. (2001). Despite such efforts on his part and ours, in the end we were unable to retrieve the complete necessary data and the study could not be included in this meta-analysis.

5. The only descriptive statistics this study reported were on the assessment of learners' confidence level. We reasoned that this measure assesses a different construct from other measures employed by the rest of the studies included in the present meta-analysis, which measure learners' pragmatic performance, and therefore decided to exclude this study from the aggregate analysis.

6. The first round of codings and refinement of the coding scheme was done by the two authors and Elif Demirel, who was our co-researcher in the first phase of this study.

7. Spada (1986) is not usually considered to be directly relevant to instructed pragmatics. However, this study was included because the syllabus of the program in which the study was conducted "aimed for the learner to produce language that is formally and functionally correct, situationally appropriate and accompanied by suitable paralinguistic features" (p. 184), a description which resonates with Kasper's (2001) comment on current interventional L2 pragmatic research; "several of the (L2 pragmatic) interventional studies illustrate that might better be termed FonFF in pragmatics – a focus on form and function" (p. 53) Therefore, we argue that the instruction involved in Spada (1986) can be interpreted to reflect instruction of L2 pragmatics.

8. We thank the editors for bringing this issue to our attention.

9. As can be seen in Table 6, the effect sizes obtained for the three explicit conditions in Lyster (1994) are unusually high (5.93, 4.80, 2.69). We speculate that these unusually high effect sizes may have been caused by the characteristics of study participants, in combination with the nature of the target of instruction and by the operationalization of explicit instruction. Specifically, the study participants were already proficient speakers of French and had been using French as a medium of instruction for their primary and secondary education. Considering their high level of L2 proficiency, teaching the appropriate and accurate use of two second person pronouns of French (tu/vous) according to the formality of the context was a fairly easier target of instruction when compared to the target of instruction of other ILP studies included in this meta-analysis. Furthermore, Table 3 shows that the explicit instructional treatments in this study were markedly more explicit than most other conditions across studies. Thus, in our opinion, Lyster's (1994) results should not be considered representative of the true instructional effectiveness of explicit ILP conditions in general.

* Of the 35 references initially considered for meta-analysis, the 21 marked with one asterisk (*) did not meet some or several of the inclusion criteria; the 13 studies marked with two asterisks (**) were those which met the criteria and were included in the final meta-analysis.

References

*Armstrong, R. (1995). Pragmatics and politeness in the second language classroom. *PASAA, 25*, 33–42.

Bardovi-Harlig, K. (1999). Exploring the interlanguage of interlanguage pragmatics: A research agenda for acquisitional pragmatics. *Language Learning, 49*, 677–713.

Bardovi-Harlig, K., & Hartford, B. S. (1993). Learning the rules of academic talk: A longitudinal study of pragmatic development. *Studies in Second Language Acquisition, 15*, 279–304.

Beebe, L. M., & Cummings, M. C. (1985). Speech act performance: A function of the data collection procedure? Paper presented at the TESOL Convention, New York.

**Billmyer, K. (1990). "I Really Like Your Lifestyle": ESL learners learning how to compliment. *Penn Working Papers in Educational Linguistics, 6*, 31–48. (ERIC Document Reproduction Service No. ED335937).

**Bouton, L. F. (1994). *Can NNS skill in interpreting implicature in American English be improved through explicit instruction? – A pilot study.* In L. F. Bouton & Y. Kachru (Eds.), *Pragmatics and Language Learning Monograph Series.* Vol. 5 (pp. 89–109). Urbana-Champaign, IL: Division of English as an International Language, University of Illinois, Urbana-Champaign. (ERIC Document Reproduction Service No. ED398742).

*Bouton, L. F. E. (1996). *Pragmatics and language learning. Monograph series volume 7.* Illinois: English as an International Language, University of Illinois at Urbana-Champaign.

*Brice, A., & Absalom, D. (1997). Classroom pragmatic skills: Investigating adolescents learning English as a Second Language. *Journal of Children's. Communication Development, 18,* 2 19–29.

Brown, J. D. (2001). Pragmatics tests: Different purposes, different tests. In K. Rose, & Kasper, G. (Eds.), *Pragmatics in Language Teaching* (pp. 301–325). Cambridge, UK: Cambridge University Press.

Cordella, M. (1991). Spanish speakers apologizing in English: A cross-cultural pragmatics study. *Australian Review of Applied Linguistics, 14,* 2, 115–138.

Cooper, H. M., & Hedges, L. V. (1994). Research synthesis as a scientific enterprise. In F. Cooper & L. Hedges (Eds). *The handbook of research synthesis* (pp. 3–14). New York: Russell Sage Foundation.

Eisenstein, M., & Bodman, J. (1986). "I very appreciate": Expressions for gratitude by native and non-native speakers of American English. *Applied Linguistics, 7,* 157–185.

Ellis, R. (1994). *The study of second language acquisition.* Oxford: Oxford University Press.

Ellis, R. (1997). *SLA research and language teaching.* Oxford: Oxford University Press.

Fotos, S. (1993). Consciousness-raising and noticing through Focus on Form: Grammar task performance versus formal instruction. *Applied Linguistics 14,* 385–407.

**Fukuya, Y. (1998). Consciousness-raising of downgraders in requests. Paper presented at Second Language Research Forum, University of Hawai'i at Mānoa. (ERIC Document Reproduction Service No. ED466100).

**Fukuya, Y., & Clark, M. K. (2001). A comparison of input enhancement and explicit instructin of mitigators. In L. Bouton (Ed.), *Pragmatics and Language Learning Monograph Series,* Vol. 10 (pp. 111–130). Urbana-Champaign, IL: Division of English as an International Language, University of Illinois Urbana-Champaign.

**Fukuya, Y., Reeve, M., Gisi, J., & Christianson, M. (1998). Does focus on form work for teaching sociopragmatics? Hawaii. (ERIC Document Reproduction Service No. ED452736).

**Fukuya, Y., & Zhang, Y. (2002). Effects of recasts on EFL learners' acquisition of pragmalinguistic conventions of request. *Second Language Studies, 21,* 1, 1–47.

Hinkel, E. (1994). Pragmatics of Interaction: Expressing Thanks in a Second Language. *Applied Language Learning, 5* (1), 73–91.

*House, J. (1996). Developing pragmatic fluency in English as a foreign language. *Studies in Second Language Acquisition, 18* (2), 225–252.

*House, J. & Kasper, G. (1981). Politeness markers in English and German. In F. Coulmas (Ed.), *Conversational Routine* (pp.157–185). The Hague: Mouton.

Hudson, T. (2001). Indictors for pragmatic instruction: Some quantitative tools. In K. Rose & G. Kasper (Eds.), *Pragmatics in Language Teaching* (pp. 283–300). New York: Cambridge University Press.

Kasper, G. (2001). Classroom research on interlanguage pragmatics. In K. Rose & G. Kasper (Eds.), *Pragmatics in Language Teaching* (pp. 33–60). Cambridge, UK: Cambridge University Press.

Kasper, G., & Dahl, M. (1991). Research methods in interlanguage pragmatics. *Studies in Second Language Acquisition, 13*, 215–247.

Kasper, G., & Roever, C. (2005). Pragmatics in second language learning. In E. Hinkel (Ed.), *Handbook of research in second language teaching and learning* (pp. 317–334). Mahwah, NJ: Lawrence Erlbaum.

Kasper, G. & Rose, K. (2001). Pragmatics in language teaching. In K. Rose & G. Kasper (Eds.), *Pragmatics in language teaching* (pp.1–9). Cambridge, UK: Cambridge University Press.

Kasper, G., & Rose, K. R. (2002). The role of instruction in learning second language pragmatics. *Language Learning, 52*, 237–273.

Kasper, G., & Schmidt, R. (1996). Developmental issues in interlanguage pragmatics. *Studies in Second Language Acquisition, 18*, 149–169.

Kasper, N., & Dahl, M. (1991). Research methods and interlanguage pragmatics. *Studies in Second Language Acquisition, 13*, 215–247.

*King, K. A., & Silver, R. E. (1993). "Sticking points": Effects of instruction on NNS refusal strategies. *Working Papers in Educational Linguistics, 9*, 47–82.

*Kondo, S. (2001, October). Instructional effects on pragmatic development: Interlanguage refusal. Paper presented at PacSLRF, University of Hawai'i at Mānoa.

**Kubota, M. (1995). Teachability of conversational implicature to Japanese EFL learners. *Institute for Research in Language Teaching Bulletin, 9*, 35–67. (ERIC Document Reproduction Service No. ED397640).

Light, R. J. & Pillemer, D. B. (1984). *Summing up: The science of reviewing research.* Cambridge, MA: Harvard University Press.

Lipsey, M. W., & Wilson, D. B.(2001). *Practical meta-analysis.* Thousand Oaks, CA: Sage Publications, Inc.

*LoCastro, V. (1997). Pedagogical intervention and pragmatic competence development. *Applied Language Learning, 8* (1), 75–109.

LoCastro, V. (2000). Evidence of accommodation to L2 pragmatic norms in peer review tasks of Japanese learners of English. *JALT Journal, 22* (2), 245–270.

**Lyster, R. (1994). The effect of functional-analytic teaching on aspects of French immersion students' sociolinguistic competence. *Applied Linguistics, 15*, 263–287.

McGroarty, M. (Ed.). (2004). *Advances in language pedagogy. Annual Review of Applied Linguistics, 24.*

*Mollering, M., & Nunan, D., (1995). Pragmatics in interlanguage: German modal particles. *Applied Language Learning, 6* (1&2), 41–64.

*Morrow, C. (1996). *The pragmatic effects of instruction on ESL learners' production of complaints and refusal speech acts.* Unpublished doctoral dissertation. State University of New York at Buffalo.

Norris, J. M., & Ortega, L. (2000). Effectiveness of L2 instruction: A research synthesis and quantitative meta-analysis. *Language Learning, 50,* 417–528

Olshtain, E., & Blum-Kulka, S. (1985). Degree of approximation: Non-native reactions to native speech act behavior. In S. Gass, & C. Madden (Eds.), *Input in second language acquisition* (pp. 303–325). Rowley, MA: Newbury House.

*Olshtain, E., & Cohen, A. (1990). The learning of complex speech act behaviour. *TESL Canada Journal, 7* (2), 45–65.

*Pearson, L. (2001). *Pragmatics in foreign language teaching: The effects of instruction on L2 learners' acquisition of Spanish expressions of gratitude, apologies, and directives.* Unpublished doctoral dissertation. University of Texas at Austin.

Rintell, E., & Mitchell, C. (1989). Studying requests and apologies: An inquiry into method. In S. Blum-Kulka, J. House, & G. Kasper (Eds.), *Cross-cultural pragmatics: Requests and apologies* (pp. 248–272). Norwood, NJ: Ablex.

*Robinson, P., Strong, G., Whittle, J., & Nobe, S. (2001). The development of EAP oral discussion ability. In J. Flowerdew & M. Peacock (Eds.), *Research perspectives on English for Academic Purposes* (pp. 347–359). Cambridge, UK: Cambridge University Press.

*Rose, K. R., & Kwai-fong, C. N. (1999). Inductive and deductive approaches to teaching compliments and compliment responses. *Perspectives, 11* (2), 124–169.

**Rose, K. R., & Kwai-fong, C. N. (2001). Inductive and deductive teaching of compliments and compliment responses. In K. R. Rose & G. Kasper (Eds.), *Pragmatics in language teaching* (pp. 145–170). Cambridge, UK: Cambridge University Press.

*Rueda, L. Y. T. (2004). *Effects of pedagogical intervention on the development of pragmatic competence in adult learners of English as a Foreign Language (EFL).* Unpublished doctoral dissertation. University of Arizona, Tucson, AZ.

Schiefflin, B. B., & Ochs, E. (1986). *Language socialization across cultures.* Cambridge, UK: Cambridge University Press.

Schmidt, R. (1995). Consciousness and foreign language learning: A tutorial on the role of attention and awareness. In R. Schmidt (Ed.), *Attention and awareness in foreign language teaching and learning (Technical Report No. 9)* (pp. 1–64). Honolulu: University of Hawai'i at Mānoa.

**Spada, N. (1986). The interaction between types of contact and type of instruction: Some effects on the L2 proficiency of adult learners. *Studies in Second Language Acquisition, 8,* 181–200.

Stock, W. (1994). Systematic coding for research synthesis. In H. Cooper & L. Hedges (Eds.), *The handbook of research synthesis* (pp.125–138). New York: Russell Sage Foundation.

Swain, M. (1995). Three functions of output in second language learning. In G.. Cook & B. Seidlhofer (Eds.), *Principle and practice in applied linguistics: Studies in honour of H. G. Widdowson* (pp. 125–144). Oxford: Oxford University Press.

Swain, M. (1998). Focus on form through conscious reflection. In C. Doughty, & J. Williams (Eds.), *Focus on form in classroom second language acquisition* (pp. 64–81). Cambridge, UK: Cambridge University Press.

Swain, M. (2000). The output hypothesis and beyond: Mediating acquisition through collaborative dialogue. In J. P. Lantolf (Ed.), *Sociocultural theory and second language learning* (pp. 97–114). Oxford: Oxford University Press.

Tabachnick, B. G., & Fidell, L. S. (2001). *Using Multivariate Statistics* (4th ed.). Needham Heights, MA: Pearson.

*Takahashi, S. (2001). The role of input enhancement in developing pragmatic competence. In K. R. Rose & G. Kasper (Eds.), *Pragmatics in language teaching* (pp. 171–199). Cambridge, UK: Cambridge University Press.

Takahashi, S. (2005). Pragmalinguistic awareness: Is it related to motivation and proficiency? *Applied Linguistics, 26*, 90–120.

**Tateyama, Y. (2001). Explicit and implicit teaching of pragmatic routines; Japanese sumimasen. In K. R. Rose & G. Kasper (Eds.), *Pragmatics in language teaching* (pp. 200–222). Cambridge, UK: Cambridge University Press.

*Tateyama, Y., Kasper, G., Mui, L. P., Tay, H., & Thananart, O. (1997). Explicit and implicit teaching of pragmatic routines. *Pragmatics and Language Learning, 8*, 163–178.

Thomas, M. (1994). Review article: Assessment of L2 proficiency in second language acquisition research. *Language Learning, 44*, 307–336.

*Tochon, F. V., & Dionne, J.-P. (1994). Discourse analysis and instructional flexibility: A pragmatic grammar. (ERIC Document Reproduction Service No. ED398741).

*Wijeyewardene, I. (2001). Interaction in learner interlanguage: An approach to the practice and self-assessment of oral skills. *English Australia Journal 19* (1), 50–64.

**Wildner-Bassett, M. (1984). *Improving pragmatic aspects of learner's interlanguage.* Tübingen: Gunter Narr Verlag.

*Wildner-Bassett, M. (1986). Teaching 'polite noises': Improving advanced adult learners' repertoire of gambits. In G. Kasper (Ed.), *Learning, teaching and communication in the foreign language classroom* (pp. 163–178). Århus: Aarhus University Press.

*Wishnoff, J. R. (2000). Hedging your bets: L2 academic writing and computer-mediated discourse. *Second Language Studies 19* (1), 119–148.

**Witten, C. (2000). Using video to teach for sociolinguistic competence in the foreign language classroom. *Texas Papers in Foreign Language Education, 5* (1), 143–175. (ERIC Document Reproduction Service No. ED468314).

*Yoshimi, D. R. (2001). Explicit instruction and JFL learners' use of interactional discourse markers. In K. R. Rose & G. Kasper (Eds.), *Pragmatics in language teaching* (pp. 223–244). Cambridge, UK: Cambridge University Press.

Appendix 1: Journals checked manually

	Years searched	Potentially relevant studies that did not meet inclusion criteria (marked by one asterisk in the references)	Studies included in meta-analysis (marked by two asterisks in the references)
Annual Review of Applied Linguistics	1992, 1994, 1998, 2000	0	0
Applied Language Learning	2000–2001	2	0
Applied Linguistics	1986–2003	0	1
Australian Review of Applied Linguistics	1999–2002	0	0
Canadian Modern Language Review	1985–2003	0	0
International Journal of Applied Linguistics	1999–2002	0	0
Issue in Applied Linguistics	2000–2002	0	0
Language in Society	1996–2003	0	0
Language Learning	1997–2003	0	0
Modern Language Journal	2002–2003	0	0
Pragmatics and Language Learning	1989, 1993, 1994, 1996	1	2
Second Language Research	2000–2002	0	0
Studies in Second Language Acquisition	1986–2003	1	1
System	1985–2003	0	0
Working Papers in Educational Linguistics	Volumes 10, 13, 16, 17, 18	1	0
World Englishes	1993–2000	0	0

Appendix 2: 13 included studies

Study	Teaching goal	Proficiency	L1	Research focus	Design	Assessment procedure/instrument
Billmeyer 1990	Compliments	Intermediate, advanced	Japanese	Explicit	Pre-instructional observation, post-instructional observation, control	Frequency of appropriate production
Bouton 1994	Implicature	University level	Mixed	Explicit	Pretest, posttest, control	Multiple choice test
Fukuya 1998	Downgrader	TOEFL: 430–512	Japanese, Korean, Chinese	Teachability, explicit, consciousness raising	Pretest, posttest	Role play, DCT
Fukuya &Clark 2002	Mitigator	TOEFL: 410–600	Japanese, Korean, Chinese, Iranian	Explicit, input enhancement, Focus on Form vs. Focus on Forms	Pretest, posttest, control	Multiple choice test
Fukuya et al. 1998	Request	TOEFL: 500–599	Japanese, Chinese, Korean, Russian	Focus on Form vs. Focus on Forms	Pretest, posttest, control	DCT
Fukuya &Zhang 2002	Request	8 years of EFL instruction	Chinese	Recast	Pretest, posttest, control	DCT
Kubota 1995	Implicature	6–7 years of EFL instruction	Japanese	Explicit vs. consciousness raising	Pretest, posttest, control	Multiple choice test, sentence composing test
Lyster 1994	Sociopragmatically appropriate address	8 years of bilingual schooling in French	English	Explicit	Pretest, posttest, delayed posttest, comparison	Written production test, oral production test, multiple choice test

Study	Feature	Level	L1	Instruction	Design	Assessment
Rose &Kwai-fong 2001	Compliment	University level	Cantonese	Inductive vs. deductive	Pretest, posttest, control	Self assessment, DCT, meta-pragmatic assessment
Spada 1986	Formally and functionally correct, and situationally appropriate language	Intermediate	Arabic, Chinese, French, German, Greek, Indonesian, Japanese, Maly, Portugese, Spanish, Taiwanese	More explicit vs. less explicit	Pretest, posttest	Speaking test consisting of an interview and interaction task
Tateyama 2001	Formulaic expressions	Beginning	English, Chinese, Korean	Explicit vs. Implicit	Pretest, posttest	Multiple choice test, role play, self reports
Wildner-Bassett 1984	Gambits on agreement and dis-agreement	Daily or weekly use of English, residence in English speaking countries	German	Suggestopedia	Pretest, postttest	Role play
Witten 2000	Socioprag-matic competence, formality	Beginning	English	Explicit, consciousness raising, implicit	Posttest, control	Self assessment, oral discourse elicitation, multiple choice test

CHAPTER 6

The effects of Explicit Reading Strategy Training on L2 reading comprehension

A meta-analysis

Alan Taylor, John R. Stevens, and J. William Asher

Brigham Young University-Idaho / Utah State University /
Purdue University

A number of studies have been conducted to investigate whether or how the conscious use of reading strategies can enhance second language (L2) reading comprehension. A potentially effective intervention in reading classes is to teach the use of such strategies explicitly to second and foreign language students, a type of pedagogical intervention that we call Explicit Reading Strategy Training (ERST) in the present study. Although research bearing on this question has accumulated, the findings are hardly conclusive. The present meta-analysis attempted to take stock of how effective ERST really is, and it also investigated the question of whether certain variables, such as the nature of the strategies taught, the type of test used to measure comprehension benefits, and so on, exert a systematic influence on the effects of ERST on L2 reading comprehension observed across primary studies to date. Twenty-three unique sample studies were identified as appropriate for inclusion, and their results were meta-analyzed. It was found that, on average, participants who received ERST training comprehended L2 texts better than those who did not receive such training, with a mean effect of $d = .54$, which can be interpreted as 68% of the average students receiving ERST exceeding the average reading comprehension of students not receiving such training on measures of L2 reading comprehension. Of the moderating variables examined, statistically significant effects were found only for overall length of the texts employed in the reading post-tests and for proficiency level and age of the L2 readers who received the ERST training across studies. The findings are discussed and implications for L2 reading pedagogy are suggested.

Introduction

Second language reading is an important skill that can facilitate or hinder academic success to many second language (L2) learners across educational contexts. Reading is also a crucial source of input for L2 development. Because of the centrality of L2 reading, many beginning and intermediate L2 textbooks have some form of L2 reading component. In addition, some include reading strategies, such as brainstorming and planning before reading. These tips are offered on the assumption that strategies can positively improve L2 reading comprehension and help L2 learners become better L2 readers. Ideally, indeed, skillful use of strategies necessary for effective L2 reading can potentially empower readers to become autonomous in L2 learning by exploiting reading as a source of L2 input for further learning.

A number of studies have been conducted to investigate whether or how the conscious use of reading strategies can enhance L2 reading comprehension. For example, in a classic study, Carrell, Pharis, and Liberto (1989) found that readers provided with training in the use of semantic mapping, a metacognitive strategy, performed significantly better than those without such training. Pappa, Zafiropoulou, and Metallidou (2003) obtained similar results. Although these and other studies have shown that strategy training can be effective in L2 reading comprehension, the degree of effectiveness of such training is still unclear, and the overall effectiveness when compared to no strategy training is currently ambiguous. Other variables, such as type of strategy training and age of the L2 readers, may moderate the study outcomes. In light of such uncertainty, meta-analytic research can enable us to come to more concrete conclusions. The present study, a quantitative meta-analysis, is an exploratory attempt to synthesize the available literature and to shed more light on the effects of explicit reading strategy instruction (ERST) – a term we adopt in the present meta-analysis following Bimmell et al. (2001) – on L2 reading comprehension.

Theoretical motivation for the meta-analysis

Explicit Reading Strategy Training defined

For the purpose of this study, strategies are defined as techniques explicitly taught to L2 learners with the goal to enhance L2 reading comprehension (for similar definitions, see Chamot 2001; O'Malley & Chamot 1990; Oxford 1990). The term Explicit Reading Strategy Training (ERST) is thus introduced to underscore that these techniques are explicitly communicated to the L2 reader to enhance reading comprehension. Strategy training that is *explicit* is the focus of this meta-analysis because we are interested in action-oriented, proactive assistance for the L2 reader. The criterion of explicitness is based on whether or not the strategy is openly communicated to the learner, who is purportedly aware that a strategy is being conveyed and is usable. The following example from Kemper (1989) illustrates the strategy of "activating prior knowledge" operationalized as an ERST treatment:

> The experimental treatment promoted the activation and the use of the subjects' existing background knowledge and experience, that which they already know about their native language and culture to learn the new English language and American culture. This treatment instructed students to rely on and use their individual experiences of their native language, culture, and world knowledge. (p. 28)

Another example of an ERST treatment can be found in the following intervention by Pappa et al. (2003), where students were taught the reading strategy of "semantic mapping":

> The procedural steps of this method generally include a brainstorming session in which students verbalise 110 associations on a topic or a key concept as the teacher writes them on the board. The teacher then facilitates the students' discussion to organise or categorise the associations into the form of a map, activating thus their prior knowledge of the topic and helping them to focus on the relevant content schema. Students develop a map of the story's topic before reading both to learn the key vocabulary and to activate their prior knowledge bases of that topic. (p. 774)

In the above study, at the end of the ERST session, the L2 readers were also explicitly told "that semantic mapping would be particularly useful for dealing with reading passages that contain a lot of details" (p. 781). Explicitness is considered important because it is more certain that learners' attention is focused on the strategies in question. The focus of the present meta-analysis, therefore, is on intervention as opposed to observation. If it was not apparent to the learner that a strategy was being presented, the treatment was not included in the present meta-analysis.

Strategies can be of different types. Oxford's (1990) model of direct, indirect, and social strategies is used in the present meta-analysis because it has been shown to be consistent with learners' strategy use (Tsung-Yuan & Oxford 2002). For the purposes of this study, however, only direct and indirect strategies were considered, since social strategies have not been manipulated as independent variables in experimental L2 reading studies. Direct strategies are those that learners apply to the language itself. Generally, these are also called *cognitive* strategies. Indirect strategies are those that are applied to the language learning process. One of the major categories under the rubric of indirect strategies, as applied to L2 reading comprehension, is *metacognitive* strategies. Metacognitive strategies are those used for planning, monitoring, or reviewing how the interaction with the L2 text will take place. As Neil Anderson (2002) puts it:

> Metacognition can be defined simply as thinking about thinking. Learners who are metacognitively aware know what to do when they don't know what to do; that is, they have strategies for finding out or figuring out what they need to do. The use of metacognitive strategies ignites one's thinking and can lead to more profound learning and improved performance, especially among learners who are struggling. (p. 1)

Understanding the effectiveness of metacognition provides insight into the general L2 reading process, and assists researchers in understanding learners' reasons for learning the L2 (Wenden 2001). For the purposes of the present meta-analysis cognitive strategies are simply those used to interact with the L2 text, and metacognitive strategies are those used to manage how the interaction with the L2 text takes place.

We should mention that the distinction between which general type of strategy is actually used – whether cognitive or metacognitive – is often difficult to truly measure. Also, the fact that many ERST studies have multiple mixtures of cognitive and meta-cognitive strategies further muddies the research water. How do we know, for instance, which strategy is actually having the dominant effect on L2 reading comprehension? The distinction is made in the present study, however, because most primary researchers seem to construe the difference as salient in their studies. That is, there may be a differential effect of ERST on L2 reading comprehension depending on whether or not metacognitive ERST is conducted.

The need for the present meta-analysis

Grabe (1991) expressed the difficulty of drawing overall conclusions from research on L2 reading strategy use because of several important moderating variables that potentially influence the results:

> A major problem with strategy training is that there are so many potential training strategies, interactions with student learning styles, and training

> contexts. Establishing consistent results in second language situations will be difficult until many more reading strategy experiments are conducted. (p. 393)

Since the publication of Grabe (1991), more experiments on ERST in the contexts of foreign language and ESL learning have been conducted. However, although extensive, the research is hardly conclusive. Some studies have found a statistically significant difference between groups with ERST and groups without such instruction (Ghenghea 1985; Hamp-Lyons & Proulx 1982; Kemper 1989; Kern 1989; Kitajima 1997; Kusiak 2001; Pappa et al. 2003; Park-Oh 1994; Porter 1992; Raymond 1993; Tanaka 1985). Conversely, other studies have found that there is no statistically significant difference between such groups (see Arellano 1991; Barnett 1988a, 1988b; Bimmel et al. 2001; Evans 2002; Prinz 1998). It is therefore not surprising that Grabe's skepticism is echoed more recently by Brantmeier (2002):

> The interactive nature of L2 reading, in and of itself, reveals the difficulty in designing studies that examine the L2 process as well as the complexity involved in formulating generalizations across L2 reading strategy studies. Both the nature of the sample and the setting within which a study takes place must be considered when thinking about generalizability. (p. 12)

The difficulty in comparing across studies is clear, because of important moderating variables that influence the results. Yet, meta-analytic procedures, including systematic coding of primary studies and homogeneity tests, provide information that can facilitate explanations of such differences among and between studies. Through rigorous selection of experimental and quasi-experimental studies, systematic coding of relevant moderating variables, and aggregation of findings across accumulated studies, the present meta-analytical approach provides more insight and more qualified results than any narrative review or any single empirical study would be able to provide. The use of meta-analytic procedures will enable us to determine the overall effect of ERST on L2 reading comprehension as well as the differing influence of other potentially important variables on the results of ERST primary studies.

Moderating variables of interest in the meta-analysis of ERST

In experimental research, many variables may influence results, though controls are introduced to enable a focus on those variables of most interest. Meta-analytic research on L2 reading has thus far found that much variance in experimental results depends on how the independent and dependent variables are manipulated by the primary researcher (Taylor 2002). Consequently, a number of experimental methodology variables were considered of potential interest in the present meta-analysis. Conceptually, these moderating variables were derived from consideration of discussions and observations made in publications on L2 reading and L2 reading strategies. All primary studies included in the meta-analysis were then coded for these variables, in order to eventually inspect the extent to which they affected the results observed across studies. (Readers will find the complete list of variables and codes used in Table 3.)

A good deal of variance most likely depends on the manner and type of treatment provided to the experimental group versus that of the control group. Thus, for example, it is possible that a major difference exists between studies that teach L2 readers how to go about interacting with the text (thus focusing on metacognitive strategies) and those that teach L2 readers how to interact directly with the text (thus emphasizing cognitive strategies).

Some variance may be also explained by how the experimental effects are measured, as suggested in published discussions of L2 reading tests (see Bernhardt 1983, 1991; Shohamy 1984; Wolf 1993). Testing instruments can easily provide varying degrees of precision concerning how much L2 text has actually been understood, and, consequently, how much effect the treatment really has had on the experimental group. For example, Bernhardt (1983) demonstrated how, on a poorly-constructed multiple-choice test, L2 participants who have not read an L2 text can perform nearly as well as those who have read it. This occurs because the instrument contains additional information regarding the text. Using logic and the information provided in the test items, the reader can simply choose the most plausible answers based on how the questions are posed. Of course, multiple-choice instruments can be as reliable and valid as many other types of standardized tests, provided they were developed through extensive preparation and pilot-testing. However, some instruments, such as the L1 recall protocol, may be more telling than others of how much effect a certain treatment has had on L2 reading comprehension (Bernhardt 1983, 1991; Shohamy 1984; Wolf 1993). A broader feature of L2 reading comprehension tests is whether they require a productive (e.g., recall) or a receptive (e.g., multiple choice) response from the readers.

The amount of time intervening between pre-test and post-test administrations, as well as the time length of the treatment, are two other variables that may affect the results of ERST studies. L2 readers who are provided with more time to improve their ERST may perform better than those without such prolonged training. Conversely, readers provided with lengthy ERST training may perform worse than non-ERST readers because they rely too heavily on certain strategies (i.e., activating background knowledge) and may forget other fundamental strategies (such as guessing vocabulary words from context) for improving L2 reading comprehension.

How and when the L2 is used may be an equally important variable in this meta-analysis, and thus several so-called language variables were included (see Table 3). The level of the L2 reader may be the most critical of all the language variables. For example, Laufer (1996) claims that unless an L2 reader has a basic vocabulary of at least 3,000 words, it makes little difference which strategies are used. Thus, there may be a threshold at which an L2 reader needs to be in order for ERST to really have an important effect on L2 reading comprehension (Alderson 1984; Laufer 1996; Laufer & Sim 1985).

Age may also play a part in how or whether a certain strategy or combination of strategies is used. Younger learners may be more accepting of in-class teaching, such as strategies, and this predisposition can decrease with age (Nikolov 1999). Conversely, because they have normally spent more time reading, older students have had a greater chance of developing reading strategies. For L2 readers, cognitive and literacy maturity in the L1 may be essential for development of reading strategies in the L2. For bilingual readers, research has shown that L1 strategic behaviors undergird those in the L2 (Hardin 2001). Thus, ERST studies may yield different results if they focus on young children who are still in the process of developing reading skills in their L1 (with the conventional cut-off point below 12 years of age), as opposed to relatively mature but still developing readers who are in high school (between 12 and 18 years of age), or on college-level adults.

The language context of the study also needs to be considered, since language behavior and language learning are so closely tied to culture and context (see Abu-Rabia 1996, 1998). For instance, one could argue that ESL learners may have much more motivation to become more effective readers than EFL learners because the former live in the target language and culture. Further, learners of other (non-English) foreign languages may not generally have enough motivation to learn the L2 as either ESL or EFL learners. As Pappa et al. (2003) have suggested, the language context can influence the results reported across ERST studies.

Finally, the length of the L2 texts used to measure L2 reading comprehension on the posttest was also identified as a potentially important moderating variable in the current study. For example, a text that is very short may not afford enough opportunities for the L2 reader to use the newly learned strategies. On the other hand, if a text is too long, the L2 reader may give up on the ERST and just try to finish the test, perhaps because of fatigue. In both hypothetical cases, the effects of ERST would not be truly known because the inappropriate choice of text length would have hampered researchers' ability to measure how effective the ERST really is.

Obviously, variables influence or are related to other variables. Also, some variables may have more influence on results of studies than others. The present meta-analysis sought to discern what seem to be the most influential moderating variables in studies about the effects of ERST on L2 reading comprehension. By including a wide net of potentially relevant variables, the present meta-analysis sought to uncover issues that can then be studied more in depth in subsequent primary and meta-analytic studies.

Research questions

The following questions guided the present meta-analysis:

1) What is the overall effectiveness of ERST on L2 reading comprehension?
2) Does the use of metacognitive ERST make a difference in promoting L2 reading comprehension?
3) Which tests are best for determining the effects of ERST on L2 reading comprehension?
4) Does context (i. e., FL, EFL, ESL) make a difference in ERST studies?
5) Is ERST as effective for first year learners as it is for second and third year learners?
6) Does age of the L2 readers make a difference in ERST?
7) How might issues of test timing and treatment time length influence ERST studies?
8) Does overall length of the texts employed to measure effects of ERST matter?

The first research question is the most important because it is causal and is the core question of all the primary studies included in this meta-analysis. The subsequent questions are primarily methodological and language-based questions. They are considered correlational in nature and are key in determining potential moderating variables that may influence the results of studies.

To our knowledge, some of the questions have never been directly studied. However, this does not mean they should not be studied. First, they seem to be the key variables explaining a substantial proportion of the variability among studies. Second, meta-analysis as a research methodology need not only synthesize; it can also provide new ideas and directions for future studies.

Method

Inclusion and exclusion criteria and literature search

Studies relevant and included in the present meta-analysis had to meet certain criteria: (a) the study had to be either an experiment or a quasi-experiment, (b) the study had to be written in English, (c) at least one of the dependent variables of the study was reading comprehension, (d) the effect of ERST versus no ERST on L2 reading was tested, and (e) it was possible to extract an effect size from the data provided. Studies lacking any of these qualities were not included. One study (Boonyaratapan 2000) was excluded because it was published in French. At least several studies were discarded because two explicit strategy instruction groups (in other words, two experimental groups) were compared without a control group (e.g., Carrell 1985; Tang 1974). Bilingual studies (e.g., Padron 1985) were also excluded because this meta-analysis is concerned with language learning, and learners that are characterized as bilingual can be considered already competent in the L2.

Quasi-experiments featured intact classes who were administered a pretest and post-test and experienced a treatment versus no treatment. Quasi-experiments as well as true experiments (that is, where subjects were randomly assigned to experimental or control groups) were included because they increased the number of types of comparisons available across studies, providing more insight into the effects of the conditions under which the studies were done. Likewise, unpublished sources were included because using them markedly increased the number of studies available and, consequently, the number of participants used in the statistical tests, thus reducing the possibility of Type II errors. We conducted a test of homogeneity, which revealed no significant difference between published and non-published sources (see Appendix A). This result suggests the magnitudes resulting from ERST treatments contributed by the unpublished sources were in no particularly systematic way different from the magnitudes of effects yielded by the published sources.

A variety of electronic search methods were used to find relevant studies for this meta-analysis. The most important of these were Proquest Digital Dissertations, part of Dissertation Abstracts International (DAI), Languages and Literatures Behavior Abstracts (LLBA), and The Educational Resources Information Center (ERIC). Once a study was found, its bibliography was checked in order to identify further potential studies for inclusion. Approximately 400 abstracts were read and analyzed, along with the bibliographies and literature reviews of studies found to meet the above criteria. Twenty-one studies were found, out of which twenty-three unique outcomes were extracted. An outcome, or study report, is essentially a study within a study, which was obtained when a researcher reported multiple experiments within the same publication.

Calculation of effect sizes

A measure of effect size, Hedges' g, was extracted for all outcomes using DSTAT (Johnson 1993). The effect size is the standardized difference between two means and is the backbone of causal meta-analysis. They are, in essence, adjusted normal curve deviants of the differences between the means of the experimental and comparison groups divided by the pooled standard deviations of the two groups (see Table 1):

$$g = \frac{\overline{X}_E - \overline{X}_C}{s_P}$$

The pooled standard deviation, or s_P, is represented as

$$s_P = \sqrt{\frac{(n_{G1}-1)s_{G1}^2 + (n_{G2}-1)s_{G2}^2}{(n_{G1}-1) + (n_{G2}-1)}}$$

where the square root is taken of the sum of the degrees of freedom of each group multiplied by its own variance and divided by the sum of the overall degrees of freedom (see Lipsey & Wilson 2001). The adjusted g includes a correction for study sample size (see Hedges 1981, 1982).

Basic descriptive statistics are generally needed in order to calculate the effect size. The sample size, the means for each group, and their respective standard deviations are the most important statistics to include in a study. Yet, in many cases, the g was not as easily obtainable. It was found, as shown in the footnotes of Table 1, that many primary researchers in this domain failed to include the standard deviation. In some cases, only the p or F-value and the sample size were reported. Since means and standard deviations are used in calculating p or F-values, it was often possible to deductively extract effect sizes. The g was extracted from the F-ratio using the following formula:

$$g = \sqrt{\frac{F(n_1 + n_2)}{n_1 n_2}}$$

where g is the effect size estimate, F is the test statistic, and n represents the sample size of the respective groups, whether control or experimental (for formulas, see Appendix B in Lipsey & Wilson 2001). Alternately the p-value was taken and converted, given the degrees of freedom, to the t-value, from which the effect size was calculated with the following formula:

$$g = t\sqrt{\frac{n_{\cdot 1} + n_2}{n_1 n_2}}$$

where the t-value is multiplied by the square root of the total study sample divided by the product of the sample sizes.

Once extracted, the effect size was entered into the software Comprehensive Meta-Analysis (Biostat 2001), from which all other statistics, including the Hedges adjusted g, the weighting of studies, fixed and random effects, confidence intervals and homogeneity tests were derived (see Table 2). Since Comprehensive Meta-Analysis requires a Cohen's d to be initially entered, we converted the Hedges g to a Cohen's d with the following formula:

$$g = \frac{d}{\sqrt{\dfrac{n_1 + n_2}{df}}}$$

where Cohen's d is divided by the square root of the sum of the population divided by the degrees of freedom (for more detail on how Hedges' g and Cohen's d are related, see Appendix B). It should be pointed out that the footnotes in Table 1 explain precisely how the g was calculated in the event of a lack of data. Notice, also, that Table 1 includes two studies that had two outcomes each.

Table 1 provides information as to the kind of studies that were included in the present meta-analysis. Interestingly, most studies were quasi-experiments, meaning that intact classes were used, along with a pre and posttest, instead of random assignment of subjects to experimental or control groups. Random assignment assures that the groups are at a relatively equal competency level before a treatment is administered. However, the degree of equality or comparability of groups can also be ensured when pre and posttests are conducted because one can simply subtract the difference (as measured by the effect size g) between the control and experimental groups on the pretest from the difference between the respective groups on the posttest ($g_{posttest} - g_{pretest}$). This procedure was used for all quasi experiments in the present meta-analysis. Ran-

Table 1. Basic descriptive statistics

Key: true exp = true experiment; gn score = gain scores reported; *p*-value = only *p*-value reported; *F* – value = only F-value reported

Primary Study Outcome	*Ne*	*Nc*	Pre Xe	Pre Xc	Post Xe	Post Xc	*g*
Arellano (1991) 3rd grade	17	16	51.53	49.12	41	36.44	.09
Arellano (1991) 6th grade	29	14	54.86	42.64	49.21	43.93	−.25
Barnett (1988a)[1]	90	73	31.86	32.53	35.23	34.15	.28
Barnett (1988b)	51	213	true exp	true exp	21.04	20.31	.07
Bimmel & al. (2001)[2]	12	119	83.88	82.02	89.07	86.06	.11
Brown (1991)	15	15	28	27	32	20	.95
Carrell et al. (1989)[3]	9	8	gn score	gn score	3.33	−.63	1.35
Evans (2002) Beginning level	12	15	true exp	true exp	3.67	4.53	−.55
Evans (2002) Intermediate level	6	7	true exp	true exp	4.83	4.86	−.02
Ghenghea (1985)[4]	15	15	*p*-value	*p*-value	*p*-value	*p*-value	1.14
Hamp-Lyons & Proulx (1982)	8	8	84.1	83.9	103	115.25	.56
Kemper (1989)	84	56	41.50	38.51	49.77	40.75	.83
Kern (1989)	26	27	61.92	72.22	83.08	75.26	1.49
Kitajima (1997)[5]	13	15	30.69	25.53	2.52	1.67	.77
Kusiak (2001)[6]	78	80	11.56	12.78	14.49	13.81	.48
Pappa et al. (2003)[7]	30	29	54.90	61.50	60.90	62.00	.49
Park-Oh (1994)	24	21	97.13	123	114.72	119.93	.55
Porter (1992)	17	17	true exp	true exp	4.45	1.52	1.65
Prinz (1998)	14	12	14.00	19.85	12.33	15.62	−.29
Raymond (1993)	21	22	48.43	46.41	50.91	37.82	.47
Talbot (1995)	183	61	52.00	54.00	67.60	60.90	.53
Tanaka (1985)	30	30	7.43	9.07	8.07	7.93	1.00
Zhicheng (1992)[8]	15	14	true exp	true exp	*F*-value	*F*-value	1.13

Note. Random Effects, Hedges adjusted *g* = .54

[1] This study is considered a true experiment (confirmed 12-8-2003). The *F*-test was used to calculate the *g*.

[2] In this study the standard deviation for calculating the *g* was derived from the standard error.

[3] The *g* was estimated via a ratio method with the effect size of the difference between the control pre and posttest.

[4] The *g* was calculated using the sample size *n* and the, *p*-value with the program DSTAT (Johnson 1993).

[5] The reader will notice that the means in this study are on a different scale. This is because the pre and posttests were not the same. However, the pretest was an indicator of group differences and was therefore used. ($g_{posttest} - g_{pretest}$).

[6] There was a slight discrepancy with regard to the sample size in Kusiak (2001). The author marked the control group as 80 and the experimental group as 78. Later in the article in the table of basic statistics, the sample size numbers were reversed.

[7] An effect size of .46 is reported by Pappa et al. (2003). We are simply reporting our own calculation. The effect size of the control group was subtracted from the effect size of the experimental group: −.09−(−.58) = .49.

[8] For each experimental group, a g was obtained and then the mean *g* was calculated.

domized, true experiments without pretests (e.g., Barnett 1998b; Evans 2002; Porter 1992; Zhicheng 1992) could simply be calculated with only the posttest results.

Table 2. Overall meta-analysis

	Citation	N1	N2	Effect	StdErr	Lower	Upper	PValue
	Arellano (1991) 3rd grade	17	16	.091	.349	−.620	.802	.791
	Arellano (1991) 6th grade	29	14	−.251	.327	−.911	.408	.436
	Bamett (1988a)	90	73	.280	.158	−.033	.592	.076
	Barnett (1988b)	51	231	.070	.155	−.235	.374	.651
	Bi mmel et al . (2001)	12	119	.110	.303	−.489	.710	.715
	Brown (1991)	15	15	.947	.388	.152	1.741	.013
	Carrell et al. (1989)	9	8	1.351	.553	.172	2.530	.010
	Evans (2002) Beginning	12	15	−.555	.396	−1.370	.261	.152
	Evans(2002) Intermediate	6	7	−.020	.556	−1.245	1.204	.969
	Ghenghea (1985)	15	15	1.138	.398	.324	1.953	.003
	Hamp-Lyons & Proulx (1982)	8	8	.556	.513	−.544	1.655	.259
	Kemper (1989)	84	56	.831	.180	.476	1.187	.000
	Kem (1989)	26	27	1.488	.313	.859	2.116	.000
	Kitajima (1997)	13	15	.776	.395	−.036	1.588	.045
	Kusiak (2001)	78	80	.481	.161	.162	.800	.003
	Pappa et al. (2003)	30	29	.492	.265	−.037	1.022	.060
	Park-Oh (1994)	24	21	.553	.305	−.062	1.168	.066
	Porter (1992) Semantic Map	17	17	1.650	.404	.828	2.472	.000
	Prinz (1998)	12	14	−.292	.396	−1.109	.525	.450
	Raymond (1993)	21	22	.472	.310	−.153	1.098	.123
	Talbot (1995)	183	61	.530	.150	.235	.825	.000
	Tanaka (1985)	30	30	.997	.275	.447	1.547	.000
	Zhicheng (1992)	15	14	1.127	.404	.298	1.957	.004
Fixed	Combined (23)	797	907	.487	.054	.380	.593	000
Random	Combined (23)	797	907	.535	.101	.336	.734	.000

Coding of primary studies

The basis for making comparisons across studies was to use the codes representing differing conditions among the studies and categorized as moderator variables. Two researchers, the first author of the present study and a research assistant, scrutinized the initial selection of the codes. Notably, after some initial discussion early in the process, the variable "Independent Variables as defined by the primary researcher" was discarded because it was (a) in many cases not really defined, and (b) there were almost as many different names for the ERST as there were studies. Similarly, several other coding categories were considered only to be discarded, because it became clear they would lead to too many codes with only one or two studies to make the comparison statistically justifiable (e.g., whether a treatment involved "Direct versus Indirect" strategies). In addition, the two variables of "Language Context of Study" and "Dependent Variable" spurred several disagreements and led to refinements of coding definitions. After discarding the above-mentioned variables, the simple percent agreement rate between the two coders was 82%. Another research assistant outside of our research group, with statistical expertise and several years of foreign language experience, checked the codes. After further discussion between the primary researcher and the second research assistant, the discrepancies were resolved until an overall agreement rate of 100% was obtained. The final coding categories, which represented both research methodology and linguistic attributes, are listed in Table 3. Table 4 displays the values assigned to each study for each coding category.

Homogeneity tests

In order to explore the nature of differences between and among groups of studies, two different tests of homogeneity were considered. The first, the test of homogeneity of effect sizes, tested whether all of the studies under consideration shared a common effect size. The test statistic here is

$$Q_T = \sum w_i(g_i - g)^2,$$

where g_i is the effect size estimate from study i, w_i is the inverse of the corresponding variance, and g is the fixed effects overall effect size estimate. When all of the 23 studies here share a common effect size, Q_T is approximately distributed as chi-square with 22 degrees of freedom.

The second test of homogeneity considered whether different classes of studies shared a common effect size. For any such variable characterizing K different classes of effect sizes in the meta-analysis, a test of homogeneity of effect sizes across classes can be considered. The test statistic here is

$$Q\beta = \sum w_k(g_k - g)^2$$

where g_k is the fixed effects overall effect size estimate for class k, w_k is the inverse of the corresponding variance, and g is the fixed effects overall effect size estimate. When all of the K classes share a common effect size, $Q\beta$ is approximately distributed as chi-square with $K-1$ degrees of freedom. This test is analogous to the F-test of equality of class means in an analysis of variance (see Hedges & Olkin 1985: 153–154).

Table 3. Variables and codes

Experimental Methodology Variables	Codes
A. Metacognitive Elements	1-Yes 2-No
B. Dependent Variable	1-L1 Recall 2-L2 Recall 3-Cloze Test 4-Mix 5-Standardized Test 6-Multiple-Choice 7-Open-ended questions 8-Sentence Translation
C. Productive versus Receptive Variable	1-Productive 2-Receptive 3-Both
D. Total Time of Experiment, Pretest to Posttest	1- One to Four Weeks 2-Five to Eight Weeks 3-Nine to Twelve Weeks 4-Twelve weeks or more
E. Total Hours of Treatment	1-Zero to Five 2-Six to Ten 3-Eleven to Twenty 4-Thirty or more
Language Variables	
F. Average Level of Participants[1]	1-First Year 2-Second Year 3-Third Year or ESL
G. Average Age of Participants	1-Zero to 12 2-Twelve to Eighteen 3-Eighteen or more or University Student
H. Language Context of Study	1-ESL 2-EFL 3-FL
I. Words in Text(s) of Testing Instrument	0-no data 1-Zero to four hundred 2-Four hundred to eight hundred 3-Eight hundred or more

[1] This is the year of their personal L2 study during which they are participating in the primary study

Table 4. Variables codes assigned across studies

Study Outcomes	Variables & Codes								
	A	B	C	D	E	F	G	H	I
Arellano (1991) 3rd grade	2	5	2	3	3	3	1	2	2
Arellano (1991) 6th grade	2	5	2	3	3	3	1	2	2
Barnett (1988a)	2	5	2	4	2	1	3	3	0
Barnett (1988b)	1	1	1	3	4	1	3	3	2
Bimmel et al. (2001)	2	5	3	4	3	3	2	2	0
Brown (1991)	1	2	1	2	2	3	3	2	3
Carrell et al. (1989)	1	7	1	1	1	3	3	1	3
Evans (2002) Beginning level	2	1	1	2	1	1	3	3	1
Evans (2002) Intermediate level	2	1	1	2	1	2	3	3	1
Ghenghea (1985)	1	4	3	3	3	3	2	3	1
Hamp-Lyons & Proulx (1982)	1	3	1	4	4	3	3	1	3
Kemper (1989)	1	5	2	2	4	3	3	1	0
Kern (1989)	2	1	1	4	4	2	3	3	1
Kitajima (1997)	2	1	1	4	4	2	3	3	2
Kusiak (2001)	1	4	3	1	2	2	2	2	1
Pappa et al. (2003)	1	4	3	1	1	3	2	2	3
Park-Oh (1994)	1	2	1	2	2	3	3	1	3
Porter (1992)	2	1	1	1	3	3	2	3	3
Prinz (1998)	2	5	2	3	3	3	2	1	0
Raymond (1993)	1	1	1	2	1	2	3	3	2
Talbot (1995)	1	2	1	2	2	3	3	1	3
Tanaka (1985)	2	4	3	4	4	3	3	2	2
Zhicheng (1992)	1	6	2	1	1	3	3	1	3

Note. A 0 value was assigned when no data were provided in the study for the given coded variable.

Results

The overall random-effects effect size, Hedges g, of the effects of ERST on L2 reading comprehension was .54 with considerable heterogeneity among studies ($Q = 63.92$; $p < .001$). These statistics indicate that on posttests, learners with ERST on average comprehend L2 texts more than one-half of a standard deviation above those without such training. We can generalize and situate the magnitude of ERST in a more practical interpretive context by converting this effect size of .54 into a percentage scale. If we do so, the prediction is that 68% of the average students receiving ERST will exceed the average reading comprehension of students not receiving such training on measures of L2 reading comprehension.

Table 5. Test of homogeneity for "Metacognitive Elements" variable

Group	Point estimate		
Yes (12)	.4050		
No (11)	.5318		
Combined (23)	.4866		
Source	Q-Value	*df*	PValue
Between classes	1.24800	1.0000	.2642

Type of ERST: Cognitive vs. metacognitive strategy training

As shown in Table 5, the mean effect size for the 11 studies which delivered cognitive strategies only was .53, whereas the mean effect size for the 12 studies that featured some metacognitive strategy in the ERST training was .41, and this was a non-statistically-significant difference ($Q\beta = 1.25$; $p = .26$). Thus, whether or not a primary ERST treatment included at least some metacognitive strategy training led to no statistically significant differences in observed L2 reading comprehension results.

Tests employed to measure reading comprehension

Six of the 23 primary samples meta-analyzed measured L2 reading comprehension via standardized tests such as the TOEFL (Kemper 1989; Park-Oh 1994), the Gates-MacGinitie Reading test (Prinz 1998), and the Iowa Test of Basic Skills (ITBS) (Arellano 1991). Most of the other studies used the recall protocol, generally considered a very valid measure of L2 reading comprehension (Bernhardt 1983, 1991; Taylor 2002) in either the L1 (used in seven studies) or the L2 (used in three studies). Some studies employed a combination of different measurement instruments (e.g., Bimmel et al. 2001). As shown in Table 6, however, the type of post-test measure employed did not seem to statistically significantly influence the results of ERST studies ($Q\beta = 10.29$; $p = .11$). These results should be interpreted with caution, since some codes only had one study. There was a large effect size of 1.35 for studies that used an open-ended instrument, and an equally large effect size of 1.13 for studies using a multiple-choice instrument. For all other test types, mean effect sizes were considerably smaller (.64 for studies employing researcher-made mixture of various tests; .58 for studies using L2 recall; .56 for studies with cloze tests; and .41 for the studies using the L1 recall). A strikingly low average effect size of .33 resulted from the six studies that featured standardized tests.

Table 6. Test of homogeneity for "Dependent Variable" variable

Group	Point estimate		
Cloze Test (1)	.5559		
L1 recall (7)	.4081		
L2 recall (3)	.5790		
Multiple-Choice (1)	1.1275		
Open-ended Questions (1)	1.3506		
Researcher Mix (4)	.6352		
Standardized Test (6)	.3275		
Combined (23)	.4866		
Source	**Q-Value**	*df*	*P*Value
Between classes	10.2930	6.0000	.11283

Table 7. Test of homogeneity for "Productive versus Receptive" variable

Group	Point estimate		
Both (5)	.5664		
Productive (12)	.5007		
Receptive (6)	.3994		
Combined (23)	.4866		
Source	**Q-Value**	*df*	*P*Value
Between classes	1.3280	2.0000	.5147

Similarly, the test design feature of receptive versus productive response format had little influence on the results of ERST studies, as can be seen in Table 7. There was an effect size of .57 for studies with both productive and receptive test tasks, an effect size of .50 for studies with productive test tasks only, and an effect size of .40 for studies with receptive test tasks only. There was no statistically significant difference between groups according to this variable and its respective codes ($Q\beta = 1.33$; $p = .51$). Furthermore, a post hoc test of homogeneity between only productive and receptive variables did not indicate statistical significance ($Q\beta = .63$; $p = .43$). Taking the evidence in Tables 6 and 7 together, it can be concluded that the type of posttest used to measure L2 reading comprehension did not make a statistically significant difference in explaining ERST study variance, at least for the present 23 studies.

Length of study and length of treatment

The 23 studies meta-analyzed were grouped into four balanced groups according to the total time it took to conduct a given study: up to four weeks (five studies), five to eight weeks (seven studies), nine to twelve weeks (five studies), and fifteen or sixteen weeks (six studies). As seen in Table 8, average effect sizes of around half a standard deviation unit were found for the various study lengths, except for the five studies lasting between 9 and 12 weeks, which yielded a negligible mean effect size of .09. This difference was statistically significant ($Q\beta = 15.08$; $p = .00$). Some unknown quality in these five ERST studies must be invoked to explain this result.

More closely related to the effectiveness of an ERST treatment is the number of hours of exposure to the strategy training. Table 9 shows that the largest mean effect size was observed with studies involving the longest ERST treatments (30 or more hours), with studies of shorter lengths yielding similar smaller effect sizes. These differences, however, were not statistically significant ($Q\beta = 2.89$; $p = .41$).

Table 8. Test of Homogeneity for "Total Time of Experiment, Pretest to Posttest" Variable

Group	Point estimate		
0–4 Weeks (5)	.6882		
5–8 Weeks (7)	.5571		
9–12 Weeks (5)	.0921		
15–16 weeks (6)	.5662		
Combined (23)	.4866		
Source	**Q-Value**	*df*	*P*Value
Between classes	15.0830	3.0000	.0018

Table 9. Test of homogeneity for "Total Hours of Treatment" variable

Group	Point estimate		
0–5 (6)	.4498		
6–10 (5)	.4669		
11–20 (6)	.3180		
30 or more (6)	.6027		
Combined (23)	.4866		
Source	**Q-Value**	*df*	*P*Value
Between classes	2.8940	3.0000	.4082

Proficiency level, age, and learning context

Language variables related to learner populations and contexts were also examined. The participants' proficiency level was considered a potentially influential moderating variable in our pool of studies. As shown in Table 10, studies focusing on participants in their second year or third year and beyond resulted in reasonable effect sizes of over half a standard deviation unit, whereas studies that featured first-year participants resulted in a negligible average effect size of .12, and this difference between groups was statistically significant ($Q\beta = 16.06$; $p = .00$). Post hoc comparisons reveal the difference was located specifically between studies involving first-year and second-year students.

The average age of the participants also seemed to influence the results of the studies in the present meta-analysis, as displayed in Table 11. Whereas the overall effectiveness of ERST was about half a standard deviation unit for studies with adolescent and adult participants, the ERST treatment received by the 3rd and 6th graders studied by Arellano (1991) seemed to lead to no improvement in their L2 reading comprehension (–.09). These results should be interpreted with caution, as they come from just one study report and two independent samples (the young learners investigated by Arellano 1991). Nev-

Table 10. Test of homogeneity for "Average Level of Participants" variable

Group	Point estimate		
First Year (3)	.1197		
Second Year (5)	.6330		
Third Year or more (15)	.6096		
Combined (23)	.4866		
Source	**Q-Value**	*df*	*P*Value
Between classes	16.0640	2.0000	.0003

Table 11. Test of homogeneity for "Average Age of Participants" variable

Group	Point estimate		
0–12 (2)	–.0913		
12–18 (6)	.5114		
18+ (15)	.5208		
Combined (23)	.4866		
Source	**Q-Value**	*df*	*P*Value
Between classes 6.2080 2.0000	.0450		

Table 12. Test of homogeneity for "Language Context of Study" variable

Group	Point estimate		
EFL (4)	.4410		
ESL (10)	.6319		
FL (9)	.4042		
Combined (23)	.4866		
Source	Q-Value	df	PValue
Between classes	3.3320	2.0000	.1890

ertheless, it might be that cognitive and literacy maturity in the L1 is desirable before readers can benefit from ERST in their L2.

By contrast, the language context in which the respective studies were conducted seemed not to have an effect on the results of the studies, as shown in Table 12.

Overall text length

The amount of words in the respective texts used to test the effects of ERST on reading comprehension was thought to be a potentially relevant variable. It should be noted that this information was not available for four studies (cf. Table 1), which had to be treated as missing data in this analysis. As shown in Table 13, effect sizes were obtained of .70 for studies with test texts of 801 or more words, .57 for studies with test texts of 0–400 words, and .27 with texts of 401–800 words. There was a statistically significant difference among groups according to this variable ($Q\beta = 8.60$; $p = .01$). If the studies were further divided up as in Table 14, one can see, purely from a descriptive standpoint, how the effect sizes generally (not in all cases) go up with the larger posttest texts. The difference among groups noted in Table 14 ($p = .00$) should be interpreted with caution, because there are some codes with only one, two, or three studies. The four studies employing texts of 601–800 words yielded such a low mean effect size because of the two Arellano (1991) studies, which were long studies with very young participants. Thus, this may have affected the outcomes disproportionately. If the 601–800 studies and the missing data studies are excluded, the difference is not statistically significant ($p = .17$). Outliers and anomalies notwithstanding, the results presented in Tables 13 and 14 consistently point to a trend for an increase in average effect size as longer texts are employed in the tests.

Table 13. Test of homogeneity for "Number of Words in Posttest Text" variable

Group	Point estimate		
0–400 (5)	.5768		
401–800 (6)	.2728		
801+ (8)	.6954		
Source	**Q-Value**	*df*	*P*Value
Between classes	8.6020	2.0000	.0135

Table 14. Test of homogeneity for "Number of Words in Posttest Text" variable

Group	Point estimate		
0–200 (3)	.2252		
201–400 (2)	.6922		
401–600 (2)	.9250		
601–800 (4)	.0893		
801–1000 (4)	.9553		
1001–1200 (3)	.6770		
1200 or more (1)	.5304		
Source	**Q-Value**	*df*	*P*Value
Between classes	25.1530	6.0000	.00035

Discussion

Several points can be made on the basis of the results obtained in the present meta-analysis. Overall, participants who received ERST training comprehended L2 texts better than those who did not receive such training. From this general result it can be easily concluded that some ERST is better than none. We can also claim, with a certain degree of confidence, that learners who are provided with ERST can actually perform approximately half a standard deviation above those that do not receive ERST. Moreover, if the observed effect size of .54 were converted to a percentage scale, 68% of the average-performing students receiving ERST will exceed the average reading comprehension of students not receiving such training on measures of L2 reading comprehension. This finding, previously ambiguous, now sheds light on approximately how much influence L2 instructors can have on their L2 students' reading performance just by explicitly training them in the use of reading strategies. The accumulated empirical evidence suggests that those who are provided with ERST gain knowledge that provides them with a better capability for L2 reading. However, considering how ERST has been operationalized to date, it was generally difficult to identify one outstanding strategy, as most of the strategies were combinations of individual ones. Such combinations seem to be effective for L2 reading comprehension. In terms of best reading strategies to teach, perhaps the most basic conclusion is that any type of ERST is better than nothing.

Given the relatively low sample of studies included in this meta-analysis, considerable caution must be employed in interpreting any subsequent disambiguation of the specific study variables associated with greater or lower magnitudes of effect. Findings did reveal several patterns of potential interest, though the potential error associated with calculating multiple statistical significance tests on the same small sample of studies cannot be ignored; therefore, the following points should be taken as suggestive rather than indicative.

There was no statistically significant difference between studies that did and did not use metacognitive ERST. As mentioned earlier, it is difficult to truly ascertain which strategy – whether cognitive or metacognitive – is being used by the learner, especially when multiple strategies are taught. An anonymous reviewer also pointed out that this distinction has been eschewed in reading research as problematic, a stance that is hinted at in the use of "metacognition" (rather than metacognitive strategies) by Anderson (2002) in the quote presented in our introduction. It would seem that the above results of no difference between cognitive and metacognitive strategy training support this alternative interpretation as well. Future primary studies should investigate this null finding more in depth.

This meta-analysis found no statistically significant difference between studies that used different measurement instruments. It is uncertain to what extent most of the instruments used in the respective studies were valid and reliable for measuring the effects of ERST on L2 reading comprehension. Quite a few instruments were used in the pool of studies. While the recall protocol is perhaps one of the best instruments for testing L2 reading comprehension, very reliable tests such as the TOEFL reading comprehension section and other standardized reading tests are probably fairly accurate measures of what is truly comprehended by the L2 reader. Similarly, there was no statistically significant difference between studies that used receptive and productive testing instruments. It was interesting to note, however, that the higher effect sizes were found for studies that used both productive and receptive tests. A matter worth investigating in future primary studies is whether a combination of tests provides more telling data on how much effect ERST is having on L2 reading comprehension.

By contrast, how much time a study lasted, from pretest to posttest, made a statistically significant difference in observed study outcomes. Despite the difference, however, there appeared to be no strong direction in the results verifying this, as the effect sizes for this variable were not consistent. Interestingly, the largest effect size was for the group of studies with the shortest study length whereas the second largest average effect size was for the group of studies with the longest study length. Superficially, it seems possible that within a short period of time, participants provided with ERST are able to perform as well as those with longer training periods, but this assertion remains unproven. Evidently, there are latent variables associated with idiosyncratic individual study results (e.g., the two young samples in Arellano 1991), other than study length, that are influencing the results.

With regard to treatment length, there was no statistically significant difference between studies according to the number of hours of ERST, although the largest mean effect size was found for lengthy treatments of 30 hours or more. This seems to be a surprising finding, as one would expect to see better results for longer, more intensive treatments. Perhaps quality is more important than quantity, and more is not necessarily better when it comes to ERST. Alternatively, future studies should investigate the possibility that time is an important factor in ERST only if researchers address how participants react to it and how motivational issues affect L2 learners in the studies that feature long-lasting ERST treatments. More specifically, perhaps the ability to promote and keep motivational interest in using the techniques learned in ERST is an important factor in L2 studies. This finding is in line with that of Pappa, Zafiropoulou, and Metallidou (2003), who found that ERST accompanied by a motivational treatment provided superior results to ERST only:

> Moreover, results showed that, while training only in metacognitive strategy use had a small effect on students' posttest performance, the boosting in motivation had a moderated effect on students' performance. This implied that the presence of this kind of motivational orientation facilitates performance by activating subjects' intention to invest time and effort in this specific cognitive domain. (p. 784)

Pappa et al. (2003) used an extra motivational component which entailed (a) inclusion of a sociocultural component in the foreign language syllabus, (b) developing the learners' cross-cultural awareness, and (c) promotion of students' contact with foreign language speakers. All these aspects were part of what was called "motivational boosting" (Pappa et al. 2003:781). These components, which distinguished their study from other ERST studies, may enhance the effects of ERST, and particularly of long-lasting ERST interventions.

The statistically significant difference observed between studies with participants of differing levels suggests that L2 readers may need to have attained a certain L2 competency level before ERST can have an important role. This finding may be explained by threshold L2 reading theories, in which L2 learners need to be at a certain level, sometimes called the "threshold", in order for L2 reading strategies to be effective (Alderson 1984; Laufer 1996; Laufer & Sim 1985). Based on our data, the L2 readers' threshold at which ERST can be most effective is generally reached sometime in the second year or later of L2 instruction, at which time the 3,000 word-level may be reached. This corroborates to a certain degree the research of Laufer (1996), who found that if L2 learners do not know at least 3,000 words, no amount of skills in the L1 can help them to understand mainstream L2 texts.

There was a statistically significant difference between studies with participants of differing ages. A priori, this difference appears problematic, as younger children can be considered effective language learners (Long 1990). However, this does not necessarily mean they are effective strategy users. These differences may be the result of the language competency and level of the participants in the respective studies. Older students, especially those who have competency in the language, seem to use ERST much more effectively than younger students. The only negative effect size, −.09, was found for learners in the 0–12 group. This result should be interpreted with some caution, however, as the 0–12 group only had two studies. It is possible that with age, L2 readers may be more open to ERST. This tentative finding comes as a boost for adult learners, who generally consider themselves at a disadvantage when their L2 ability is compared to younger learners. The effects of age in using ERST should be further studied in future primary studies and meta-analyses. With age generally comes maturity, and reaching literacy and cognitive maturity may exert a facilitative influence on how effective ERST can be in the L2 (as well as the L1). Thus, in answer to our research question: "Does age of the L2 readers make a difference in ERST?" we tentatively find that age can be important and may be influencing the results of our studies.

The language context of the individual study resulted in non-statistically-significant differences between studies. It was noteworthy, however, that the overall effect size was highest (although not significantly so) for ESL studies. Perhaps this is because ESL learners are generally more advanced than the "foreign language" student, such as North-American students learning French in the United States. Thus, advanced ESL students may make more use of ERST because there is less dependence on lower-level, bottom-up processing. If a larger pool of studies were available to meta-analyze context effects, one might discover important motivational reasons for learning an L2 depending on the context (second, foreign, English, non-English) of language learning.

There was a statistically significant difference for studies that used post-test L2 texts of differing lengths. It is possible that strategies are more useable as there is more text on which to use them. This is disputable, however, because the groups of studies with posttest lengths of 401–800 words did not have a very large average effect size. A closer look at the descriptive data (cf. Table 14) reveals that this variable may need further study because the effect sizes seem to generally increase (although this is not always the case) as the number of words in the posttest text increases. This in part corroborates Taylor's (2002) research, which suggested that longer texts provide more opportunity for the learner to make use of the independent variable. The present meta-analysis was less clear, however. This no doubt is related to a weakness in the current state of research in this domain: There are simply not enough studies to produce verifiable evidence as to which variables are truly affecting the results. More primary studies are needed in the future to better ascertain a clearer pattern of accumulated findings regarding moderating variables.

Conclusion and future research

It is important to mention that a meta-analysis can only be as good as the available accumulated primary studies on which it is based. In the present meta-analysis, the inclusion of more studies would have provided more sure conclusions – especially concerning which moderator variables were influencing the results of studies. Further, more studies would have indicated other future research directions to pursue. Some of the studies included in the present meta-analysis were unpublished. While these studies can be considered usable (cf. Appendix A), it may have been preferable to have included only published studies, as they generally undergo much more scrutiny than unpublished studies.

An essence of science is replicability, and this principle holds as true for meta-analysis as it does for primary research. In the interest of replicability, all of the studies in this meta-analysis are cited and can be readily accessed online or in libraries. The statistics, codes, and sample sizes used in our analyses can also be reproduced. The methods and sources for the calculation of the effect sizes and weighting methods have been given in this report. The coding methods used have been operationally defined. The basic data extracted from each study have been presented. It is likely that some readers of this meta-analysis may disagree with the codes we have used, and if this is the case, they can certainly use the data presented here and add their own codings to test alternative hypotheses. Still other readers may believe that different variables will better explain the observed differences across primary studies and support their theories of L2 reading comprehension. If this is the case, they can follow our detailed methodological procedures to pursue the meta-analysis of new variables across studies. Finally, readers may perhaps suggest additional experimental studies not included in this summary of the ERST L2 literature. They can be included in future meta-analytic studies.

In the context of our purposes for the present meta-analysis, we have offered empirical evidence that ERST can make a difference in amount of L2 text understood. In general, these results shed light on the substantial influence L2 instructors can have on L2 readers. L2 instructors can provide effective ERST to students. Generally, it seems as though ERST in some way softens the learning curve of L2 readers. Perhaps the key is continual improving and honing of strategy use rather than simply teaching. In addition, it may be necessary to continually be reminded of the importance of already learned strategies, as they may be forgotten or less effective in some way. Thus, there may be a kind of "honeymoon effect" in which the learners are excited at first to be privy to new information on improving their L2 reading, and subsequently lose interest as time progresses. Future studies should be conducted on interest attrition and other motivational factors in ERST.

In sum, language educators should be aware of important variables that can influence the effectiveness of ERST on L2 reading comprehension. The use of metacognition, the use of high quality tests, the L2 level and age of the student, keeping students motivated to continue using the strategies, and the choice and use of texts, are some of the potentially essential variables that can improve L2 students' learning experiences. With the proper strategy training, more input can be gleaned from L2 texts and a greater variety of texts can be read. As research on specific ERST types (e.g., semantic mapping and so on) accumulates, it is our hope that future meta-analyses can shed light on the relative effectiveness of providing students with explicit training on a variety of L2 reading strategies.

Note

* The studies included in the meta-analysis proper are indicated by an asterisk.

References

Abu-Rabia, S. (1996). Attitudes and cultural background and their relationship to reading comprehension in a second language: A comparison of three different social contexts. *International Journal of Applied Linguistics, 6,* 81–107.

Abu-Rabia, S. (1998). Social and cognitive factors influencing the reading comprehension of Arab students learning Hebrew as a second language in Israel. *Journal of Research in Reading, 21,* 201–212.

Alderson, J. C. (1984). Reading in a foreign language: A reading problem or a language problem? In J. C. Alderson, & A. H. Urquhart (Eds.), *Reading in a Foreign Language* (pp. 1–27). London: Longman.

Anderson, N. J. (2002). *The role of metacognition in second language teaching and learning.* (ERIC Document Reproduction Service No. ED 463659).

*Arellano, E. M. (1991). *The effects of retelling as an instructional strategy with expository text for nonnative English speakers.* Unpublished doctoral dissertation. Memphis State University.

*Barnett, M. A. (1988a). Teaching reading strategies: How methodology affects language course articulation. *Foreign Language Annals, 21,* 109–119.

*Barnett, M. A. (1988b). Reading through context: How real and perceived strategy use affects L2 comprehension. *Modern Language Journal, 72,* 150–162.

Bernhardt, E. B. (1983). Testing foreign language reading comprehension: The immediate recall protocol. *Die Unterrichtspraxis, 16,* 27–33.

Bernhardt, E. B. (1991). *Reading development in a second language: Theoretical, empirical and classroom perspectives.* Norwood, NJ: Ablex.

*Bimmel, P. E., Van den Berg, H., & Oostdam, R. J. (2001). Effects of strategy training on treading comprehension in first and foreign language. *European Journal of Psychology of Education, 16,* 509–529.

Brantmeier, C. (2002). Second language reading strategy research at the secondary and the university levels: Variations, disparities, and generalizability. *Reading Matrix: An International Online Journal, (2)3.* Retrieved January 31 2004 from http://www.readingmatrix.com/articles/brantmeier/article.pdf

Boonyaratapan, M. (2000). *L'impact de l'entraînement à l'utilisation des stratégies de lecture sur la compréhension de textes chez des élèves thailandais.* Unpublished doctoral dissertation. University of Laval.

*Brown, R. L. (1991). *The effects of teaching a multicomponent reading strategy on university ESL students' reading comprehension and reports of reading strategies.* Unpublished doctoral dissertation. Michigan State University.

Carrell, P. L. (1985) Facilitating ESL reading by teaching text structure. *TESOL Quarterly, 19,* 727–52.

*Carrell, P. L., Pharis, B. G., & Liberto, J. C. (1989). Metacognitive strategy training for ESL reading. *TESOL Quarterly, 23,* 647–678.

Chamot, A. U. (2001). The role of learning strategies in second language acquisition. In M. P. Breen (Ed.), *Learner contributions to language learning: New directions in research* (pp. 25–43). New York: Longman/Pearson.

Comprehensive Meta-Analysis 1.12. [Computer software]. (2001). Englewood, NJ. Biostat.

*Evans, C. (2002). *The effects of computer-assisted main idea instruction on foreign language reading comprehension.* Unpublished doctoral dissertation. University at Albany, State University of New York.

*Ghenghea, V. (1985). Relationships between mother tongues (Romanian) and a foreign language (German) in developing rational reading skills in German. *Rassegna Italian di Linguistica Applicata, 17,* 125–134.

Grabe, W. (1991). Current developments in second language reading research. *TESOL Quarterly, 25,* 375–406.

*Hamp-Lyons, L. & Proulx, G. (1982). *A comparison of two methods of teaching advanced ESL reading.* Paper presented at the TESOL Summer Meeting, Evanston, IL, July 16–17. (ERIC Document Reproduction Service No. ED 227 678).

Hardin, V. B. (2001). Transfer and variation in cognitive reading strategies of Latino fourth-grade students in a late-exit bilingual program. *Bilingual Research Journal, 25,* 539–561.

Hedges, L. V. (1981). Distribution theory for Glass's estimator of effect size and related estimators. *Journal of Educational Statistics, 6,* 107–128.

Hedges, L. V. (1982). Estimation of effects size from a series of independent experiments. *Psychological Bulletin, 92,* 490–499.

Hedges L. V., & Olkin, I. (1985). *Statistical methods for meta-analysis.* Orlando, FL: Academic Press.

Johnson, B. T. (1993). *DSTAT: Software for Meta-Analytic Review of Research Literatures (Version 1.11)* [Computer Software]. Hillsdale, NJ: Lawrence Erlbaum.

*Kemper, S. E. (1989). *Metacognition reading strategies for English as a second language: The reading mode.* Unpublished doctoral dissertation. California State University.

*Kern, R. G. (1989). Second language reading strategy instruction: Its effects on comprehension and word inferences ability. *Modern Language Journal, 73,* 135–149.

*Kitajima, R. (1997). Referential strategy training for second language reading comprehension of Japanese texts. *Foreign Language Annals, 30,* 84–97.

*Kusiak, M. (2001). The effect of metacognitive strategy training on reading comprehension and metacognitive knowledge. *Eurosla Yearbook, 1,* 255–274.

Laufer, B. (1996). The lexical threshold of second language reading comprehension: What it is and how it relates to L1 reading ability. *Jyvaskyla Cross-Language Studies, 17,* 55–62.

Laufer, B., & Sim, D. D. (1985). Measuring and explaining the reading threshold needed for English for academic purposes texts. *Foreign Language Annals, 18,* 405–411.

Lipsey, M. W. & Wilson, D. B. (2001). *Practical meta-analysis.* Thousand Oaks, CA: Sage.

Long, M. H. (1990). Maturational constraints on language development. *Studies in Second Language Acquisition, 12,* 251–286.

Nikolov, M. (1999). Why do you learn English?' 'Because the teacher is short.' A study of Hungarian children's foreign language learning motivation. *Language Teaching Research, 3,* 33–56.

O'Malley, J. M., & Chamot, A. U. (1990). *Learning strategies in second language acquisition.* Cambridge, UK: Cambridge University Press.

Oxford, R. L. (1990). *Language learning strategies: What every teacher should know.* Boston: Heinle & Heinle.

Padron, Y. N. (1985). *Utilizing cognitive reading strategies to improve English reading comprehension of Spanish-speaking bilingual students.* Unpublished doctoral dissertation. University of Houston.

*Pappa, E., Zafiropoulou, M. & Metallidou, P. (2003). Intervention on strategy use and on motivation of Greek pupils' reading comprehension in English classes. *Perceptual and Motor Skills, 96,* 773–786.

*Park-Oh, Y. (1994). *Self-regulated strategy training in second language reading: Its effects on reading comprehension, strategy use, reading attitudes, and learning styles of college ESL students.* Unpublished doctoral dissertation. University of Alabama.

*Porter, L. P. (1992). *An investigation of the effectiveness of two prior knowledge-based vocabulary teaching strategies on vocabulary knowledge and reading comprehension in an advanced foreign language class.* Unpublished doctoral dissertation. Kent State University.

*Prinz, P. (1998). *The influence of strategic teaching on reading in a second language.* Unpublished doctoral dissertation. Boston University.

*Raymond, P. M. (1993). The effects of structure strategy training on the recall of expository prose for university students reading French as a second language. *Modern Language Journal, 77,* 445–458.

Shohamy, E. (1984). Does the testing method make a difference? The case of reading comprehension. *Language Testing, 1,* 147–170.

*Talbot, D. C. (1995). *Metacognitive strategy training for reading: Developing second language learners' awareness of expository test patterns.* Unpublished doctoral dissertation. University of Hong Kong.

*Tanaka, C. (1985). *A study of the effectiveness of reading instruction at the college level in Japan based on psycholinguistic theory.* Unpublished doctoral dissertation. University of Kansas.

Tang, B. T. (1974). A psycholinguistic study of the relationships between children's ethnic-linguistic attitudes and the effectiveness of methods used in second-language reading instruction. *TESOL Quarterly, 8,* 233–251.

Taylor, A. M. (2002). *A meta-analysis on the effects of L1 glosses on L2 reading comprehension.* Unpublished doctoral dissertation. Purdue University.

Tsung-Yuan, H., & Oxford, R. (2002). Comparing theories of language learning strategies: A confirmatory analysis. *Modern Language Journal, 86,* 368–383.

Wenden A. L. (2001). Metacognitive knowledge in SLA: The neglected variable. In M. P. Breen (Ed.), *Learner contributions to language learning: New directions in research* (pp. 44–64). New York: Longman/Pearson.

Wolf, D. F. (1993). A comparison of assessment tasks used to measure FL reading comprehension. *Modern Language Journal, 77,* 473–489.

*Zhicheng, Z. (1992). *The effects of teaching reading strategies on improving reading comprehension for ESL learners.* Paper presented at the annual meeting of the Mid-South Educational Research Association, Knoxville, TN, November 11–13. (ERIC Document Reproduction Service No. ED 356 643).

Appendix A

Table A. Test of Homogeneity of Published versus Non-published Studies

Group	Point estimate		
Non-published (**13**)	.5575		
Published (**10**)	.4258		
Combined (**23**)	.4866		
Source	**Q-Value**	*df*	*P*Value
Between classes	1.4550	1.0000	.2277

Appendix B

The difference between Hedges' g and Cohen's d is a subtle one. Consider a study with treatment condition measurements $X_1, \ldots, X_n$ and control condition measurements $Y_1, \ldots, Y_m$. It is assumed that the X measurements are a representative sample from a population with mean μ_x and variance σ^2_x. Also, the Y measurements are assumed to come from some population with mean μ_y and variance σ^2_y.

Then the effect size parameter to be estimated is of the form $\delta = \dfrac{\mu_x - \mu_y}{\sigma_{pop}}$, where σ_{pop} is some measure of the average population standard deviation (see Table 16.2 in Cooper & Hedges 1994:237). For both g and d, the difference $\mu_x - \mu_y$ is estimated by the difference in sample means, $\bar{X} - \bar{Y}$.

It is assumed that $\sigma^2_x \neq \sigma^2_y$, i.e., that the standard deviations for the treatment and control populations are not necessarily equal. The difference between g and d is how this "average population standard deviation" is estimated (see the second paragraph on p. 234 of Cooper & Hedges 1994).

In g, the estimate of σ_{pop} is

$$S_p = \sqrt{\frac{(n-1)s_x^2 + (m-1)s_y^2}{n+m-2}} = \sqrt{\frac{\sum\limits_{i=1}^{n}(X_i - \bar{X})^2 + \sum\limits_{i=1}^{m}(Y_i - \bar{Y})^2}{n+m-2}}$$

In d, the estimate of σ_{pop} is

$$\sigma = \sqrt{\frac{(n-1)s_x^2 + (m-1)s_y^2}{n+m}} = \sqrt{\frac{\sum\limits_{i=1}^{n}(X_i - \bar{X})^2 + \sum\limits_{i=1}^{m}(Y_i - \bar{Y})^2}{n+m}}$$

Then $d = g\sqrt{\frac{n+m}{n+m-2}}$ (as in equation 16–28 on p. 239 of Cooper & Hedges 1994).

CHAPTER 7

A meta-synthesis of qualitative research on effective teaching practices for English Language Learners

Kip Téllez and Hersh C. Waxman
University of California, Santa Cruz / University of Houston

Qualitative studies in second language teaching are increasing in both number and quality. Such studies are addressing familiar questions regarding effective teaching practices as well as underscoring the importance of context in language learning. Yet there have been no systematic compilations or analyses of this body of research literature. This chapter reviews and synthesizes the qualitative research studies in the field of second language instruction with a focus on effective practices for English Language Learners in US schools.

Using techniques for coding and categorizing qualitative data suggested by Noblit and Hare (1988) and others (Flinspach 2001), we synthesized the results of 25 studies. Our synthesis revealed practices congealed around four instructional orientations: (a) communitarian teaching, a manner of instruction built around community; (b) protracted language events, a strategy in which teachers work to maximize verbal activity; (c) building on prior knowledge, an overall approach to teaching in which teachers work to connect students' lives to school themes; and (d) the use of multiple representations, a method designed to support language with objects and indexes.

In addition to our review, we compare our findings with results of quantitative research syntheses, noting important methodological differences between qualitative and quantitative approaches. Finally, we explore the role of the future of qualitative research syntheses in second language teaching and learning.

Introduction

In a 1995 special issue of the *TESOL Quarterly*, Lazaraton (1995) suggested that the number and quality of qualitative studies in second language learning was bound to increase and, consequently, have a greater impact in the instructional domain. In the years since this publication, this prediction has been only partly realized. Qualitative studies in educational settings have indeed become more commonplace, and the quality of such studies, although difficult to assess, seems to be improving. More important perhaps is the type of research that qualitative methods and analyses encourage. Qualitative studies in second language instructional settings have paid attention to important contextual features (e.g., the cultural backgrounds of learners) of second language learning that quantitative studies often failed to recognize. Educational ethnographies, in particular, have allowed researchers to explore nuances of learners and learning environments and explain their work in "thick descriptions," allowing their readers to gain an appreciation for the complexity of language learning under varied conditions and contexts.

In addition, a new focus on teacher research in second language education suggests a new source of qualitative investigations, although teacher research studies thus far have been largely descriptive in nature only (Bailey & Nunan 1996). Lazaraton also pointed out that qualitative research holds great potential for assisting practitioners in their work. Instead of the manipulation of experimental conditions using large data sources (important features of any educational research program, but largely inaccessible to teachers), the naturalistic and contextualized nature of qualitative research has more appeal to teachers and other educators who work directly with students in classrooms. Further, using the inductive logic assumed in most qualitative studies, policymakers may find in this body of research literature recommendations for restructuring and thereby improving existing language learning programs.

The potential yield of findings taken from qualitative research in second language settings suggested to us that it was time to consider what qualitative researchers had found with respect to effective instructional practices for English Language Learners (ELLs). The present review addresses what the recent qualitative literature adds to our understanding of good teaching practices for second language learners.

Focus on effective teaching practices

In conducting the present meta-synthesis, our interest was in illuminating best teaching practices for ELLs. Thus, we are not concerned with studies that focused on effective *programs* for ELLs, preferring instead to inform the practices of teachers in classrooms. For instance, we did not include research evaluating the relative success of bilingual education vs. English immersion, or studies that addressed the ongoing debate over early exit vs. late exit bilingual programs. We anticipated that the qualitative research in English language instruction would yield studies more focused on context and the direct experiences of teachers and students. We were interested in how educators can increase ELLs' achievement in English, but we did not expect to find, for instance, qualitative researchers reporting growth in standardized test scores in their studies. Rather, we anticipated that we would locate studies focused on broad and innovative teaching practices that encouraged language growth in a variety of contexts. We also expected that qualitative studies would consider the role of the teacher as a crucial element in effective practices.

Qualitative researchers, perhaps by nature, tend to focus on the experiences of actors as they negotiate their worlds. Consequently, we predicted that all of the studies we found would examine the effect of practices that required much teacher direction. On the other hand, we anticipated finding studies interested in more than descriptions of context alone. Contemporary English Language Development (ELD) teachers in the US and elsewhere are under increasing pressure to teach English more quickly and efficiently (Brennan, Kim, Wenz-Gross, & Siperstein, 2001), in no small part owing to the federal No Child Left Behind legislation (Goertz & Duffy 2003). This pressure has encouraged teachers to seek practices that yield broad gains.

New accountability pressures notwithstanding, teachers of school-aged children, in contrast to those working with adults, have always been concerned with knowing and using a wide range of teaching practices. This concern is reflected in the importance of methods courses in teacher education programs (Mosenthal 1996). In the early elementary grades, specifically, ELLs possess few individual learning strategies. For instance, an adult learner might naturally make a set of flashcards to memorize terms. By contrast, young learners lack the capacity for such a task. Of course, teaching methods can take a teacher only so far (Bartolome 1994), but teachers of younger ELLs must devote a significant part of their professional planning to linking curriculum with an appropriate teaching practice or technique.

ELLs and the importance of context

Recently, the focus and interest in effective practices has increased among educational researchers (Fisher, Frey, & Williams 2002). However, this new emphasis on experimentally based "best practices" is receiving much attention, with controversy at every turn (Howe 2004). The primary disagreements emerge not from the search for effective practices, but the experimental procedures used to assess them, and whether effective practices, once discovered, should be mandated for use in all contexts. One of the persistent problems in education is that we often talk about best practices in education without consideration of context or possible interaction effects (Eisner 1998, 2001). Unfortunately much of the research on effective teaching practices as well as in other substantive areas does not address important contextual differences. For example, in the area of ELLs, many studies and reviews of research have merely prescribed generalized best practices for ELLs without taking into account the important individual and contextual variables that represent the great diversity of conditions or risk factors that students encounter. There is much variability, however, within the population of ELLs. G. N. García (2001), for example, pointed out that 45% of the current ELL school-aged student population is foreign-born immigrants, while the remaining 55% are U.S.-born. Foreign- and native-born students as well as other subgroups of students have different dialects, levels of schooling, and degrees of access to preschool experiences, all of which differentially impact their achievement in school. This heterogeneity makes it highly problematic to describe a "typical" ELL and therefore appropriate interventions. Many conceptual articles and studies generalize to a larger population without taking into account the great diversity among types of ELLs. Consequently, recommendations from research should take into account this diversity among ELLs.

Whatever disagreements might exist with respect to best practices, all sides agree that the academic achievement of ELLs in the US is unacceptably low. The academic achievement scores of the 4.5 million "Limited English Proficient" students in US K-12 schools – a figure that grows at an annual rate of about three percent (Kindler 2002) – suggest that ELLs are struggling. Although such data are less than complete (state and federal agencies tend to report on racial/ethnic differences rather than language status), studies show that ELLs are well below their native-English-speaking counterparts on tests of literacy (Kindler 2002). Mexican American ELLs, who comprise by far the largest group of ELLs, fare worst of all (Schmid 2001), with dropout rates as high as 40 % in some regions (Hispanic Dropout Project 1998). Teacher professional development is falling short in providing teachers with the preparation required to address the needs of ELLs. A recent national survey showed that in many states, even those with large and growing ELL populations, less than 10 % of the teachers had received more than eight hours of English development in-service in the previous three years (U.S. Department of Education 2002). Given these data, it is no surprise that educators and policymakers are in search of the most effective and efficient practices for ELLs (e.g., August & Hakuta 1997).

Meta-analysis and meta-synthesis in education

It is also obvious why there is such interest in meta-analytic studies and other research syntheses. Quantitative research meta-analyses in education have led to findings important to both researchers and policymakers. For instance, Elbaum, Vaughn, Hughes, and Moody (2000) conducted a meta-analysis of Reading Recovery, a literacy program distinguished by one-to-one tutoring with a highly trained teacher. The resources needed to maintain Reading Recovery had made it somewhat controversial. To the surprise of many, the meta-analysis revealed that other one-on-one tutoring produced results similar to those of Reading Recovery and that small-group tutoring programs yielded similar results. The results of this study have altered tutoring programs in many schools.

Research syntheses of effective instruction may lead to the adoption of more efficient techniques or offer proof of the benefits (both social and academic) of instructional practices such as cooperative learning (e.g., Nath, Ross, & Smith 1996). Indeed, meta-analyses hold the potential to alter many large-scale instructional practices. However, we must point out that in the US educational research context, all studies of educational practice, both original research studies and meta-analyses, are now part of an ongoing discussion regarding what constitutes a valid scientific study in education (Eisenhart & Towne, 2003). The federal No Child Left Behind Act of 2001, for example, is placing a new emphasis on scientifically based research and requires states and school districts to choose "evidence-based" programs for their schools and classrooms. This change is providing support to the growing numbers of researchers (Glass 2000; Wang, Haertel, & Walberg 1993) and organizations, such as the Campbell Collaboration (2002), to synthesize findings from research. It is argued that these systematic reviews of the research will firm up the "soft science" of education and finally begin to provide empirical evidence that certain programs or approaches are effective in improving student outcomes (Viadero 2002).

An important role of research in language teaching is the evaluation of teaching practices. Historically, such research has guided teachers to the most effective instructional methods. However, much of the research on effective language teaching practices has used quantitative methods, employing large data sets or experimental conditions unfamiliar to practitioners. Qualitative research strategies, on the other hand, typically reflect and illustrate the classroom conditions teachers recognize. This present review of research suggests that new, qualitative research may provide a different set of instructional strategy recommendations for English language teachers working in a wide variety of settings.

The methods for conducting a research synthesis of qualitative studies are not so well developed as those for aggregating quantitative research. A qualitative research synthesis cannot, for instance, rely upon an agreed upon treatment metric such as effect size (e.g., Glass, McGaw & Smith 1981; Norris & Ortega 2000). Indeed, in the most widely cited paper on qualitative reviews, Noblit and Hare (1988) argued that the goal of a qualitative and interpretive research synthesis is less about generalizing what constitutes effective practices across contexts than informing readers of the contexts themselves. To wit, one of the most widely read ethnographies in education, Shirley Brice Heath's "Ways With Words" (Heath 1983), compelled educators not because it was a prescription for how schools should use language, but rather a description of how the language of the school fit or failed to fit with the language of the family.

Another primary difference between our review and other, more quantitative works is the size of the research base. It is true that qualitative studies are growing in number, but we found that our exhaustive review of the literature did not yield the number of studies typically found in most meta-analyses of quantitative studies in the field of educational research (cf. Bus & van Ijzendoorn 1999; Swanson, Trainin, Necoechea, & Hammill 2003), though this phenomenon may be related to the incipient nature of work on language learning per se (as indicated by the sample sizes in chapters in the current volume).

In addition to lacking great numbers of previous studies, qualitative researchers have struggled to fit the terms of quantitative work to their purposes. Recently, Finfgeld (2003) developed a set of definitions unique to qualitative reviews. First, she recommended that qualitative reviewers avoid the term *meta-analysis* when referring to their work. In its place, she suggested that qualitative research summaries use the term *meta-synthesis*, an "umbrella term referring to the synthesis of findings across multiple qualitative reports to create a new interpretation" (p. 895). This term's meaning implies that researchers engaged in meta-syntheses are bound to inform the results of their work with additional analytic and theoretical frames. On the basis of Finfgeld's typology, we henceforth refer to our work as a meta-synthesis.

Methodology

The literature search

Despite the variations from a typical meta-analysis, we began our meta-synthesis in the manner common to all literature reviews: by circumscribing a time period for inclusion (1990–2000, in our case) and selecting indexing tools for our search.

Although we recognize that many studies predate this period and that many important works have been published since, the time frame we chose coincides with the rapid growth of qualitative studies in education. Our review begins at 1990, at the same time several influential works on qualitative data analysis were published (e.g., Strauss & Corbin 1990). Whereas a decade seems an arbitrary period, we believe that it allowed us to find enough quality studies to develop themes useful for language educators.

We relied on five primary search source indexes or databases in preparing this meta-synthesis: Education Abstracts, Educational Resources Information Center, California Digital Library Social Science Citation Index, and Dissertation Abstracts. Table 1 describes our search indexes in detail. We did not limit our search to articles published in English, but found none published in other languages. Neither did we limit our search to studies conducted in the US, but most of the research we found had been conducted there. Search terms used in the meta-synthesis were all combinations of the following terms: English, English Language Learner(s) (ELLs), ESL, ELD, Instruction, Instructional, Effective, Ethnography, Qualitative, and Second Language.[1] We did not exclude studies because they did not fit the document type typically indexed in a database. For instance, if we found a book or dissertation of topical relevance in Education Abstracts, we did not exclude that work. In addition, we conducted several "cross-checks" of our searches, finding that research articles found in Education Abstracts were also found in the Web of Science database.

Table 1. Sources used to search for studies

Index/Database	Description	Usage
Ovid Technology's Education Abstracts[a]	Education Abstracts is a bibliographic database that indexes and abstracts articles of at least one column in length from English-language periodicals and yearbooks published in the United States and elsewhere from 1983-present. Abstracting coverage begins with January 1994. Abstracts range from 50 to 300 words and describe the content and scope of the source documents.	Education Abstracts was used primarily to locate published, often refereed research papers, typically found in academic journals (e.g., *Reading Research Quarterly*).
Educational Resources Information Center (ERIC)	ERIC is a national information system designed to provide ready access to an extensive body of education-related literature. Established in 1966, ERIC is supported by the US Department of Education's Office of Educational Research and Improvement and is administered by the National Library of Education (NLE). At the heart of ERIC is the largest education database in the world containing more than 1 million records of journal articles, research reports, curriculum and teaching guides, conference papers, and books.	ERIC served to locate primarily unpublished reports and references to papers presented at conferences. In addition, ERIC will often index evaluation reports not published in journals.
California Digital Library (CDL)	CDL is a collaborative effort of the UC campuses, organizationally housed at the University of California Office of the President. It is responsible for the design, creation, and implementation of systems that support the shared collections of the University of California. CDL includes Melvyl Union Catalog (CAT) and the California Periodicals database (PE). Library materials are owned by UC and others.	CDL served to locate books and book chapters.
Web of Science's Social Science Citation Index (SSCI)	The Social Science Citation Index is a multidisciplinary index to the journal literature of the social sciences. It indexes more than 1,725 journals across 50 social sciences disciplines.	SSCI was used to locate additional works or citations by specific authors, as well as searches using keywords and subjects.

Table 1. (*continued*)

Index/Database	Description	Usage
Dissertation Abstracts	Dissertation Abstracts indexes US dissertations and theses completed in the past 30 years.	This index was particularly useful because many qualitative research projects in education generally and second language education specifically are lengthy and therefore unlikely to be compressed to journal form from their original length.

[a] Ovid is no longer the title of the database we used for our search. It is now known as Wilson Web's Education Index.

Inclusion and exclusion of studies

Our literature search yielded approximately 50 studies that initially appeared relevant. The full text of eight of the papers could not be located (typically ERIC documents). Twelve of the studies were oriented more towards sociocultural themes or structural elements of schooling (e.g., Chintapalli-Tamirisa 1995) than classroom practices. We acknowledge that many of these studies addressed critical issues in the education of ELLs, but their focus was not on classroom practices, and therefore they were excluded from the meta-synthesis.[2]

With the remaining studies both found in full text and relevant to our theme, we then applied several criteria for selection in the review. First, the study was required to have provided a rationale for choosing its participants and context. Why did the author(s) select a particular school or group of students or teachers instead of others? We believed that such a requirement was reasonable given the importance of context in qualitative research. We did not, however, require studies to have engaged in efforts to find a "representative" context or participant. Such an effort is often impossible given the wide and open access needed for qualitative – especially ethnographic – research. In one instance, the researcher had chosen a specific school because she had formerly been a teacher there and was promised free and unfettered access to interview students and teachers, take field notes, and review certain school curricula (Giacchino-Baker 1992). Often the level of familiarity and trust needed between the qualitative researcher and the research participants dictates or even

mandates the use of a particular context. Therefore, we did not eliminate studies in which the author(s) acknowledged a previous personal or professional
connection to the context. We did, however, require that the author(s): (a) describe the process in selecting a research site, (b) acknowledge any previous
relationships with the site and its participants (if applicable), and (c) provide
a clear description of the research context, including those features that might
limit the generalizability of the findings. The parallel to this criterion found in
the quantitative research syntheses criteria might be whether a study made use
of a valid sampling strategy.

Second, data had to be collected using a systematic strategy; that is, primary data were collected using a recognized qualitative technique (e.g., Miles
& Huberman 1994). Studies that did not make clear their data collection methods, or those that failed to use any systematic procedure, were not included in
the analysis. For instance, we excluded a study that addressed literacy strategies
for early elementary ELLs. The topic was clearly of interest to the synthesis, but
the author simply offered strings of quotes from learners and teachers but provided no evidence on how or when the interviews were conducted, whether or
not the interviewees were given a chance to review their comments (member
check), or even context of the interviews.

Third, to be included, the study had to apply some sort of careful, systematic analysis and interpretation of the data. We hoped that this criterion
would offer us a measure of rigor, tantamount to the fidelity of treatment
groups required of a quantitative, experimental study. Of course, rigor cannot
be fully determined in a qualitative study report, just as qualified researchers
may have disagreements over whether experimental groups represent the effect
of treatment or merely existing differences. Nevertheless, we found that Wolcott's (1994) typology of qualitative research, in which a researcher engages in
description, analysis, and interpretation, is a good proxy for rigor in the qualitative realm. Wolcott argued that qualitative research has the responsibility
first to describe its data; that is, to treat descriptive data as a matter of fact. Using this guide, we insisted that the study be comprehensive and coherent in its
presentation of the data.

Next, we required the included studies to contain a comprehensive analysis of the data. Wolcott called for the qualitative researcher to "extend beyond a
purely descriptive account [...] that proceeds in some careful, systematic way
to identify key factors and relationships among them" (Wolcott 1994: 10). Finally, Wolcott suggested that qualitative research "reach out for understanding
or explanation beyond the limits of what can be explained with the degree of
certainty usually associated with analysis" (p. 11). The use of this final feature

in Wolcott's typology required the studies to have an analytic lens that connected the data and theory to larger implications (i.e., corroborate their data with extant theory or existing research).

The application of these criteria excluded another 10 studies, most of which were presentations at professional meetings. Several of these studies were of interest, but their method of data analysis was not fully reported. It was difficult to eliminate relevant studies, but we argue that these requirements served the purpose of including only those studies that represent sound qualitative strategies. This final round left us with 25 studies in the meta-synthesis, all marked with an asterisk in the reference list.

In spite of our strict criteria, we did not discriminate based on a study's adherence to a particular ontology of qualitative research. For instance, we did not quarrel with whether a study began with explicit hypotheses or instead allowed the results to emerge, refining the analysis *en route*. We recognize that this is an important point of disagreement in the way that qualitative researchers analyze data (Glaser & Straus 1967) but decided that we should not be drawn into the merits of inductive vs. deductive research logic. Nor did we constrain our review to studies published in refereed journals. Indeed, eliminating relevant works uncovered in doctoral dissertations – publications not routinely considered refereed – would have severely curtailed the number of studies in the analysis. Some meta-analyses have excluded such "fugitive" studies (cf. Norris & Ortega 2000), but we found that the space needed to convey fully the results of a qualitative study is often found only in dissertations. We included only one mixed-method research study (Ochoa & Pérez 1995) but were open to including additional such studies had they emerged from the search process.

Coding and development of study themes

Once the papers had been selected, we faced the task of determining how the studies might coalesce into themes of effective instruction. In the quantitative world, one might rely on algorithms of matrix algebra (i.e., exploratory factor analysis) to determine which studies fit together, but qualitative studies offer no comparative strategy. Instead, we looked to other qualitative research syntheses from education and other social sciences. For instance, Sandelowski, Docherty, and Emden (1997), in their review of methods used in "qualitative meta-syntheses," suggest three general strategies for synthesizing qualitative studies. The first strategy integrates the findings of one researcher's work over time. A second integrates the results of studies across both time and researchers. The third strategy transforms qualitative data into counts and frequencies, which can then be analyzed using quantitative methods. The task we faced suggested the second strategy, integrating the results of studies across time (1990–2000) and researchers. Flinspach's (2001) work was also useful in determining a strategy for coding and organizing the studies. Baumann and Duffy's (2001) synthesis of themes in the teacher education research literature provided an important insight. Using the constant comparative method applied to written documents (cf. Glaser & Straus 1967), their iterations of category identification suggested that our syntheses would benefit from a similar strategy.

We began with an a priori list of codes and categories (Miles & Huberman 1994). The results section of each study was examined and classified into one of the following initial categories, themselves based on what previous meta-analyses found. Our initial categories included: (a) effective literacy practices, (b) effective speaking/listening practices, (c) practices promoting pragmatic skills, and (d) other. We then engaged the open and axial coding scheme common to original research in qualitative studies (Straus & Corbin 1990).[3] In the open coding procedure, we tried to fit the studies into our a priori categories.

This strategy forced us to fit the studies to previous work in large-scale reviews of the literature, but it soon became clear that these categories were not taking advantage of the specialized themes of these qualitative studies. The inadequacy of these initial categories compelled us to consider the analytic nature of a meta-synthesis. We maintained that with the aid of some general theoretical references, we could recode the studies into categories more meaningful and coherent. We should also point out that our task was made both easier and more difficult because we had only 25 studies to sort.

Based on the failure of our original, open coding strategy, we proceeded to an axial coding of the studies, in which we now used our theoretical frames as guides. With the aid of foundational works (e.g., Dewey 1916), the coding was made both easier and coherent. For instance, a large number of the studies dealt with student-teacher, student-student, and, in one case (Clark 1999), teacher-teacher interactions. In several of the studies, the practice affiliated with such interaction was not specific to literacy or oral development but rather focused on the linguistic value of the interaction itself. The axial coding informed by the frames taken from the theoretical literature revealed that several of the studies could be considered part of a new "interaction" category, and thus a new, meta-synthetic category was developed, which we named "communitarian" teaching practices. Continuing using a wider analytic lens afforded us in the axial coding, four additional categories were developed.

As a test of the reliability of these new categories, we returned to the original categories (e.g., literacy, speaking/listening) and tried to "retrofit" the studies. This attempt failed, largely because the second set of categories held more explanatory value and appeared to us as a more coherent set. Most important, these new categories fit better the results of the qualitative research.

Results

Four effective teaching practices emerged from the meta-synthesis. They are: (a) communitarian teaching practices, (b) protracted language events, (c) multiple representations designed for understanding target language, and (d) building on prior knowledge. The following sections summarize the research in these four areas in addition to exploring a fifth theme, structural obstacles to effective instruction, often addressed in the literature.

Communitarian teaching practices

The first effective teaching strategy uncovered by the qualitative research synthesis was related to, but extended well beyond, what is commonly known as cooperative learning. Many experimental (and most often quantitative) studies have demonstrated the positive effects of cooperative learning among ELLs (e.g., Calderon, Hertz-Lazarowitz, & Slavin 1998). However, the qualitative research reviewed here suggested a broader and more comprehensive role for cooperative learning. Each of the papers addressing the importance of social interactions for learning language considered group tasks as crucial experiences for language learning. However, they generally believed that interactional learning encouraged a strong form of social cooperation and discourse that *in turn drove language learning*. This is a crucial difference between experimental studies of cooperative learning among language learners and qualitative and ethnographic studies of the same; that is, the difference between the ethnographers' perspective on group learning and the traditional perspective on cooperative learning turns on the distinction between teaching practices alone and much broader views of teaching based on social relationships. Perhaps it is because of the way that ethnographers approach their research, or perhaps it is simply their predisposition to see all interactions as socially meaningful, whether or not such relations serve a learning function. But for the most part, they saw genuine social relationships and the talk that emerged from these relationships as the primary engine of language learning.

The term cooperative learning fails to capture fully the type of learning under study by these researchers. Because the qualitative researchers' focus is trained on the social aspects of language use, the term *communitarian learning*, first used by Kahne (1996) in the educational context, appears to be a more apt description. Communitarian thought in education has its roots in John Dewey's vision of community as a society in which rational and democratic decision-making processes enable the pursuit of common goals (Dewey 1961). Communitarians of this type see open discourse as an essential feature of democracy. Further, communitarian ideals call for community norms and values that help open to public critiques. In essence, a communitarian belief in human societies suggests that open discourse leads to shared social values and free, unfettered social intercourse. Clearly, the goals and interests of a communitarian society are not necessarily the development of language, but such social interactions cannot proceed without a heavy reliance on language.

The qualitative and often ethnographic research studies reviewed here began their interest in language and literacy growth among ELL students but in many cases discovered that the social growth resulting from students from diverse language and cultural backgrounds preceded and sometimes overshadowed language learning. For instance, Goatley, Brock, and Raphael (1995) found that inviting ELLs to join native English speaking book clubs not only improved their language skills but also allowed them an opportunity to share their cultural frame with other students. For one particular student, a Vietnamese immigrant, the effect was profound. Naturally, she made great language gains but also came to understand her role in the larger class as a spokesperson on many issues unknown to her native US classmates. Their ethnography revealed important language and social development made by the native US students as well.

The movement for conversation as a primary means of learning has its roots in Socrates' view of the function of language, which, stated plainly, was to communicate from individual mind to individual mind, resulting in ontological agreements. More recently, the work of Vygotsky (1934/1986) has been called upon to support the notion that language development is yoked to the development of thought, with language doing the pulling. And Vygotsky's now famous refutation of Piaget's theory of private speech as sharply limited in function supports the view that our early private language "serves mental orientation, conscious understanding [...] in overcoming difficulties" (p. 228). Egocentric speech becomes inner speech, which transforms into dialogue with others, each transition resulting in more complex thinking. In this model, language, spoken language in particular, drives understanding. Contemporary educational researchers have built on this body of theory and research by promoting academic discourse as one important tool for learning in formal schooling settings (e.g., Barnes 1976; Hall & Verplaetse 2000; Wells 1986).

A study by Tujay, Jennings, and Dixon (1995) represents well this traditional research line of shared language use as a means for language growth. These researchers based their year-long ethnography of a third-grade classroom of diverse language learners on principles more aligned with language learning goals than communitarian ideals. Nevertheless, their conclusions sound remarkably like those found by Goatley, Brock, and Raphael (1995). As they observed a group of third-grade students who varied in their English language proficiency, they found that although a focus on common task (creating a "planet" story) did not necessarily offer each student the same opportunities to learn, it allowed students varied ways in which they could organize their own learning, essentially creating an individual learning plan. Hruska (2000) also used ethnography to show the relationship between social identity and language use for enhanced language achievement. As a study of communitarian language learning, this line of research also suggests that the interaction of the students served to create an important solidarity among the students that encouraged language events. A focus on communitarian learning practices seems to enhance language learning even when no student in the group has strong proficiency in English (McConnell 1996). More evidence comes from Joyce's (1997) study of ELL writers in which text production and accuracy increased when peers were responsible for each other's work, guided in part by teacher direction. In addition, the introduction of computers as a mediating factor in language development seems to enhance language development insofar as students remain in groups – or at least dyads – while working at the computer (González-Edfelt 1990).

The effectiveness of the communitarian strategy has an historical and sociological rationale. For the better part of our history as a species, the only reason to learn another language was to communicate with people who spoke that language. Before nation-states identified "official" languages and enforced the learning of these privileged languages in formal schools, people learned additional languages because the people who spoke other languages had something they wanted, did something they thought was fascinating, or maybe were members of a group they needed in alliance against yet another group, among dozens of other purposes. The research reviewed in this section seems to build upon this ancient tradition. By creating conditions in which dialogue is genuine and in which social solidarity (i.e., getting to know these different people who speak this different language) and a shared goal are the primary purposes of interaction, educators who use communitarian teaching practices enhance language learning.

The conclusion from these studies suggests that inviting students who are learning English to engage in academic conversations with their peers is a fundamental tool of language learning. These studies suggest that the teacher should serve as a language model, but that the teacher is merely one model of many. It is perhaps more important that the students understand the teacher's role in the classroom discourse as part of the community's discourse rather than the arbiter of accuracy in the language.

A final observation suggests that cooperative, communitarian practices have long been associated with Latino culture, but communitarian knowledge-building practices may in fact be a key element in all immigrant households. Mikyong (1995) argued that Asian families demonstrated a distinct propensity for cooperative strategies. Of course, Asian cultures, which are very often built on the Confucian value of filial piety, might be expected to rely on family learning structures (Sue & Okazaki 1990). But it has been suggested that all immigrant families, irrespective of ethnicity, are more likely to rely on family members (both nuclear and extended) during the stressful acculturation process (Kwak 2003). Therefore, teachers who use communitarian teaching practices are using a teaching strategy familiar to immigrant families. A full explanation for communitarian practices among recent immigrants need not be fully explored here; however, schools must be cognizant of the value placed on cooperative knowledge-building among ELLs' families and exploit teaching practices that resonate with this learning tool.

Protracted language events

Language is learned through its use. Dialogic interaction is the primary tool through which we learn language. The research reviewed here supports this assertion but also suggests that effective second language instruction must be built upon lengthy dialogues, referred to in this chapter as *protracted language events*. This concept is similar to Gallimore and Goldenberg's (1992) instructional conversations in language learning classrooms. In these qualitative studies, however, the specific form of the language events seemed to be less important than its expansiveness.

In some ways, the use of protracted language events mirrors the essential features of first language development. Brown and Bellugi (1964), in their landmark research of children learning language, found an essential pattern to syntax and semantic speech when children are learning language with an

Table 2. Child-adult language event (adapted from Brown & Bellugi 1964)

Speech Act (Child)	Notes
Child: "Look, doggy run."	Using this form of telegraphic speech maintains the word order of a more proficient speaker of English.
Adult: "Yes, that funny dog is running fast. Look at him go."	Adult repeats meaning of speech act, but expands using target form of the dialect, adding additional information and correcting form if necessary. The child is supported in her observation by having her meaning repeated. In addition, the adult has built additional meaning upon the child's initial statement. Brown and Bellugi noted that many rounds of this pattern provide enough language for the child to acquire the syntax – among other proficiencies – of the target language.
Adult protracts the language event by asking a question of the *child*: "Why is that funny dog running after that stick?"	Many child/adult interactions continue in this way. The adult has invited the dialogue to expand further, providing yet another opportunity for the child to learn both syntax and meaning.
Child: "He want stick."	Child's response is focused on meaning in spite of incorrect form.
Adult: "Yes, he wants to get that stick so that he can bring it back to the boy."	Again, adult repeats meaning of speech act, expands using target form of the dialect, and adds additional information.

adult (or more capable speaker). Table 2 offers an example of this pattern with explanatory notes. We can assume that children raised in this language environment are better prepared for the language events of the classroom.

As we consider the application of Brown and Bellugi's research when working with ELLs, we must first note that the content and complexity of protracted language events will be age appropriate. We must also note that the social relationship among teachers and students is certainly different than that between a parent and a child. However, teachers who utilize protracted language events understand the value of "keeping the conversation going," a feature of language acquisition that not only bonds teacher and student socially but also enhances the development of language comprehension (Bridges, Sinha, & Walkerdine 1981). They set in motion for their students a dialogue that continues moving. They engender conversations that offer ELLs an opportunity to be understood, a chance for their speech acts to be valued, and the occasion to be corrected for form without humiliation.

Several of the studies fit this category of protracted language use. Giacchino-Baker (1992), for instance, discovered that secondary ELLs reported that they needed more time and more interactions with their teacher to learn English. The students noted that in large classes, those in which teacher-directed lessons were common, they had few experiences of simply talking with a native speaker. A similar concern was reported in another study of secondary ELLs (Poglinco 1997). These students understood that when teachers were able to engage in protracted language events with them they acquired more language. Villar (1999) found that the methods of instructional conversation when combined with the time to engage in expansive lessons served to improve English language acquisition.

Pilgreen and Krashen (1993) found that protracted language events with text alone encouraged increased English skills. After implementing a sustained silent reading program with secondary ELLs, they found that students enjoyed books more, read more, and understood more of what they read. Even protracted language events when discussing mathematics appeared to advance English skills, as shown by Kaplan and Patino (1996). This study examined ELLs' achievement in both mathematics (word-problem solving) and English when teachers guided students through a "linguistic warm-up" to the problem (i.e., encouraging the students to use the terms of the problem in context), a breakdown of the problem into natural grammatical phrases, cooperative problem solving, and the creation of like problems of their own. Finally, Clark (1999) found that teachers who committed to language interactions created a schoolwide environment for language learning. This study implies that protracted language events among teachers results in increased achievement among ELLs.

Returning to the meta-synthetic lens, we find additional theoretical evidence for the category of research cited here. Wells (1986), for instance, is among those who argue that protracted speech acts form the foundation upon which all academic learning is built. He suggested that the "co-construction of meaning" between teacher and students (and among students) must be at the center of all schooling endeavors. His research, among many others (e.g., Tharp & Gallimore 1988), offers evidence that effective instruction among all learners begins with genuine and protracted discourse. ELLs may simply need more.

Multiple representations designed for understanding target language

A third instructional strategy suggested by the meta-synthesis is the heavy reliance on multiple representations in second language instruction. The wholly symbolic nature of all oral languages and most written languages makes linking the meaning of words with some other representation of meaning mandatory for learning. Instructional practices that build on this linkage include the use of graphic organizers, juxtaposed text and images, multi- and hyper-media, and film (e.g., Tang 1992).

Although not working from the tradition of second language education, Tufte (1990), whose work has become popular among cognitive theorists who study comprehension of scientific concepts, helps us to understand the valuable role visual images can play in learning:

> Visual displays of information encourage a diversity of individual viewer styles and rates of editing, personalizing, reasoning, and understanding. Unlike speech, visual displays are simultaneously a wide-band and a perceiver-controllable channel. (p. 31)

Tufte's point is particularly germane to students learning a second language, for whom rate of delivery, comprehensible input, and self-regulated attention are key factors in developing competence. Qualitative researchers have begun to explore the role of images, most notably among these is Kinsella (1996). This research found that struggling secondary school ELLs engaged in "coping" strategies that included the use of visual aids as "bootstraps" to comprehension, even when the instruction failed (or perhaps even discouraged) the use of images as a tool to aid language learning.

The use of multiple media, primarily video, has not been lost on teachers, many of whom have discovered that video language support is highly effective in promoting language skills (e.g., Clovis 1997). The rationale for combining words and images as aids to comprehension has come largely from Mayer's (1997; Mayer, Heiser, & Lonn 2001) generative theory of multimedia learning. This research tradition, largely based on experimental and quantitative measures, has now been applied to L2 settings (Jones & Plass 2002), where researchers have found that images enhance comprehension. In a qualitative study, Astorga (1999) investigated the role of pictures in promoting second language acquisition and found that pictures illustrating the written narrative facilitated the decoding process for children learning English.

Although the study of visual images such as pictures and word learning is an important part of language teaching, learning a language is clearly more than acquiring the meaning of discrete words. Rhythm, meter, and phonology are also language elements the thoughtful teacher must understand, suggesting that music may play a role in developing L2. McMullen and Saffran (2004) made a compelling argument, suggesting that language and music development are not only similar, but in fact yoked to one another. The quantitative research has shown that music aids language learning (Lowe 1998), and Medina (1990), working in the qualitative tradition, found that music can benefit second language learners by helping students to learn the rhythm and diction of a new language. Finally, in their ethnography on several kindergarten ELLs, Toohey and Day (1999) found that music "seduced" the learners into language activities, encouraging participation by even the most reticent learners.

The meta-analysis conducted by Moore and Readence (1984) suggests that non-ELL students benefit greatly (effect sizes up to .68) from text accompanied by graphic organizers. We anticipate that qualitative research will soon produce research supporting the general effects of graphic organizers as an effective teaching practice. To date, however, we could not locate such a paper.

The study of multiple representations deserves more attention from the research literature. Media sources that provide an important context for language learning appear to make instruction more effective.

Building on prior knowledge

Nearly every effective lesson design model suggests that one of the first tasks of the teacher in the instructional event is the activation of prior knowledge. The simplicity of the phrase *activate prior knowledge* belies the deep complexity and multiple interpretations the phrase suggests. For one teacher, activating prior knowledge may be simply reminding students of what was covered in yesterday's lesson. For another, it means investigating the most sacred cultural values held by the students and creating lessons incorporating what she has learned. For yet another, it means simply teaching what you know because your own cultural background mirrors the students'. So the operational definition of *activate prior knowledge* is quite indeterminate in the educational community. Yet in spite of this indeterminacy, the rationale runs clear: Teachers must understand what students already know, so that they may build on the knowledge students have. This crucial idea in the formation of any educational experience has been repeated in one form or another since the formal study of education began. Plato, in his "Meno's Paradox," made the problem of prior knowledge the centerpiece of his epistemology. Dewey, in *Experience and Education*, noted "that the beginning of instruction shall be made with the experiences learners already have" (1938:74). Contemporary cognitive psychologists point out the centrality of prior knowledge when they use terms such as *schema*. And each time educators talk of constructivism, they are admitting to the importance of prior knowledge (Windschitl 2002).

The role of prior knowledge and its importance in working with ELLs is the focus of several papers in this review. Most notably, G. E. Garcia (1991) found that prior knowledge played an important role when Latino ELLs were asked to demonstrate their knowledge on several tests of literacy. The qualitative evidence reported in this study indicated that students' limited background knowledge of the content (knowledge assumed by the teacher to be held by all students) reduced their performance on questions that required use of background knowledge, impacting most their understanding of vocabulary and literal interpretation of the test. Because it was found that students used Spanish to interpret vocabulary and understand English reading passages, it was suggested that literacy in Spanish should not be overlooked when trying to improve English reading comprehension.[4] In another study of Mexican American high school ELLs, Godina (1998) found that teachers who used Mexicano culture were much more successful than those teachers who ignored the cultural and linguistic knowledge altogether.

Hornberger's (1990) work demonstrates how literacy teachers can interpret and use the concept of prior knowledge in diverse ways and contexts. After spending a year in two classrooms, Hornberger noted that in the classroom where several native Spanish speaking children were placed together, the teacher was more likely to use cultural knowledge as prior knowledge in making text comprehensible. In the other classroom, where only a few ELLs of diverse native languages were placed, the teacher used more immediate instances of prior knowledge of which all the students had knowledge (e.g., a story they had read earlier in the school year). In both cases, the teachers' use of prior knowledge created an effective tool for English literacy. Floriani (1994) arrived at a similar finding, pointing out that learners who shared both a local (i.e., socioeconomic, ethnic, and native language) and classroom (i.e., students working at the same table group for the school year) background were more successful in negotiating the meaning of texts than those learners who shared a classroom only. Olmedo (1996) also found strong evidence for the importance of a common context.

Aninao (1993) tested the effectiveness of metacognitive strategies among secondary ELLs. Although metacognitive strategies are not typically considered building on prior knowledge, Aninao's research had the best fit in this category. In a year-long study designed to test the effectiveness of cognitive and metacognitive strategies, each student was instructed in the use of imagery (the use of visualization techniques to help them remember vocabulary words), transfer (the development of semantic connections with their native language), recombination (the use of known words rearranged within sentences), and reciprocal teaching (the use of strategies designed to prepare students to ask questions to assess comprehension, summarize, and clarify). The metacognitive strategies used were self-monitoring and self-evaluation. Students were instructed to ask themselves the following questions: "What do I already know?", "Am I sure that I know this?", "What do I still need to learn?," "How am I going to learn this?" and "How can I be sure that I have learned this?" By extensive interviewing and classroom observation, Aninao found that students were able to use recombination and imaging effectively, but strategies of cognitive transfer and reciprocal teaching were more difficult. Students were not successful in using the metacognitive strategies of self-evaluation and self-monitoring. It was suggested that metacognitive strategies such as planning, self-monitoring and self-evaluation should be taught before cognitive strategies in order to maximize student achievement. It was also emphasized that because of the complexity of some of the tasks, teachers who use learning strategy training need to be fluent in the student's native language. The overall results of the study were equivocal. The fact that the students were able to use imagery and recombination effectively (while other strategies were less successful) suggests that the metacognitive strategies used in this study are part of a larger effort to connect students to their previous knowledge. Varela (1997) found that learning strategies were beneficial in providing students with the language tools they needed in content classes taught in English. These learning strategies, similar to those studied by Aninao, enhanced performance in English and content courses.

Several of the studies suggested that the students' native language (as a form of prior knowledge) is an important component of English instruction. For instance, Ochoa and Pérez (1995) reported that teachers in schools where ELLs were very successful had sufficient materials in assisting their students in the transition from Spanish to English. This study also notes that the successful schools were those in which teachers understood clearly the transition to English processes salient in US bilingual education. Huang and Chang (1998) found that instruction based on prior knowledge in the form of self-efficacy (confidence in one's capacity to learn) also served to enhance English learning.

Building on students' cultural and linguistic knowledge remains one of education's greatest mysteries. The role of prior knowledge, far from being a specific strategy, is one that will require much more research. Qualitative studies, such as those reviewed here, have begun a line of inquiry that may bring us closer to understanding how effective instructional practices make use of the knowledge students already have.

Corollary category: Structural obstacles to effective instruction

The themes of the qualitative and ethnographic studies included here, at least in this point in their development, tend to draw a particular focus on the structural educational supports and barriers encountered by ELLs. Many of these studies set out to study classroom practices but also were bound to lay bare the structural elements that *prevented* effective practice. For instance, many studies of ELLs find that their achievement is limited because their teachers are not specifically prepared for working with them. Godina (1998) interviewed a teacher who was quite willing to share her ignorance of instructional practices for language teaching, in spite of teaching many ELLs: "It's really hard for me because I am not trained in ESL. And, it's really frustrating for me since I don't know how to deal with it" (p. 95). This dilemma presents itself as a clear structural barrier rather than the use of an ineffective teaching strategy. This teacher could not implement effective language teaching practices because she had no knowledge of them. This structural barrier could be removed if the school were able to provide training for such teachers.[5]

In addition to unprepared teachers, several studies pointed to inappropriate placement in ESL classes or lower track courses, an uninspired curriculum, a lack of thematic instruction and a general failure in helping ELLs in making personal and cultural connections (e.g., Giacchino-Baker 1992; Godina 1998).

Given the contextual nature of qualitative and ethnographic studies, we were not surprised that the authors chose to point out the lack of preparation among teachers in their studies. Conducting interviews, taking field notes, and engaging in other qualitative strategies provide the researcher access to the greater universe of the learner, and it is sometimes the case that the teachers or features of school hinder learning. Qualitative researchers tend to point these out.

Closing remarks

Qualitative research in education has explored new concepts of effective instruction. Further, it has exposed new relationships among familiar ideas. It has encouraged educators, researchers, and policymakers alike to reconsider some of our common assumptions about second language learning. Listening to the voices of ELLs, teachers, and the community, qualitative studies have encouraged us to pay closer attention to the context and processes of learning while also attending to outcomes. Far removed from the process-product research that once dominated educational research, qualitative studies have, to the lament of some, complicated our views of schooling. But the full realization of qualitative research in the study of effective teaching practice in language education will require more time.

The use of meta-syntheses in education is even more inchoate, and our work here is best considered a first attempt at using the strategies for compiling qualitative works into coherent themes. As such, we recognize several limitations of our study. For example, we remain concerned that our coding schemes and categories would be replicated by other researchers examining the same studies. The choice of external theoretical frames in the development of research themes (Wolcott 1994), in particular, remains a challenge to replication, but we came to recognize that, without such frames, our categories would not have the coherence they do. However, it is easy to imagine that other researchers would select alternative frames and perhaps arrive at different conclusions. These limitations caused us to wonder at times that our meta-syntheses could be distinguished from a simple research narrative. Like many qualitative researchers, we kept in mind the so-called objectivity found in meta-analyses and had doubts about the external validity of our study when compared to compilations of quantitative research. But these are problems that all meta-syntheses in educational research will be required to face, and we anticipate that future work in this area will help forge a more common method for the development of themes, as well as an analog to the effect size we find in traditional meta-analyses. Finally, in spite of our best efforts, we have likely missed studies that should have been included in the meta-synthesis. To the authors of studies we overlooked, we send our apologies and kindly ask for a notice or update of their work.

The themes that we derived, we admit, do not necessarily break new ground in the effective practices realm of second language teaching. For instance, building on prior knowledge is a common practice validated by both quantitative and qualitative research. Nevertheless, we believe that this meta-synthesis has emphasized the key role these practices play in teaching ELLs. On the basis of anecdotal evidence, teachers who read a previous version of our work have reported that the meta-synthesis has given them a tool to promote communicative forms of teaching they favor over the form-based drills promoted by their administration.

While the primary purpose of our meta-synthesis was to identify features of teaching practices for ELLs that have been shown to be effective, a secondary purpose was to explore the potential for qualitative studies to inform such practice. The studies reviewed here found that communitarian teaching practices, protracted language events, using multiple representations designed for teaching new languages, and building on prior knowledge are practices likely to increase learning among ELLs. These practices are less determinate than the instructional methods often uncovered in a quantitative review. Teachers who wish to adopt these practices will likely find that they must adapt and fit them to their own context and purposes. Some may even encounter an incommensurable gap between their own beliefs about teaching language and these practices. Such adaptations are likely to be a consequence of a meta-synthesis. McCormick, Rodney, and Varcoe (2003) suggested that the results of meta-synthesis, rather than point to clear and unambiguous social and educational practices, will require practitioners to consider their praxis, the terrain between theory and practice but informed by both.

It remains to be seen if practitioners will implement practices revealed in a meta-synthesis with more enthusiasm than those identified in meta-analytic studies. Educational theorists (e.g., Robinson 1998; Winch 2001) are increasingly troubled by the apparent lack of relevance of educational research for practice. Researchers conducting meta-analyses have wondered whether practitioners will trust their work sufficiently to inform classroom practice (Gersten & Baker 1999). This same concern applies to meta-syntheses.

Our review revealed what we believe to be several effective practices based on a limited number of studies. The future of research in effective teaching practices for ELLs may be well represented in the mixed-methods approach taken by Yedlin (2003). This study assessed first-grade ELLs' achievement in English literacy using quantitative measures while using a qualitative, ethnographic approach to understand how the teacher orchestrated an approach to literacy development using multiple, concurrent zones of proximal development and the myriad informal assessments needed to facilitate children's comprehension and language development. The growth of mixed-method studies such as Yedlin's suggests that a new type of research synthesis, neither meta-analysis nor meta-synthesis, but a weaving together of multiple practices, may reveal the overarching strategies needed to improve the academic achievement of ELLs. Some of the new conceptual frameworks and models for incorporating mixed methods hold great promise for the future of educational research (Cresswell 2003; Johnson & Onwuegbuzie 2004; Tashakkori & Teddlie 2003).

Finally, given the effective practices we found in this meta-synthesis, what might be the implications for English language teachers and teaching? First, preservice teacher education can help beginning educators to understand the ways in which non directive approaches to teaching (e.g., communitarian practices) foment language development for ELLs. This knowledge may also help beginning teachers overcome their impulse to consider effective instruction as "teacher talk" (Goodlad 1984). Practicing teachers may also enhance their teaching effectiveness by considering how their current practices are corroborated (or contradicted) by the practices we found in this meta-synthesis. If experienced teachers lack faith in protracted language events, for instance, why do they think this way and what might change their minds?

Conducting this meta-syntheses and sharing our results with other educators has reminded us of the crucial nature of instructional context and the importance of teachers' beliefs and practices, as well as the power of questions and reflection to enhance teaching practice. On the basis of our experiences, we suggest that rather than mandate "proven" practices, meta-syntheses in education should seek to provoke deep reflection and debate. In the main, the goal of the meta-synthesis in education recalls Geertz's (1973) comment on the fruitless search for "truths" in anthropology: "What gets better is the precision with which we vex each other" (p. 29).

Acknowledgement

This research was supported by the Mid-Atlantic Regional Laboratory for Student Success (LSS), funded by the Institute of Education Sciences, US Department of Education. The views expressed are those of the authors and not necessarily shared by any of the above funding agencies. We would like to thank Susan Leigh Flinspach, an anonymous reviewer, and the editors for their thoughtful critique of earlier versions of the chapter.

Notes

1. Whereas our search terms did not include *bilingual* or *biliteracy*, we do not want readers to conclude that we are opposed to programs promoting bilingualism. On the contrary, we are very troubled by the English-only movement in the US and have proposed strategies for reestablishing bilingual education in those states where it has been legislatively erased (Téllez, Flinspach, & Waxman 2005). Nevertheless, teaching English is a key goal for ELLs in the U.S.; students who lack strong English skills will struggle, especially when they reach secondary school. We were also concerned that a focus on both L2 (English in our case) and bilingual teaching practices would result in a set of papers too large for a coherent review. Finally, the practices we identified could apply to teaching English in bilingual settings and perhaps be useful in other language teaching contexts.

2. Many classic qualitative studies have been conducted that deal with ELL issues and are not reviewed in this meta-synthesis because they fall outside the scope of what we set out to synthesize. For example, Fillmore's (1982) oft-cited study was out of our date range, as was Duff (2001). Other excellent ELL qualitative studies published between 1990 and 2000 are not about teaching practices but instead focus on peer support (Beaumont 1999), social-

ization (Willett 1995), program quality (Freeman 1996), school policies (Harklau 2000), or teachers and culture (Jimenez & Gersten 1999).

3. Coding was conducted by the researchers; the themes were validated by two second language specialists.

4. Whereas we have not specifically considered the role of L1 development as an instructional practice, some research has shown that L1 competence in reading, in particular, predicts success in L2 literacy (van Gelderen et al. 2004). However, other studies (e.g., Bernhardt & Kamil 1995) attribute L2 reading capacity to a more global metalinguistic capacity. This important debate in the field of bilingual and dual language education is beyond the scope of our chapter, mostly because we consider the development of L1 literacy skills as part of a program rather than a teaching practice.

5. One compelling study demonstrated the importance of an expert teacher in the education of ELLs. Fitzgerald & Noblit (1999) shared a qualitative work written in the "confessional" style of the anthropological literature. Because this chapter was constructed more as personal narrative, choosing not to employ qualitative methods, we did not include it in our meta-synthesis but nevertheless consider it noteworthy for two reasons. First, it showed the importance of a well-qualified teacher for ELLs, one who takes care to document and reflect on student achievement and its relation to instructional practice. Second, it raised issues regarding the criteria for inclusion in a meta-synthesis. Should narratives and confessional accounts, clearly qualitative in nature, be considered scientific, qualitative research?

* Studies included in the meta-synthesis are marked with an asterisk (*).

References

*Aninao, J. C. (1993). *Training high school ESL students to use language learning strategies.* Unpublished doctoral dissertation. Stanford University.

*Astorga, M. C. (1999). The text-image interaction and second language learning. *Australian Journal of Language and Literacy, 22* (3), 212–233.

August, D., & Hakuta, K. (Eds.). (1997). *Improving schooling for language-minority children: A research agenda.* Washington, DC: National Academy Press.

Bailey, K. M., & Nunan, D. (1996). *Voices from the language classroom: Qualitative studies in second language education.* Cambridge, UK: Cambridge University Press.

Barnes, D. (1976). *From communication to curriculum.* New York: Penguin.

Bartolome, L. I. (1994). Beyond the methods fetish: Toward a humanizing pedagogy. *Harvard Education Review, 64*(2), 173–194.

Baumann, J. F., & Duffy, A. M. (2001). Teacher-researcher methodology: Themes, variations, and possibilities. *The Reading Teacher, 54*(6), 608–615.

Beaumont, C. (1999). Dilemmas of peer assistance in a bilingual full inclusion classroom. *The Elementary School Journal, 99*(3), 233–254.

Bernhardt, E. B., & Kamil, M. L. (1995). Interpreting relationships between L1 and L2 reading – consolidating the linguistic threshold and the linguistic interdependence hypotheses. *Applied Linguistics, 16*, 15–34.

Brennan, R. T., Kim, J., Wenz-Gross, M., & Siperstein, G. N. (2001). The relative equitability of high-stakes testing versus teacher-assigned grades: An analysis of the Massachusetts Comprehensive Assessment System (MCAS). *Harvard Educational Review, 71*(2), 173–216.

Bridges, A., Sinha, C., & Walkerdine, V. (1981). The development of comprehension. In G. Wells (Ed.), *Learning through interaction: The study of language development* (pp. 116–156). Cambridge, UK: Cambridge University Press.

Brown, R., & Bellugi, U. (1964). Three processes in the child's acquisition of syntax. *Harvard Education Review, 34* (2), 133–151.

Bus, A. G., & van Ijzendoorn, M. H. (1999). Phonological awareness and early reading: A meta-analysis of experimental training studies. *Journal of Educational Psychology, 91* (3), 403–414.

Calderon, M., Hertz-Lazarowitz, R., & Slavin, R. (1998). Effects of cooperative integrated reading and composition on students making the transition from Spanish to English reading. *Elementary School Journal, 99*(2), 153–165.

Chintapalli-Tamirisa, P. (1995). *Contexts of learning in second language classrooms: An ethnographic study of a high school ESL class.* Unpublished doctoral dissertation. University of Houston.

*Clark, S. T. (1999). *Factors promoting literacy development of first-grade English language learners in monolingual-English classes at one elementary school.* Unpublished doctoral dissertation. The Claremont Graduate University.

*Clovis, D. L. (1997). Lights, television, action! Utilizing electronic media for teaching English as a second language. *Educational Leadership, 55*(3), 38–41.

Cresswell, J. W. (2003). *Research design: Qualitative, quantitative, and mixed method approaches.* Thousand Oaks, CA: Sage.

Dewey, J. (1916). *Democracy and education: An introduction to the philosophy of education.* New York: Macmillan.

Dewey, J. (1938). *Experience and education.* New York: Macmillan.

Dewey, J. (1961). *Democracy and education.* New York: Macmillan.

Duff, P. A. (2001). Language, literacy, content, and (pop) culture: Challenges for ESL students in mainstream courses. *Canadian Modern Language Review, 58*, 103–122.

Eisenhart, M., & Towne, L. (2003). Contestation and change in national policy on "scientifically based" education research. *Educational Researcher, 32* (7), 31–38.

Eisner, E. W. (1998). *The kinds of schools we need: Personal essays.* Portsmouth, NH: Heinemann.

Eisner, E. W. (2001). Concerns and aspirations for qualitative research in the new millenium. *Qualitative Research, 1* (2), 135–145.

Elbaum, B., Vaughn, S., Hughes, M. T., & Moody, S. W. (2000). How effective are one-to-one tutoring programs in reading for elementary students at risk for reading failure? A meta-analysis of the intervention research. *Journal of Educational Psychology, 92*(4), 605–619.

Fillmore, L. W. (1982). Instructional language as linguistic input: Second-language learning in classrooms. In L. C. Wilkinson (Ed.), *Communicating in the classroom* (pp. 283–296). New York: Academic Press.

Finfgeld, D. L. (2003). Metasynthesis: The state of the art – so far. *Qualitative Health Research, 13*, 893–904.

Fisher, D., Frey, N., & Williams, D. (2002). Seven literacy strategies that work. *Educational Leadership, 60*(3), 70–73.

Fitzgerald, J., & Noblit, G. W. (1999). About hopes, aspirations, and uncertainty: First-grade English-language learners' emergent reading. *Journal of Literacy Research, 31* (2), 133–182.

Flinspach, S. (2001). *Interpretive synthesis: A methodology for reviewing qualitative case study research*. Unpublished doctoral dissertation. The University of Chicago.

*Floriani, A. (1994). Negotiating what counts: Roles and relationships, texts and contexts, content and meaning. *Linguistics and Education, 5*(3–4), 241–274.

Freeman, R. D. (1996). Dual-language planning at Oyster bilingual school: "It's much more than language." *TESOL Quarterly, 30*, 557–582.

Gallimore, R., & Goldenberg, C. N. (1992). Tracking the developmental path of teachers and learners: A Vygotskyan perspective. In F. K. Oser, A. Dick, & J-L. Patry (Eds.), *Effective and responsible teaching: The new synthesis* (pp. 203–221). San Francisco: Jossey-Bass.

*Garcia, G. E. (1991). Factors influencing the English reading test performance of Spanish-speaking Hispanic children. *Reading Research Quarterly, 26*(4), 371–392.

García, G. N. (2001). The factors that place Latino children and youth at risk of educational failure. In R. E. Slavin & M. Calderón (Eds.), *Effective programs for Latino students* (pp. 307–329). Mahwah, NJ: Lawrence Erlbaum.

Geertz, C. (1973). *The interpretation of culture*. New York: Basic.

Gersten, R., & Baker, S. (1999.) *Effective instruction for English language learners: A multi-vocal approach toward research synthesis*. (ERIC Document Reproduction Service No. ED 430 019).

*Giacchino-Baker, R. (1992). *Recent Mexican immigrant students' opinions of their use and acquisition of English as a second language in an "English-Only" American high school: A qualitative study*. Unpublished doctoral dissertation. The Claremont Graduate University.

Glaser, B. G., & Strauss, A. L. (1967). *The discovery of grounded theory: Strategies for qualitative research*. Chicago: Aldine.

Glass, G. V. (2000). *Meta-analysis at 25*. Retrieved December 9, 2005, from http://glass.ed. asu.edu/gene/papers/meta25.html

Glass, G. V., McGaw, B., & Smith, M. L. (1981). *Meta-analysis in social research*. Thousand Oaks, CA: Sage.

*Goatley, V. J., Brock, C. H., & Raphael, T. E. (1995). Diverse learners participating in regular education "book clubs". *Reading Research Quarterly, 30*, 352–380.

Goertz, M., & Duffy, M. (2003). Mapping the landscape of high-stakes testing and accountability programs. *Theory into Practice, 42* (1), 4–11.

*Godina, H. (1998). *Mexican-American high-school students and the role of literacy across home school-community settings*. Unpublished doctoral dissertation. University of Illinois.

*González-Edfelt, N. (1990). Oral interaction and collaboration at the computer: Learning English as a Second language with the help of your peers. *Computers in the Schools, 7* (1–2), 53–90.

Goodlad, J. I. (1984). *A place called school: Prospects for the future.* New York: McGraw-Hill.

Hall, J. K., & Verplaetse, L. S. (Eds.). (2000). *Second and foreign language learning through classroom interaction.* Mahwah, NJ: Lawrence Erlbaum.

Harklau, L. (2000). From the "good kids" to the "worst": Representations of English language learners across educational settings. *TESOL Quarterly, 34,* 35–67.

Heath, S. B. (1983). *Ways with words: Language, life, and work in communities and classrooms.* Cambridge, UK: Cambridge University Press.

Hispanic Dropout Project. (1998). *Final report.* Available online at http://www.ncela. gwu.edu/miscpubs/hdp/final.htm.

*Hornberger, N. (1990). Creating successful learning contexts for bilingual literacy. *Teachers College Record, 92*(2), 212–229.

Howe, K. R. (2004). A critique of experimentalism. *Qualitative Inquiry 10*(1), 42–61.

*Hruska, B. L. (2000, March). *Bilingualism, gender, and friendship: Constructing second language learners in an English dominant Kindergarten.* Paper presented at the annual meeting of the American Association for Applied Linguistics, Vancouver, BC, Canada.

*Huang, S. C., & Chang, S. F. (1998). Self-efficacy in learners of English as a second language: Four examples. *Journal of Intensive English Studies, 12,* 23–40.

Jimenez, R., & Gersten, R. (1999). Lessons and dilemmas derived from the literacy instruction of two Latino/a teachers. *American Educational Research Journal, 36,* 265–301.

Johnson, R. B., & Onwuegbuzie, A. (2004). Mixed methods research: A paradigm whose time has come. *Educational Researcher, 33*(7), 14–26.

Jones, L. C., & Plass, J. L. (2002). Supporting listening comprehension and vocabulary acquisition in French with multimedia annotations. *Modern Language Journal, 86,* 546–561.

Joyce, D. C. (1997). *Strategies for responding to the writing of ESL students.* (ERIC Document Reproduction Service No. ED 421 014).

Kahne, J. (1996). *Reframing educational policy: Democracy, community, and the individual.* New York: Teachers College Press.

*Kaplan, R. G., & Patino, R. A. (1996, April). *Teaching mathematical problem solving to students with limited English proficiency.* Paper presented at the annual meeting of the American Educational Research Association, New York.

Kindler, A. L. (2002). *Survey of the state's Limited English Proficient Students and available educational programs and services: 2000–2001 summary report.* Washington, DC: National Clearinghouse for English Language Acquisition & Language Instruction Educational Programs.

*Kinsella, K. M. (1996). *The reading-to-learn strategies and experiences of high school ESL students.* Unpublished doctoral dissertation. University of San Francisco.

Kwak, K. (2003). Adolescents and their parents: A review of intergenerational family relations for immigrant and non-immigrant families. *Human Development, 46*(2/3), 115–36.

Lazaraton, A. (1995). Qualitative research in applied linguistics: A progress report. *TESOL Quarterly, 29,* 455–472.

Lowe, A. S. (1998). Teaching music and second languages: Methods of integration and implications for learning. *Canadian Modern Language Review, 54,* 218–238.

Mayer, R. E. (1997). Multimedia learning: Are we asking the right questions? *Educational Psychologist, 32*(1), 1–19.

Mayer, R. E., Heiser, J., & Lonn, S. (2001). Cognitive constraints on multimedia learning: When presenting more material results in less understanding. *Journal of Educational Psychology, 93*(1), 187–198.

McCormick, J., Rodney, P., & Varcoe, C. (2003). Reinterpretations across studies: An approach to meta-analysis. *Qualitative Health Research, 13*, 933–944.

McMullen, E., & Saffran, J. R. (2004). Music and language: A developmental comparison. *Music Perception, 21*(3), 289–311.

*Medina, S. (1990, March). *The effects of music upon second language vocabulary acquisition.* Paper presented at the annual meeting of the Teachers of English to Speakers of Other Languages, San Francisco.

Mikyong, K. (1995). Serving Asian-American children in school: An ecological perspective. In S. Rothstein (Ed.), *Class, culture, and race in American schools* (pp. 145–160). Westport, CT: Greenwood.

Miles, M. B., & Huberman, A. M. (1994). *Qualitative data analysis: An expanded sourcebook.* Thousand Oaks, CA: Sage.

Moore, D. W., & Readence, J. E. (1984). A quantitative and qualitative review of graphic organizer research. *Journal of Educational Research, 78* (1), 11–17.

Mosenthal, J. (1996). Situated learning and methods coursework in the teaching of literacy. *Journal of Literacy Research 28*(3), 379–403.

Nath, L. R., Ross S., & Smith, L. (1996). A case study of implementing a cooperative learning program in an inner-city school. *Journal of Experimental Education, 64*(2), 117–136.

Noblit, G. W., & Hare, R. D. (1988). *Meta-ethnography: Synthesizing qualitative studies.* Newbury Park, CA: Sage.

Norris, J. M., & Ortega, L. (2000). Effectiveness of L2 instruction: A research synthesis and quantitative meta-analysis. *Language Learning, 50*, 417–528.

*Ochoa, H. S., & Pérez, R. J. (1995). Appraising curriculum and instruction practices of bilingual programs in elementary schools varying in effectiveness: A qualitative and quantitative comparison. *Journal of Educational Issues for Language Minority Students, 15*, 49–63. Available at http://www.ncbe.gwu.edu/miscpubs/

*Olmedo, I. M. (1996). Creating contexts for studying history with students learning English. *Social Studies, 87*(1), 39–43.

*Pilgreen, J., & Krashen, S. (1993). Sustained silent reading with English as a second language high school students: Impact on reading comprehension, reading frequency, and reading enjoyment. *School Library Media Quarterly, 22* (1), 21–23.

*Poglinco, S. M. (1997). *La meta, el desvío, and la superación: Student images of success and achievement: A qualitative study of Latina second language learners in high school.* Unpublished doctoral dissertation. New York University.

Robinson, V. M. J. (1998). Methodology and the research-practice gap. *Educational Researcher, 27*(1), 17–26.

Sandelowski, M., Docherty, S., & Emden, C. (1997). Qualitative metasynthesis: Issues and techniques. *Research in Nursing and Health, 20*, 365–371.

Schmid, C. L. (2001). Educational achievement, language-minority students, and the new second generation. *Sociology of Education*, Special Issue, no number, 71–87.

Strauss, A. L., & Corbin, J. (1990.). *Basics of qualitative research: Grounded theory procedures and techniques*. Newbury Park, CA: Sage.

Sue, S., & Okazaki, S. (1990). Asian-American educational achievements: A phenomenon in search of an explanation. *American Psychologist, 45*(8), 913–920.

Swanson, H. L., Trainin, G., Necoechea, D. M., & Hammill, D. D. (2003). Rapid naming, phonological awareness, and reading: A meta-analysis of the correlation evidence. *Review of Educational Research, 73,* 407–440.

*Tang, G. (1992). The effect of graphic representation of knowledge structures on ESL reading comprehension. *Studies in Second Language Acquisition, 14,* 177–195.

Tashakkori, A., & Teddlie, C. (Eds.) (2003). *Handbook of mixed methods in social and behavioral research*. Thousand Oaks, CA: Sage.

Téllez, K., Flinspach, S., & Waxman, H. C. (2005). Resistance to scientific evidence: Program evaluation and its lack of influence on policies related to language education programs. In R. Hoosain & F. Salili (Eds.), *Language in multicultural education* (pp. 57–76). Greenwich, CT: Information Age Publishing.

Tharp, R. G., & Gallimore, R. (1988). *Rousing minds to life: Teaching, learning, and schooling in social context*. New York: Cambridge University Press.

*Toohey, K., & Day, E. (1999). Language-learning: The importance of access to community. *TESL Canada Journal, 17*(1), 40–53.

Tufte, E. R. (1990). *Envisioning information*. Cheshire, CT: Graphics Press.

*Tujay, S., Jennings, L., & Dixon, C. (1995). Classroom discourse and opportunities to learn: An ethnographic study of knowledge construction in a bilingual third grade class. *Discourse Processes, 19,* 75–110

US Department of Education. (2002). *Schools and Staffing Survey 1999–2000*. Washington, DC: Author.

van Gelderen, A., Schoonen, R., de Glopper, K., Hulstijn, J., Simis, A., Snellings, P., et al. (2004). Linguistic knowledge, processing speed, and metacognitive knowledge in first- and second-language reading comprehension: A componential analysis. *Journal of Educational Psychology, 96* (1), 19–30.

*Varela, E. E. (1997). *Speaking solo: Using learning strategy instruction to improve English language learners' oral presentation skills in content-based ESL*. Unpublished doctoral dissertation. Georgetown University.

Viadero, D. (2002, September 4). Education department picks groups to develop database of effective practices. *Education Week*. Retrieved December 9, 2002, from http://www.edweek.org/ew/ew_printstory.cfm?slug=01whatworks.h22

*Villar, J. A. (1999). *A model for developing academic language proficiency in English language learners through instructional conversations*. Unpublished doctoral dissertation. University of Connecticut.

Vygotsky, L. (1934/1986). *Thought and language*. Cambridge, MA: MIT Press.

Wang, M. C., Haertel, G. D., & Walberg, H. J. (1993). Toward a knowledge base for school learning. *Review of Educational Research, 63,* 249–294.

Wells, G. (1986). *The meaning makers: Children learning language and using language to learn*. Portsmouth, NH: Heinemann.

Willett, J. (1995). Becoming first graders in an L2: An ethnographic study of L2 socialization. *TESOL Quarterly, 29,* 473–503.

Winch, C. (2001). Accountability and relevance in educational research. *Journal of Philosophy of Education, 35* (3), 443–459.

Windschitl, M. (2002). Framing constructivism in practice as the negotiation of dilemmas: An analysis of the conceptual, pedagogical, cultural, and political challenges facing teachers. *Review of Educational Research, 72,* 131–175.

Wolcott, H. F. (1994). *Transforming qualitative data.* Thousand Oaks, CA: Sage.

Yedlin, J. A. (2003). *Teacher talk and writing development in an urban first-grade English as a second language classroom.* Unpublished doctoral dissertation. Harvard University.

CHAPTER 8

Research synthesis and historiography

The case of assessment of second language proficiency

Margaret Thomas
Boston College

In the words of Light and Pillemer (1984: ix), research synthesis allows us to "learn from existing findings, to 'discover what is known." That is to say, it reviews the outcomes of multiple, independent (but comparable), research projects, so as to provide a context for the interpretation of individual results within the total body of research. The broad-scope perspective of this kind of scholarship, and its synthetic reflection on the products of a research community, are also characteristic of the work of historians, especially in the various sub-fields subsumed under "the history of ideas." Study of the history of a discipline requires one to engage in some of the same activities entailed in research synthesis. This chapter examines one aspect of research on second language learning, the assessment of target-language proficiency. My orientation is historical in that I compare the results of two studies, carried out twelve years apart, that survey conventions of second language proficiency assessment; the goal is to investigate whether, and if so, how practices of proficiency assessment have changed over that time interval. While not participating in all the conventional features of research synthesis, this chapter illustrates overlaps and gaps between research synthesis and historiography, taken as two partially-intersecting tools we can employ to "discover what is known."

Introduction

John Norris and Lourdes Ortega advocate the virtues of research synthesis as a means of evaluating the complex, often contradictory, findings of modern scientific study of second language (L2) learning and teaching. In particular, they have championed the power of meta-analysis to summarize and quantify the results of multifarious individual studies (Norris & Ortega 2000, 2001). The chapters of this book demonstrate something of the range of what research synthesis and meta-analysis reveal about second language (L2) learning and teaching.

My purpose in this chapter is to point out the virtues of a different, but related, kind of secondary research, namely work that inquires into the history of the study of L2 acquisition. In trying to understand the development of a field of study over time, historiographers do not carry out research synthesis exactly as Norris and Ortega envision it. But historiography and research synthesis have certain traits in common. Applied to the case at hand, investigation into the history of L2 acquisition tries to understand how people in other times and places have conceived of the nature of language learning: What kinds of questions did they raise about the acquisition of a second language, and how did they seek answers to those questions? To what extent were they satisfied with the answers they found?[1] In performing this kind of research, the historian has to attend open-mindedly to a wide array of materials, derived from many sources, then to look for patterns and relationships that emerge among them (Andresen 1985; Koerner 1976; Law 2003). Likewise, research synthesis wrestles with a body of literature in the hope of achieving an integrated overview of different approaches scholars have taken to a complex and heterogeneous object of inquiry. That overview must go beyond a simple "literature review," to present the object of inquiry coherently while respecting the integrity of its constituent parts and the individuality of different approaches to it. In these ways, historiography and research synthesis both draw on, and develop, similar intellectual skills; they also face similar threats to their validity.

On the other hand, there is enough dissimilarity between research synthesis in the social-scientific tradition as presented by (for example) Cooper and Hedges (1994), Glass (1976), or Light and Pillemer (1984), and the kind of integrated overview of research entailed in historiography, such that each provides a kind of parallax on the conventions of the other. Comparison of the two, therefore, has the potential to bring both into sharper focus.

In this chapter I present a small study of one detail of modern research on L2 acquisition. I then introduce a historical dimension by recapitulating that study after twelve years, an interval long enough in this context to count as meaningful. The chapter is organized in three subsections. First, I review the motivation, methodology, and results of Thomas (1994), a research synthesis-like study that surveyed techniques of assessing target language proficiency in empirical research on L2 acquisition published in four academic journals between 1988 and 1992. Next, I present the results that emerged when that study was repeated a dozen years later, and explore what continuities and gaps between the two sets of results might mean. I conclude by returning to the relationship of research synthesis to historical study.

Assessment of L2 proficiency in second language acquisition research 1988–1992: A liminal work of research synthesis

Thomas (1994) was not conceived as a research synthesis, nor as a work of historiography. Rather, it was conceived in the course of searching for a model on which to design a cross-sectional study of the acquisition of anaphors in L2 English and L2 Japanese (Thomas 1993). To discover how learners develop their knowledge of reflexive pronouns in L2, I needed a reliable means of assessing the global target-language proficiency of each member of a large subject pool ($n = 174$), recruited from eleven different schools and language-instructional programs, in two countries. Trolling through literature in the field, I found that published work differed along several dimensions with respect to proficiency assessment. Not only did researchers differ in the range of learners' L2 abilities they assessed and in how they carried out the assessment, but they also differed in how they incorporated assessment of proficiency into their research design, and in the depth of their investment in assessing it. I eventually settled on a methodology that seemed adequate for the purposes of the research I was carrying out. But my curiosity about conventions for assessing proficiency in the context of L2 research persisted.

To satisfy that curiosity I later returned to the issue, taking as my universe of study all articles that appeared during a five-year interval between 1988 and 1992 in four key journals published in English: *Applied Linguistics* (Vols. 9–13), *Language Learning* (Vols. 38–42), *Second Language Research* (Vols. 4–8), and *Studies in Second Language Acquisition* (Vols. 10–14). The question I sought to answer was "What are the conventions for assessment of target-language proficiency in empirical research on L2 acquisition, as represented in contemporary Euro-American-oriented scholarship?" That I worked with four journals (rather than five, or fifteen) within a five-year time span (rather than a longer or shorter interval) were not principled decisions, but rather decisions based on convenience and an estimate of how much data might suffice to answer the question. Similarly, the choice of these four sources followed largely from their availability, and from my subjective sense that they constitute a representative sample of refereed literature. These criteria for selection of materials did not, of course, define what is relevant and irrelevant to the research question in any independent sense. Inevitably, they isolated a subset of the relevant material, bounded by both arbitrary limits (for example, because a particular piece of research appeared too late or too early to be included in the corpus I analyzed) and limits imposed by my tacit judgment (because judgment is involved in, for example, decisions about what journals count as "representative," and about how long an interval would likely capture a decent amount of variability). Farther afield, decisions I made at the outset to exclude other plausible sources of information about proficiency assessment – unpublished papers; theses and dissertations; books; texts published in other languages – all need to be recognized as limiting the value of the analysis I produced.

Acknowledging these limits, I plunged into this material, and, as a first step, established guidelines for excluding certain categories of texts published in the journals: book reviews; articles that do not address L2 acquisition; essays that interpret or review already-published data rather than presenting new findings; editorial commentary that introduces articles gathered into thematic issues of the journals. I also excluded articles that analyze research not conducted by the authors themselves (i.e. texts that comment on data collected by other researchers), because these virtually never include sufficient detail about the original study. An exception to the latter exclusion is that I admitted into the body of research that I would analyze journal articles based on massive, collaborative, studies of L2 acquisition (e.g. the European Science Foundation and ZISA projects) even if the author(s) of those articles had not been directly involved in data collection, because information about the subjects' proficiency, insofar as it was assessed, is widely available.

The corpus thus defined included 157 experimental or observational studies. I examined each one to determine how the authors represented the character of L2 proficiency within the learner population in question, and how they incorporated that information into their research design. Four major categories of proficiency-assessment techniques emerged, which I defined as follows:

(1) Impressionistic judgment
   (Seemingly) spontaneous, unsupported, characterization of learners' competence in L2 (e.g. "The subjects in this study were beginners"). Sometimes – but not always – these characterizations would be corroborated (only) by reports of learners' length of residence in L2-speaking environments

(2) Institutional status
   Learners' membership in a specific group (typically, an academic course),

or assignment to a particular rank within some research-external social structure, used as a proxy for achieved proficiency

(3) In-house assessment

Proficiency defined by locally-developed instruments such as program-internal placement tests, or by the outcome of research-specific tests designed to measure skills considered prerequisite to the target of inquiry (e.g. syntactic movement; past-tense morphology; familiarity with particular vocabulary items)

(4) Standardized test

Assessment of proficiency through standardized instruments in the public domain: for example, the Peabody Picture Vocabulary Test, TOEFL, Michigan Test of English Language Proficiency; see Thomas (1994:325) for an exhaustive listing[2]

I first posited these four categories of assessment techniques on the basis of a preliminary survey of the corpus, then refined them by inspecting each of the 157 articles in turn. Many individual studies fell cleanly into one or the other category. However, classification was not always a straightforward task, opening up the possibility that inconsistency in coding distorts my results. Among other threats, there were cases where authors did not clearly communicate the means by which they assessed proficiency, or where they defined proficiency by multiple means, or defined it differently at different stages of a multi-dimensional research design. In ambiguous or complex instances, I tried to locate what seemed to be the researchers' primary basis for assessment of proficiency, by:

> ...record[ing] all the various means of defining proficiency, but assign[ing] the study as a whole to the class representing the first step of proficiency assessment. That is, I classified a given study according to the first means used by the researchers in defining or describing their participants. I then sub-classified the study according to any additional means of assessment employed. This resulted in a branching taxonomy of proficiency-assessment practices within some of the four major classes...   (Thomas 1994:313)

Working through these kinds of complexities in the corpus, I eventually assigned each of the 157 studies to one of these four techniques of assessment, save for 4 studies that fell into a heterogeneous "Other" category. In Table 1, the left hand column tallies the incidence of each technique within the total corpus analyzed in Thomas (1994).

Figure 1 depicts the distribution of studies, by technique, across the four journals, indicating the percentage of each journal's total contribution to the

Table 1. Incidence of four techniques of assessing L2 proficiency, 1988–92 versus 2000–04 corpora

Means of Assessment	1988–92 Corpus $n = 157$ No. Articles in Corpus (% of Total Corpus)		2000–04 Corpus $n = 211$ No. Articles in Corpus (% of Total Corpus)	
Impressionistic Judgment	33	(21.0)	40	(19.0)
Institutional Status	63	(40.1)	70	(33.2)
In-House Assessment	22	(14.0)	41	(19.4)
Standardized Test	35	(22.3)	49	(23.2)
Other	4	(2.5)	11	(5.2)

1998–92 data from Thomas (1994:312)

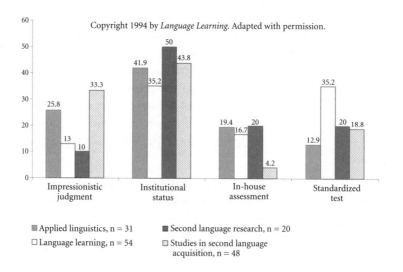

Copyright 1994 by *Language Learning*. Adapted with permission.

- ■ Applied linguistics, n = 31
- □ Language learning, n = 54
- ■ Second language research, n = 20
- ▨ Studies in second language acquisition, n = 48

Figure 1. Distribution of articles in the 1988–92 corpus = (153), across four major classes of proficiency assessment techniques, by journal, as the percent of relevant publications in a given journal (From Thomas 1994:312)

corpus assigned to each of the four techniques, excluding those classified as "Other" (so that, henceforth, the 1988–92 corpus will be treated as consisting of 153 studies).

Thomas (1994: 313–27) discussed examples of the four proficiency assessment techniques, indicating instances of what seem to be appropriate and inappropriate employment of each one. I also cited instances where researchers appeared to have insufficiently considered the impact of L2 proficiency on their results – either because they admitted research participants with too little L2 competence, or too much, or the wrong profile of skills, or who constituted an overly heterogeneous subject pool. The article closed by speculating about why proficiency seemed sometimes to be inadequately controlled in L2 research, and provided some examples where clever research design appeared to achieve that control in a satisfying and economical manner. My conclusion is that although it is obviously advantageous to have more, rather than less, information about the learners whose L2 is being investigated, the choice about whether, and if so how and to what extent, to assess proficiency needs to be made strategically, with thoughtful reference to research goals and design.

I conceived and executed this investigation of the assessment of L2 proficiency without awareness of the tradition of research synthesis as it is represented in, for example, Light and Pillemer's (1984) influential introduction to the subject (provocatively titled *Summing up: The science of reviewing research*). In retrospect, Thomas (1994) represents a kind of liminal research synthesis, in the sense of being positioned on a threshold: it is oriented toward its object of inquiry in ways that resemble the orientation of research synthesis, but it does not fully enter into the conventions of that technique. On the one hand, like a typical research synthesis, the 1994 study surveys and reflects on existing research. Moreover, it sets criteria for isolating a body of work from the literature, then reviews and assesses that work in search of generalizations that provide insight into the relationship of individual studies to the corpus as a whole. The 1994 study has this in common with research synthesis. On the other hand, research synthesis in its classic form weighs the empirical evidence, pro and con, a controversial finding. That is to say, it is directed at identifying what are the best-supported outcomes within a body of research that arrives at contradictory outcomes; it "sums up" the products of diverse research to determine which works come out on top. In contrast, the target of interest in Thomas (1994) – how L2 proficiency is assessed – is an aspect of the methodology of empirical studies of L2 acquisition, rather than the outcome of those studies. Moreover, my objective in surveying the means of proficiency assessment was to depict a range of viable options, variously applicable in different research contexts, not to discern any single "best" technique.

In these ways, the 1994 study approached research synthesis without participating in the full constellation of its practices and goals, at least as they are conventionally depicted. As Norris and Ortega elaborate in the Introduction to this collection – and as they demonstrate in Norris and Ortega (2000) – research synthesis can be defined more broadly so that it is not inevitably directed at "summing up," in the sense of calculating the differential values of opposing points of view. It is within this more liberal definition of research synthesis that Thomas (1994) can be included, and that parallels between secondary research and historical study are worth exploring.

Revisiting assessment of L2 proficiency in second language acquisition research twelve years later

Thomas (1994) was designed as a portrait of proficiency assessment techniques used in L2 research during a particular five-year period, without reference to how those practices might change over time. But another use to which those data might be put would be as one of two legs spanning an interval across which the maintenance or modification of proficiency assessment practices might be revealed. It should be clear that although occasional citations of Thomas (1994) appeared in subsequent literature, there is no reason to believe that its publication marked a turning point in the methodology of L2 research. Rather, in the intervening years, the study of L2 acquisition overall has grown in size, diversified, and increased in sophistication, driven by large-scale changes in the social and intellectual climate, and in the training and interests of the research community. As a witness to the growth and elaboration of study of L2 acquisition, one might compare pairs of introductory textbooks that span more than a decade, such as White (1989, 2003) (about which see Thomas 2003), or even those re-issued in new editions after a shorter interval, such as Gass and Selinker (1994, 2001), Lightbown and Spada (1993, 1999), or Mitchell and Myles (1998, 2004). Differences between the first and second members of each of these pairs of texts give ample evidence for "substantial developments that have taken place in the field in the last few years" (Mitchell & Myles 2004: 1) and for a recent "enormous increase in research" (White 2003: xii). What is of special interest here is whether these substantial developments and the increased volume of research have entailed changes in how scholars operationalize proficiency. To investigate this matter, I set out to repeat the 1994 study using the five most recent volumes of the same four journals: *Applied Linguistics* (Vols. 21–25), *Language Learning* (Vols. 50–54, excluding Supplements), *Second Language Research* (Vols. 16–20), and *Studies in Second Language Acquisition* (Vols. 22–26). I extracted from the journals all the relevant empirical studies of L2

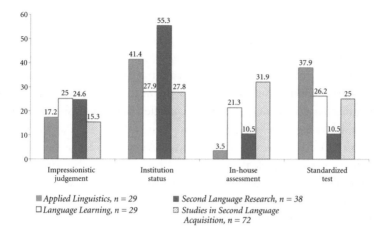

Figure 2. Distribution of articles in the 2000–04 corpus (n = 200), across four major classes of proficiency assessment techniques, by journal, as the percent of relevant publications in a given journal

acquisition published from 2000 to 2004, relying on the criteria for inclusion established in Thomas (1994). The new corpus contained 211 articles. The right hand column in Table 1 depicts the incidence of articles that employ each technique of proficiency assessment, and the proportional contribution of each technique within the total corpus of the second study. Figure 2 depicts the distribution of each of the 211 studies by technique for each of the four journals, excluding 11 studies classified as "Other" (so that henceforth the 2000–04 corpus will be taken to contain exactly 200 studies).

Comparison of the left and right hand columns in Table 1 reveals that there has been relatively little aggregate change in the proportion of published articles that employ these four techniques. The largest shift is a 7% reduction in reliance on Institutional Status, balanced by a 5% increase in In-House Assessment techniques. Comparison of Figures 1 and 2 shows that all four journals have continued to publish work that employs each of the four techniques. There has been some instability in the distribution of assessment techniques across the four journals over time, but a reduction of the prevalence of one technique in one journal is compensated for by an increase in research using that technique in other journals.

Perhaps the outstanding difference between Figures 1 and 2 concerns the two journals that contribute the largest numbers of studies, *Language Learning* (61 articles, amounting to 31% of the 2000–4 corpus) and *Studies in Second Language Acquisition* (72 articles, 36%). Comparing their profiles in 1988–92 and 2000–04, both journals have moved in the direction of publishing research that is more evenly distributed across the four categories of proficiency assessment techniques. *Second Language Research* and *Applied Linguistics*, on the other hand, have not participated in this trend. If anything, *Second Language Research* now depends even more heavily on research that employs Institutional Status as a proxy for L2 proficiency, while work published in *Applied Linguistics* shows an increased reliance on Standardized Tests at the expense of Impressionistic Judgment and In-House Assessment. Since the choice of a proficiency assessment technique is often bound up in the conventions – or perhaps, folkways – of particular sub-streams of research, the proficiency-assessment profiles of *SLR* and *AL* may be a consequence of editorial decisions to specialize in certain approaches to the study of L2 acquisition. Or it may derive from the related factor of the kinds of submissions each journal attracts. Whatever its explanation, because *SLR* and *AL* contribute fewer articles to the total 2000–4 corpus (19% and 14.5%, respectively), shifts in the complexion of work published in these journals have a relatively small impact overall, as indicated by the stability of the percentages reported in Table 1.

However, the apparent consistency of the 1988–92 and 2000–04 corpora viewed this way provides only one perspective on these data. In order to establish an initial basis for comparison, I approached the 2000–04 corpus assuming the relevance of the four categories of assessment techniques developed for the 1988–92 corpus. But I anticipated that those categories might offer a less-than-ideal fit to research as it is being carried out now, twelve years later. A demonstrated need to re-define the categories of classification could be taken as evidence for change in the object of study and, moreover, might offer insight into the nature of that change. What I found was that although those categories still sufficed as a crude instrument for analysis, they were rendered less revealing in the 2000–04 corpus, for several reasons.

One such reason is that the techniques by which researchers gather data about L2 proficiency now seem less consequential than the operations they perform on those data. Many studies in the 2000–04 corpus collect richer information about proficiency and exploit it more fully relative to how proficiency was addressed in the 1988–92 corpus. Twelve years ago, a typical move was to target learners judged to have neither too little nor too much knowledge of the L2 by setting floor and ceiling limits on their standardized test scores or assigned levels in some institutional context (e.g. second-year versus fourth-year students of the target language), then to admit participants from within that range in such a way as to establish an appropriate number of subgroups of roughly equal sizes.[3] This cleared the way for the research to proceed, under

the assumption that the participants' proficiency had been adequately characterized – even if (1) the content of the test instrument, or the basis for
assignment of learners to institutional levels, bore no particular relevance to
the target of research; and (2) only indirect or suggestive evidence existed that
the groups represented internally-consistent levels of knowledge of the L2, and
that each group possessed substantively different competence relative to the
other groups.

In contrast, studies in the 2000–04 corpus frequently probe learners' proficiency in finer detail, then integrate those data into the research in more
complex ways. One indication of this trend is the fact that many researchers
who either divide a sample of learners into sub-groups, or assemble a cohort of
learners treated as commensurate with respect to proficiency, employ statistical
tests to estimate the validity of how they have partitioned or aggregated learners. For example, both De Groot and Keijzer (2000) and Roca de Larios, Marín,
and Murphy (2001) analyzed the variance of L2 proficiency around the mean
for their sample of learners. In the case of De Groot and Keijzer, the data were
the learners' self-reported L2 proficiency ratings, on which the researchers performed an ANOVA to confirm the overall homogeneity of their subject pool (p.
48). Roca de Larios et al., on the other hand, conducted an ANOVA on learners'
scores on the Oxford Placement Test by way of justifying division of them into
three proficiency levels (pp. 204–5). I assigned De Groot and Keijzer's study to
the category of Impressionistic Judgment, since no corroborating evidence was
sought to support the learners' self-ratings. In contrast, I assigned Roca de Larios et al.'s study to the category of Standardized Test, since they selected learners
for participation on the basis of standardized test scores. One might therefore
place these two studies quite far apart insofar as the array of techniques listed in
(1) through (4) form a continuum from the most private, subjective, basis on
which to assess proficiency, to the most public, mechanical, basis. But viewed
in another light, both projects' authors have manipulated their data about proficiency in parallel ways, for similar reasons. In this sense, they are not so far
apart in how they have made use of the information at their disposal. Assignment of De Groot and Keijzer (2000) to category (1) and Roca de Larios et
al. (2001) to category (4) masks the fact that their authors went beyond simple collection of proficiency data, acting on a similar impulse to investigate the
validity of their proficiency-assessment techniques.[4]

Hancin-Bhatt's (2000) study of L2 English syllable codas in the interlanguage of native speakers of Thai provides a more elaborate example of how research in the 2000–04 corpus sometimes reaches across categories (1) through
(4) to gather data about proficiency, then manipulates those data in finer detail.

I assigned this article to the Institutional Status category, because the author used learners' participation in "beginner or intermediate" (p. 216) level English classes as the first and central criteria for inclusion in the study. In addition, she reported TOEFL scores for 10 of the 11 subjects, and indicated each one's length of study of English and of residence in English-speaking environments. Hancin-Bhatt also reported each participant's score on a grammaticality judgment task. In this task, learners listened to 72 pairs of near-identical sentences while reading along silently with the tape. One member of each pair contained a single syntactic error. The learners' job was to repeat into a tape recorder the sentence they considered grammatically correct. Hancin-Bhatt indicates that the task was "taken to provide an additional [intra-group] comparison of the learners' English knowledge" (p. 217), in particular, as a measure of learners' L2 syntax, since the ungrammatical stimuli contained *that*-trace effects, and violations of constraints on agreement, case, word order, *do*-support, auxiliary inversion and adverb placement (p. 218). But although this exercise was presented to the research participants as a grammaticality judgment task, Hancin-Bhatt's real interest in it was as a record of their capacity to produce L2 codas, because she had strategically constructed the stimuli to contain an array of the critical syllable structures. Hancin-Bhatt tabulated the rates of epenthesis, deletion, and substitution attested on the tapes, incorporating those data into her analysis of L2 coda production. As an aside, she also reported each learner's overall success rate at identifying grammatical versus ungrammatical stimuli. In these ways, Hancin-Bhatt gathered diverse information about the participants' L2 skills. In fact, her methodology affords her rather more information about proficiency than she makes use of. Granted that the learners' TOEFL scores range from 423 to 587, and the percentage of correct grammaticality judgment task scores range from 77.8 to 94.4, she might have exploited this fairly wide span of proficiency to infer a developmental sequence in the acquisition of L2 codas.

Hancin-Bhatt (2000) exemplifies a trend in proficiency assessment within recent research on L2 acquisition: that it probes proficiency in ways that go beyond mechanical recording of learners' scores or memberships in particular institutional groups. In this sense it is less liable to containment within the boundaries of the four categories established for analyzing the 1988–92 corpus. Although Thomas (1994: 313) emphasized the approximate and permeable nature of those boundaries, categorization of recent work must be done even more tentatively. In particular, in the examples we have seen so far, research subsumed under different categories may have more in common than meets the eye, a trend obscured by the apparent congruence between the 1988–92 and 2000–04 corpora displayed in Table 1.

A second trend inverts this relationship. Among studies in the 2000–04 corpus that fall into a particular category are some which employ that proficiency-assessment technique in quite different ways, different enough to challenge the generalization that they belong together. For example, the category of In-House Assessment subsumes a variety of measures of L2 proficiency, incorporated variously into a variety of research designs. Daller, van Hout, and Treffers-Daller (2003) employ several in-house measures of proficiency in a complex study of lexical skills. Their work compares two groups of Turkish / German bilinguals, one of which returned to Turkey after having been educated in Germany up to an average age of 13, while the other continued living in Germany. The researchers conducted an error analysis of the German language competence of both groups, and analyzed their spontaneous speech in Turkish for syntactic complexity. In addition, both groups completed a C-(cloze) test of German. The combined results of these measures confirmed (according to Daller et al., pp. 204–7) that the returnee group is dominant in Turkish while those who have remained in Germany are dominant in German. Because these proficiency-assessment instruments were privately-developed and research-specific, this study belongs under the In-House Assessment rubric.[5] So does Leeser (2004). In research on future tense in L2 Spanish, Leeser (pp. 592–3) created a translation task to reduce a pool of 648 potential participants down to the 266 who actually participated, eliminating all who had already acquired some knowledge of the target grammatical feature. Montrul (2000: 249–53) re-wrote an English-language cloze test in Spanish and in Turkish, then administered it to separate cohorts of learners of all three languages (plus native-speaking controls), in an ambitious attempt to characterize each of 6 groups of learners (3 L2s times 2 L1s) by level of L2 proficiency, and, where possible, partition them into low-intermediate, intermediate, and high-intermediate sub-groups. Jensen and Vinther (2003) used a pre-test / post-test design to study the effects of two different types of input enhancement among L1 Danish learners of Spanish enrolled in three schools. When the pre-test, an elicited-imitation task, revealed that the learners differed significantly in L2 proficiency, Jensen and Vinther measured differences between each individual's pre- versus post-test scores to discern the efficacy of particular input enhancement practices (pp. 394–6).

All four of these studies were assigned to In-House Assessment, even though they assess proficiency in heterogeneous manners, and then incorporate the data they gather into research design in idiosyncratic ways: Daller et al. analyzed spontaneous speech and cloze-test results to justify division of the subjects into German- versus Turkish-dominant groups; Leeser used a translation to exclude learners with prior knowledge of a specific L2 feature; Montrul's cloze test partitioned a diverse subject pool; and Jensen and Vinther gathered elicited imitation data from learners before and after one of several treatments, so as to compare their relative efficacy. In these ways, the 2000–04 corpus encompasses a lot of variety even within a single ostensibly unified proficiency-assessment technique. That variety was not absent in the 1988–92 corpus, but it has increased in the intervening years.

A third difference between the two corpora has to do with the overall role of proficiency assessment in research on L2 acquisition, an issue that complexifies extraction of information that one might, at a distance, expect to be embedded as a matter of course in the methodology of these 200 studies. When I reiterated this analysis, I discovered not only that the categories established for the 1988–92 corpus characterized many individual cases more awkwardly than they did earlier, but also that a subset of research in the 2000–04 corpus downplayed the value of assessing learners' L2 competence, a phenomenon referenced in Norris and Ortega (2003).

A trend to background or downplay the assessment of proficiency in recent study of L2 acquisition may be driven forward by several forces. First, certain research questions can be defined and answered without reference to information about learners' proficiency beyond their identification as L2 learners. This includes, for example, questions about universals or implicational relationships proposed to hold for all learners over the whole course of acquisition. Work in this vein was already a substantial presence in the 1988–92 corpus; for example, in Thomas (1994) I cited Eckman's (1991) study of Greenbergian constraints on L2 phonology as a case where "more precise data about language proficiency would be dispensable (albeit advantageous)" (p. 317). In the years since 1994, research on universals and implicational relationships in interlanguage grammars has flourished, plausibly contributing to an academic culture that is more tolerant of under-definition of proficiency in empirical work on L2 acquisition.[6]

Second, for some researchers, emancipation from Bley-Vroman's (1983) famous "comparative fallacy" renders suspect any evaluation of learners' grammars that relativizes them to the grammars of native speakers, because to do so fails to acknowledge the essential internal consistency of what learners know about their L2 independent of whatever knowledge they share with native speakers. This commitment erodes confidence in many kinds of assessment techniques, without providing either alternatives or a rationale for L2 research to proceed in the absence of assessment.

Third, for some scholars, the salient features of a person's capacity to produce and comprehend language are that it is a dynamic, multi-dimensional, and context-dependent phenomenon. From this vantage point, to characterize language proficiency as a static trait, independently quantifiable in the manner of a variable like height or age, seems so reductionistic as to lack all usefulness.

In the 2000–04 corpus, I encountered work by scholars who seemed to leave proficiency undefined, or under-defined, for one or the other of the reasons adverted to above, although they did not always explicitly object to proficiency assessment in these terms. For instance, Platt and Brooks' (2002) work on task engagement in L2 learner dyads within a Vygotskian framework remarks only that one pair of their participants had had six hours of L2 instruction, while another, three years of high school L2 classes; Platt and Brooks neither depict the learners' proficiency nor provide an explanation why no such depiction is needed (p. 375). Others researchers sometimes remarked that there was no need to inquire in depth into learners' knowledge of the L2. Hulstijn and Laufer (2001:547–8, 554) asserted that if their two groups of learners (one in the Netherlands, the other in Israel) were not equivalent in proficiency, the fact that they were able to perform the experimental task provided sufficient evidence for their competence. Izumi (2003:296) prescinded from analyzing his data on learners' processing of relative clauses according to proficiency, on the grounds that different levels of proficiency do not necessarily implicate different knowledge of relative clauses. Research that desists from proficiency assessment in these manners usually characterizes participants' knowledge of the L2 either impressionistically or in terms of learners' institutional status without probing further, so that such work augments categories (1) and (2). Moreover, in the 2000–04 corpus, 6 of the 11 studies that comprised the "Other" category were so assigned because their authors provided *no* characterization at all of the L2 proficiency of the participants, other than to identify them as L2 learners. In Thomas (1994) none of the 4 studies in the Other category were placed under that rubric due to lack of characterization of L2 proficiency.

Of these three differences between the 1988–92 and 2000–04 corpora, none indicates an unprecedented departure. Rather, they constitute shifts of emphasis and the extension of trends already present within the proficiency-assessment practices surveyed in Thomas (1994). However, projecting forward the direction of the small attested differences between the 1988–92 and 2000–04 corpora, what emerges is a kind of incipient dichotomization in how researchers assess L2 proficiency. On the one hand, some research on L2 acquisition seems to be moving toward more detailed investigation of learners' proficiency, relative to what was typical in 1988–92, and to incorporation of that information into the design of empirical studies in research-specific ways. On the other hand, there also exists a seemingly paradoxical movement toward devaluing, or even dispensing with, efforts to assess what research participants know about the target language on the grounds that such information is unnecessary, unreliable, or unrevealing.

Research synthesis in relation to historiography

The differences unearthed by comparison of research published in 1988–92 with that published in 2000–04 are modest. But repeating the survey of proficiency assessment practices across a twelve-year interval suggests some changes in this aspect of modern research on L2 acquisition, within the context of a rapidly expanding discipline. Recapitulating the study after an even longer interval would very likely reveal more change, eventually forcing a revision of the categories of analysis in (1) through (4), or possibly inducing a full reorientation of the approach taken in Thomas (1994) and repeated here. Moreover, each successive iteration of the study would likely provide a new prospect on earlier results, in the same way that arriving at point C on a trip from A to D provides one with a fresh view of A and B.

These are the common ways in which studying the passage of a phenomenon through time increments our understanding of it. Research synthesis, on the other hand, does not routinely attend to historical matters. Rather, it increments our understanding of phenomena in complementary ways. But like the work exemplified here, research synthesis looks out across large expanses of research in search of patterns that no individual study can reveal. Research synthesis as well as historical inquiry requires immersion in the products of other people's thought. To do that both exposes one to the hazards of trying to understand questions others have posed and the answers they have arrived at, and opens up the rewards of attempting to see the world through other people's eyes.

Light and Pillemer (1984) assert the need to "improve . . . efforts to learn from existing findings, to 'discover what is known'" (p. ix), even if to do so diverts attention from the collection of new scientific results. Light and Pillemer set the stage for their text by narrating how colleagues and students often recruit them to help design new research. Their first response to such requests is:

... [to] ask what has been learned in that particular area from earlier studies. After all, new investigations should build upon existing knowledge. The response, nearly always, is that a group of earlier studies is complex and even contradictory. Indeed, the contradictions are an important reason for conducting the new study.

Our questioners seldom consider investing time and resources to synthesize the information that already exists. We wondered why not. This seems a sensible first step. Without a clear picture of where things now stand, simply adding one new study to the existing morass is unlikely to be very useful.

(Light & Pillemer 1984: vii–viii)

When, in these terms, Light and Pillemer promote the value of attending to "a fundamental component of the scientific process: the systematic accumulation of knowledge" (p. viii), they might very well be speaking in the voice of historiographers. What historiographers would add is that by attending to the accumulation of knowledge one comes to better understand one's own position: Andresen (1985: 362) wrote that linguistic historiography "aims to serve the on-going study of language [as] . . . a method of gaining perspective." Historian of linguistics Vivien Law seems to build on this point, in a passage that can be read as reiterating a classic motivation to try to "improve [our] efforts to learn from existing findings, to 'discover what is known'":

...that sense of perspective [gained from historical study] should help us to find our right place in time too. Of course we see the whole of history as conspiring to bring about the present, and in a sense this is true. At the same time, though, we are part of a present which is conspiring to bring about a whole series of futures; we are in transition, just as much as every past era was part of a process of transition and change leading ultimately to us. If in studying the history of linguistics we avoid the temptation to focus only on the bits that foreshadow our own preoccupations, but look too at the ideas which didn't live on to the present, we will develop a much stronger sense of the ebb and flow of ideas, an ebb and flow of which we are part, just as our predecessors were.

(Law 2003: 7–8)

Research synthesis and historiography similarly inquire into the ebb and flow of ideas. In this chapter I have considered them as two partially-intersecting instruments applicable in our attempts to "discover what is known." By these lights, their distinguishing characteristic is that research synthesis aims to locate and articulate what is most effective, revealing, and powerful in the results existing research, according to locally-determined standards of what makes research effective, revealing, and powerful. In contrast, historical study doesn't carry that evaluative burden. In fact, as Law points out, the historian is charged with attending equally to "ideas which didn't live on to the present" and those that have survived and flourished. In the case at hand, a research synthesis directed at proficiency-assessment techniques might survey published literature to weigh the benefits of methods that are in use, then recommend the adoption of whatever seemed most effective in particular contexts. Historical inquiry into proficiency assessment in research on L2 acquisition would survey the range of methods scholars have employed, with reference to how and why those methods have shifted across time.

In the Introduction to this collection, Norris and Ortega assume a somewhat different definition of research synthesis under which its evaluative characteristic is not criterial. That would have the effect of positioning historical inquiry, alongside meta-analysis, as members of a family of techniques for investigating scientific study, all subsumed under a broadly-defined rubric of research synthesis. To someone interested in the history of ideas, competing definitions of terms are provocative grist for the mill. Here, the question that follows is not so much "Which is a better definition of the relationship between historical study and research synthesis?" as it is "How do these two definitions provide us with differing frameworks for understanding research on L2 acquisition?" The chapters in this volume build up the body of literature showing what we can learn from trying to "discover what is known." Whether we view historical study as belonging alongside research synthesis, or as subsumed within it, that literature opens up new ways of looking at research on how people acquire a second language.

Notes

1. Thomas (2004) constitutes one approach to these issues.

2. Note that in the 2000–04 corpus (described below) a wider variety of standardized tests were employed, for example the ACTFL Oral Proficiency Interview, the University of Athens' Greek Language Proficiency Test, and the Diploma de Español como Lengua Extranjera. Thomas (1994:327) remarked on the need for more tests that can assess L2 proficiency in languages other than English, so it is gratifying to see that such tests are now in use.

3. Poulisse and Schils (1989:19), for example, established advanced, intermediate, and beginning groups of participants in this way, drawing equal numbers of learners from three institutional levels of L2 instruction; later they concluded that their lowest level group "may not have been low enough to bring out the expected difference to light" (p. 40). Schneider and Connor (1990:415) randomly selected 15 learners' essays from those assigned scores of 3, 4, and 6 on the Test of Written English, using these data as their basis for analyzing topic structures in high, mid, and low rated texts.

4. The fact that De Groot and Keijzer (2000) and Roca de Larios et al. (2001) attend to potential sources of error in the measurement or labeling of learners' knowledge of L2 may indicate that they are grappling with some of the problems facing L2 research that Norris and Ortega (2003) point out, problems which were less acknowledged at the time of the 1994 study.

5. Note that the In-House Assessment tests Daller, van Hout, and Treffers-Daller (2003) employ seem mostly aimed at validating their preemptory division of the participants into two groups on the basis of their different life histories, so that in the absence of those tests the study would have been subsumed under the rubric of Impressionistic Judgment. However, I reserved Impressionistic Judgment for studies where only the researchers' unsupported judgment is involved in characterizing learners' proficiency, with or without reference to the learners' length of residence in L2-speaking environments.

6. With reference to this trend, note that Figures 1 and 2 suggest that articles published in the journal *Second Language Research* have drifted in the direction of assessing proficiency by way of impressionistic judgment, and away from the use of standardized tests. *Second Language Research* is a popular venue for publication of studies on language universals in L2.

References

Andresen, J. (1985). Why do we do linguistic historiography? *Semiotica, 56*, 357–370.

Bley-Vroman, R. (1983). The comparative fallacy in interlanguage studies: The case of systematicity. *Language Learning, 33*, 1–17.

Cooper, H., & Hedges, L. V. (Eds.). (1994). *The handbook of research synthesis.* New York: Russell Sage Foundation.

Daller, H., van Hout, R., & Treffers-Daller, J. (2003). Lexical richness in the spontaneous speech of bilinguals. *Applied Linguistics, 24*, 197–222.

De Groot, A. M. B., & Keijzer, R. (2000). What is hard to learn is easy to forget: The roles of word concreteness, cognate status, and word frequency in foreign-language vocabulary learning and forgetting. *Language Learning, 50*, 1–56.

Leeser, M. J. (2004). The effects of topic, familiarity, mode, and pausing on second language learners' comprehension and focus on form. *Studies in Second Language Acquisition, 26*, 587–615.

Gass, S. M., & Selinker, L. (1994). *Second language acquisition: An introductory course.* Mahwah, NJ: Lawrence Erlbaum.

Gass, S. M., & Selinker, L. (2001). *Second language acquisition: An introductory course* (2nd ed.). Mahwah, NJ: Lawrence Erlbaum.

Glass, G. V. (1976). Primary, secondary, and meta-analysis of research. *Educational Researcher, 5* (10), 3–8.

Hancin-Bhatt, B. (2000). Optimality in second language phonology: Codas in Thai ESL. *Second Language Research, 16*, 210–232.

Hulstijn, J. H., & Laufer, B. (2001). Some empirical evidence for the Involvement Load Hypothesis in vocabulary acquisition. *Language Learning, 51*, 539–558.

Izumi, S. (2003). Processing difficulty in comprehension and production of relative clauses by learners of English as a second language. *Language Learning, 53*, 285–323.

Jensen, E. D., & Vinther, T. (2003). Exact repetition as input enhancement in second language acquisition. *Language Learning, 53*, 373–428.

Koerner, E. F. K. (1976). The importance of linguistic historiography and the place of history in linguistic science. *Foundations of Language, 14*, 541–574.

Law, V. (2003). *The history of linguistics in Europe from Plato to 1600*. Cambridge, UK: Cambridge University Press.

Light, R. J., & Pillemer, D. B. (1984). *Summing up: The science of reviewing research*. Cambridge, MA: Harvard University Press.

Lightbown, P., & Spada, N. (1993). *How languages are learned*. Oxford: Oxford University Press.

Lightbown, P., & Spada, N. (1999). *How languages are learned* (Rev. ed.). Oxford: Oxford University Press.

Mitchell, R., & Myles, F. (1998). *Second language learning theories*. London: Arnold.

Mitchell, R., & Myles, F. (2004). *Second language learning theories* (2nd ed.). London: Arnold.

Montrul, S. (2000). Transitivity alternations in L2 acquisition: Toward a modular view of transfer. *Studies in Second Language Acquisition, 22*, 229–273.

Norris, J. M. & Ortega, L. (2000). Effectiveness of L2 instruction: A research synthesis and quantitative meta-analysis. *Language Learning, 50*, 417–528.

Norris, J. M. & Ortega, L. (2001). Does type of instruction make a difference? Substantive findings from a meta-analytic review. *Language Learning, 51*, 157–213.

Norris, J. M. & Ortega, L. (2003). Defining and measuring SLA. In C. J. Doughty and M. H. Long (Eds.), *The handbook of second language acquisition* (pp. 717–761). Malden, MA: Blackwell.

Platt, E., & Brooks, F. B. (2002). Task engagement: A turning point in foreign language development. *Language Learning, 52*, 365–400.

Poulisse, N., & Schils, E. (1989). The influence of task- and proficiency-related factors on the use of compensatory strategies: A quantitative analysis. *Language Learning, 39*, 15–48.

Roca de Larios, J., Marín, J., & Murphy, L. (2001). A temporal analysis of formulation processes in L1 and L2 writing. *Language Learning, 51*, 497–538.

Schneider, M., & Connor, U. (1990). Analyzing topical structure in ESL essays. *Studies in Second Language Acquisition, 12*, 411–427.

Thomas, M. (1993). *Knowledge of reflexives in a second language*. Amsterdam: John Benjamins.

Thomas, M. (1994). Assessment of L2 proficiency in second language acquisition research. *Language Learning, 44*, 307–336.

Thomas, M. (2003). Two textbook representations of second language acquisition and Universal Grammar: "Access" versus "constraint." *Second Language Research, 19*, 359–376.

Thomas, M. (2004). *Universal grammar in second language acquisition: A history*. London: Routledge.

White, L. (1989). *Universal Grammar and second language acquisition*. Amsterdam: John Benjamins.

White, L. (2003). *Second language acquisition and Universal Grammar*. Cambridge, UK: Cambridge University Press.

Commentaries

Introduction to Section III

In the final two chapters, Nick Ellis and Craig Chaudron reflect on and fore-
cast the future of research synthesis in LL&LT. These respected voices are well
known for their primary research in the field. However, each has also contributed considerably to establishing, fostering, and maintaining a milieu of L2
research synthesis: Chaudron particularly through his 1988 book on classroom
research, and Ellis particularly through his editorship of *Language Learning*.
It is fitting that, in the final chapters, these authorities offer us their critical –
indeed, their synthetic – perspectives, based on their broad, deep, and lengthy
interactions with L2 research. Each commentary also addresses patterns in both
the substantive findings and the methodologies of the current collection, and
each raises important questions about the role to be played by synthesis in
applied linguistics.

CHAPTER 9

Meta-analysis, human cognition, and language learning

Nick C. Ellis

University of Michigan

This chapter considers the virtues and pitfalls of meta-analysis in general, before assessing the particular meta-analyses/syntheses in this collection, weighing their implications for our understanding of language learning. It begins by outlining the argument for meta-analytic research from rationality, from probability, and from the psychology of the bounds on human cognition. The second section considers the limitations of meta-analysis, both as it is generally practised and as it is exemplified here. Section 3 reviews the seven chapter syntheses. By properly summarizing the cumulative findings of that area of second language learning, each individually gives us an honest reflection of the current status, and guides us onwards by identifying where that research inquiry should next be looking. Taken together, these reviews provide an overview of second language learning and teaching, a more complex whole that usefully inter-relates different areas of study. For, as with all good syntheses, the whole emerges as more than the sum of the individual parts.

Meta-analysis, research synthesis, and human cognition

Our knowledge of the world grows incrementally from our experience. Each new observation does not, and should not, entail a completely new model or understanding of the world. Instead, new information is integrated into an existing construct system. The degree to which a new datum can be readily assimilated into the existing framework, or conversely that it demands accommodation of the framework itself, rests upon the congruence of the new observation and the old. Bayesian reasoning is a method of reassessing the probability of a proposition in the light of new relevant information, of updating our existing beliefs as we gather more data. Bayes' Theorem (e.g., Bayes 1763) describes what makes an observation relevant to a particular hypothesis and it defines the maximum amount of information that can be got out of a given piece of evidence. Bayesian reasoning renders rationality; it binds reasoning into the physical universe (Jaynes 1996; Yudkowsky 2003). There is good evidence that human *implicit* cognition, acquired over natural ecological sampling as natural frequencies on an observation by observation basis, is rational in this sense (Anderson 1990, 1991a, b; Gigerenzer & Hoffrage 1995; Sedlmeier & Betsc 2002; Sedlmeier & Gigerenzer 2001).

The progress of science, too, rests upon successful accumulation and synthesis of evidence. Science itself is a special case of Bayes' Theorem; experimental evidence is Bayesian evidence. Although from our individual perspectives, the culture and career structure of research encourages an emphasis on the new theoretical breakthrough, the individual researcher, and the citation-classic report, each new view is taken from the vantage of the shoulders of those who have gone before, giants and endomorphs alike. We educate our researchers in these foundations throughout their school, undergraduate, and postgraduate years. Yet despite these groundings, the common publication practice in much of applied linguistics, as throughout the social sciences, is for a single study to describe the 'statistical significance' of the data from one experiment as measured against a point null hypothesis (Morrison & Henkel 1970). Sure, there is an introduction section in each journal article which sets the theoretical stage by means of a narrative review, but in our data analysis proper, we focus on single studies, on single probability values.

In our statistical analysis of these single studies, we do acknowledge the need to avoid Type I error, that is, to avoid saying there is an effect when in fact there is not one. But the point null hypothesis of traditional Fisherian statistics entails that the statistical significance of the results of a study are the product of the size of the effect and the size of the study; any difference, no matter how small, will be a significant difference providing that there are enough participants in the two groups (Morrison & Henkel 1970; Rosenthal 1991). So big studies find significant differences whatever. Conversely, the costs and practicalities of research, when compounded with the pressure to publish or perish, entail that small studies with concomitantly statistically insignificant findings never get written up. They languish unobserved in file drawers and thus fail to be integrated with the rest of the findings. Thus our research culture promotes Type II error whereby we miss effects that we should be taking into account, because solitary researchers often don't have the resources to look hard enough, and because every research paper is an island, quantitatively isolated from the community effort. Traditional reporting practices therefore fail us in two ways: (i) significance tests are confounded by sample size and so fail as pure indicators of effect, and (ii) each empirical paper assesses the effects found in that one paper, with those effects quarantined from related research data that have been gathered before.

One might hope nevertheless that the readers of each article will integrate the new study with the old, that human reasoning will get us by and do the cumulating of the research. Not so I'm afraid, or not readily at least. However good human reasoners might be at *implicitly* integrating *single new observations* into their system, they are very bad at *explicitly* integrating *summarized data*, especially those relating to proportions, percentages or probabilities. Given a summary set of new empirical data of the type typical in a research paper, human conscious inference deviates radically from Bayesian inference. There is a huge literature over the last 30 years of cognitive science demonstrating this, starting from the classical work of Kahneman and Tversky (1972). When people approach a problem where there's some evidence X indicating that hypothesis A might hold true, they tend to judge A's likelihood solely by how well the current evidence X seems to match A, without taking into account the prior frequency or probability of A (Tversky & Kahneman 1982). In this way human statistical/scientific reasoning is not rational because it tends to neglect the base rates, the prior research findings. "The genuineness, the robustness, and the generality of the base-rate fallacy are matters of established fact" (Bar-Hillel 1980:215). People, scientists, applied linguists, students, scholars, all are swayed by the new evidence and can fail to combine it properly, probabilistically, with the prior knowledge relating to that hypothesis.

It seems then that our customary statistical methodologies, our research culture, our publication practices, and our tendencies of human inference all conspire to prevent us from rationally cumulating the evidence of our research! Surely we can do better than this. Surely we must.

As the chapters in this volume persuasively argue and illustrate, our research progress can be bettered by applying a Bayesian approach, a cumulative view where new findings are more readily integrated into existing knowledge. And this integration is not to be achieved by the mere gathering of prose conclusions, the gleaning of the bottom lines of the abstracts of our research literature into a narrative review. Instead we need to accumulate the results of the studies, the empirical findings, in as objective and data-driven a fashion as is possible. We want to take the new datum relating to the relationship between variable X and variable Y as an effect size (a sample-free estimate of magnitude of the relationship), along with some estimate of the accuracy or reliability of that effect size (a confidence interval [CI] about that estimate), and to integrate it into the existing empirical evidence. We want to decrease our emphasis on the single study, and instead evaluate the new datum in terms of how it affects the pooled estimate of effect size that comes from meta-analysis of studies on this issue to date. As the chapters in this volume also clearly show, this isn't hard. The statistics are simple, providing they can be found in the published paper. There is not much simpler a coefficient than Cohen's d, relating group mean difference and pooled standard deviation, or the point biserial correlation, relating group membership to outcome (Clark-Carter 2003; Kirk 1996). These statistics are simple and commutable, and their combination, either weighted or unweighted by study size, or reliability, or other index of quality, is simply performed using readily googled freeware or shareware, although larger packages can produce more options and fancy graphics that allow easier visualization and exploratory data analysis.

And there are good guides to be had on meta-analytic research methods (Cooper 1998; Cooper & Hedges 1994; Lipsey & Wilson 2001; Rosenthal 1991; Rosenthal & DiMatteo 2001). Rosenthal (1984) is the first and the best. He explains the procedures of meta-analysis in simple terms, and he shows us why in the reporting of our research we too should stay simple, stay close to the data, and emphasize description. Never, he says, should we be restricting ourselves to the use of F or chi square tests with degrees of freedom in the numerator greater that 1, because then, without further post-hocs, we cannot assess the size of a particular contrast. "These omnibus tests have to be overthrown!" he urges (Rosenthal 1996). Similarly, he reminds us that "God loves the .06 nearly as much as the .05" (ibid.), exhorting the demise of the point null hypothesis, the dichotomous view of science. The closer we remain to the natural frequencies, the more we support the rational inference of our readers (Gigerenzer & Hoffrage 1995; Sedlmeier & Gigerenzer 2001), allowing a 'new intimacy' between reader and published data, permitting reviews that are no longer limited to authors' conclusions, abstracts and text, and providing open access to the data themselves. Thus for every contrast, its effect size should be routinely published. The result is a science based on better synthesis with reviews that are more complete, more explicit, more quantitative, and more powerful in respect to decreasing Type II error. Further, with a sufficient number of studies there is the chance for analysis of homogeneity of effect sizes and the analysis and evaluation of moderator variables, thus promoting theory development.

During my term as Editor of the journal *Language Learning* I became convinced enough of these advantages to act upon them. We published a number of high citation and even prize-winning meta-analyses (Blok 1999; Goldschneider & DeKeyser 2001; Masgoret & Gardner 2003; Norris & Ortega 2000), including that by the editors of this current collection. And we changed our instructions for authors to require the reporting of effect sizes:

> The reporting of effect sizes is essential to good research. It enables readers to evaluate the stability of results across samples, operationalizations, designs, and analyses. It allows evaluation of the practical relevance of the research outcomes. It provides the basis of power analyses and meta-analyses needed in future research. This role of effect sizes in meta-analysis is clearly illustrated in the article by Norris and Ortega which follows this editorial statement.
>
> Submitting authors to *Language Learning* are therefore required henceforth to provide a measure of effect size, at least for the major statistical contrasts which they report.
> (N. C. Ellis 2000a)

Our scientific progress rests on research synthesis, so our practices should allow us to do this well. Individual empirical papers should be publishing effect sizes. Literature reviews can be quantitative, and there is much to gain when they are. We might as well do a quantitative analysis as a narrative one, because all of benefits of narrative are found with meta-analysis, yet meta-analysis provides much more. The conclusion is simple: *meta-analyses are Good Things*.

There's scope for more in our field. I think there's probably enough research done to warrant some now in the following areas: (1) critical period effects in SLA, (2) the relations between working memory/short-term memory and language learning, (3) orders of morphosyntax acquisition in L1 and L2, (4) orders of morphosyntax acquisition in SLA and Specific Language Impairment, investigating the degree to which SLA mirrors specific language impairment, (5) orders of acquisition of tense and aspect in first and second acquisition of differing languages, summarizing work on the Aspect Hypothesis (Shirai & Andersen 1995), (6) comparative magnitude studies of language learner aptitude and individual differences relating to good language learning, these being done following 'differential deficit' designs (Chapman & Chapman 1973, 1978; N. C. Ellis & Large 1987) putting each measure onto the same effect-size scale and determining their relative strengths of prediction. This is by no means intended as an exhaustive inventory, it is no more than a list of areas that come to my mind now as likely candidates.

Meta-analysis in practice: Slips twixt cup and lip

However Good a Thing in theory, meta-analysis can have problems in practice. Many of these faults are shared with those generic "fruit drinks" that manufacturers ply as healthy fare for young children – they do stem from fruit, but in such a mixture it's hard to discern which exactly, tasting of everything and nothing; they are so heavily processed as to loose all the vitamins; organic ingredients are tainted by their mixing with poor quality, pesticide-sprayed crops; and there is too much added sugar. Meta-analysis is like this in that each individual study that passes muster is gathered: three apples, a very large grapefruit, six kiwi-fruit, five withered oranges, and some bruised and manky bananas. Behold, a bowl of fruit! Into the blender they go, press, strain, and the result reflects. . ., well, what exactly (Cooper et al. 2000; Field 2003; George 2001; Gillett 2001; Lopez-Lee 2002; Pratt 2002; Schwandt 2000; Warner 2001)? Most meta-analyses gather together into the same category a wide variety of operationalizations of both independent and dependent variables, and a wide range of quality of study as well.

At its simplest, meta-analysis collects all relevant studies, throws out the sub-standard ones on initial inspection, but then deals with the rest equally. To paraphrase British novelist George Orwell, although all studies are born equal, some are more equal than others. So should the better studies have greater weight in the meta-analysis? Larger n studies provide better estimates than do smaller n studies, so we could weight for sample size. Two of the chapters here report effect sizes weighted for sample size (Dinsmore; Taylor et al.), one reports both weighted and unweighted effects (Russell & Spada), and the others only report unweighted effect sizes.

Statistical power is just one aspect of worth. Good meta-analyses take quality into account as moderating variables (Cooper & Hedges 1994; Cooper et al. 2000). Studies can be quality coded beforehand with points for design quality features, for example: a point for a randomized study, a point for experimenters blind, a point for control of demand characteristics, etc. Or two methodologists can read the method and data analysis sections of the papers and give them a global rating score on a 1–7 scale. The codings can be checked for rater-reliability and, if adequate, the reviewer can then compute the correlation between effect size and quality of study. If it so proves that low quality studies are those generating the high effect sizes, then the reviewer can weight each study's contribution according to its quality, or the poorest studies can be thrown out entirely. Indeed there are options for weighting for measurement error of the studies themselves (Hunter & Schmidt 1990; Rosenthal 1991; Schmidt & Hunter 1996).

We don't see many of these measures evident in the current collection. I suspect that this is not because of any lack of sophistication on the part of the reviewers but rather that it belies a paucity of relevant experimental studies which pass even the most rudimentary criteria for design quality and the reporting of statistics. Keck et al. start with a trawl of over 100 studies, and end up with just 14 unique samples. Russell and Spada start with a catch of 56 studies, but only 15 pass inspection to go into the analysis proper. The other meta-analyses manage 16, 13, and 23 included studies respectively. Not many on any individual topic. Our field has clearly yet to heed relevant recommendations for improved research and publication practices (Norris & Ortega 2000: 497–498). But nevertheless, such slim pickings failed to daunt our meta-analysts from pressing onwards to investigate moderator effects. Of course they did, after all that effort we would all be tempted to do the same. Heterogeneous effect sizes – Gone fishing! One moderator analysis looked for interactions with 5 different moderator variables, one of them having six different levels, and all from an initial 13 studies. These cell sizes are just too small. And we have to remember that these are not factorially planned contrasts – studies have self-selected into groups, there is no experimental control, and the moderating variables are all confounded. Any findings might be usefully suggestive, but there's nothing definitive here. We would not allow these designs to pass muster in individual experimental studies, so we should be sure to maintain similar standards in our meta-analyses. Admittedly, all of the authors of these studies very properly and very explicitly acknowledge these problems, but it's the abstracts and bottom lines of a study that are remembered more than are design cautions hidden in the text.

Which brings us to consider the final potential pitfall of meta-analyses. First the good, then the bad. Their good effects include a complete and representative summary of a research area to date, plus guided future research development through the identification of moderating variables in ways that would not be possible otherwise, and the identification of gaps in the literature where we don't know enough, where there aren't enough studies on particular aspects of the independent or dependent variables in question. A good example, again, is the Norris & Ortega (2000) meta-analysis. This gave us a timely and comprehensive analysis of the cumulative research findings on L2 instruction to that date. It told us that focused L2 instruction results in substantial target-oriented gains ($d = 0.96$), that explicit types of instruction are more effective than implicit types, and that the effectiveness of L2 instruction is durable. And this is the bottom-line we first recall. And then the moderator analyses showed that there were interactions with outcome measure, with, for example, implicit, fluent processing in free response situations producing rather smaller effect sizes ($d = 0.55$ for free response measures, Norris & Ortega 2000: 470). Only 16% of the studies in their meta-analysis used this type of response, so the overall effect size rather inflates the bottom line if it's implicit, fluent language processing that SLA instructors are usually trying to effect (Doughty 2004). From any meta-analysis, along with its major findings, we have to remember the details.

Forget these details, and we risk the bad effects whereby meta-analyses might actually close down research on a given topic, at least temporarily. However paradoxical, this could be a natural psychological reaction. It would require a temerity greater than that found in the average postgraduate student, I believe, to embark upon the next experimental study in an area which has recently been subject to a exhaustive and substantial meta-analysis. If so, we should certainly not be undertaking these exercises prematurely, before there are sufficient studies of like-type to make the game worth the candle. And we should not condone any beliefs in meta-analyses as being the final chapters or bottom lines. In properly remembering their generalities and their details, they are, as with other good reviews, substantial stepping-stones on our research path. It is their exhaustiveness and their explicitness which allows their support.

Meta-synthesis and meta-analyses: The implications of these chapters for language learning

So saying, the seven research syntheses gathered in this volume present useful overviews of areas of research into second language acquisition (SLA) at the beginning of the twenty-first century. In my retelling of them here, my narrative follows the order of humankind in its evolutionary influences of biology, interaction, language, consciousness, and culture. I begin with the theme set in Dinsmore's chapter.

Much of SLA research at the end of the twentieth century was driven by a linguistic framework which held that there is a human biological endowment for language and that the aspects of language that are innately specified comprise a Universal Grammar (UG). The theory of UG holds that the primary linguistic evidence is indecisive, noisy, and poorly specified (the "poverty of the stimulus" argument). Yet children seem universally to adhere to linguistic principles despite this considerable latitude in the evidence of the input which forms the evidence for their native language learning. Therefore these linguistic principles must somehow be innately prespecified, thus to constrain language growth (Crain & Thornton 1998; Pinker 1984). Linguistic theory of the particular nature of these innate constraints as they operate in first language acquisition has seen marked changes over the last three decades, from Government and Binding theory (the "Principles and Parameters" model, Chomsky 1981), through early Minimalism (Chomsky 1995) and its subsequent developments (Hauser et al. 2002). During this same period, there have also been challenges both to the poverty of the stimulus argument (MacWhinney 2004; Pullum 2002) and to innatist accounts of linguistic universals (Elman et al. 1996; Goldberg 2003; MacWhinney 1999; Tomasello 2003) from emergentist and constructionist views of child language acquisition. Nevertheless, such theories had considerable impact upon the study of SLA because of their natural corollaries: "Is SLA also constrained by these innate principles?", and, if so, "What is the nature of the second language learner's access to UG?" (White 1989, 2003).

Various positions were defended in various forms, the three main stances being broadly: (1) "Full Access/No Transfer" (e.g., Flynn 1996) whereby UG constrains L2 acquisition just as it does L1. (2) "Full Access/Full Transfer" positions (e.g., Schwartz & Sprouse 1996) which believes that L2 learners have full access to UG principles and parameters but in early stages of learning they transfer the parameter settings of their first language, only subsequently revising their hypotheses as the L2 input fails to conform to these L1 settings. (3) "No-Access" positions (e.g., Bley-Vroman 1990; Clahsen 1988) whereby the language faculty that drives first language acquisition is only available during an initial critical developmental period (Johnson & Newport 1989, 1991) after which it atrophies and is no longer available to adult second language learners who must resort to general problem-solving and cognitive skills. According to the "No-Access" view, SLA is fundamentally different from first language acquisition in that it is achieved using all-purpose learning processes rather than being guided by modular constraints.

Dinsmore's meta-analysis gathers together the findings of primary empirical studies designed to compare first and second language learners' performance on linguistic structures which instantiate various principles or parameters held to be part of UG in the Government and Binding version of the theory. If, Dinsmore argued, there was no difference in the performance of first and second language learners on these structures, with the mean effect size for this contrast being close to zero, then this would be evidence for second language learners having Full Access to UG. Instead, the meta-analysis resulted in a substantial overall effect size at 1.25, the Full Access model does not hold, and we are left with the conclusion that second language learners are not constrained in their learning in the same way as is posited for first language learners. We cannot tell from this meta-analysis whether there is Partial Access, mediated by L1 settings, or none at all, as in the Fundamental Difference hypothesis, but what we do know is the SLA is of a different kind from L1A: Learners left to their own devices to acquire a second language from naturalistic input usually fare much less successfully than child L1 learners, and they stabilize or fossilize at a stage far short of native language competence.

Consequently, for adults to develop beyond these limits, they require something further to successfully guide subsequent development of their grammars – some additional form-focused instruction. Why is this necessary for successful adult L2 acquisition but not for child L1 acquisition? As Dinsmore explains, generative answers to this question revolve around lack of full access to UG. Alternative cognitive accounts argue that these limitations stem from the phenomena of learned attention and transfer from L1 (N. C. Ellis, in press-b, in press, 2006). Children approach the task of first language learning with a neural apparatus ready to optimally represent the language input they are exposed to (N. C. Ellis, in press-a), whereas adults bring to the task of second language learning not a *tabula rasa* but a *tabula repleta* and they perceive the second language evidence through structures that are tuned to the L1 and automatized to process linguistic input accordingly (N. C. Ellis 2002a, b). Implicit language learning thus fails to rationally optimize L2 representation. Modules, whether innately given or learned, automatically and irrepressibly process their input in their well-tuned ways, their implicit, habitual processes being highly adaptive in predictable situations, but less so in the uncertainty that comes with novelty. Their operation is only preventable upon a realization of cognitive failure when there is the chance of their being overridden by conscious control. When automatic capabilities fail, there follows a call recruiting additional collaborative conscious support (Baars & Franklin 2003): We only think about walking when we stumble, about driving when a child runs into the road, and about language when communication breaks down. In unpredictable conditions, the capacity of consciousness to organize existing knowledge in new ways is indispensable. The resources of consciousness and explicit learning must thus be brought to bear in order to overcome L1 transfer (N. C. Ellis 2005), but these are only recruited when there is sufficient negative evidence of the failure of the old ways to be perceivable, when there is a noticeable gap in our competences. Thus the research findings that discount the Full Access view imply that implicit SLA from communicative naturalistic input cannot suffice, and that negative evidence, conscious learning, and explicit instruction may be additional necessary components of successful second language acquisition.

Next, the meta-analysis of Keck et al. investigating the empirical links between interaction and acquisition provides important insights into the role of conscious processing in SLA. All theories of language acquisition posit that the primary evidence for SLA is the linguistic input. Input is necessary, though not all input becomes intake (Corder 1967). There is good reason to believe that this is because not all of the input is appropriately processed by learners' existing language habits, that consciousness is necessary for the learning of new information, and that learners must notice a new linguistic construction in order to consolidate a unitized representation of it (N. C. Ellis 2005; Schmidt 2001). White (1987) emphasizes that it is comprehension difficulties that provide the learner with the negative feedback that she believes necessary for L2 acquisition. At the point of incomprehension, the learner's conscious resources are brought to bear, often as a result of the social resources of their interlocutor. The usual social-interactional or pedagogical reactions to non-nativelike utterances involve an interaction-partner (Gass & Varonis 1994) or instructor (Doughty & Williams 1998) intentionally bringing additional evidence to the attention of the learner. Analyses of native-speaker / non-native-speaker (NS-NNS) interactions demonstrate how conversation partners scaffold the acquisition of novel vocabulary and other constructions by focusing attention on perceptual referents or shades of meaning and their corresponding linguistic forms (Chun et al. 1982; R. Ellis 2000; Gass 1997; Long 1983; Oliver 1995), often making salient the particular features of the form that are pertinent. The interlocutor has various means of making the input more comprehensible: (1) by modifying speech, (2) by providing linguistic and extralinguistic context, (3) by orienting the communication to the 'here and now' and, (4) by modifying the interactional structure of the conversation (Long 1982). Thus SLA is dialectic, involving the learner in a conscious tension between the conflicting forces of their current interlanguage productions and the evidence of feedback, either linguistic, pragmatic, or metalinguistic, that allows socially scaffolded development.

Keck et al. synthesize the findings of the last 25 years of experimental studies investigating whether such interaction facilitates the acquisition of specific linguistic structures. Their meta-analysis shows that treatment groups involving negotiated interactions substantially outperformed control groups with large effect sizes in both grammar and lexis on both immediate and delayed posttests. Their analysis of the moderating variables additionally demonstrated that, as Loschsky and Bley-Vroman (1993) had initially proposed, communication tasks in which the target form was essential for effective completion yielded larger effects than tasks in which the target form was useful but not required. The first conclusion then is that successful usage of a construction that is essential for communication promotes acquisition; if that construction is initially unknown by the learner, interaction with a native speaker can help shape it, scaffolding its use and acquisition by allowing the learner to consciously notice and explore its form. But there is more to this chapter. The *comprehensible output hypothesis* (Swain 1985, 1993, 1995, 1998) proposed that in addition to comprehensible input, comprehensible output contributes towards L2 acquisition because learners make their output more comprehensible if obliged to do so by the demands of communication. Eight of the unique sample studies in the meta-analysis of Keck et al. involved *pushed output*, where participants were required to attempt production of target features, often because they played the role of information-holders in jigsaw, information-gap, or narrative tasks. On immediate posttests, the tasks involving pushed output produced larger effect sizes ($d = 1.05$) than those without ($d = 0.61$). Taking these findings together, this meta-analysis demonstrates the ways in which conscious learning, recruited in social negotiations that scaffold successful learner comprehension and, particularly, production, promotes the acquisition of targeted linguistic constructions.

The next chapter in the story presents the evidence for the role of negative evidence. Russell and Spada synthesize three decades of empirical research into the effects of corrective feedback upon second language grammar acquisition. Their meta-analysis assesses the effectiveness of negative evidence, i.e. feedback from any source which provides evidence of learner error of language form, isolated from other aspects of instruction. Typical of such feedback is the recast, where the learner's ill-formed utterance is reformulated by their interlocutor. Recasts provide implicit negative evidence that the learner has erred, in conjunction with the positive evidence of a better-formed expression. Other forms of feedback can be more explicit, for example where the learner is clearly told that they have made an error and are provided with an explicit correction, or, at the extreme, where additionally a metalinguistic explanation of the underlying grammatical rule is provided. The average effect sizes for treatments that provided negative evidence over those that did not were large, with a weighted mean of 1.16. This well-focused review clearly substantiates a role for corrective feedback in SLA.

These analyses have concerned grammar, a shared focus of generative and cognitive theories of SLA alike. But what of other aspects of SLA which all agree are peripheral to UG? Do they behave any differently in respect of the need for interaction, negative evidence, conscious learning, and explicit instruction in their successful acquisition? The chapters that follow suggest not. First there is the meta-analysis of Jeon and Kaya on the effects of L2 instruction on interlanguage pragmatic (ILP) development, that is, how second language learners come to accomplish their goals and attend to interpersonal relationships while using a second language. Psychology, applied linguistics, and second language studies alike all show that non-verbal communication and the processing of native interpersonal interaction cues is largely implicit. But there are clear cultural differences in pragmatics, and just as is the case for interlanguage grammar, the endstate ILP of second language learners can be quite limited (Kasper & Schmidt 1996). Implicit naturalistic learning of L2 pragmatics can stabilize or fossilize too, with clear differences between second language and nativelike performance, and thus, as with grammar, there have been calls for the consideration of the role of instruction in L2 pragmatics (Bardovi-Harlig 1999; Kasper & Rose 2002). The last decade has seen a couple of dozen empirical studies of instructed ILP using a variety of teaching methods, and it is these which Jeon and Kaya gather in their meta-analysis. L2 pragmatic instruction produced a large improvement from pre-test to post-test in the treatment groups ($d = 1.57$), and instruction groups outperformed their controls at post-test ($d = 0.59$). These significant effects of instruction on pragmatics are in broad agreement with the findings of the meta-analysis of Norris and Ortega (2000) demonstrating large effects of instruction on L2 grammar development.

Taylor et al. next present a meta-analysis of experimental studies investigating whether instruction in the conscious use of reading strategies can enhance L2 reading comprehension. Explicit Reading Strategy Training (ERST) involves the explanation of various metacognitive and cognitive reading strategies to learners along with instruction in their use. For example, 'semantic mapping' strategy training informs students that organizing and activating their prior knowledge of a particular conceptual area can help their reading comprehension, and it shows them how to achieve this by class brainstorming followed by collaborative categorization of this shared knowledge into a semantic map. Other ERST programs involved the training of metacognitive strategies such as the conscious planning, monitoring or reviewing of reading comprehension. The combined results of 23 such studies showed that, on average, participants who received ERST comprehended L2 texts better than those who did not. Effective reading and sentence comprehension are a major goal of advanced SLA; such comprehension is far more advanced than the decoding skills of early literacy or the focus on individual lexis and grammatical forms that comprise much of introductory levels. Accordingly, Taylor et al. found that the proficiency level of the L2 learners significantly moderated the outcomes of ERST training, with effects that were superior for higher proficiency learners. Consciousness is a means to learning new things, but compared to the vast number of unconscious neural processes happening in any given moment, conscious capacity evidences a very narrow bottleneck (Baars 1997; N. C. Ellis 2005). If the learner's conscious learning mechanisms are devoted to decoding novel orthography or the inhibition of irrelevant L1 symbol-sound mappings and the controlled substitution of L2 alternatives, there is no residual capacity for inferencing and comprehension. It is necessary to have these lower-level L2 skills acquired and automatized before the resources of working memory can properly be devoted to inferencing, the construction of meanings and the accommodation of larger schematic and propositional representations (LaBerge 1995; LaBerge & Samuels 1974).

Téllez and Waxman follow with a meta-synthesis of qualitative research on effective teaching practices for English language learners. Their methods, like their findings, remind us of the need for an ecological perspective on learning (Kramsch 1993, 2002) whereby all language and all cognition are situated in particular cultural contexts that imbue these activities with meaning. When the language of the school fails to fit the language of the family, language learning fails (Heath 1983). Téllez and Waxman identify the following emergent themes of current qualitative research into effective practices for English Language Learners in US schools; their common theme is the integrity of home, school, and language: (a) communitarian teaching, a manner of instruction built around community, (b) teachers working to maximize verbal ability in protracted language events (echoing the advantages of negotiated interaction and pushed output as studied in the meta-analysis of Keck et al.), (c) building on prior knowledge, with teachers working to connect students' lives to school themes, and (d) the use of multiple representations, supporting language with objects and indexes. From the point of view of the individual learners, these practices make sense of language in their culture, their community, their selves and their embodiment. But why, from a cognitive analysis, do these methods facilitate learning? Simply, as Sir Frederic Bartlett explained nigh on a century ago in his experimental and social psychological analyses of memory, because "memory is an effort after meaning" (Bartlett 1932:44). Such contextual elaboration and relevance has profound cognitive reverberations in the greater memorability of deeply processed information (Craik & Lockhart 1972), in the facilitated recall of multiply coded, imageable information (Paivio 1990), in the remindings of context-dependent memory (Baddeley 1976), and in transfer-appropriate processing (Lockhart 2002). Consciousness is ever contextualized, as intelligence is socially situated. Information comes usefully to mind when it is relevant.

The final chapter is that of Thomas who investigates the relevance of information in time. Historiographic analysis is a particular type of research

synthesis which investigates the evolution of theoretical ideas in the development of a field of study, analyzing these changes by the detailed investigation
of representative corpora of published research at different points in time. By
comparing the results of Thomas (1994), a research synthesis-like survey of
techniques of assessing target language proficiency in empirical research on
L2 acquisition published between 1988 and 1992, with a recapitulation of that
project a dozen years later, she is able to describe theories of second language
learning as they influence language proficiency assessment at these different
points in time. The continuities and gaps between these two sets of results
throw light on the evolution of the field of SLA itself. Despite an enormous
increase in the amount of SLA research and a number of substantial new
theoretical developments over that 12 year period, Thomas identifies a consistency over time in the proportion of published articles using the different
categories of proficiency assessment (impressionistic judgment, institutional
status, in-house assessment or standardized tests). A noted change, however,
was an emergent incipient dichotomization in how researchers assess L2 proficiency. Some of more recent research tends to probe learners' proficiency in
finer detail and then integrate those data into the research in more complex
ways. Yet over the same period, there is a seemingly paradoxical movement
toward devaluing efforts to assess what research participants know about the
target language on the grounds that language proficiency is a dynamic, multi-
dimensional, and context-dependent phenomenon. Both of these trends reflect
a recognition of individual differences and the complexity of interlanguage development: the first to the degree that individual differences in learner types or
levels of proficiency exist at a level of stability that they might be analyzed as
a demonstrable source of variation, the second to the degree that they are so
ubiquitous, chaotic, and uncontrollable as to constitute noise. The latter, to my
mind, is too pessimistic in its resignation. There are methods in dynamic systems research that can help us analyze the forces of change and their non-linear
interactions (Elman et al. 1996:Chapter 4; Holland 1998; Scott Kelso 1997).
Even so, we do indeed face a considerable conceptual challenge in moving from
the acknowledgment of interlanguage as a dynamic system to the development
of a range of methodologies appropriate to its study (N. C. Ellis 1998, in press,
2006; Larsen-Freeman 1997, in press; Larsen-Freeman & Ellis, in press, December 2006; MacWhinney 1999). The practical challenges are considerable
too. Determining general principles is difficult enough, determining patterns
of individual difference with the same degree of reliability necessitates a much
larger scale of sample.

Whatever the field of study, whatever the point in its evolution, there is a tension between the search for general laws and the acknowledgement of individuality, between the lumpers and the splitters, between nomothetic and idiographic approaches, between the overall effect size, the identification of moderating variables, the individual study, and the qualitative description of the individual case. So too there is always the tension between current research fashion and the errors of the prior generation recalled as something to react against. But the fallabilities of memory let us ignore that earlier research in the more misty past, far enough back in the history of the field to be forgotten, thus to allow George Bernard Shaw's "The novelties of one generation are only the resuscitated fashions of the generation before last." Synthesis across the history of the field is as important as synthesis across its breadth.

Meta-synthesis of meta-analyses

So this book presents us with a variety of secondary research techniques (meta-analytic, metasynthetic, and historiographic) to gather what is known about SLA. These exemplars should serve well as models for others interested in the essential task of systematic synthesis. So too, this collection provides a picture of current research relating to second language learning and teaching. But this is no mere snapshot of today's news. Instead, these chapters provide an integration, a weighted summary, a hologram as it were, of the last three decades or so of work on these issues. Some of the collections are a little slim, and some of the moderator analyses acknowledgedly rather lacking in power, but as long as we remember their limitations, these methods provide the best summaries that are possible of this research to date.

And as we recall the need for more studies with a more representative range of populations, treatments, contexts, and outcome variables, as we remember the hints that are provided by the significantly heterogeneous effect sizes and subsequent analyses of moderators, they help us identify the gaps, weaknesses, and themes which research could next profitably explore. Meanwhile, as I have argued here, I believe that some additional understanding emerges from the affinity of these seven syntheses when taken together. The story of language that they tell makes biological, phenomenological, ecological, psychological, sociological, and pedagogical sense.

Acknowledgements

Thanks to David Ingledew for aerobic and productive discussions about meta-analysis whilst running through the beautiful countryside of Llangoed.

References

Anderson, J. R. (1990). *The adaptive character of thought*. Hillsdale, NJ: Lawrence Erlbaum.

Anderson, J. R. (1991a). Is human cognition adaptive? *Behavioral & Brain Sciences, 14*, 471–517.

Anderson, J. R. (1991b). The adaptive nature of human categorization. *Psychological Review, 98*, 409–429.

Baars, B. J. (1997). In the theatre of consciousness: Global workspace theory, a rigorous scientific theory of consciousness. *Journal of Consciousness Studies, 4*, 292–309.

Baars, B. J., & Franklin, S. (2003). How conscious experience and working memory interact. *Trends in Cognitive Science, 7*, 166–172.

Baddeley, A. D. (1976). *The psychology of memory*. New York: Harper and Row.

Bar-Hillel, M. (1980). The base rate fallacy in probability judgments. *Acta Psychologica, 44*, 211–233.

Bardovi-Harlig, K. (1999). Exploring the interlanguage of interlanguage pragmatics: A research agenda for acquisitional pragmatics. *Language Learning, 49*, 677–713.

Bartlett, F. C. (1932). *Remembering: A study in experimental and social psychology*. Cambridge, UK: Cambridge University Press.

Bayes, T. (1763). An essay towards solving a problem in the doctrine of chances. *Philosophical Transactions of the Royal Society of London, 53*, 370–418.

Bley-Vroman, R. (1990). The logical problem of foreign language learning. *Linguistic Analysis, 20*, 3–49.

Blok, H. (1999). Reading to young children in educational settings: A meta-analysis. *Language Learning, 49*, 343–371.

Chapman, L. J., & Chapman, J. P. (1973). *Disordered thought in schizophrenia*. New York: Appleton-Century-Crofts.

Chapman, L. J., & Chapman, J. P. (1978). The measurement of differential deficit. *Journal of Psychiatric Research, 14*, 303–311.

Chomsky, N. (1981). *Lectures on government and binding*. Dordrecht: Foris.

Chomsky, N. (1995). *The minimalist program*. Cambridge, MA: MIT Press.

Chun, A. E., Day, R. R., Chenoweth, N. A., & Luppescu, S. (1982). Errors, interaction, and corrections: A study of native-nonnative conversations. *TESOL Quarterly, 16*, 537–546.

Clahsen, H. (1988). Parameterized grammatical theory and language acquisition: A study of the acquisition of verb placement and inflection by children and adults. In S. Flynn & W. O'Neil (Eds.), *Linguistic theory in second language acquisition* (pp. 47–75). Dordrecht: Kluwer.

Clark-Carter, D. (2003). Effect size: The missing piece in the jigsaw. *The Psychologist, 16*, 636–638.

Cooper, H. (1998). *Synthesizing research: A guide for literature reviews* (3rd ed.). Thousand Oaks, CA: Sage.

Cooper, H., & Hedges, L. V. (Eds.). (1994). *The handbook of research synthesis.* New York: Russell Sage Foundation.

Cooper, H., Valentine, J. C., & Charlton, K. (2000). The methodology of meta-analysis. In R. M. Gersten & E. P. Schiller (Eds.), *Contemporary special education research: Syntheses of the knowledge base on critical instructional issues* (pp. 263–280). Mahwah, NJ: Lawrence Erlbaum.

Corder, S. P. (1967). The significance of learners' errors. *International Review of Applied Linguistics, 5,* 161–169.

Craik, F. I. M., & Lockhart, R. S. (1972). Levels of processing: A framework for memory research. *Journal of Verbal Learning and Verbal Behavior, 11,* 671–684.

Crain, C., & Thornton, R. (1998). *Investigations in Universal Grammar: A guide to experiments on the acquisition of syntax.* Cambridge, MA: MIT Press.

Doughty, C. (2004). Effects of instruction on learning a second language: A critique of instructed SLA research. In B. VanPatten, J. Williams, S. Rott & M. Overstreet (Eds.), *Form-meaning connections in second language acquisition.* Mahwah, NJ: Lawrence Erlbaum.

Doughty, C., & Williams, J. (Eds.). (1998). *Focus on form in classroom second language acquisition.* Cambridge, UK: Cambridge University Press.

Ellis, N. C. (1998). Emergentism, connectionism and language learning. *Language Learning, 48,* 631–664.

Ellis, N. C. (2000a). Editorial statement. *Language Learning, 50*(3), xi–xiv.

Ellis, N. C. (2002a). Frequency effects in language processing: A review with implications for theories of implicit and explicit language acquisition. *Studies in Second Language Acquisition, 24,* 143–188.

Ellis, N. C. (2002b). Reflections on frequency effects in language processing. *Studies in Second Language Acquisition, 24,* 297–339.

Ellis, N. C. (2005). At the interface: Dynamic interactions of explicit and implicit language knowledge. *Studies in Second Language Acquisition, 27,* 305–352.

Ellis, N. C. (in press-a). Language acquisition as rational contingency learning. *Applied Linguistics, 27*(1).

Ellis, N. C. (in press-b). Selective attention and transfer phenomena in SLA: Contingency, cue competition, salience, interference, overshadowing, blocking, and perceptual learning. *Applied Linguistics, 27*(2).

Ellis, N. C. (in press, 2006). Cognitive perspectives on SLA: The associative cognitive CREED. *AILA Review.*

Ellis, N. C., & Large, B. (1987). The development of reading: As you seek so shall you find. *British Journal of Psychology, 78,* 1–28.

Ellis, R. (2000). *Learning a second language through interaction.* Amsterdam: John Benjamins.

Elman, J. L., Bates, E. A., Johnson, M. H., Karmiloff-Smith, A., Parisi, D., & Plunkett, K. (1996). *Rethinking innateness: A connectionist perspective on development.* Cambridge, MA: MIT Press.

Field, A. P. (2003). Can meta-analysis be trusted? *The Psychologist, 16,* 642–645.

Flynn, S. (1996). A parameter-setting approach to second language acquisition. In W. Ritchie & T. Bhatia (Eds.), *Handbook of second language acquisition* (pp. 121–158). San Diego, CA: Academic Press.

Gass, S. (1997). *Input, interaction, and the development of second languages.* Mahwah, NJ: Lawrence Erlbaum.

Gass, S., & Varonis, E. (1994). Input, interaction and second language production. *Studies in Second Language Acquisition, 16,* 283–302.

George, C. A. (2001, February 1–3). *Problems and issues in meta-analysis.* Paper presented at the Paper presented at the Annual Meeting of the Southwest Educational Research Association, New Orleans, LA.

Gigerenzer, G., & Hoffrage, U. (1995). How to improve Bayesian reasoning without instruction: Frequency formats. *Psychological Review, 102,* 684–704.

Gillett, R. (2001). Meta-analysis and bias in research reviews. *Journal of Reproductive & Infant Psychology, 19* (4), 287–294.

Goldberg, A. E. (2003). Constructions: A new theoretical approach to language. *Trends in Cognitive Science, 7,* 219–224.

Goldschneider, J. M., & DeKeyser, R. (2001). Explaining the "Natural order of L2 morpheme acquisition" in English: A meta-analysis of multiple determinants. *Language Learning, 51,* 1–50.

Hauser, M. D., Chomsky, N., & Tecumseh Fitch, W. (2002). The faculty of language: What is it, who has it, and how did it evolve? *Science, 298,* 1569–1579.

Heath, S. B. (1983). *Ways with words: Language, life, and work in communities and classrooms.* Cambridge, UK: Cambridge University Press.

Holland, J. H. (1998). *Emergence: From chaos to order.* Oxford: Oxford University Press.

Hunter, J. E., & Schmidt, F. L. (1990). *Methods of meta-analysis: Correcting error and bias in research findings.* Newbury Park, CA: Sage.

Jaynes, E. T. (1996). Probability theory with applications in science and engineering. Available at http://bayes.wustl.edu/etj/science.pdf.html

Johnson, J., & Newport, E. L. (1989). Critical period effects in second language learning and the influence of the maturational state on the acquisition of ESL. *Cognitive Psychology, 21,* 215–258.

Johnson, J., & Newport, E. L. (1991). Critical period effects on universal properties of language: The status of subjacency in the acquisition of a second language. *Cognition, 39,* 215–258.

Kahneman, D., & Tversky, A. (1972). Subjective probability: A judgment of representativeness. *Cognitive Psychology, 3,* 430–454.

Kasper, G., & Rose, K. R. (2002). The role of instruction in learning second language pragmatics. *Language Learning, 52,* 237–273.

Kasper, G., & Schmidt, R. (1996). Developmental issues in interlanguage pragmatics. *Studies in Second Language Acquisition, 18,* 149–169.

Kirk, R. E. (1996). Practical significance: A concept whose time has come. *Educational and Psychological Measurement, 56,* 746–759.

Kramsch, C. (1993). *Context and culture in language teaching.* Oxford: Oxford University Press.

Kramsch, C. (Ed.). (2002). *Language acquisition and language socialization: Ecological perspectives*. London: Continuum.

LaBerge, D. (1995). *Attentional processing: The brain's art of mindfulness*. Cambridge, MA: Harvard University Press.

LaBerge, D., & Samuels, S. J. (1974). Toward a theory of automatic information processing in reading. *Cognitive Psychology, 6*, 293–323.

Larsen-Freeman, D. (1997). Chaos/complexity science and second language acquisition. *Applied Linguistics, 18*, 141–165.

Larsen-Freeman, D. (in press). On the need for a new metaphor for language and its development. *Aplied Linguistics, 27*.

Larsen-Freeman, D., & Ellis, N. C. (Eds.). (in press). Language emergence: Implications for applied linguistics. Special Issue of *Aplied Linguistics, 27*.

Lipsey, M. W., & Wilson, D. B. (2001). *Practical meta-analysis*. Thousand Oaks, CA: Sage.

Lockhart, R. S. (2002). Levels of processing, transfer-appropriate processing, and the concept of robust encoding. *Memory, 10*, 397–403.

Long, M. H. (1982). Native speaker/non-native speaker conversation in the second language classroom. In M. Long & J. Richards (Eds.), *Methodology in TESOL: A book of readings* (pp. 339–354). Rowley, MA: Newbury House.

Long, M. H. (1983). Linguistic and conversational adjustments to non-native speakers. *Studies in Second Language Acquisition, 5*, 177–193.

Lopez-Lee, D. (2002). Indiscriminate data aggregations in meta-analysis: A cause for concern among policy makers and social scientists. *Evaluation Review, 26*, 520–544.

Loschsky, L., & Bley-Vroman, R. (1993). Grammar and task-based methodology. In G. Crookes & S. Gass (Eds.), *Tasks and language learning* (pp. 123–167). Clevedon, Avon: Multilingual Matters.

MacWhinney, B. (2004). A multiple process solution to the logical problem of language acquisition. *Journal of Child Language, 31*, 883–914.

MacWhinney, B. (Ed.). (1999). *The emergence of language*. Hillsdale, NJ: Lawrence Erlbaum.

Masgoret, A.-M., & Gardner, R. C. (2003). Attitudes, motivation, and second language learning: A meta-analysis of studies conducted by Gardner and associates. *Language Learning, 53*, 123–163.

Morrison, D. E., & Henkel, R. E. (Eds.). (1970). *The significance test controversy*. London: Butterworths.

Norris, J. M., & Ortega, L. (2000). Effectiveness of L2 instruction: A research synthesis and quantitative meta-analysis. *Language Learning, 50*, 417–528.

Oliver, R. (1995). Negative feedback in child NS/NNS conversation. *Studies in Second Language Acquisition, 18*, 459–481.

Paivio, A. (1990). *Mental representations: A dual coding approach*. Oxford: Oxford University Press.

Pinker, S. (1984). *Language learnability and language development*. Cambridge, MA: Harvard University Press.

Pratt, T. C. (2002). Meta-analysis and its discontents: Treatment destruction techniques revisited. *Journal of Offender Rehabilitation, 35*, 127–137.

Pullum, G. K. (2002). Empirical assessment of stimulus poverty arguments. *Linguistic Review, 19*, 9–50.

Rosenthal, R. (1984). *Meta-analytic procedures for social research*. Beverly Hills: Sage.

Rosenthal, R. (1991). *Meta-analytic procedures for social research* (Revised ed.). Newbury Park, CA: Sage.

Rosenthal, R. (1996). Meta-analysis: Concepts, corollaries and controversies. *World Congress of Psychology*. Montreal.

Rosenthal, R., & DiMatteo, M. R. (2001). Meta-analysis: Recent developments in quantitative methods for literature reviews. *Annual Review of Psychology, 52*, 59–82.

Schmidt, F. L., & Hunter, J. E. (1996). Measurement error in psychological research: Lessons from 26 research scenarios. *Psychological Methods, 1*.

Schmidt, R. (2001). Attention. In P. Robinson (Ed.), *Cognition and second language instruction* (pp. 3–32). Cambridge, UK: Cambridge University Press.

Schwandt, T. A. (2000). Meta-analysis and everyday life: The good, the bad, and the ugly. *American Journal of Evaluation, 21*, 213–219.

Schwartz, B. D., & Sprouse, R. A. (1996). L2 cognitive states and the full transfer/full access model. *Second Language Research, 12*, 40–72.

Scott Kelso, J. A. (1997). *Dynamic patterns: The self-organization of brain and behavior*. Cambridge, MA: A Bradford Book, MIT Press.

Sedlmeier, P., & Betsc, T. (2002). *Etc. – frequency processing and cognition*. Oxford: Oxford University Press.

Sedlmeier, P., & Gigerenzer, G. (2001). Teaching Bayesian reasoning in less than two hours. *Journal of Experimental Psychology: General, 130*, 380–400.

Shirai, Y., & Andersen, R. W. (1995). The acquisition of tense–aspect morphology. *Language, 71*, 743–762.

Swain, M. (1985). Communicative competence: Some roles of comprehensible input and comprehensible output in its development. In S. M. Gass & C. G. Madden (Eds.), *Input in second language acquisition* (pp. 235–253). Rowley, MA: Newbury House.

Swain, M. (1993). The output hypothesis: Just speaking and writing aren't enough. *Canadian Modern Language Review, 50*, 158–164.

Swain, M. (1995). Three functions of output in second language learning. In G. Cook & B. Seidlhofer (Eds.), *Principle and practice in applied linguistics: Studies in honour of H. G. Widdowson* (pp. 125–144). Oxford: Oxford University Press.

Swain, M. (1998). Focus on form through conscious reflection. In C. Doughty & J. Williams (Eds.), *Focus on form in classroom second language acquisition* (pp. 64–81). Cambridge, UK: Cambridge University Press.

Thomas, M. (1994). Assessment of L2 proficiency in second language acquisition research. *Language Learning, 44*, 307–336.

Tomasello, M. (2003). *Constructing a language*. Boston, MA: Harvard University Press.

Tversky, A., & Kahneman, D. (1982). Evidential impact of base rates. In D. Kahneman, P. Slovic & A. Tversky (Eds.), *Judgment under uncertainty: Heuristics and biases* (pp. 153–160). Cambridge, UK: Cambridge University Press.

Warner, J. (2001). Quality of evidence in meta-analysis. *British Journal of Psychiatry, 178*, 79.

White, L. (1987). Against comprehensible input: The Input Hypothesis and the development of L2 competence. *Applied Linguistics, 8*, 95–110.

White, L. (1989). *Universal Grammar and second language acquisition*. Amsterdam: John Benjamins.

White, L. (2003). *Second language acquisition and Universal Grammar.* Cambridge, UK: Cambridge University Press.

Yudkowsky, E. (2003). An intuitive explanation of Bayesian reasoning. Retrieved May 2005 from http://yudkowsky.net/bayes/bayes.html

Some reflections on the development of (meta-analytic) synthesis in second language research

Craig Chaudron

University of Hawai'i at Mānoa

In my commentary on this volume, I offer a historical reflection on the status of research syntheses and meta-analysis in applied linguistics. Following primitive beginnings of such research in the late 1960s and 1970s, the accumulation of both theoretical models and consistently focused studies allowed for influential reviews of second language acquisition, the effects of L2 instruction, reading processes, and individual differences in L2 acquisition. Nonetheless, these developments have also revealed the difficulties in our furthering knowledge about such processes, as a result of the need in many domains for (1) a common conceptual or descriptive basis for quantitative measurement, (2) sufficient comparable studies in order to conduct meta-analysis, (3) adequate and appropriate sampling and selection within reviews, and (4) an orientation on the part of researchers to integrate findings within a common framework.

As the articles in this volume reveal, a superior level of sophistication has at last been attained in the applications of meta-analytic procedures to second language research. Not only the diversity of conceptual fields addressed by these authors, but also the extent of their quantitative and conceptual synthesis of information derived from a wide range of studies, demonstrates that in less than thirty years the knowledge base for understanding language acquisition processes and language education has evolved substantially, with great refinement of conceptual frameworks, methods in description and measurement, and precision in the presentation of findings. The approaches to research synthesis illustrated here can be applied to a wide range of topics and research domains, such that few researchers can afford to fail to develop a full synthesis of findings prior to engaging in the next research project. The growing awareness of the power of meta-analytical techniques to focus and reformulate research questions and identify critical factors and phenomena to investigate should lead most to initiate their next work based on a careful application of findings of this sort to a well-developed theoretical base.

Because these developments in methodology of research synthesis are relatively new, evidenced in the general field of social sciences only in the past 20–25 years,[1] it should not be surprising that there has been so little such development until recently in the field of applied linguistics.

In my brief remarks here, I feel nonetheless compelled to place some of these newer developments in the context of the evolution of approaches to research synthesis and integrative reviews in the second language acquisition and education field. We can see how topics that may initially have appeared not to be conducive to quantitative meta-analyses have become so, at times owing only to the gradual increment in number of studies adopting similar procedures, at times because of evolution in the methodology available to the research field. I will also attempt to illustrate some of the problems that exist with the conduct of meta-analyses, and to note some areas in our field which do not appear as yet to lend themselves to quantitative meta-analysis, but could be reconceived in order to make them so, and which may in any case be amenable to other approaches to synthesis and integrative review. I will focus on four areas of research, which are for the most part represented in this volume: L2 grammatical development, instructional effects, reading instruction, and individual differences. These serve to illustrate the issues of the evolution of a conceptual or descriptive basis for quantitative measurement, the need for sufficient comparable studies in order to conduct meta-analysis, the adequacy of sampling and selection, and the orientation to integrating findings within a common framework.

L2 grammatical development

One of the earliest and perhaps most influential research syntheses in second language acquisition was surely Krashen's (1977) proposal of a fixed order of acquisition of English grammatical morphemes. This study, which was not the first to propose such a "natural order," was however remarkable for the way in which it applied the order derived from several earlier empirical studies in a quantitative comparison (by way of rank-order correlational analyses and implicationally ordered relations) with the order of acquisition of the same forms that had been observed in about two dozen L1 and L2 studies, both longitudinal and cross-sectional, several with different measures within them. Krashen then argued for the consistency of findings across these studies, when viewed in the light of the theoretical constructs of the Monitor Model, which explained where and why there might be variance from the natural order. Krashen's summary thus represented a standard for research synthesis, in which (1) a fundamental question is identified and constrained by theory, then (2) a (nearly complete) sampling of empirically adequate studies addressing the question is obtained, (3) the studies are classified according to basic categories of subject samples and contexts, and finally (4) a synthesizing metric is applied to all studies, with comparison of results that suggest uniformity/consistency of the claimed natural order. At the time, Krashen could avail himself only of one primary criterion for consistency in findings, in this case the acceptable level of significance of the correlation coefficients obtained. What was however missing from this proposal was a matter that proceeded to vex researchers for the next thirty years: what was the *source* of such a natural order? How could it be viewed more generically as a phenomenon applicable across languages? Krashen's Monitor Model could not provide either the linguistic or psychological account for it, and it was not evident how any research synthesis might go about finding this out.

An early attempt at a conceptual synthesis of findings with morpheme orders was Andersen's (1978) detailed quantitative (implicational) analysis that led to linguistically motivated groupings (free/bound, NP/VP) of the morphemes in question, which would make independent sense perhaps with other languages. But it was not until Goldschneider and DeKeyser's (2001) study, 23 years later, that a more closely meta-analytic approach was applied to this question, with a rigorous sampling of studies of morpheme order and reduction of the data to those which could be compared across studies. The value of the analysis lay, however, not in an obvious quantitative comparison of accuracy orders (the authors admittedly did not attempt, in fact, an average in the classic meta-analytic fashion), but in the researchers' application of conceptually underlying psychological and linguistic factors by which each morpheme could be coded for its relative frequency, phonological salience, syntactic category, semantic complexity, and morphophonological regularity – all conceived in the end as measures of "salience." These were then employed to predict, in a standard regression model, the individual outcomes of each selected study (with a respectable R-squared of 0.71). Although this is not a true "meta-analysis" in the now-classic Rosenthal/Glass mode (because the accuracy findings were not evaluated with respect to their central tendencies and variances, although the morpheme scores were weighted for the different sample sizes), it is the necessary approach to uncovering systematic sources of variability, which is a major purpose of integrative reviews and theoretical progression. This study thus stands as an example of the power of a meta-analytic procedure to reveal underlying factors in second language acquisition, but since *all* the variance is not "explained," and, as acknowledged by the authors, there remain problems with the methodology of morpheme order analysis in any case, further steps in research are needed. But the next steps should proceed by incorporating or modifying the conceptual frameworks that have been found to provide such a degree of explanatory value.

It is clear that complex linguistic questions in acquisitional sequences are quite difficult to describe, much less to measure in specific numerical terms, and even if a particular feature can be measured, the interaction of many components of meaning and syntactic form do not easily lend themselves to systematic quantified comparisons. An example of such complexity is the extensive review and analysis by Bardovi-Harlig (1999, 2000) of the cross-linguistic acquisition of tense-aspect systems. It is evident in her detailed displays of learner data that a quantitative meta-analysis of such phenomena lies yet somewhere in the future, when a substantially larger number of studies have been conducted to obtain comparable data. At best, Bardovi-Harlig can demonstrate that, in several studies across languages, within similar genres, similar orders of development of aspectual features occur. With such data, once the descriptive apparatus has been developed, the next stage of synthesis might involve a co-efficient of concordance among rank orders across studies as the verification of a hypothesized order of development (rather than, say, calculating means or effect sizes for the accuracy of a given structure among learners on a specific task, which would not integrate the developmental trends).

Instructional effects

An area of applied linguistics research that lends itself better to quantitative comparisons between effect sizes has been approached for some forty years with integrative reviews and syntheses of findings: the study of the effects of instruction on L2 acquisition. This area is evidenced in several of the chapters in this volume (Jeon & Kaya; Keck et al.; Russell & Spada; and Taylor et al.), as well as, obviously, Norris and Ortega (2000). In my view, this line of integrative review research has its origins in the methods comparisons studies of the 1960s and 1970s (Levin 1972; Smith 1970) and the classic conceptually organized integrative study of L1 education by Dunkin and Biddle (1974), which dealt however with all contents of instruction, the research on language as a subject matter being rather limited at the time. These early studies were resigned to simply comparing, by means of a vote-count method (Hedges & Olkin 1980), the relative advantage of, say, "deductive" and "inductive" instruction, while the factors that might influence the outcomes were too many to allow for conclusions as to the primary contrasting variables, due to the paucity of sufficiently examined moderator variables or analyses of instructional processes, and due to too diverse measurement procedures.

Long (1983) adopted a similar vote-counting approach with L2 research, while exerting a greater effort to restrict the studies to be considered to those which could contrast the relative amount of exposure or instruction provided to the learners. This publication inspired a considerable amount of research and a great deal of the subsequent efforts of classroom researchers to document and explain the mechanisms by which instruction could lead to superior acquisition. His study suffered again, however, from the paucity of empirically rigorous studies directly investigating this contrast, as well as the lack of sufficient measurement of the relevant variables and additional factors which were likely moderators (such as proficiency – cf. Thomas, this volume). Long had insufficient "data" to conduct a more meta-analytically quantitative comparison of effects.[2]

In my book on classroom research (Chaudron 1988), I made a similar effort to synthesize a number of features of instruction by vote-counting, but in addition, in some cases sufficient studies had been conducted to provide some quantitative comparisons of factors, such as speech rate and complexity of teacher talk. A few meta-analyses of specific instructional effects in L1 education that were pertinent to L2 studies were available as models at that time, in particular Redfield and Rousseau's (1981) analysis of the effects of higher order cognitive questioning on student performance (a re-analysis of the data in the earlier integrative, vote-counting review by Winne 1979). Nonetheless, due to different approaches to measurement and non-consistent design in L2 research, even the most quantified variables of teacher talk were best displayed and compared as ranges of values. These studies had for the most part not involved experimental means comparisons. Averaging of medians of observed variables would barely have provided a more useful summary, because the visible variation and ranges of values for the few measures available was sufficient information to identify the trends toward, for example, simpler speech to lower level learners. (Compare this, for example, to the later vote-counting integrative review presented in Yano, Long, & Ross 1994.) Such questions as the effects of feedback, which also lacked descriptive uniformity, appeared not amenable to any meta-analytical synthesis from the studies then extant. It is therefore all the more notable that Russell and Spada (this volume), not even twenty years later, can achieve the quantitative reduction and comparison among more recent studies of feedback in classrooms. Yet they are also limited in their findings by the fact that their summary of effects could only be made on a comparison of conditions of instruction with feedback versus no feedback (rather than by comparison of the internal features of the feedback). Perhaps in a further round of analysis, if the data are available, Russell and Spada (or another researcher) could examine the study-internal *types* of corrective feedback (shown in their Table 5) with a multiple regression prediction size of effect (as done in Goldschneider & DeKeyser 2001).[3]

Keck et al. (this volume) also have benefited from the very recently evolving research program in task-based language instruction, which allowed them to conduct their meta-analysis. Of particular value to this study is the growing consistency in descriptive classifications of the factors that are involved in such instruction, such as the linguistic focus of tasks and the output and task essential/utility factors that could distinguish among groups of studies. Indeed, the conceptual apparatus for identifying such features has only been developed in the last decade (see Loschky & Bley-Vroman 1993; and other articles in Crookes & Gass 1993).

Reading instruction

Likewise, in the area of reading research, the study in this volume by Taylor et al., demonstrates the recency of the opportunity to investigate this focused area through a meta-analysis.[4] When sufficient research on a unified topic has accumulated, this sort of summary becomes possible. Yet it is notable that approximately half of the studies reviewed in this paper were as yet unpublished (dissertations or conference papers), which raises a different question about research syntheses, namely, the adequacy of the sampling procedures employed. Comparing this with a related integrative review of reading instruction for ESL learners in the United States (Fitzgerald 1995a; cf. Fitzgerald 1995b, a study of ESL learners' cognitive reading strategies), published approximately mid-way through the period covered by Taylor et al.'s sample of studies, one sees that Fitzgerald includes nearly 100% published studies. This is despite the fact that she also searched both ERIC Documents, *Dissertation Abstracts,* and relevant conference programs in order to write to authors, exactly as did Taylor et al. Moreover, Fitzgerald covered a large range of topics about reading instruction (process descriptions, timing of L2 instructional intervention, general methods, and materials), more inclusive than Taylor et al.'s narrower focus on reading strategy training and studies with calculable effect sizes in addition (although they also included other language and country data, which were not sought by Fitzgerald). One would expect, then, that Fitzgerald would at least find and include the same studies as analyzed by Taylor et al. (within the same available time frame and excluding FL studies).

But Fitzgerald's review found only four studies of metacognitive/strategy training from 1979 up to 1994, of which only one – Carrell, Pharis, and Liberto (1989) – was included by Taylor et al., while two others were excluded on the basis of their not dealing with L2 learners. One of these was identified by Taylor et al. as a study of bilinguals, but the other (Au 1979), I must presume, may have been excluded because it dealt not with second language learners, rather with second dialect learners – Hawaii Creole English speakers. And a fourth (Swicegood 1990) was a dissertation with the keywords "metacognitive reading strategy" and "Spanish-dominant students" in the title, but which may also have been excluded on the basis of it dealing probably with bilingual learners. On the other hand, among the ESL studies reviewed by Taylor et al. and within the time period of Fitzgerald (1995a; up through 1993 to be fair), there were four dissertations and one ERIC document not included in the earlier review. We cannot speculate easily why Fitzgerald, whose research methods certainly appear thorough, would have missed these studies (computer-based search potential was already widely available at the time), nor why Taylor et al. missed one dissertation. We have only to be mindful of the possibility of failure to uncover relevant literature; therefore we must be cautious in drawing "final" conclusions of what appear to be rigorous and complete reviews.

Although there is a positive finding from comparing these two quite distinct reviews, in that they arrive at a similar conclusion with respect to the generally positive effects of reading strategy training on comprehension, Fitzgerald's conclusions are much less qualified than those of Taylor et al., owing both to the lack of summative quantification of findings, of course, and to the more limited data set with no further internal moderating factors – Taylor et al. examined 7 different moderating variables. The desirable result of integrative reviews and meta-analyses is that not only do more comparable findings accumulate, but with additional time, more suspected moderating variables can be examined for their effects. We will, nevertheless, always be left with further research and refinement of variables and constructs, in order to make the maximum sense of all the data obtained.

Individual differences

A final area of considerable interest, and in dire need of meta-analytic syntheses of findings, is research on individual difference (ID) variables in language acquisition. Thomas' article in the current volume deals with an ID, but it is not directed at an analysis of the role of proficiency in acquisition or instruction, rather at the measurement of it for the sake of research.[5] Although the impact of her earlier work has taken its time in appearing, once researchers take stock of the revelations brought out by Thomas, there may yet be more significant research on proficiency that merits meta-analysis, insofar as it might examine the correlation between specific measures of proficiency and various acquisitional patterns.

We see developing on the near horizon as well, the potential of various IDs related to aptitude (such as working memory) to be subjected to meta-analysis, as the number of studies employing similar measures is rapidly accumulating (see Robinson 2005, for an important review, which links basic psycholinguistic research to SLA-related research to instructional contexts, in relation to aptitude). Yet the reasons for a lack of quantitative and advanced syntheses of research on IDs and second language acquisition include some of the previously mentioned factors of insufficient accumulation of studies, variation or inadequate conceptualization of phenomena for the sake of comparability, difficulties in measurement, and so on.

The evidence is in that if sufficient studies *are* available in which adequate statistical measures have been taken, meta-analytic techniques can be applied to great advantage. An example is Masgoret and Gardner's (2003) correlation-based meta-analysis of studies conducted using their attitude/motivation test battery (AMTB). One might question the *use* of such an analysis, since they set out to validate several hypotheses, but from within the context only of the employment of their own battery as a measure, rather than from a synthesis of a wider range of studies of attitudes and motivation. Their procedure, however, is valuable and sets a comparative standard and challenge for similar studies that might wish to contest their hypotheses.

Such a challenge can be posed in the case of language learning strategy research, where we first of all see a clear need for a synthesis of conceptual formulation, and more specifically some reconciliation between the two distinct traditions in this domain that have been developing in parallel for many years, that of Chamot and her colleagues (Chamot & El-Dinary 1999; Chamot, Barnhardt, El-Dinary, & Robbins 1999; O'Malley & Chamot 1990), and that of Oxford and her colleagues (Bedell & Oxford 1996; Oxford 1990, 1996; Oxford

& Burry-Stock 1995; cf. Chaudron 2003b). The conceptual and descriptive apparatus that has evolved out of these two traditions has appeared on the surface to be quite similar, as often comparable behaviors are labeled in similar ways ("planning," "organizing" "transferring," "deducting"), yet the approaches to measurement in the two have kept their distance. The favored measurement approach in Oxford's tradition has been the self-reported rating scales of the Strategy Inventory for Language Learning (SILL), whereas Chamot and colleagues have tended to employ behavioral observation and frequency measures.

Whereas in the earlier stages of conceptual development of learner strategies (begun in the "good language learner" era, as in Naiman, Fröhlich, Stern, & Todesco 1978), identification and classification, along with behavioral observation and description, were needed, the work of Oxford led to a measurement approach to learner strategies, where the SILL instrument incorporated at first as many as 135 items for self-rating of frequency of use (now usually limited to smaller batteries of 50 or 80 items, but grouped into six major groupings). The SILL has now been employed in numerous studies, and translated even into several other languages (see reviews in the work of Oxford and her colleagues, above). So, just as Masgoret and Gardner (2003) could now make quantitative syntheses of findings from numerous applications of the AMTB, so too it behooves the employers of the SILL to attempt some form of cross-study comparisons. Remarkably, however, although several of the reviews cited here have the surface appearance of being integrative, they have not taken advantage of the data derived from studies with the SILL to draw more synthetic quantitative or conceptual conclusions.

To illustrate, in Figure 1 (analysis taken from Chaudron 2003b) I have made a comparison of the factor analysis results from use of the SILL in different contexts (as indicated in the citations above each column). By far the most common approaches to use of results from the SILL have been to examine the factor structure of responses to the instrument, followed by correlational analyses between components and other (independent or predicted) variables. The various researchers employing the SILL have preferred to assess the underlying structure of the instrument by means of principal components factor analysis, with oblique (Varimax) rotations. Standard practice has involved identifying factor solutions with eigenvalues greater than 1.0, according to the predominant types of items with high loadings (> 0.30) on a given factor. As described and cited in both Oxford and Burry-Stock (1995) and Bedell and Oxford (1996), and summarized in Figure 1, a comparison of factor analyses conducted on seven data sets (mostly unpublished work) from the 50-item SILL and one from Bedell's Chinese translation of the 80-item instrument, displays quite distinct factor structures across cultural and FL and SL contexts.

Much of the pattern of these analyses is common to all, thus the stuff of a serious meta-analysis, with the first factor providing the largest component of variance in the entire data sets (as low as 10.7%, but the remainder from 16.6% to 26.3%), and the rest of the factors (2 through 8) explaining much smaller proportions, of almost equal value (range from 2.0% to 8.5%; mean for all these factors = 3.64%, SD 1.29%). The combined explained variance of the 9 factors in each case account for between 41% and 53.3% of the variability in the questionnaire responses (mean 48.2%, SD. 5.1%). A final notable common pattern is the prevalence of "active language use" (which Oxford and Burry-Stock [1995] refer to as "active, naturalistic language use"), "metacognitive planning," and "sensory memory strategies" among the top factors observed. Namely, two of these three are always the first and second factors obtained, and in two studies of the seven, the third one is the third factor.

Nevertheless, there are numerous differences among the data sets, and difficulties with this approach to the analysis of such data. The most obvious difference in interpretation is the discrepancy in terminology across studies, compared with the original terms used to refer to the strategy components on the SILL. That is, whereas the SILL identifies Memory Strategies, the distinct factor classifications related to these are often different factors and terminology on the same study: from Bedell (1993) – "review and repetition" and "memory-vocabulary;" from Zhang (1994) – "sensory memory," "sensory (visual) memory," and "general memory;" from Yang (1999) – "memory and analysis" and "general memory;" from Watanabe (1990) – "sensory memory;" from Boraie et al. (1994) – "sensory memory," "sensory memory and anxiety," [the items on the SILL that reflect anxiety are for "lowering" it] "general memory," and "sensory memory" (again!). Similarly, among Cognitive Strategies are the following: "functional practice–productive," "functional practice–receptive," "formal practice," and "cognitive-analytic" (Bedell); "active language use" (all of the remaining studies), "formal oral practice" (Watanabe, Yang). Further, besides several groupings of social and affective together on single factors (Zhang, Boraie et al., Green & Oxford), several other "factors" are identified by combined types of strategies, which appear on occasion to be quite distinct from one another: "social and affective", and "social and error correction" (Bedell), "metacognitive and affective" (Zhang), "metacognitive and social/affective" (Watanabe), "reflection (analysis and anxiety)" (Watanabe, and Green & Oxford), "social/cognitive conversation" and "cognitive and relaxation" (Green & Oxford), "request and repetition" (Boraie et al.), "compensation and analysis"

	PRChina (Bedell 1993) 353 H.S./Univ. 80 items	PR China (Zhang 1994) 741 H.S. 50 items	Taiwan (Yang 1999) 590 Univ. 50 items	Japan (Watanabe 1990) 255 Univ. 50 items	Egypt (Boraie et al. 1994) 761 adult 50 items	Puerto Rico (Green & Oxford 1995) 374 Univ. 50 items	Combined U.S. (various) 137 Univ. 50 items
Factors ("Strategies" classifications for each Factor)							
1	Functional practice-productive # 18% *	Active language use 18.9%	Metacognitive planning 26.3%	Active language use 23.3%	Metacognitive planning 10.7%	Active language use 21.6%	Active language use 16.6%
2	Metacognitive – 3.8%	Metacognitive planning – 4.7%	Active language use – 4.9%	Sensory memory – 6.7%	Sensory memory – 5.0%	Metacognitive planning – 7.1%	Metacognitive planning – 8.5%
3	Compensation – 3.5%	Affective & social – 3.8%	Memory & analysis – 4.2%	Metacognitive/ Social/Affective – 5%	Affective & social – 5.3%	Affective & social – 4.8%	Affective 5.4%
4	Functional practice-Receptive – 3.3%	Sensory memory – 3.3%	Formal oral practice – 3.8%	Compensation & analysis – 3.8%	Active language use – 4.7%	Reflection (analysis & social) – 3.8%	Sensory memory – 5.2%
5	Review & Repetition – 2.6%	Compensation in reading – 2.9%	Social 3.3%	Formal oral practice – 3.5%	Request & repetition – 4.4%	Sensory memory – 3.7%	Social 4.1%
6	Memory-Vocabulary – 2.6%	Metacognitive & affective – 2.7%	Compensation in reading – 2.9%	Affective 3.3%	Sensory memory & anxiety – 3.6%	Social/cognitive conversation – 3.1%	Compensation & analysis – 3.8%
7	Formal practice & Affective 2.4%	Sensory (visual) memory 2.55	Affective 2.6%	Compensation in speaking 2.8%	Compensation in reading & listening – 4.4%	Sensory (visual) memory 2.6%	Metacognitive planning 3.2%
8	Social & Error-Correction 2.1%	Attention to key details 2.55	Compensation in speaking 2.4%	Attention to key details 2.6%	General memory 3.1%	Cognitive & relaxation 2.5%	General memory 3.2%
9	Cognitive-Analytic – 2.0%	General memory 2.4%	General memory 2.3%	Reflection (analysis & anxiety) 2.5%	Sensory memory 3.4%	General compensation 2.4%	Compensation & non-analytic 3.0%
Total Variance Accounted for by 9 Factors	41%	43.7%	51.9%	53.3%	44%	51.6%	51.9%

Labels are the authors' * Percentages refer to proportion of variance attributed to each factor, and total variance explained by all 9 factors

Figure 1. Factor structure of SILL in seven studies

(summarized from Oxford & Burry-Stock 1995; Bedell & Oxford 1996) Location (author; N of type of learner; n of items) and "compensation and non-analytic" (Combined U.S.). While the original data or factor loadings from most of these are unavailable, it is evident from these terminological differentiations and combinations of descriptors chosen for the different factors that many of them are derived from loadings on only a small number (one or two) of individual SILL questions, sometimes quite restrictively defined, and occasionally conceptually separate.

Another difficulty in making much sense of these analyses across studies is that in virtually all the studies, the tapering off of explained variances after the first factor, and once or twice the second, reveals the limited additional contribution of the subsequent factors, as seen in the "scree plots" of these factors. In all but the top three cases, the very level decline from Factor 2, or 3, to Factor 9 shows that there is little that truly distinguishes any of these factors from one another, in terms of their relative contribution to the overall variance in the instrument.

Moreover, none of the evident differences (or similarities) across these studies have been interpreted in any systematic way with respect to the supposed differences (or similarities) in the contexts and populations studied in them. Yet such an effort, if it were to be made, may be moot, because perhaps a more substantial concern with this display of the supposed "factor structure" of the SILL is that, since the instrument has been found to have high overall reliability, thereby entailing that all items have strong inter-item correlations, one should not in fact expect there to be separate factors among the items, each one contributing separate variances to the entire instrument. Moreover, if somewhere between 41% and 53.3% of the variance in respondents' scores on the SILL is "explained" by as many as nine factors, one is led to question what sort of strategy types or groups, or other characteristics of learners' self-perceptions in response to the SILL items, "explain" the remaining 46.7% to 59% of variance (in responses to highly consistent – reliable – questions). There seems to be a considerable amount of entirely unexplained, possibly random, variance in these learners' responses to this instrument measuring learner strategies, and those who have used the SILL for primary data collection have not offered theoretical constructs to interpret additional variability.

This brief display of a possible meta-analytic approach to correlational data such as that found in strategy, attitude, and motivation research points primarily to the inadequacy of the measures employed in the absence of well-developed and systematically employed constructs, which are needed for valid interpretation of the results. These inadequacies would have been revealed, had the primary researchers or a colleague made the effort to conduct a simple quantitative synthesis or comparison across the studies.

Conclusion

I have pointed here to various ways in which and reasons why research syntheses in our field have been slow to develop, noting as well different potential shortcomings of efforts, owing to insufficiently evolved conceptual apparatus, limited number of consistent studies following similar methodologies and measures, inexplicable or haphazard omission of research within reviews, and at times simply a lack of perspective to recognize the potential of the meta-analytical tools that are available. We are fortunate, however, to have here at last some exceptional models of what is possible.

As emphasized at the beginning of this chapter, although there is a substantial set of predecessors in the development of research syntheses, integrative reviews, and meta-analyses in applied linguistics, this volume should represent not only a guide and a standard against which to judge future research, but perhaps the prime mover and impetus to researchers to adopt more focused and directed endeavors, leading them to decline to engage in individual studies without the greatest effort made initially to ensure that the theoretical and empirical grounds for the research are justified by a thorough examination of our existing knowledge.

Notes

1. Jackson's (1980) summary of procedures for "integrative reviews," notes the virtual lack of any substantial statement of theory or practice on the topic until the late 1970s, with the appearance, for example, of Glass's (1976, 1977) arguments for quantitative meta-analysis serving as something of a benchmark, reinforced by the work of Rosenthal (1984), though credit is due to the early study of Light and Smith (1971). The first meta-analysis published in the *Review of Educational Research* appears to be that of Roberts (1980), just a few issues prior to Jackson's argument.

2. This is not to say that highly rigorous meta-analysis was not possible on second language learning data in the early period of development of the methodology. A notable meta-analysis of program effects in bilingual education was conducted by Willig (1985). She was able to accomplish this review due to the much more extensive funding and large-scale efforts directed toward program evaluation in this domain. Nonetheless, Willig's study was conducted on a relative small number of the existing evaluations, because, in order to determine whether quantitative meta-analysis would result in the same finding as a previous, government-sponsored non-quantitative analysis (Baker & de Kanter 1981) that had concluded a fairly weak effect of bilingual programs, she preferred to adopt the stringent selection criteria of the latter. Her careful analysis revealed a much more positive strength of the effect of bilingual programs. Yet this study could not examine more specific aspects

of the internal nature of those programs, nor the sources of effects of instruction, in the direction desired by L2 research.

3. Compare the coverage and approach of Bangert-Drowns et al. (1991), who conducted a meta-analysis of L1 feedback types on test-like instruction (including computer-delivered types), where learners were provided various types of feedback on their responses, and then subsequently tested on the content covered.

4. There are also increasing numbers of meta-analyses in other areas of instruction and learning which can contribute to our understanding of related areas in L2 research, such as the review of small-group work and applications of technology by Lou, Abrami, and d'Apollonia (2001), or the meta-analysis of incidental vocabulary learning in reading processes by Swanborn and de Glopper (1999), which could contribute greatly to the integrative reviews seen in, for example, Wesche and Paribakht (1999).

5. A number of research summaries and syntheses of note in the L2 literature have, of course, examined methodological issues; the majority of these pose questions and derive conceptual factors in ways that are not easily conceived of as sources for more quantitative meta-analyses (such as the study of metalinguistic judgments or data collection methods by Chaudron 1983, 2003a; cf. L1 research shown in Menn & Bernstein Ratner 2000, and L2 research in Kasper & Grotjahn 1991).

References

Andersen, R. W. (1978). An implicational model for second language research. *Language Learning, 28,* 221–282.

Au, K. H.-P. (1979). Using the experience-text-relationship method with minority children. *Reading Teacher, 32,* 677–679.

Baker, K. A., & de Kanter, A. A. (1981). *Effectiveness of bilingual education: A review of the literature.* Washington, DC: Office of Planning, Budget and Evaluation, U.S. Department of Education.

Bangert-Drowns, R. L., Kulik, C.-L. C., Kulik, J. A., & Morgan, M. T. (1991). The instructional effect of feedback in test-like events. *Review of Educational Research, 61,* 213–238.

Bardovi-Harlig, K. (1999). From morpheme studies to temporal semantics: Tense-aspect research in SLA. *Studies in Second Language Acquisition, 21,* 341–382.

Bardovi-Harlig, K. (2000). *Tense and aspect in second language acquisition: Form, meaning, and use.* A Supplement to *Language Learning, 50.*

Bedell, D. A. (1993). *Cross-cultural variation in choice of language learning strategies: A mainland Chinese investigation with comparison to previous studies.* Unpublished master's thesis. University of Alabama, Tuscaloosa, AL.

Bedell, D. A., & Oxford, R. L. (1996). Cross-cultural comparisons of language learning strategies in the People's Republic of China and other countries. In R. L. Oxford (Ed.), *Language learning strategies around the world: Cross-cultural perspectives* (pp. 47–60). Honolulu: Second Language Teaching and Curriculum Center, University of Hawai'i.

Boraie, D., Kassabgy, O., & Oxford, R. (1994). *Empowering teachers and learners: Style and strategy awareness.* Paper presented at the annual meeting of Teachers of English to Speakers of Other Languages, Baltimore, Maryland.

Carrell, P. L., Pharis, B. G., & Liberto, J. C. (1989). Metacognitive strategy training for ESL reading. *TESOL Quarterly, 23,* 647–678.

Chamot, A. U., & El-Dinary, P. B. (1999). Children's learning strategies in language immersion classrooms. *Modern Language Journal, 83,* 319–338.

Chamot, A. U.; Barnhardt, S., El-Dinary, P. B., & Robbins, J. (1999). *The learning strategies handbook.* New York: Addison Wesley Longman.

Chaudron, C. (1983). Research on metalinguistic judgments: A review of theory, methods, and results. *Language Learning, 33,* 343–377.

Chaudron, C. (1988). *Second language classrooms: Research on teaching and learning.* Cambridge, UK: Cambridge University Press.

Chaudron, C. (2003a). Data collection in SLA research. In C. Doughty & M. H. Long, (Eds.), *The handbook of second language acquisition* (pp. 762–828). Malden, MA: Blackwell.

Chaudron, C. (2003b). *Learner strategies.* Unpublished review paper commissioned by the Diagnostic Assessment Procedure Project, University of Hawai'i, Honolulu.

Crookes, G., & Gass, S. M. (Eds.). (1993). *Tasks and language learning: Integrating theory and practice.* Clevedon, UK: Multilingual Matters.

Dunkin, M. J., & Biddle, B. J. (1974). *The study of teaching.* New York: Holt, Rinehart and Winston.

Fitzgerald, J. (1995a). English-as-a-second language reading instruction in the United States: A research review. *Journal of Reading Behavior* (now *Journal of Literacy Research), 27*(2), 115–152

Fitzgerald, J. (1995b). English-as-a-second-language learners' cognitive reading processes: A review of research in the United States. *Review of Educational Research, 65,* 145–190.

Glass, G. V. (1976). Primary, secondary, and meta-analysis of research. *Educational Researcher, 5*(10), 3–8.

Glass, G. V. (1977). Integrating findings: The meta-analysis of research. *Review of Research in Education, 5,* 351–379.

Goldschneider, J. M., & DeKeyser, R. M. (2001). Explaining the "Natural Order of L2 Morpheme Acquisition" in English: A meta-analysis of multiple determinants. *Language Learning, 51,* 1–50.

Green, J. M., & Oxford, R. (1995). A closer look at learning strategies, L2 proficiency, and gender. *TESOL Quarterly 29,* 2, 261–297.

Hedges, L. V., & Olkin, I. (1980). Vote counting methods in research synthesis. *Psychological Bulletin, 88,* 359–369.

Jackson, G. B. (1980). Methods for integrative reviews. *Review of Educational Research, 50,* 438–468.

Kasper, G., & Grotjahn, R. (Eds.). (1991). *Methods in second language research.* Special Issue of *Studies in Second Language Acquisition, 13*(2).

Krashen, S. D. (1977). Some issues relating to the Monitor Model. In H. D. Brown, C. A. Yorio, & R. H. Crymes, (Eds.), *On TESOL '77: Teaching and learning English as a second language: Trends in research and practice* (pp. 144–158). Washington, D.C.: TESOL.

Levin, L. (1972). *Comparative studies in foreign language teaching*. Stockholm: Almqvist and Wiksell.

Light, R. J., & Smith, P. V. (1971). Accumulating evidence: Procedures for resolving conflicts among different research studies. *Harvard Educational Review, 41*, 429–471.

Long, M. H. (1983). Does second language instruction make a difference? A review of research. *TESOL Quarterly, 17*, 359–382.

Loschky, L., & Bley-Vroman, R. (1993). Grammar and task-based methodology. In G. Crookes & S. M. Gass (Eds.), *Tasks and language learning: Integrating theory and practice* (pp. 123–167). Clevedon, UK: Multilingual Matters.

Lou, Y., Abrami, P. C., & d'Apollonia, S. (2001). Small group and individual learning with technology: A meta-analysis. *Review of Educational Research, 71*, 449–521.

Masgoret, A.-M., & Gardner, R. C. (2003). Attitudes, motivation, and second language learning: A meta-analysis of studies conducted by Gardner and associates. *Language Learning, 53*, 123–163.

Menn, L., & Bernstein Ratner, N. (Eds.). (2000). *Methods for studying language production*. Mahwah, NJ: Lawrence Erlbaum.

Naiman, N., Fröhlich, M., Stern, H. H., & Todesco, A. (1978). *The good language learner*. Toronto: Ontario Institute for Studies in Education.

Norris, J. M., & Ortega, L. (2000). Effectiveness of L2 instruction: A research synthesis and quantitative meta-analysis. *Language Learning 50*, 417–528.

O'Malley, J. M., & Chamot, A. U. (1990). *Learning strategies in second language acquisition*. Cambridge, UK: Cambridge University Press.

Oxford, R. L. (1990). *Language learning strategies: What every teacher should know*. Rowley, MA: Newbury House.

Oxford, R. L., (Ed.). (1996). *Language learning strategies around the world: Cross-cultural perspectives*. Honolulu: Second Language Teaching and Curriculum Center, University of Hawai'i.

Oxford, R. L., & Burry-Stock, J. A. (1995). Assessing the use of language learning strategies worldwide with the ESL/EFL version of the Strategy Inventory for Language Learning (SILL). *System, 23*, 1–23.

Redfield, D. L., & Rousseau, E. W. (1981). A meta-analysis of experimental research on teacher questioning behavior. *Review of Educational Research, 51*, 237–245.

Roberts, D. M. (1980). The impact of electronic calculators on educational performance. *Review of Educational Research, 50*, 71–98.

Robinson, P. (2005). Aptitude and second language acquisition. *Annual Review of Applied Linguistics, 25*, 45–73.

Rosenthal, R. (1984). *Meta-analytic procedures for social research*. Beverly Hills, CA: Sage.

Smith, P. D. (1970). *A comparison of the cognitive and audiolingual approaches to foreign language instruction: The Pennsylvania Foreign Language project*. Philadelphia: Center for Curriculum Development.

Swanborn, M. S. L., & de Glopper, K. (1999). Incidental word learning while reading: A meta-analysis. *Review of Educational Research, 69*, 261–285.

Swicegood, M. A. (1990). *The effects of metacognitive reading strategy training on the reading performance and student reading analysis strategies of third-grade Spanish-dominant students*. Dissertation Abstracts International *52*, p. 449A.

Watanabe, Y. (1990). *External variables affecting language learning strategies of Japanese EFL learners: Effects of entrance examinations, years spent at college/university, and staying overseas.* Unpublished master's thesis, Lancaster University, Lancaster, U.K.

Wesche, M., & Paribakht, T. S. (Eds.). (1999). *Incidental L2 vocabulary acquisition: Theory, current research, and instructional implications.* Special Issue of *Studies in Second Language Acquisition, 21*(2).

Willig, A. C. (1985). A meta-analysis of selected studies on the effectiveness of bilingual education. *Review of Educational Research, 55,* 269–317.

Winne, P. H. (1979). Experiments relating teachers' use of higher cognitive questions to student achievement. *Review of Educational Research, 49,* 13–50.

Yang, N.-D. (1999). The relationship between EFL learners' beliefs and learning strategy use. *System 27,* 515–535.

Yano, Y., Long, M. H., & Ross, S. (1994). The effects of simplified and elaborated texts on foreign language reading comprehension. *Language Learning, 44,* 189–219.

Zhang, W. (1994). *Data on university EFL language use.* Unpublished manuscript, Ohio University, Athens, Ohio.

Author index

Subject index

In the series *Language Learning & Language Teaching* the following titles have been published thus far or are scheduled for publication: